# MznLnx

*Missing Links Exam Preps*

Exam Prep for

## Financial Statement Analysis

Wild & Subramanyam & Halsey, 8th Edition

The MznLnx Exam Prep is your link from the texbook and lecture to your exams.
The MznLnx Exam Preps are unauthorized and comprehensive reviews of your textbooks.

All material provided by MznLnx and Rico Publications (c) 2010
Textbook publishers and textbook authors do not particpate in or contribute to these reviews.

## MznLnx

### Rico Publications

*Exam Prep for Financial Statement Analysis*
8th Edition
Wild & Subramanyam & Halsey

*Publisher:* Raymond Houge
*Assistant Editor:* Michael Rouger
*Text and Cover Designer:* Lisa Buckner
*Marketing Manager:* Sara Swagger
*Project Manager, Editorial Production:* Jerry Emerson
*Art Director:* Vernon Lowerui

*Product Manager:* Dave Mason
*Editorial Assitant:* Rachel Guzmanji
*Pedagogy:* Debra Long
*Cover Image:* Jim Reed/Getty Images
*Text and Cover Printer:* City Printing, Inc.
*Compositor:* Media Mix, Inc.

(c) 2010 Rico Publications

ALL RIGHTS RESERVED. No part of this work covered by the copyright may be reproduced or used in any form or by an means--graphic, electronic, or mechanical, including photocopying, recording, taping, Web distribution, information storage, and retrieval systems, or in any other manner--without the written permission of the publisher.

Printed in the United States
ISBN:

For more information about our products, contact us at:
Dave.Mason@RicoPublications.com

For permission to use material from this text or product, submit a request online to:
Dave.Mason@RicoPublications.com

# Contents

**CHAPTER 1**
*Overview of Financial Statement Analysis* — 1

**CHAPTER 2**
*Financial Reporting and Analysis* — 41

**CHAPTER 3**
*Analyzing Financing Activities* — 71

**CHAPTER 4**
*Analyzing Investing Activities* — 113

**CHAPTER 5**
*Analyzing Investing Activities: Special Topics* — 152

**CHAPTER 6**
*Analyzing Operating Activities* — 182

**CHAPTER 7**
*Cash Flow Analysis* — 219

**CHAPTER 8**
*Return on Invested Capital* — 242

**CHAPTER 9**
*Profitability Analysis* — 262

**CHAPTER 10**
*Prospective Analysis* — 279

**CHAPTER 11**
*Credit Analysis* — 299

**CHAPTER 12**
*Equity Analysis and Valuation* — 333

**ANSWER KEY** — 352

# TO THE STUDENT

### COMPREHENSIVE

The *MznLnx* Exam Prep series is designed to help you pass your exams. Editors at MznLnx review your textbooks and then prepare these practice exams to help you master the textbook material. Unlike study guides, workbooks, and practice tests provided by the texbook publisher and textbook authors, *MznLnx* gives you **all** of the material in each chapter in exam form, not just samples, so you can be sure to nail your exam.

### MECHANICAL

The MznLnx Exam Prep series creates exams that will help you learn the subject matter as well as test you on your understanding. Each question is designed to help you master the concept. Just working through the exams, you gain an understanding of the subject--its a simple mechanical process that produces success.

### INTEGRATED STUDY GUIDE AND REVIEW

MznLnx is not just a set of exams designed to test you, its also a comprehensive review of the subject content. Each exam question is also a review of the concept, making sure that you will get the answer correct without having to go to other sources of material. You learn as you go! Its the easiest way to pass an exam.

### HUMOR

Studying can be tedious and dry. MznLnx's instructional design includes moderate humor within the exam questions on occassion, to break the tedium and revitalize the brain

## Chapter 1. Overview of Financial Statement Analysis

1. _____ is a structured methodology that is focused on completely understanding the customer's needs, identifying how best to meet those needs, and then "reinventing" the stream of processes to meet those needs.
   a. Thing
   b. Business analysis1
   c. Undefined
   d. Undefined

2. _____ refers to a summary of all the transactions that have occurred over a particular period.
   a. Thing
   b. Financial statement1
   c. Undefined
   d. Undefined

3. In finance, _____ is the process of estimating the market value of a financial asset or liability. They can be done on assets (for example, investments in marketable securities such as stocks, options, business enterprises, or intangible assets such as patents and trademarks) or on liabilities (e.g., Bonds issued by a company).
   a. Valuation1
   b. Event
   c. Undefined
   d. Undefined

4. _____ refers to a market in which, at a minimum, current price changes are independent of past price changes, or, more strongly, price reflects all available information.
   a. Efficient market1
   b. Thing
   c. Undefined
   d. Undefined

5. A _____ is, as defined in economics, a social arrangement that allows buyers and sellers to discover information and carry out a voluntary exchange of goods or services.
   a. Thing
   b. Market1
   c. Undefined
   d. Undefined

6. _____ is a measure of a company's earning power from ongoing operations, equal to earnings before the deduction of interest payments and income taxes.
   a. Thing
   b. Operating profit1
   c. Undefined
   d. Undefined

7. A significant decline in economic activity. In the U.S., _____ is approximately defined as two successive quarters of falling GDP, as judged by NBER.
   a. Thing
   b. Recession1
   c. Undefined
   d. Undefined

8. _____ refers to the return to the resource entrepreneurial ability; total revenue minus total cost.
   a. Thing
   b. Profit1
   c. Undefined
   d. Undefined

9. _____ usually refers to characteristics that permit a firm to compete effectively with other firms due to low cost or superior technology, perhaps internationally.
   a. Competitiveness1
   b. Thing
   c. Undefined
   d. Undefined

10. _____ characterizes the process of leading and directing all or part of an organization, often a business, through the deployment and manipulation of resources. Early twentieth-century _____ writer Mary Parker Follett defined _____ as "the art of getting things done through people."

## Chapter 1. Overview of Financial Statement Analysis

a. Management1
b. Thing
c. Undefined
d. Undefined

11. In financial terminology, _____ is the capital raized by a corporation, through the issuance and sale of shares.
a. Stock1
b. Thing
c. Undefined
d. Undefined

12. _____ refer to an equity security, representing a shareholder's ownership of a corporation. _____ are one of a finite number of equal portions in the capital of a company, entitling the owner to a proportion of distributed, non-reinvested profits known as dividends and to a portion of the value of the company in case of liquidation.
a. Thing
b. Shares1
c. Undefined
d. Undefined

13. A _____ is an individual or company (including a corporation) that legally owns one or more shares of stock in a joined stock company.
a. Thing
b. Shareholder1
c. Undefined
d. Undefined

14. In finance, _____ refers to the amounts of cash being received and spent by a business during a defined period of time, sometimes tied to a specific project. Most of the time they are being used to determine gaps in the liquid position of a company.
a. Thing
b. Cash flow1
c. Undefined
d. Undefined

15. Amount of corporate profits paid out for each share of stock is referred to as _____.
a. Dividend1
b. Thing
c. Undefined
d. Undefined

16. A group of products that are physically similar or are intended for a similar market are called the _____.
a. Product line1
b. Thing
c. Undefined
d. Undefined

17. _____ is a business magazine published by McGraw-Hill. It was first published in 1929 under the direction of Malcolm Muir, who was serving as president of the McGraw-Hill Publishing company at the time. It is considered to be the standard both in industry and among students.
a. Business Week1
b. Organization
c. Undefined
d. Undefined

18. _____ refers to spending for the production and accumulation of capital and additions to inventories. In a financial sense, buying an asset with the expectation of making a return.
a. Investment1
b. Thing
c. Undefined
d. Undefined

19. The consumer's appraisal of the product or brand on important attributes is called _____.

*Chapter 1. Overview of Financial Statement Analysis*  3

a. Evaluation1
b. Thing
c. Undefined
d. Undefined

20. Assistance provided by countries and by international institutions such as the World Bank to developing countries in the form of monetary grants, loans at low interest rates, in kind, or a combination of these is called _____. _____ can also refer to assistance of any type rendered to benefit some group or individual.
a. Thing
b. Aid1
c. Undefined
d. Undefined

21. In business and engineering, new _____ is the complete process of bringing a new product to market. There are two parallel aspects to this process : one involves product engineering ; the other marketing analysis. Marketers see new _____ as the first stage in product life cycle management, engineers as part of Product Lifecycle Management.
a. Thing
b. Product development1
c. Undefined
d. Undefined

22. _____ is the corporate management term for the act of partially dismantling and reorganizing a company for the purpose of making it more efficient and therefore more profitable.
a. Restructuring1
b. Thing
c. Undefined
d. Undefined

23. The sum of fixed cost and variable cost is referred to as _____.
a. Thing
b. Total cost1
c. Undefined
d. Undefined

24. The term _____ is commonly used to describe business and market activity in industrializing or emerging regions of the world. It is sometimes loosely used as a replacement for emerging economies, but really signifies a business phenomenon that is not fully described by or constrained to geography or economic strength; such countries are considered to be in a transitional phase between developing and developed status.
a. Thing
b. Emerging markets1
c. Undefined
d. Undefined

25. The term _____ is commonly used to describe business and market activity in industrializing or emerging regions of the world.
a. Emerging market1
b. Thing
c. Undefined
d. Undefined

26. _____ refers to an undertaking by two parties for a specific purpose and duration, taking any of several legal forms.
a. Thing
b. Joint venture1
c. Undefined
d. Undefined

27. In 2000 _____ and Time Warner announced plans to merge, and the deal was approved by the Federal Trade Commission on January 11, 2001. This merger was primarily a product of the Internet mania of the late-1990s, known as the Internet bubble. The deal is known as one of the worst corporate mergers in history, destroying over $200 billion in shareholder value.

a. Organization
b. America Online1
c. Undefined
d. Undefined

28. In the common law, a _____ is a type of business entity in which partners share with each other the profits or losses of the business undertaking in which they have all invested.
a. Thing
b. Partnership1
c. Undefined
d. Undefined

29. A company's purchase of the property and obligations of another company is an _____.
a. Acquisition1
b. Thing
c. Undefined
d. Undefined

30. In accounting, an _____ represents an event in which an asset is used up or a liability is incurred. In terms of the accounting equation, expenses reduce owners' equity.
a. Expense1
b. Thing
c. Undefined
d. Undefined

31. _____ Corporation, founded in 1968 and based in Santa Clara, California, USA, is the world's largest semiconductor company. _____ is best known for its PC microprocessors, where it maintains roughly 80% market share.
a. Organization
b. Intel1
c. Undefined
d. Undefined

32. All the individuals or households that want goods and services for personal consumption or use are a _____.
a. Consumer market1
b. Thing
c. Undefined
d. Undefined

33. A person to whom a debt or legal obligation is owed, and who has the right to enforce payment of that debt or obligation is referred to as _____.
a. Creditor1
b. Thing
c. Undefined
d. Undefined

34. _____ is the process whereby interested parties resolve disputes, agree upon courses of action, bargain for individual or collective advantage, and/or attempt to craft outcomes which serve their mutual interests.
a. Thing
b. Negotiation1
c. Undefined
d. Undefined

35. People's physical and mental talents and efforts that are used to help produce goods and services are called _____.
a. Thing
b. Labor1
c. Undefined
d. Undefined

36. A worker association that bargains with employers over wages and working conditions is called a _____.
a. Union1
b. Thing
c. Undefined
d. Undefined

37. _____ refers to a recording as positive in the balance of payments, any transaction that gives rise to a payment into the country, such as an export, the sale of an asset, or borrowing from abroad.
   a. Thing
   b. Credit1
   c. Undefined
   d. Undefined

38. _____ specialize in information either to bring together two parties to a transaction or to buy in order to sell again.
   a. Intermediaries1
   b. Thing
   c. Undefined
   d. Undefined

39. _____ refers to a financial organization that specializes in selling primary offerings of securities. Investment bankers can also perform other financial functions, such as advising clients, negotiating mergers and takeovers, and selling secondary offerings.
   a. Thing
   b. Investment banker1
   c. Undefined
   d. Undefined

40. _____ refers to the combination of two firms into a single firm.
   a. Thing
   b. Merger1
   c. Undefined
   d. Undefined

41. _____ is the name given to the set of legal principles, in countries following the English common law tradition, which supplement strict rules of law where their application would operate harshly, so as to achieve what is sometimes referred to as "natural justice."
   a. Thing
   b. Equity1
   c. Undefined
   d. Undefined

42. Suppliers and financial institutions that lend money to companies is referred to as a _____.
   a. Thing
   b. Lender1
   c. Undefined
   d. Undefined

43. A detailed written statement that describes the nature of the business, the target market, the advantages the business will have in relation to competition, and the resources and qualifications of the owner is referred to as a _____.
   a. Thing
   b. Business plan1
   c. Undefined
   d. Undefined

44. _____ refers to a person or tool with a primary function of information analysis, generally with a more limited, practical and short term set of goals than a researcher.
   a. Analyst1
   b. Person
   c. Undefined
   d. Undefined

45. _____ refers to a claim on the borrower future income that is sold by the borrower to the lender. A _____ is a type of transferable interest representing financial value.
   a. Security1
   b. Thing
   c. Undefined
   d. Undefined

46. Independent accounting entity with a self-balancing set of accounts segregated for the purposes of carrying on specific activities is referred to as a _____.

a. Fund1 b. Thing
c. Undefined d. Undefined

47. In finance and economics, _____ is the price paid by a borrower for the use of a lender's money. In other words, _____ is the amount of paid to "rent" money for a period of time.
   a. Interest1 b. Thing
   c. Undefined d. Undefined

48. A group of firms that produce identical or similar products is an _____. It is also used specifically to refer to an area of economic production focused on manufacturing which involves large amounts of capital investment before any profit can be realized, also called "heavy _____".
   a. Industry1 b. Thing
   c. Undefined d. Undefined

49. _____ refers to a "non tangible product" that is not embodied in a physical good and that typically effects some change in another product, person, or institution. Contrasts with good.
   a. Thing b. Service1
   c. Undefined d. Undefined

50. _____ refers to a discount offered on merchandise sold to encourage prompt payment; offered by sellers of merchandise and represents sales discounts to the seller when they are used and purchase discounts to the purchaser of the merchandise.
   a. Thing b. Cash discount1
   c. Undefined d. Undefined

51. _____ refers to an amount that is loaned to an exporter to be repaid when the exports are paid for by the foreign importer.
   a. Thing b. Trade credit1
   c. Undefined d. Undefined

52. The difference between the face value of a bond and its selling price, when a bond is sold for less than its face value it's referred to as a _____.
   a. Thing b. Discount1
   c. Undefined d. Undefined

53. _____ refers to an out-of-court settlement in which creditors agree to allow the firm more time to meet its financial obligations. A new repayment schedule will be developed, subject to the acceptance of creditors.
   a. Extension1 b. Thing
   c. Undefined d. Undefined

54. _____ indicates whether a borrower has in the past made loan payments when due.
   a. Creditworthiness1 b. Thing
   c. Undefined d. Undefined

55. _____ refers to a debt instrument, issued by a borrower and promising a specified stream of payments to the purchaser, usually regular interest payments plus a final repayment of principal.

a. Bond1  
b. Thing  
c. Undefined  
d. Undefined

56. _____ is the difference between the intrinsic value of a stock (i.e. value based on stock valuation and what the company is actually worth) and the price that the market sets on a stock (i.e. stock price is a matter of market participants' opinions and is different from the intrinsic value).
   a. Thing
   b. Margin of safety1
   c. Undefined
   d. Undefined

57. A deposit by a buyer in stocks with a seller or a stockbroker, as security to cover fluctuations in the market in reference to stocks that the buyer has purchased but for which he has not paid is a _____. Commodities are also traded on _____.
   a. Margin1
   b. Thing
   c. Undefined
   d. Undefined

58. _____ refers to the capacity to turn assets into cash, or the amount of assets in a portfolio that have that capacity.
   a. Thing
   b. Liquidity1
   c. Undefined
   d. Undefined

59. _____ refers to a debt that can reasonably be expected to be paid from existing current assets or through the creation of other current liabilities, within one year or the operating cycle, whichever is longer.
   a. Current liability1
   b. Thing
   c. Undefined
   d. Undefined

60. A _____ is an asset on the balance sheet which is expected to be sold or otherwise used up in the near future, usually within one year.
   a. Current asset1
   b. Thing
   c. Undefined
   d. Undefined

61. A _____ is a present obligation of the enterprise arizing from past events, the settlement of which is expected to result in an outflow from the enterprise of resources embodying economic benefits.
   a. Liability1
   b. Thing
   c. Undefined
   d. Undefined

62. An item of property, such as land, capital, money, a share in ownership, or a claim on others for future payment, such as a bond or a bank deposit is an _____.
   a. Asset1
   b. Thing
   c. Undefined
   d. Undefined

63. The ability of a company to pay interest as it comes due and to repay the face value of debt at maturity is called _____.
   a. Solvency1
   b. Thing
   c. Undefined
   d. Undefined

64. In economic models, the _____ time frame assumes no fixed factors of production. Firms can enter or leave the marketplace, and the cost (and availability) of land, labor, raw materials, and capital goods can be assumed to vary.

# Chapter 1. Overview of Financial Statement Analysis

a. Long run1  
b. Thing  
c. Undefined  
d. Undefined

65. _____ generally refers to financial wealth, especially that used to start or maintain a business. In classical economics, _____ is one of four factors of production, the others being land and labor and entrepreneurship.
    a. Capital1
    b. Thing
    c. Undefined
    d. Undefined

66. A _____ is a "promise" or an "agreement" that is enforced or recognized by the law. In the civil law, a _____ is considered to be part of the general law of obligations.
    a. Contract1
    b. Thing
    c. Undefined
    d. Undefined

67. _____ is the process of determining the fair price of a bond. As with any security, the fair value of a bond is the present value of the stream of cash flows it is expected to generate.
    a. Thing
    b. Bond valuation1
    c. Undefined
    d. Undefined

68. In agency law, one under whose direction an agent acts and for whose benefit that agent acts is a _____.
    a. Thing
    b. Principal1
    c. Undefined
    d. Undefined

69. The effect of the background under which a message often takes on more and richer meaning is a _____. _____ is especially important in cross-cultural interactions because some cultures are said to be high _____ or low _____.
    a. Context1
    b. Thing
    c. Undefined
    d. Undefined

70. In finance, _____ is a profit or an increase in value of an investment such as a stock or bond. _____ is calculated by fair market value or the proceeds from the sale of the investment minus the sum of the purchase price and all costs associated with it.
    a. Gain1
    b. Thing
    c. Undefined
    d. Undefined

71. A _____ refers to a layout accurate in size, color, scheme, and other necessary details to show how a final ad will look. For presentation only, never for reproduction.
    a. Comprehensive1
    b. Thing
    c. Undefined
    d. Undefined

72. _____ refer to people in the organization who actually use the product or service purchased by the buying center.
    a. Users1
    b. Thing
    c. Undefined
    d. Undefined

73. Uses price and volume data to determine past trends, which are expected to continue into the future is called _____.

## Chapter 1. Overview of Financial Statement Analysis

a. Thing
c. Undefined
b. Technical analysis1
d. Undefined

74. _____ is a security or stock valuation method that uses financial and economic analysis to predict the movement of security prices such as Bond prices, but more commonly stock prices. The fundamental information that is analyzed can include a company's financial reports, and non-finanical information such as estimates of the growth of demand for competing products, industry comparisons, analysis of the effects of new regulations or demographic changes, and economy-wide changes.
a. Thing
c. Undefined
b. Fundamental analysis1
d. Undefined

75. _____ refers to as applied to a warrant, this represents the market value of common stock minus the exercise price. The difference is then multiplied by the number of shares each warrant entitles the holder to purchase.
a. Intrinsic value1
c. Undefined
b. Thing
d. Undefined

76. _____ refers to the price of an asset agreed on between a willing buyer and a willing seller; the price an asset could demand if it is sold on the open market.
a. Thing
c. Undefined
b. Market value1
d. Undefined

77. _____ refers to the sale of securities directly to a financial institution by a corporation. This eliminates the middleman and reduces the cost of issue to the corporation.
a. Private placement1
c. Undefined
b. Concept
d. Undefined

78. _____ generally refers to the buying and holding of shares of stock on a stock market by individuals and funds in anticipation of income from dividends and capital gain as the value of the stock rises.
a. Equity investment1
c. Undefined
b. Thing
d. Undefined

79. The phrase _____ refers to the aspect of corporate finance strategy and management dealing with the merging and acquiring of different companies as well as other assets. Usually mergers occur in a friendly setting where executives from the respective companies participate in a due diligence process to ensure a successful combination of all parts.
a. Thing
c. Undefined
b. Mergers and acquisitions1
d. Undefined

80. Firms in the process of becoming publicly traded companies will issue shares of stock using an _____, which is merely the process of selling stock for the first time to interested investors.
a. Thing
c. Undefined
b. Initial public offering1
d. Undefined

81. Cash flow activities that include obtaining cash from issuing debt and repaying the amounts borrowed and obtaining cash from stockholders and paying dividends is referred to as _____.

a. Thing  
c. Undefined  
b. Financing activities1  
d. Undefined

82. Other organizations in the same industry or type of business that provide a good or service to the same set of customers is referred to as a _____.
a. Competitor1  
c. Undefined  
b. Thing  
d. Undefined

83. A standardized method or technique that is performed repetitively, often on different materials resulting in different finished goods is called an _____.
a. Operation1  
c. Undefined  
b. Thing  
d. Undefined

84. In finance the term _____ has two distinct meanings, both relating to securities. The first is a designation for a 'class' of common or preferred stock. _____ of common or preferred stock typically has enhanced voting rights or other benefits compared to the other forms of shares that may have been created. The equity structure, or how many types of shares are offered, is determined by the corporate charter.
a. Thing  
c. Undefined  
b. A share1  
d. Undefined

85. An examination of the financial reports to ensure that they represent what they claim and conform with generally accepted accounting principles is referred to as _____.
a. Thing  
c. Undefined  
b. Audit1  
d. Undefined

86. A _____ describes a business that functions without the intention or threat of liquidation for the foreseeable future. Accountants and auditors may be required to evaluate and disclose whether a company is no longer a _____, or is at risk of ceasing to be one.
a. Thing  
c. Undefined  
b. Going concern1  
d. Undefined

87. _____ is a multinational computer technology corporation with 2004 global annual sales of US$39.79 billion and 71,553 employees in 102 countries and regions as of July 2006. It develops, manufactures, licenses, and supports a wide range of software products for computing devices.
a. Microsoft1  
c. Undefined  
b. Organization  
d. Undefined

88. Government intervention to alter market structure or prevent abuse of market power is called _____.
a. Thing  
c. Undefined  
b. Antitrust1  
d. Undefined

89. _____ is a U.S. business term for the amount of money that a company receives from its activities, mostly from sales of products and/or services to customers.
a. Revenue1  
c. Undefined  
b. Thing  
d. Undefined

90. In 1862, during the Civil War, President Lincoln and Congress created the office of Commissioner of Internal Revenue and enacted an income tax to pay war expenses. The position of Commissioner still exists today. The Commissioner is the head of the _____.
   a. Internal Revenue Service1
   b. Organization
   c. Undefined
   d. Undefined

91. _____ refers to the negotiation of labor contracts between labor unions and firms or government entities.
   a. Thing
   b. Collective bargaining1
   c. Undefined
   d. Undefined

92. A group of workers organized to advance the interests of the group is called a _____.
   a. Thing
   b. Labor union1
   c. Undefined
   d. Undefined

93. _____ refers to the percentage cost of funds used for acquiring resources for an organization, typically a weighted average of the firms cost of equity and cost of debt.
   a. Cost of capital1
   b. Place
   c. Undefined
   d. Undefined

94. The _____ used by a firm or an economy are the labor, raw materials, electricity and other resources it uses to produce its outputs.
   a. Inputs1
   b. Thing
   c. Undefined
   d. Undefined

95. _____ is the analysis of the accounts and the economic prospects of a firm.
   a. Financial analysis1
   b. Thing
   c. Undefined
   d. Undefined

96. The sequence of business functions in which usefulness is added to the products or services of a company is a _____.
   a. Value chain1
   b. Thing
   c. Undefined
   d. Undefined

97. Any product viewed by a consumer as an alternative for other products is a _____. The substitution is rarely perfect, and varies from time to time depending on price, availability, etc.
   a. Substitute product1
   b. Thing
   c. Undefined
   d. Undefined

98. _____ refers to the ability to influence the setting of prices or wages, usually arising from some sort of monopoly or monopsony position
   a. Bargaining power1
   b. Thing
   c. Undefined
   d. Undefined

99. _____ refers to the new competitors that may be induced to enter an industry if firms now in that industry are receiving large economic profits.

a. Potential competition1  
b. Thing  
c. Undefined  
d. Undefined  

100. A business is said to have a _____ when its unique strengths, often based on cost, quality, time, and innovation, offer consumers a greater percieved value and there by differtiating it from its competitors.
   a. Competitive advantage1  
   b. Thing  
   c. Undefined  
   d. Undefined  

101. An outline of how a business intends to compete with other firms in the same industry is called _____.
   a. Competitive Strategy1  
   b. Thing  
   c. Undefined  
   d. Undefined  

102. The relative proportion of an organization's fixed, variable, and mixed costs is referred to as _____.
   a. Cost structure1  
   b. Thing  
   c. Undefined  
   d. Undefined  

103. The combination of product lines offered by a manufacturer is referred to as _____.
   a. Thing  
   b. Product mix1  
   c. Undefined  
   d. Undefined  

104. An _____ is prepared by corporate management that presents financial information including financial statements, footnotes, and the management discussion and analysis.
   a. Thing  
   b. Annual report1  
   c. Undefined  
   d. Undefined  

105. A written public news announcement normally distributed to major news services is referred to as _____.
   a. Press release1  
   b. Thing  
   c. Undefined  
   d. Undefined  

106. _____ means the giving out of information, either voluntarily or to be in compliance with legal regulations or workplace rules.
   a. Thing  
   b. Disclosure1  
   c. Undefined  
   d. Undefined  

107. A long-lasting, sometimes permanent team in the organization structure created to deal with tasks that recur regularly is the _____.
   a. Committee1  
   b. Thing  
   c. Undefined  
   d. Undefined  

108. A philosophy of management that links strategic planning with dayto-day decision making. _____ seeks a fit between an organization's external and internal environments.
   a. Strategic management1  
   b. Thing  
   c. Undefined  
   d. Undefined  

109. _____ is a branch of economics that applies microeconomic analysis to specific business decisions.

a. Thing
c. Undefined
b. Managerial economics1
d. Undefined

110. _____ refers to the practice of organizing the cost-effective flow of raw materials, in-process inventory, finished goods, and related information from point of origin to point of consumption to satisfy customer requirements.
a. Thing
c. Undefined
b. Logistics Management1
d. Undefined

111. The creation of finished goods and services using the factors of _____: land, labor, capital, entrepreneurship, and knowledge.
a. Thing
c. Undefined
b. Production1
d. Undefined

112. Those activities that focus on getting the right amount of the right products to the right place at the right time at the lowest possible cost is referred to as _____.
a. Thing
c. Undefined
b. Logistics1
d. Undefined

113. Promoting and selling products or services to customers, or prospective customers, is referred to as _____.
a. Marketing1
c. Undefined
b. Thing
d. Undefined

114. The social science dealing with the use of scarce resources to obtain the maximum satisfaction of society's virtually unlimited economic wants is an _____.
a. Thing
c. Undefined
b. Economics1
d. Undefined

115. A system that collects and processes financial information about an organization and reports that information to decision makers is referred to as _____.
a. Thing
c. Undefined
b. Accounting1
d. Undefined

116. The interest rate that equates a future value or an annuity to a given present value is a _____.
a. Yield1
c. Undefined
b. Thing
d. Undefined

117. Ability to compare the accounting information of different companies because they use the same accounting principles is known as _____.
a. Thing
c. Undefined
b. Comparability1
d. Undefined

118. _____ refers to any departure from the ideal of perfect competition that interferes with economic agents maximizing social welfare when they maximize their own.
a. Distortion1
c. Undefined
b. Thing
d. Undefined

119. The pleading in a civil case in which the plaintiff states his claim and requests relief is called _____. In the common law, it is a formal legal document that sets out the basic facts and legal reasons that the filing party (the plaintiffs) believes are sufficient to support a claim against another person, persons, entity or entities (the defendants) that entitles the plaintiff(s) to a remedy (either money damages or injunctive relief).
- a. Complaint1
- b. Thing
- c. Undefined
- d. Undefined

120. _____ refers to collections of legal rules produced by the American Law Institute, covering certain subject matter areas. Although restatements are often persuasive to courts, they are not legally binding unless adopted by the highest court of a particular state.
- a. Restatement1
- b. Thing
- c. Undefined
- d. Undefined

121. An _____ is any factor (financial or non-financial) that provides a motive for a particular course of action, or counts as a reason for preferring one choice to the alternatives.
- a. Incentive1
- b. Thing
- c. Undefined
- d. Undefined

122. Similar to a script in that a _____ can be a less than completely rational decision-making method. Involves the use of a pre-existing set of decision steps for any problem that presents itself.
- a. Thing
- b. Policy1
- c. Undefined
- d. Undefined

123. A means of measuring the profitability of the firm's products, customer groups, sales territories, channels of distribution, and order sizes is called _____.
- a. Profitability analysis1
- b. Thing
- c. Undefined
- d. Undefined

124. _____ refers to the return a businessperson gets on the money he and other owners invest in the firm; for example, a business that earned $100 on a $1,000 investment would have a ROI of 10 percent: 100 divided by 1000.
- a. Thing
- b. Return on investment1
- c. Undefined
- d. Undefined

125. _____ in a financial context refers to the rate at which a provider of goods cycles through its average inventory. _____ in a human resources context refers to the characteristic of a given company or industry, relative to rate at which an employer gains and loses staff.
- a. Thing
- b. Turnover1
- c. Undefined
- d. Undefined

126. _____ through its subsidiaries and affiliates, provides capital markets services, investment banking and advisory services, wealth management, asset management, insurance, banking and related products and services on a global basis. It is best known for its Global Private Client services and its strong sales force.
- a. Organization
- b. Merrill Lynch1
- c. Undefined
- d. Undefined

127. A short-term immediate decision that, in its totality, leads to the achievement of strategic goals is called a _____.

## Chapter 1. Overview of Financial Statement Analysis

a. Thing
b. Tactic1
c. Undefined
d. Undefined

128. _____ refers to maximum total sales of a product by all firms to a segment during a specified time period under specified environmental conditions and marketing efforts of the firms.
   a. Market potential1
   b. Thing
   c. Undefined
   d. Undefined

129. _____ is using given resources in such a way that the potential positive or negative outcome is magnified. In finance, this generally refers to borrowing.
   a. Thing
   b. Leverage1
   c. Undefined
   d. Undefined

130. A _____ involves the sale or lease of any product, service, equipment, etc. that will enable the purchaser-licensee to begin a business
   a. Thing
   b. Business opportunity1
   c. Undefined
   d. Undefined

131. Cash flow activities that include the cash effects of transactions that create revenues and expenses and thus enter into the determination of net income is an _____.
   a. Operating activities1
   b. Thing
   c. Undefined
   d. Undefined

132. _____ refers to a good that has not been transformed by production; a primary product.
   a. Thing
   b. Raw material1
   c. Undefined
   d. Undefined

133. The body of knowledge and techniques that can be used to combine economic resources to produce goods and services is called _____.
   a. Technology1
   b. Thing
   c. Undefined
   d. Undefined

134. _____ refers to the function in a firm that searches for quality material resources, finds the best suppliers, and negotiates the best price for goods and services.
   a. Purchasing1
   b. Thing
   c. Undefined
   d. Undefined

135. The use of resources for the deliberate discovery of new information and ways of doing things, together with the application of that information in inventing new products or processes is referred to as _____.
   a. Thing
   b. Research and development1
   c. Undefined
   d. Undefined

136. An out-of-court settlement in which creditors agree to accept a fractional settlement on their original claim is referred to as _____.

a. Thing
b. Composition1
c. Undefined
d. Undefined

137. In economics, a _____ is a mechanism which allows people to trade money for securities or commodities such as gold or other precious metals. In general, any commodity market might be considered to be a _____, if the usual purpose of traders is not the immediate consumption of the commodity, but rather as a means of delaying or accelerating consumption over time.
a. Thing
b. Financial market1
c. Undefined
d. Undefined

138. _____ is the way in which the interrelated groups of an organization are constructed. From a managerial point of view the main concerns are ensuring effective communication and coordination.
a. Thing
b. Organizational structure1
c. Undefined
d. Undefined

139. A statement of the assets, liabilities, and net worth of a firm or individual at some given time often at the end of its "fiscal year," is referred to as a _____.
a. Thing
b. Balance sheet1
c. Undefined
d. Undefined

140. In banking and accountancy, the outstanding _____ is the amount of money owned, (or due), that remains in a deposit account (or a loan account) at a given date, after all past remittances, payments and withdrawal have been accounted for. It can be positive (then, in the _____ sheet of a firm, it is an asset) or negative (a liability).
a. Balance1
b. Thing
c. Undefined
d. Undefined

141. _____ refers to the return on an asset expected over the next period.
a. Expected return1
b. Thing
c. Undefined
d. Undefined

142. In 1986, GE acquired NBC. During the 90s, _____ helped to modernize GE by emphasizing a shift from manufacturing to services. He also made hundreds of acquisitions and made a push to dominate markets abroad. Welch adopted the Six Sigma quality program in late 1995.
a. Jack Welch1
b. Person
c. Undefined
d. Undefined

143. An _____ is a company offering debit and credit card acceptance services for merchants. Often the company is partially or wholly owned by a bank, sometimes a bank itself offers acquiring services.
a. Thing
b. Acquirer1
c. Undefined
d. Undefined

144. _____ in economics, the manner in which total output and income is distributed among individuals or factors.
a. Distribution1
b. Thing
c. Undefined
d. Undefined

*Chapter 1. Overview of Financial Statement Analysis*  17

145. _____ refers to an economic variable that is controlled by policy makers and can be used to influence other variables, called targets. Examples are monetary and fiscal policies used to achieve external and internal balance.
   a. Thing
   b. Instrument1
   c. Undefined
   d. Undefined

146. _____ refers to pro rata distributions of stock or stock rights on common stock. They are usually issued in proportion to shares owned.
   a. Thing
   b. Stock dividend1
   c. Undefined
   d. Undefined

147. A measure of the percentage of earnings paid out in dividends; found by dividing cash dividends by the net income available to each class of stock is the _____.
   a. Dividend payout ratio1
   b. Thing
   c. Undefined
   d. Undefined

148. A measure of the percentage of earnings distributed in the form of cash dividends to common stockholders is referred to as the _____. More specifically, the firm's cash dividend divided by the firm's earnings in the same reporting period.
   a. Thing
   b. Payout ratio1
   c. Undefined
   d. Undefined

149. Financing that consists of funds that are invested in exchange for ownership in the company is called _____.
   a. Equity financing1
   b. Thing
   c. Undefined
   d. Undefined

150. The trade of things of value between buyer and seller so that each is better off after the trade is called the _____.
   a. Thing
   b. Exchange1
   c. Undefined
   d. Undefined

151. Financial standards that corporations must meet before their common stock can be traded on a stock exchange are _____. _____ are not standard, but are set by each exchange. The requirements for the NYSE are the most stringent.
   a. Thing
   b. Listing requirements1
   c. Undefined
   d. Undefined

152. A _____ is a corporation or mutual organization which provides facilities for stock brokers and traders, to trade company stocks and other securities.
   a. Stock exchange1
   b. Thing
   c. Undefined
   d. Undefined

153. A person who makes economic decisions for another economic actor. A hired manager operates as an _____ for a firm's owner.
   a. Thing
   b. Agent1
   c. Undefined
   d. Undefined

154. _____ refers to the basic, normal, voting stock issued by a corporation; called residual equity because it ranks after preferred stock for dividend and liquidation distributions.
a. Common stock1
b. Thing
c. Undefined
d. Undefined

155. Obtaining financing by borrowing money is _____.
a. Thing
b. Debt financing1
c. Undefined
d. Undefined

156. A registered representative who works as a market intermediary to buy and sell securities for clients is a _____.
a. Thing
b. Stockbroker1
c. Undefined
d. Undefined

157. People who link buyers with sellers by buying and selling securities at stated prices are referred to as a _____.
a. Dealer1
b. Thing
c. Undefined
d. Undefined

158. Commercial paper or instrument in which the maker promises to pay a specific sum of money to another person, to his order, or to bearer is referred to as a _____.
a. Thing
b. Promissory note1
c. Undefined
d. Undefined

159. A _____ is something measured by a number; it is used to analyze what happens to other things when the size of that number changes.
a. Thing
b. Variable1
c. Undefined
d. Undefined

160. The rate of return on bonds, loans, or deposits. When one speaks of 'the' _____, it is usually in a model where there is only one.
a. Thing
b. Interest rate1
c. Undefined
d. Undefined

161. _____ refers to an intermediate-length loan, in which credit is generally extended from one to seven years. The loan is usually repaid in monthly or quarterly installments over its life, rather than with one single payment.
a. Thing
b. Term loan1
c. Undefined
d. Undefined

162. _____ refers to cash flow activities that include purchasing and disposing of investments and productive long-lived assets using cash and lending money and collecting on those loans.
a. Investing activities1
b. Thing
c. Undefined
d. Undefined

163. _____ are those activities involved in the running of a business for the purpose of producing value for the stakeholders. The outcome of _____ is the harvesting of value from assets owned by a business.

a. Business operations1   b. Thing
c. Undefined   d. Undefined

164. An _____ is a system whether automated or manual, that comprises people, machines, and/or methods organized to collect, process, transmit, and disseminate data that represent user information.
a. Thing   b. Information system1
c. Undefined   d. Undefined

165. _____ refers to the stock of knowledge and skill, embodied in an individual as a result of education, training, and experience that makes them more productive. The stock of knowledge and skill embodied in the population of an economy.
a. Human capital1   b. Thing
c. Undefined   d. Undefined

166. Tangible property held for sale in the normal course of business or used in producing goods or services for sale is an _____.
a. Inventory1   b. Thing
c. Undefined   d. Undefined

167. The legal right to the proceeds from and control over the use of a created product, such a written work, audio, video, film, or software is a _____. This right generally extends over the life of the author plus fifty years.
a. Thing   b. Copyright1
c. Undefined   d. Undefined

168. A _____ in the sphere of Intellectual Property Rights (IPR) is a document, contract or agreement giving permission or the 'right' to a legally-definable entity to do something (such as manufacture a product or to use a service), or to apply something (such as a trademark), with the objective of achieving commercial gain.
a. License1   b. Thing
c. Undefined   d. Undefined

169. The legal right to the proceeds from and control over the use of an invented product or process, granted for a fixed period of time, usually 20 years. _____ is one form of intellectual property that is subject of the TRIPS agreement.
a. Thing   b. Patent1
c. Undefined   d. Undefined

170. _____ refer to monetary claims or obligations by one party against another party. Examples are bonds, mortgages, bank loans, and equities.
a. Thing   b. Financial assets1
c. Undefined   d. Undefined

171. _____ are those assets usually in service over one year such as buildings, equipment, and long-term investments. These often receive favorable tax treatment over current assets. Tangible long-term assets are usually referred to as fixed assets.
a. Noncurrent assets1   b. Thing
c. Undefined   d. Undefined

## Chapter 1. Overview of Financial Statement Analysis

172. _____ is the relative proportion of labor (compared to capital) used in a process.
 a. Labor intensity1 b. Thing
 c. Undefined d. Undefined

173. A contract for the possession and use of land or other property, including goods, on one side, and a recompense of rent or other income on the other is the _____.
 a. Lease1 b. Thing
 c. Undefined d. Undefined

174. _____ is an accounting term, meaning future tax liability or asset, resulting from temporary differences between book (accounting) value of assets and liabilities, and their tax value.
 a. Thing b. Deferred tax1
 c. Undefined d. Undefined

175. _____ is an important accounting concept that describes the value of a business entity not directly attributable to its tangible assets and liabilities.
 a. Thing b. Goodwill1
 c. Undefined d. Undefined

176. A _____ is a steady income given to a person (usually after retirement). Pensions are typically payments made in the form of a guaranteed annuity to a retired or disabled employee.
 a. Pension1 b. Thing
 c. Undefined d. Undefined

177. _____ refers to the management and direction of the affairs of governments and institutions; a collective term for all policymaking officials of a government; the execution and implementation of public policy.
 a. Thing b. Administration1
 c. Undefined d. Undefined

178. _____ is the acquisition of goods or services at the best possible total cost of ownership, in the right quantity, at the right time, in the right place for the direct benefit or use of the governments, corporations, or individuals generally via, but not limited to a contract.
 a. Thing b. Procurement1
 c. Undefined d. Undefined

179. _____ is equal to the income that a firm has after subtracting costs and expenses from the total revenue. Expenses will typically include tax expense.
 a. Thing b. Net income1
 c. Undefined d. Undefined

180. Expression of the relationship between the assets and the claims on those assets is referred to as the _____, specifically Assets = Liabilities + Owners' equity.
 a. Thing b. Accounting equation1
 c. Undefined d. Undefined

## Chapter 1. Overview of Financial Statement Analysis

181. _____ is the value of funds or other consideration contributed to a company in return for an ownership interest. For instance, _____ increases when a person invests money in a company and received a stock certificate recognizing their right to share in the profits and losses of a company and increases or decreases in the equity value of the company.
   a. Thing
   b. Contributed capital1
   c. Undefined
   d. Undefined

182. Cumulative earnings of a company that are not distributed to the owners and are reinvested in the business are called _____.
   a. Retained earnings1
   b. Thing
   c. Undefined
   d. Undefined

183. The date and time on which coverage under an insurance policy takes effect is _____. Also refers to the date at which a stock or mutual fund was first traded.
   a. Inception1
   b. Thing
   c. Undefined
   d. Undefined

184. A person in possession of a document of title or an instrument payable or indorsed to him, his order, or to bearer is a _____.
   a. Holder1
   b. Thing
   c. Undefined
   d. Undefined

185. _____ refers to the time it takes for a company to purchase goods or services from suppliers, sell those goods and services to customers, and collect cash from customers.
   a. Thing
   b. Operating cycle1
   c. Undefined
   d. Undefined

186. The dollar difference between total current assets and total current liabilities is called _____.
   a. Working capital1
   b. Thing
   c. Undefined
   d. Undefined

187. Systematic and rational allocation of the acquisition cost of an intangible asset over its useful life is referred to as _____.
   a. Amortization1
   b. Thing
   c. Undefined
   d. Undefined

188. _____ is an accounting and finance term for the method of attributing the cost of an asset across the useful life of the asset. _____ is a reduction in the value of a currency in floating exchange rate.
   a. Thing
   b. Depreciation1
   c. Undefined
   d. Undefined

189. _____ refers to a financial statement that presents the revenues and expenses and resulting net income or net loss of a company for a specific period of time.
   a. Income statement1
   b. Thing
   c. Undefined
   d. Undefined

190. The _____ is net income on the last line of a income statement.

a. Thing
b. Bottom line1
c. Undefined
d. Undefined

191. _____ in contract law, a basic requirement for an enforceable agreement under traditional contract principles, defined in this text as legal value, bargained for and given in exchange for an act or promise. In corporation law, cash or property contributed to a corporation in exchange for shares, or a promise to contribute such cash or property.
a. Thing
b. Consideration1
c. Undefined
d. Undefined

192. In business organization law, the cash or property contributed to a business by its owners is referred to as _____.
a. Contribution1
b. Thing
c. Undefined
d. Undefined

193. _____ refers to the total costs of goods made or purchased and sold.
a. Cost of sales1
b. Thing
c. Undefined
d. Undefined

194. _____ is an ambiguous phrase that expresses the relationship between gross profit and sales revenue as _____ = Revenue - costs of good sold.
a. Gross margin1
b. Thing
c. Undefined
d. Undefined

195. Net sales less cost of goods sold is called _____.
a. Gross profit1
b. Thing
c. Undefined
d. Undefined

196. Method of accounting that records the effects of accounting events in the period in which such events occur regardless of when cash is exchanged is _____.
a. Accrual accounting1
b. Thing
c. Undefined
d. Undefined

197. An _____ is an accounting event in which the transaction is recognized when the action takes place, instead of when cash is disbursed or received.
a. Accrual1
b. Thing
c. Undefined
d. Undefined

198. Another name for net income is _____. That part of a company's profits remaining after all expenses and taxes have been paid and out of which dividends may be paid.
a. Thing
b. Net earnings1
c. Undefined
d. Undefined

199. _____ refers to net income plus unrealized gain or loss on securities, minimum pension liability adjustment, and foreign currency translation adjustment.

## Chapter 1. Overview of Financial Statement Analysis

a. Thing
c. Undefined
b. Comprehensive income1
d. Undefined

200. Corporate stock that has been reacquired by the corporation is _____. It is stock which is bought back by the issuing company. It reduces the number of outstanding stocks on the open market ("open market" including insiders holdings).
a. Thing
c. Undefined
b. Treasury stock1
d. Undefined

201. Reports inflows and outflows of cash during the accounting period in the categories of operating, investing, and financing is a _____.
a. Thing
c. Undefined
b. Statement of cash flow1
d. Undefined

202. Cash coming into the company as the result of a previous investment is a _____.
a. Cash inflow1
c. Undefined
b. Thing
d. Undefined

203. _____ refers to the price at which one country's currency trades for another, typically on the exchange market.
a. Exchange rate1
c. Undefined
b. Thing
d. Undefined

204. Loan origination fees that may be deductible as interest by a buyer of property. A seller of property who pays _____ reduces the selling price by the amount of the _____ paid for the buyer.
a. Thing
c. Undefined
b. Points1
d. Undefined

205. _____ refer to representation of ownership rights to the corporation.
a. Thing
c. Undefined
b. Equity securities1
d. Undefined

206. _____ refers to the long-term movement of an economic variable, such as its average rate of increase or decrease over enough years to encompass several business cycles.
a. Trend1
c. Undefined
b. Thing
d. Undefined

207. _____ refers to U.S. government agency that determines the financial statements that public companies must provide to stockholders and the measurement rules that they must use in producing those statements.
a. Organization
c. Undefined
b. Securities and exchange commission1
d. Undefined

208. _____ is generally a team of individuals at the highest level of organizational management who have the day-to-day responsibilities of managing a corporation.
a. Thing
c. Undefined
b. Senior management1
d. Undefined

209. _____ refers to the plan of organization and all the related methods and measures adopted within a business to safeguard its assets and enhance the accuracy and reliability of its accounting records.
 a. Thing
 b. Internal control1
 c. Undefined
 d. Undefined

210. A _____ is a device or set of devices that manage the behavior of other devices. Some devices or systems are not controllable.A _____ is an interconnection of components connected or related in such a manner as to command, direct, or regulate itself or another system.
 a. Control system1
 b. Thing
 c. Undefined
 d. Undefined

211. The group of individuals elected by the stockholders of a corporation to oversee its operations is a _____.
 a. Board of directors1
 b. Thing
 c. Undefined
 d. Undefined

212. _____ in corporation law, a committee of the board that recommends and supervises the public accountant who audits the corporation's financial records.
 a. Thing
 b. Audit committee1
 c. Undefined
 d. Undefined

213. _____ refers to an individual in the United States who have passed the Uniform _____ Examination and have met additional state education and experience requirements for certification as a _____.
 a. Certified Public Accountant1
 b. Thing
 c. Undefined
 d. Undefined

214. _____ refers to the standard framework of guidelines for financial accounting. It includes the standards, conventions, and rules accountants follow in recording and summarizing transactions, and in the preparation of financial statements.
 a. Generally accepted accounting principles1
 b. Thing
 c. Undefined
 d. Undefined

215. _____ refers to a written statement-also called an accountant's certificate, accountant's opinion, or audit report- prepared by an independent accountant or auditor after an audit.
 a. Thing
 b. Financial report1
 c. Undefined
 d. Undefined

216. A _____ is a specific type of option that uses the stock itself as an underlying instrument to determine the option's pay-off and therefore its value.
 a. Stock option1
 b. Thing
 c. Undefined
 d. Undefined

217. A contract that gives the purchaser the _____ to buy or sell the underlying financial instrument at a specified price, called the exercise price or strike price, within a specific period of time.
 a. Option1
 b. Thing
 c. Undefined
 d. Undefined

*Chapter 1. Overview of Financial Statement Analysis*

218. In economics, an _____ is any good or commodity, shipped or otherwise transported out of a country, province, town to another part of the world in a legitimate fashion, typically for use in trade or sale.
   a. Thing
   b. Export1
   c. Undefined
   d. Undefined

219. A _____ is an action taken by a public company that has a direct effect on the holdings of its shareholders. The most common example of a _____ is a dividend, a payment to the shareholder of company profits. Other examples include cash from the sale of rights, stock splits, and the release of warrants or options on the security.
   a. Thing
   b. Corporate action1
   c. Undefined
   d. Undefined

220. _____ refers to a person who is authorized to vote the shares of another person. Also, the written authorization empowering a person to vote the shares of another person.
   a. Thing
   b. Proxy1
   c. Undefined
   d. Undefined

221. _____ refers to a document that fully describes the matter for which the proxy is being solicited, who is soliciting the proxy, and any other pertinent information.
   a. Proxy statement1
   b. Thing
   c. Undefined
   d. Undefined

222. A financial statement showing the results of two or more successive years is called a _____.
   a. Comparative financial statement1
   b. Thing
   c. Undefined
   d. Undefined

223. A technique for evaluating a series of financial statement data over a period of time to determine the increase that has taken place, expressed as either an amount or a percentage, is a _____.
   a. Thing
   b. Horizontal analysis1
   c. Undefined
   d. Undefined

224. A comparison across time of three or more observations of a particular financial item, such as net income, is called _____.
   a. Trend analysis1
   b. Thing
   c. Undefined
   d. Undefined

225. An _____ expresses the cost of a market basket of goods relative to its cost in some 'base' period, which is simply the year or years used as a basis of comparison.
   a. Thing
   b. Index number1
   c. Undefined
   d. Undefined

226. _____ refers to the time period used for comparative analysis; the basis for indexing, e.g., of price change. A _____ may be a month, year or average of years.
   a. Thing
   b. Base period1
   c. Undefined
   d. Undefined

## Chapter 1. Overview of Financial Statement Analysis

227. In throughput accounting, the cost accounting aspect of Theory of Constraints (TOC), _____ is the money spent turning inventory into throughput. In TOC, _____ is limited to costs that vary strictly with the quantity produced, like raw materials and purchased components.
   a. Operating expense1
   b. Thing
   c. Undefined
   d. Undefined

228. The year used as the basis for comparison by a price index such as the CPI. The index for any year is the average of prices for that year compared to the _____; e.g., 110 means that prices are 10% higher than in the _____.
   a. Base year1
   b. Thing
   c. Undefined
   d. Undefined

229. _____ equals Gross Profit divided by Revenue, expressed as a percentage. The percentage represents the amount of each dollar of Revenue that results in Gross Profit.
   a. Gross profit margin1
   b. Thing
   c. Undefined
   d. Undefined

230. A market in which no buyer or seller has market power is called a _____.
   a. Competitive market1
   b. Thing
   c. Undefined
   d. Undefined

231. _____ is a measure of profitability. It is calculated using a formula and written as a percentage or a number. _____ = Net income before tax and interest / Revenue.
   a. Profit margin1
   b. Thing
   c. Undefined
   d. Undefined

232. _____ refers to an analytical tool designed to identify significant relationships; measures the proportional relationship between two financial statement amounts.
   a. Ratio analysis1
   b. Thing
   c. Undefined
   d. Undefined

233. _____ refer to securities that are readily traded in the secondary securities market.
   a. Marketable securities1
   b. Thing
   c. Undefined
   d. Undefined

234. In Keynesian economics _____ refers to personal _____ expenditure, i.e., the purchase of currently produced goods and services out of income, out of savings (net worth), or from borrowed funds. It refers to that part of disposable income that does not go to saving.
   a. Thing
   b. Consumption1
   c. Undefined
   d. Undefined

235. _____ refers to the method under which income and expenses are determined for tax purposes. Important accounting methods include the cash basis and the accrual basis.
   a. Thing
   b. Accounting method1
   c. Undefined
   d. Undefined

## Chapter 1. Overview of Financial Statement Analysis

236. Tax _____ falls into two categories: civil and criminal. Under civil _____, the IRS may impose as a penalty of an amount equal to as much as 75 percent of the underpayment.
 a. Fraud1
 b. Thing
 c. Undefined
 d. Undefined

237. A financial ratio that indicates the organization's ability to meet its current debt obligations is referred to as _____.
 a. Liquidity ratio1
 b. Thing
 c. Undefined
 d. Undefined

238. The _____ is a comparison of a firm's current assets to its current liabilities. The _____ is an indication of a firm's market liquidity and ability to meet short-term debt obligations.
 a. Current ratio1
 b. Thing
 c. Undefined
 d. Undefined

239. _____ is one of a series of accounting transactions dealing with the billing of customers which owe money to a person, company or organization for goods and services that have been provided to the customer. This is typically done in a one person organization by writing an invoice and mailing or delivering it to each customer.
 a. Thing
 b. Accounts receivable1
 c. Undefined
 d. Undefined

240. _____ refers to any distinct act of dominion wrongfully exerted over another's personal property in denial of or inconsistent with his rights therein. That tort committed by a person who deals with chattels not belonging to him in a manner that is inconsistent with the ownership of the lawful owner.
 a. Conversion1
 b. Thing
 c. Undefined
 d. Undefined

241. _____ refers to the way a corporation finances itself through some combination of equity sales, equity options, bonds, and loans. Optimal _____ refers to the particular combination that minimizes the cost of capital while maximizing the stock price.
 a. Capital structure1
 b. Thing
 c. Undefined
 d. Undefined

242. In finance, _____ occurs when a debtor has not met its legal obligations according to the debt contract, e.g. it has not made a scheduled payment, or violated a covenant (condition) of the debt contract.
 a. Thing
 b. Default1
 c. Undefined
 d. Undefined

243. Net profit after taxes per dollar of equity capital is referred to as _____.
 a. Thing
 b. Return on equity1
 c. Undefined
 d. Undefined

244. The common stock or ownership capital of the firm is _____. _____ may be supplied through retained earnings or the sale of new common stock.

a. Common equity1  
b. Thing  
c. Undefined  
d. Undefined

245. _____ - earnings before extraordinary items, less preferred-share dividends, divided by average common shareholders' equity. Shows the rate of return on the investment for the company's common shareholders, the only providers of capital who do not have a fixed return.
a. Thing  
b. Return on common Equity1  
c. Undefined  
d. Undefined

246. In finance, the _____ of a stock is used to measure how cheap or expensive share prices are. It is probably the single most consistent red flag to excessive optimism and over-investment.
a. Thing  
b. P/E ratio1  
c. Undefined  
d. Undefined

247. Cash flowing out of the business from all sources over a period of time is _____.
a. Cash outflow1  
b. Thing  
c. Undefined  
d. Undefined

248. The value today of a stream of payments and/or receipts over time in the future and/or the past, converted to the present using an interest rate. If X t is the amount in period t and r the interest rate, then _____ at time t=0 is V = ?T /t.
a. Present value1  
b. Thing  
c. Undefined  
d. Undefined

249. _____ concerns itself with the worth, utility, trading or economic value, moral value (virtue), legal value, quantitative or aesthetic value of people and things - or the combination of all these.
a. Value theory1  
b. Event  
c. Undefined  
d. Undefined

250. _____ refers to a rise in the value of a country's currency on the exchange market, relative either to a particular other currency or to a weighted average of other currencies. The currency is said to appreciate. Opposite of 'depreciation.' _____ can also refer to the increase in value of any asset.
a. Appreciation1  
b. Thing  
c. Undefined  
d. Undefined

251. Type of security acquired by loaning assets is called a _____.
a. Thing  
b. Debt security1  
c. Undefined  
d. Undefined

252. An increase in the overall price level of an economy, usually as measured by the CPI or by the implicit price deflator is called _____.
a. Thing  
b. Inflation1  
c. Undefined  
d. Undefined

253. The payment to holders of bonds payable, calculated by multiplying the stated rate on the face of the bond by the par, or face, value of the bond. If bonds are issued at a discount or premium, the _____ does not equal the interest expense.

a. Interest payment1  
b. Thing  
c. Undefined  
d. Undefined

254. _____ refers to a thing that was originally personal property and that has been actually or constructively affixed to the soil itself or to some structure legally a part of the land.
   a. Fixture1  
   b. Thing  
   c. Undefined  
   d. Undefined

255. Cash provided by operating activities adjusted for capital expenditures and dividends paid is referred to as _____.
   a. Free cash flow1  
   b. Thing  
   c. Undefined  
   d. Undefined

256. A substantial expenditure that is used by a company to acquire or upgrade physical assets such as equipment, property, industrial buildings, including those which improve the quality and life of an asset is referred to as a _____.
   a. Capital expenditure1  
   b. Thing  
   c. Undefined  
   d. Undefined

257. Major investments in long-term assets such as land, buildings, equipment, or research and development are referred to as _____.
   a. Thing  
   b. Capital expenditures1  
   c. Undefined  
   d. Undefined

258. An organization that employs resources to produce a good or service for profit and owns and operates one or more plants is referred to as a _____.
   a. Firm1  
   b. Thing  
   c. Undefined  
   d. Undefined

259. _____ is the term used to describe income received based on the production of those others who have become members of one's organization.
   a. Thing  
   b. Residual income1  
   c. Undefined  
   d. Undefined

260. _____ payments can refer to an ongoing stream of payments in respect of the completion of past achievements.
   a. Residual1  
   b. Thing  
   c. Undefined  
   d. Undefined

261. The _____ of an asset or group of assets is sometimes the price at which they were originally acquired, in many cases equal to purchase price.
   a. Thing  
   b. Book value1  
   c. Undefined  
   d. Undefined

262. In finance, the _____ of a security is the present value at a future point in time of all future cash flows. It is most often used in multi-stage discounted cash flow analysis, and allows for the limitation of cash flow projections to a several-year period.

a. Terminal value1  
b. Thing  
c. Undefined  
d. Undefined

263. _____ is an economic concept with commonplace familiarity; it is the price that a good or service is offered at, or will fetch, in the marketplace; it is of interest mainly in the study of microeconomics.
a. Thing  
b. Market price1  
c. Undefined  
d. Undefined

264. The application of the theory of rational expectations to financial markets is referred to as _____.
a. Thing  
b. Efficient market hypothesis1  
c. Undefined  
d. Undefined

265. Confidential information of a company, its products, or securities not generally available to the public gained from a source inside the company is called _____.
a. Inside information1  
b. Thing  
c. Undefined  
d. Undefined

266. A financial market in which long-term debt and equity instruments are traded is referred to as a _____. The _____ includes the stock market and the bond market.
a. Thing  
b. Capital market1  
c. Undefined  
d. Undefined

267. As used in economics, _____ means something unexpected, rather than the more extreme normal meaning of something seemingly impossible. Some paradoxes are just theoretical results that go against what one thinks of as normal.
a. Thing  
b. Paradox1  
c. Undefined  
d. Undefined

268. In economics, _____ refers to relationships between economic aggregates such as national income, government expenditure and aggregate demand. For example, the consumption function is a relationship between aggregate demand for consumption and aggregate disposable income.
a. Aggregate behavior1  
b. Thing  
c. Undefined  
d. Undefined

269. Book of original entry, in which transactions are recorded in a general ledger system, is referred to as a _____.
a. Thing  
b. Journal1  
c. Undefined  
d. Undefined

270. A _____ is sometimes thought of as perma-bears—market participants who are permanently biased to a bear market view. However, the _____ is not biased specifically towards a negative view of the price trend in a market, but rather takes a contrary position to the prevailing market trend, whether that trend is positive or negative.
a. Thing  
b. Contrarian1  
c. Undefined  
d. Undefined

271. An organized marketplace in which common stocks are traded. In the United States, the largest _____ is the New York Stock Exchange, on which are traded the stocks of the largest U.S. companies.

## Chapter 1. Overview of Financial Statement Analysis

a. Stock market1
c. Undefined
b. Thing
d. Undefined

272. Today, the _____ consists of 30 of the largest and most widely held public companies in the United States. The "industrial" portion of the name is largely historical—many of the 30 modern components have little to do with heavy industry. To compensate for the effects of stock splits and other adjustments, it is currently a weighted average, not the actual average of the prices of its component stocks.
a. Organization
c. Undefined
b. Dow Jones Industrial Average1
d. Undefined

273. _____ refers to a database that includes decision rules for use of the data, which may be qualitative as well as quantitative.
a. Knowledge base1
c. Undefined
b. Thing
d. Undefined

274. A company that conducts various aspects of securities trading, analysis and advisory services is a _____.
a. Thing
c. Undefined
b. Brokerage firm1
d. Undefined

275. The _____ is the market for securities, where companies and the government can raise long-term funds.
a. Securities market1
c. Undefined
b. Thing
d. Undefined

276. _____ is an American stock investor, businessman and philanthropist. Nicknamed the "Oracle of Omaha" or the "Sage of Omaha", he has amassed an enormous fortune from astute investments, particularly through his company Berkshire Hathaway, in which he holds a greater than 38% stake.
a. Warren Buffett1
c. Undefined
b. Person
d. Undefined

277. _____ is one of the most general and applicable methods of analytical thinking, depending only on the division of a problem, decision or situation into a sufficient number of separate cases.
a. Thing
c. Undefined
b. Case analysis1
d. Undefined

278. _____ refers to an economic theory that describes how rational investors allocate their wealth among different financial assets-that is, how they put their wealth into a 'portfolio.'
a. Thing
c. Undefined
b. Portfolio theory1
d. Undefined

279. In finance, a _____ is a collection of investments held by an institution or a private individual. Holding but not always a _____ is part of an investment and risk-limiting strategy called diversification. By owning several assets, certain types of risk (in particular specific risk) can be reduced.
a. Portfolio1
c. Undefined
b. Thing
d. Undefined

**Chapter 1. Overview of Financial Statement Analysis**

280. _____ refers to a measure of how much an economic or statistical variable varies across values or observations. Its calculation is the same as that of the covariance, being the covariance of the variable with itself.
- a. Variance1
- b. Thing
- c. Undefined
- d. Undefined

281. Investing in a collection of assets whose returns do not always move together, with the result that overall risk is lower than for individual assets is referred to as _____.
- a. Thing
- b. Diversification1
- c. Undefined
- d. Undefined

282. A _____ is a comparison of the money earned (or lost) on an investment to the amount of money invested.
- a. Rate of return1
- b. Thing
- c. Undefined
- d. Undefined

283. The anxieties felt because the consumer cannot anticipate the outcomes of a purchase but believes that there may be negative consequences is called a _____.
- a. Thing
- b. Perceived risk1
- c. Undefined
- d. Undefined

284. _____ refers to the rate of return that investors demand from an investment to compensate them for the amount of risk involved.
- a. Required rate of return1
- b. Thing
- c. Undefined
- d. Undefined

285. The _____ (sensitivity of the asset returns to market returns, relative volatility), is a key parameter in the Capital asset pricing model. It can also be defined as the risk of the stock to a diversified portfolio.
- a. Beta coefficient1
- b. Thing
- c. Undefined
- d. Undefined

286. Movements in a stock portfolio's value that are attributable to macroeconomic forces affecting all firms in an economy, rather than factors specific to an individual firm are referred to as _____.
- a. Thing
- b. Systematic risk1
- c. Undefined
- d. Undefined

287. Short-term obligations of the federal government are _____. They are like zero coupon bonds in that they do not pay interest prior to maturity; instead they are sold at a discount of the par value to create a positive yield to maturity.
- a. Treasury bills1
- b. Thing
- c. Undefined
- d. Undefined

288. _____ refers to the extent of the up and down movements of a fluctuating economic variable; that is, the difference between the highest and lowest values of the variable.
- a. Thing
- b. Amplitude1
- c. Undefined
- d. Undefined

289. The likelihood that events, including economic mismanagement, will cause drastic changes in a country's business environment that adversely affects the profit and other goals of a particular business enterprise is referred to as _____.

a. Thing
b. Economic risk1
c. Undefined
d. Undefined

290. The amount of goods that money will buy, usually measured by the CPI is referred to as _____.
a. Thing
b. Purchasing power1
c. Undefined
d. Undefined

291. _____ is the risk that the value of an investment will decrease due to moves in market factors.
a. Thing
b. Market risk1
c. Undefined
d. Undefined

292. The risk related to the inability of the firm to hold its competitive position and maintain stability and growth in earnings is _____.
a. Business risk1
b. Thing
c. Undefined
d. Undefined

293. _____ refers to the extent to which an economic variable, such as a price or an exchange rate, moves up and down over time.
a. Thing
b. Volatility1
c. Undefined
d. Undefined

294. _____ refers to the fee charged by an insurance company for an insurance policy. The rate of losses must be relatively predictable: In order to set the _____ (prices) insurers must be able to estimate them accurately.
a. Premium1
b. Thing
c. Undefined
d. Undefined

295. In finance, the _____ can be the expected rate of return above the risk-free interest rate.
a. Thing
b. Risk premium1
c. Undefined
d. Undefined

296. The _____ is a court's determination of a matter of law based on the issue presented in the particular case. In other words: under this law, with these facts, this result.
a. Holding1
b. Thing
c. Undefined
d. Undefined

297. _____ is a risk-adjusted measure of the so-called "excess return" on an investment. It is a common measure of assessing active manager's performance as it is the return in excess of a benchmark index or "risk-free" investment.
a. Thing
b. Alpha1
c. Undefined
d. Undefined

298. _____ refers to a portfolio that includes a variety of assets whose prices are not likely all to change together. In international economics, this usually means holding assets denominated in different currencies.
a. Thing
b. Diversified portfolio1
c. Undefined
d. Undefined

## Chapter 1. Overview of Financial Statement Analysis

299. _____ refers to the assignment of income for various tax purposes. A multistate corporation's nonbusiness income usually is distributed to the state where the nonbusiness assets are located; it is not apportioned with the rest of the entity's income.
- a. Allocate1
- b. Thing
- c. Undefined
- d. Undefined

300. _____ refers to provisions in a law or a contract whereby monetary payments are automatically adjusted whenever a specified price index changes.
- a. Indexing1
- b. Thing
- c. Undefined
- d. Undefined

301. _____ refers to a special type of mutual fund that engages in 'market-neutral strategies'. They are primarily organized as limited partnerships, and previously were often simply called "limited partnerships" and were grouped with other similar partnerships such as those that invested in oil development.
- a. Hedge fund1
- b. Thing
- c. Undefined
- d. Undefined

302. _____ refers to a process of offsetting risk. In the foreign exchange market, hedgers use the forward market to cover a transaction or open position and thereby reduce exchange risk. The term applies most commonly to trade.
- a. Thing
- b. Hedge1
- c. Undefined
- d. Undefined

303. A company that is controlled by another company or corporation is a _____.
- a. Thing
- b. Subsidiary1
- c. Undefined
- d. Undefined

304. _____ refers to the amount by which expenses exceed revenues. The difference between income received and expenses, when expenses are greater.
- a. Net loss1
- b. Thing
- c. Undefined
- d. Undefined

305. A _____ is a financial report that shows incoming and outgoing money during a particular period (often monthly or quarterly). The statement shows how changes in balance sheet and income accounts affected cash and cash equivalents and breaks the analysis down according to operating, investing, and financing activities.
- a. Cash flow statement1
- b. Thing
- c. Undefined
- d. Undefined

306. _____ refers to another name for a business organization. Other similar terms are business firm, sometimes simply business, sometimes simply firm, as well as company, and entity.
- a. Enterprise1
- b. Thing
- c. Undefined
- d. Undefined

307. Yield rate of bonds, which is usually equal to the market rate of interest on the day the bonds are sold is the _____.

a. Effective interest rate1
b. Thing
c. Undefined
d. Undefined

308. In accounting, a _____ is an asset that is recorded as property that creates more property, e.g. a factory that creates shoes, or a forest that yields a quantity of wood.
a. Capital asset1
b. Thing
c. Undefined
d. Undefined

309. The _____ is used in finance to determine a theoretically appropriate required rate of return (and thus the price if expected cash flows can be estimated) of an asset, if that asset is to be added to an already well-diversified portfolio, given that asset's non-diversifiable risk.
a. Capital asset pricing model1
b. Thing
c. Undefined
d. Undefined

310. _____ refers to usually the first stage in the creative process. It includes education and formal training.
a. Preparation1
b. Thing
c. Undefined
d. Undefined

311. Two or more balance sheets from the same company for consecutive accounting periods, shown together to reflect the company's financial situation over time are refrred to as _____.
a. Comparative balance sheets1
b. Thing
c. Undefined
d. Undefined

312. In accounting, the _____ describes the direct expenses incurred in producing a particular good for sale, including the actual cost of materials that comprise the good, and direct labor expense in putting the good in salable condition.
a. Thing
b. Cost of goods sold1
c. Undefined
d. Undefined

313. The nominal or par value of an instrument as expressed on its face is referred to as the _____.
a. Thing
b. Face value1
c. Undefined
d. Undefined

314. In finance, a _____ is "attached" to a bond, either physically (as with old bonds) or electronically. Each _____ represents a predetermined payment promized to the bond-holder in return for his or her loan of money to the bond-issuer. .
a. Coupon1
b. Concept
c. Undefined
d. Undefined

315. A legal entity chartered by a state or the Federal government that is distinct and separate from the individuals who own it is a _____. This separation gives the _____ unique powers which other legal entities lack.
a. Organization
b. Corporation1
c. Undefined
d. Undefined

316. Gross sales less sales returns and allowances and sales discounts are referred to as _____.

a. Thing  
c. Undefined  
b. Net sales1  
d. Undefined

317. A pro rata distribution of cash to stockholders of corporate stock is called a _____.
a. Cash dividend1  
c. Undefined  
b. Thing  
d. Undefined

318. The _____ is a financial ratio debt divided by shareholders' equity. The two components are often taken from the firm's balance sheet, but they might also be calulated as market values if both the companiy's debt and equity are publicly traded. It is used to calculate a company's "financial leverage" and indicates what proportion of equity and debt the company is using to finance its assets.
a. Debt to equity ratio1  
c. Undefined  
b. Thing  
d. Undefined

319. Measures the percentage of each dollar of sales that results in net income, computed by dividing net income by net sales are referred to as _____.
a. Profit margin ratio1  
c. Undefined  
b. Thing  
d. Undefined

320. _____ refers to obligations that are not paid within 1 year.
a. Noncurrent liabilities1  
c. Undefined  
b. Thing  
d. Undefined

321. _____ refers to net income before interest and taxes, divided by interest expense; describes a company's ability to make interest payments on its debt.
a. Thing  
c. Undefined  
b. Times interest earned1  
d. Undefined

322. At equality refers to _____. Two currencies are said to be '_____' if they are trading one-for-one.
a. Thing  
c. Undefined  
b. At par1  
d. Undefined

323. Stock that has specified rights over common stock is a _____.
a. Thing  
c. Undefined  
b. Preferred stock1  
d. Undefined

324. The central value of a pegged exchange rate, around which the actual rate is permitted to fluctuate within set bounds is a _____.
a. Thing  
c. Undefined  
b. Par value1  
d. Undefined

325. Assets defined in the broadest legal sense. _____ includes the unrealized receivables of a cash basis taxpayer, but not services rendered.
a. Thing  
c. Undefined  
b. Property1  
d. Undefined

*Chapter 1. Overview of Financial Statement Analysis*  37

326. A written record of all vendors to whom the business firm owes money is referred to as _____.
 a. Thing
 b. Accounts payable1
 c. Undefined
 d. Undefined

327. Expenses that have been incurred by the end of the current accounting period but that will not be paid until a future accounting period are _____.
 a. Accrued expenses1
 b. Thing
 c. Undefined
 d. Undefined

328. The cost a business incurs to borrow money. With respect to bonds payable, the _____ is calculated by multiplying the market rate of interest by the carrying value of the bonds on the date of the payment.
 a. Interest expense1
 b. Thing
 c. Undefined
 d. Undefined

329. In accrual basis accounting, _____ is a liability resulting from an expense for which no invoice or other official document is available yet.
 a. Thing
 b. Accrued expense1
 c. Undefined
 d. Undefined

330. An _____ is the part of a contractually due sum that is paid in advance, while the balance will only follow after receipt on the counterpart in goods or services.
 a. Advance payment1
 b. Thing
 c. Undefined
 d. Undefined

331. _____ refers to an obligation in the form of a written promissory note. It is a balance sheet term referring to a company's outstanding bank loans.
 a. Thing
 b. Notes payable1
 c. Undefined
 d. Undefined

332. _____ refers to the total number of dollars received by a firm from the sale of a product; equal to the total expenditures for the product produced by the firm; equal to the quantity sold multiplied by the price at which it is sold.
 a. Thing
 b. Total revenue1
 c. Undefined
 d. Undefined

333. A _____ is a ratio of two numbers of reported levels or flows of a company. It may be two financial flows categories divided by each other (profit margin, profit/revenue). It may be a level divided by a financial flow (price/earnings). It may be a flow divided by a level (return on equity or earnings/equity). The numerator or denominator may itself be a ratio (PEG ratio).
 a. Financial ratio1
 b. Thing
 c. Undefined
 d. Undefined

334. A professional that provides expert advice in a particular field or area in which customers occassionaly require this type of knowledge is a _____.
 a. Consultant1
 b. Concept
 c. Undefined
 d. Undefined

## Chapter 1. Overview of Financial Statement Analysis

335. Valuation method departing from the cost principle that recognizes a loss when replacement cost or net realizable value drops below cost is called _____.
- a. Lower of cost1
- b. Thing
- c. Undefined
- d. Undefined

336. A _____ is a method by which an organization sets aside money over time to retire its indebtedness. More specifically, it is a fund into which money can be deposited, so that over time its preferred stock, debentures or stocks can be retired.
- a. Sinking fund1
- b. Thing
- c. Undefined
- d. Undefined

337. A _____ is a long-term debt instrument used by governments and large companies to obtain funds. It is similar to a bond except the securitization conditions are different.
- a. Debenture1
- b. Thing
- c. Undefined
- d. Undefined

338. Reduction in the selling price of goods extended to the buyer because the goods are defective or of lower quality than the buyer ordered and to encourage a buyer to keep merchandise that would otherwise be returned is the _____.
- a. Allowance1
- b. Thing
- c. Undefined
- d. Undefined

339. In accounting and finance, _____ is the portion of receivables that can no longer be collected, typically from accounts receivable or loans. _____ in accounting is considered an expense.
- a. Bad debt1
- b. Thing
- c. Undefined
- d. Undefined

340. _____ refers to the final payment date of a loan or other financial instrument, after which point no further interest or principal need be paid.
- a. Maturity1
- b. Thing
- c. Undefined
- d. Undefined

341. _____ refers to the total depreciation that has been reported as depreciation expense for the entire life of a long-term tangible asset. It is a contra-asset account.
- a. Thing
- b. Accumulated depreciation1
- c. Undefined
- d. Undefined

342. _____ is an accounting method used to establish the dollar amount at which assets are recorded on a savings association's books. The amount established is the lower of the cost of the asset or the current market value.
- a. Thing
- b. Lower of Cost or Market1
- c. Undefined
- d. Undefined

343. The total amount of physical capital that has been accumulated, usually in a country is _____. Also refers to the total issued capital of a firm, including ordinary and preferred shares.
- a. Capital stock1
- b. Thing
- c. Undefined
- d. Undefined

## Chapter 1. Overview of Financial Statement Analysis

344. _____ refers to a process whereby the assets of a business are converted to money. The conversion may be coerced by a legal process to pay off the debt of the business, or to satisfy any other business obligation that the business has not voluntarily satisfied.
- a. Thing
- b. Liquidation1
- c. Undefined
- d. Undefined

345. The act of a debtor in paying or securing one or more of his creditors in a manner more favorable to them than to other creditors or to the exclusion of such other creditors is a _____. In the absence of statute, a _____ is perfectly good, but to be legal it must be bona fide, and not a mere subterfuge of the debtor to secure a future benefit to himself or to prevent the application of his property to his debts.
- a. Preference1
- b. Thing
- c. Undefined
- d. Undefined

346. Remuneration paid to the owners of technology, patents, or trade names for the use of same name are called _____.
- a. Thing
- b. Royalties1
- c. Undefined
- d. Undefined

347. The amount of contributed capital less the par value of the stock is _____.
- a. Capital in excess of par1
- b. Thing
- c. Undefined
- d. Undefined

348. The _____ percentage shows how profitable a company's assets are in generating revenue.
- a. Return on Assets1
- b. Thing
- c. Undefined
- d. Undefined

349. _____ refers to paid, nonpersonal communication through various media by organizations and individuals who are in some way identified in the _____ message.
- a. Thing
- b. Advertising1
- c. Undefined
- d. Undefined

350. _____ is an accounting term which is commonly used in business. It is equal to the gross revenue for a given time period minus associated expenses.
- a. Thing
- b. Net profit1
- c. Undefined
- d. Undefined

351. A _____ is a form of collective investment that pools money from many investors and invests the money in stocks, bonds, short-term money market instruments, and/or other securities. In a _____, the fund manager trades the fund's underlying securities, realizing capital gains or loss, and collects the dividend or interest income.
- a. Mutual fund1
- b. Thing
- c. Undefined
- d. Undefined

352. _____ refers to the productivity of capital or sales revenue divided by invested capital.
- a. Thing
- b. Capital turnover1
- c. Undefined
- d. Undefined

353. Dividends per share divided by market price per share are called a _____. _____ indicates the percentage return that a stockholder will receive on dividends alone.
- a. Dividend yield1
- b. Thing
- c. Undefined
- d. Undefined

354. _____, also known as property, plant, and equipment (PP&E), is a term used in accountancy for assets and property which cannot easily be converted into cash. This can be compared with current assets such as cash or bank accounts, which are described as liquid assets. In most cases, only tangible assets are referred to as fixed.
- a. Thing
- b. Fixed asset1
- c. Undefined
- d. Undefined

355. Total shareholders' equity divided by the number of outstanding common shares is referred to as _____.
- a. Book value per share1
- b. Thing
- c. Undefined
- d. Undefined

356. A _____ in business refers to one company (the acquirer) purchasing another (the target). Such events resemble mergers, but without the formation of a new company.
- a. Thing
- b. Takeover1
- c. Undefined
- d. Undefined

357. _____ refers to the cash inflows and cash outflows from the general operating activities of the business; one of the three sections in the statement of cash flows.
- a. Thing
- b. Operating cash flows1
- c. Undefined
- d. Undefined

358. Because _____ creates goods for a wide range of sports, they have competition from every sports and sports fashion brand there is. _____ has no direct competitors because there is no single brand which can compete directly with their range of sports and non-sports oriented gear, except for Reebok.
- a. Nike1
- b. Thing
- c. Undefined
- d. Undefined

359. Amounts of money put aside by corporations, nonprofit organizations, or unions to cover part of the financial needs of members when they retire is a _____.
- a. Thing
- b. Pension fund1
- c. Undefined
- d. Undefined

360. _____ refers to the financial executive primarily responsible for management accounting and financial accounting. Also called chief accounting officer.
- a. Controller1
- b. Thing
- c. Undefined
- d. Undefined

*Chapter 2. Financial Reporting and Analysis*  41

1. _____ is the branch of accountancy concerned with the preparation of financial statements for external decision makers, such as stockholders, suppliers, banks and government agencies. The fundamental need for _____ is to reduce principal-agent problem by measuring and monitoring agents' performance.
   - a. Thing
   - b. Financial accounting2
   - c. Undefined
   - d. Undefined

2. A system that collects and processes financial information about an organization and reports that information to decision makers is referred to as _____.
   - a. Thing
   - b. Accounting2
   - c. Undefined
   - d. Undefined

3. _____ refers to the standard framework of guidelines for financial accounting. It includes the standards, conventions, and rules accountants follow in recording and summarizing transactions, and in the preparation of financial statements.
   - a. Thing
   - b. Generally accepted accounting principles2
   - c. Undefined
   - d. Undefined

4. _____ is a structured methodology that is focused on completely understanding the customer's needs, identifying how best to meet those needs, and then "reinventing" the stream of processes to meet those needs.
   - a. Business analysis2
   - b. Thing
   - c. Undefined
   - d. Undefined

5. In finance, _____ is the process of estimating the market value of a financial asset or liability. They can be done on assets (for example, investments in marketable securities such as stocks, options, business enterprises, or intangible assets such as patents and trademarks) or on liabilities (e.g., Bonds issued by a company).
   - a. Valuation2
   - b. Event
   - c. Undefined
   - d. Undefined

6. _____ refers to a summary of all the transactions that have occurred over a particular period.
   - a. Financial statement2
   - b. Thing
   - c. Undefined
   - d. Undefined

7. Method of accounting that records the effects of accounting events in the period in which such events occur regardless of when cash is exchanged is _____.
   - a. Thing
   - b. Accrual accounting2
   - c. Undefined
   - d. Undefined

8. An _____ is an accounting event in which the transaction is recognized when the action takes place, instead of when cash is disbursed or received.
   - a. Accrual2
   - b. Thing
   - c. Undefined
   - d. Undefined

9. _____ refer to people in the organization who actually use the product or service purchased by the buying center.
   - a. Users2
   - b. Thing
   - c. Undefined
   - d. Undefined

10. In financial terminology, _____ is the capital raized by a corporation, through the issuance and sale of shares.

## Chapter 2. Financial Reporting and Analysis

a. Thing  
b. Stock2  
c. Undefined  
d. Undefined

11. An _____ is any factor (financial or non-financial) that provides a motive for a particular course of action, or counts as a reason for preferring one choice to the alternatives.
    a. Incentive2  
    b. Thing  
    c. Undefined  
    d. Undefined

12. _____ characterizes the process of leading and directing all or part of an organization, often a business, through the deployment and manipulation of resources. Early twentieth-century _____ writer Mary Parker Follett defined _____ as "the art of getting things done through people."
    a. Management2  
    b. Thing  
    c. Undefined  
    d. Undefined

13. _____ refers to a written statement-also called an accountant's certificate, accountant's opinion, or audit report- prepared by an independent accountant or auditor after an audit.
    a. Thing  
    b. Financial report2  
    c. Undefined  
    d. Undefined

14. _____ means the giving out of information, either voluntarily or to be in compliance with legal regulations or workplace rules.
    a. Thing  
    b. Disclosure2  
    c. Undefined  
    d. Undefined

15. A group of firms that produce identical or similar products is an _____. It is also used specifically to refer to an area of economic production focused on manufacturing which involves large amounts of capital investment before any profit can be realized, also called "heavy _____".
    a. Thing  
    b. Industry2  
    c. Undefined  
    d. Undefined

16. _____ refers to a person or tool with a primary function of information analysis, generally with a more limited, practical and short term set of goals than a researcher.
    a. Analyst2  
    b. Person  
    c. Undefined  
    d. Undefined

17. _____ refers to an input that exists as a stock, providing services that contribute to production. The stock is not used up in production, although it may deteriorate with use, providing a smaller flow of services later.
    a. Primary factor2  
    b. Thing  
    c. Undefined  
    d. Undefined

18. An _____ is prepared by corporate management that presents financial information including financial statements, footnotes, and the management discussion and analysis.
    a. Thing  
    b. Annual report2  
    c. Undefined  
    d. Undefined

## Chapter 2. Financial Reporting and Analysis

19. A _____ is an individual or company (including a corporation) that legally owns one or more shares of stock in a joined stock company.
    a. Shareholder2
    b. Thing
    c. Undefined
    d. Undefined

20. _____ refers to a "non tangible product" that is not embodied in a physical good and that typically effects some change in another product, person, or institution. Contrasts with good.
    a. Thing
    b. Service2
    c. Undefined
    d. Undefined

21. A _____ is a company owned by the public rather than by a relatively few individuals. There are two different meanings for this term: (1) A company that is owned by stockholders who are members of the general public and trade shares publicly, often through a listing on a stock exchange. Ownership is open to anyone that has the money and inclination to buy shares in the company. It is differentiated from privately held companies where the shares are held by a small group of individuals, who are often members of one or a small group of families or otherwise related individuals, or other companies. The variant of this type of company in the United Kingdom and Ireland is known as a public limited compan, and (2) A government-owned corporation. This meaning of a "_____" comes from the fact that government debt is sometimes referred to as "public debt" although there are no "public bonds", government finance is sometimes called "public finance", among similar uses. This is the less-common meaning.
    a. Public company2
    b. Thing
    c. Undefined
    d. Undefined

22. Tangible property held for sale in the normal course of business or used in producing goods or services for sale is an _____.
    a. Inventory2
    b. Thing
    c. Undefined
    d. Undefined

23. Dow Jones & Company was founded in 1882 by reporters Charles Dow, Edward Jones and Charles Bergstresser. Jones converted the small Customers' Afternoon Letter into The _____, first published in 1889, and began delivery of the Dow Jones News Service via telegraph. The Journal featured the Jones 'Average', the first of several indexes of stock and bond prices on the New York Stock Exchange.
    a. Organization
    b. Wall Street Journal2
    c. Undefined
    d. Undefined

24. A _____ is a corporation or mutual organization which provides facilities for stock brokers and traders, to trade company stocks and other securities.
    a. Stock exchange2
    b. Thing
    c. Undefined
    d. Undefined

25. The trade of things of value between buyer and seller so that each is better off after the trade is called the _____.
    a. Exchange2
    b. Thing
    c. Undefined
    d. Undefined

26. Book of original entry, in which transactions are recorded in a general ledger system, is referred to as a _____.

a. Journal2  
b. Thing  
c. Undefined  
d. Undefined

27. _____ refer to gains and losses that are both unusual in nature and infrequent in occurrence; they are reported net of tax on the income statement.
   a. Thing
   b. Extraordinary items2
   c. Undefined
   d. Undefined

28. _____ refers to a measure of income that usually excludes items that a company thinks are unusual or nonrecurring; forecast income.
   a. Pro forma income2
   b. Thing
   c. Undefined
   d. Undefined

29. _____ is the corporate management term for the act of partially dismantling and reorganizing a company for the purpose of making it more efficient and therefore more profitable.
   a. Restructuring2
   b. Thing
   c. Undefined
   d. Undefined

30. A standardized method or technique that is performed repetitively, often on different materials resulting in different finished goods is called an _____.
   a. Operation2
   b. Thing
   c. Undefined
   d. Undefined

31. _____ refers to financial results from the disposal of a major segment of the business and are reported net of income tax effects.
   a. Thing
   b. Discontinued operations2
   c. Undefined
   d. Undefined

32. Method of accounting for investments in marketable equity securities; is required when the investor owns percent to percent of the investee company. The amount of investments carried under the _____ represents a measure of the book value of the investee rather than the cost or market value of the investment security.
   a. Equity method2
   b. Thing
   c. Undefined
   d. Undefined

33. A _____ is a specific type of option that uses the stock itself as an underlying instrument to determine the option's pay-off and therefore its value.
   a. Thing
   b. Stock option2
   c. Undefined
   d. Undefined

34. A company's purchase of the property and obligations of another company is an _____.
   a. Acquisition2
   b. Thing
   c. Undefined
   d. Undefined

35. In accounting, an _____ represents an event in which an asset is used up or a liability is incurred. In terms of the accounting equation, expenses reduce owners' equity.

## Chapter 2. Financial Reporting and Analysis

    a. Thing  
    c. Undefined  
    b. Expense2  
    d. Undefined

36. _____ is the name given to the set of legal principles, in countries following the English common law tradition, which supplement strict rules of law where their application would operate harshly, so as to achieve what is sometimes referred to as "natural justice."
    a. Equity2  
    c. Undefined  
    b. Thing  
    d. Undefined

37. A contract that gives the purchaser the _____ to buy or sell the underlying financial instrument at a specified price, called the exercise price or strike price, within a specific period of time.
    a. Thing  
    c. Undefined  
    b. Option2  
    d. Undefined

38. The use of resources for the deliberate discovery of new information and ways of doing things, together with the application of that information in inventing new products or processes is referred to as _____.
    a. Thing  
    c. Undefined  
    b. Research and development2  
    d. Undefined

39. A _____ is the set of feasible allocations in an economy that cannot be improved upon by subset of the set of the economy's consumers (a coalition). In construction, when the force in an element is within a certain center section, the _____, the element will only be under compression.
    a. Core2  
    c. Undefined  
    b. Thing  
    d. Undefined

40. _____ refers to the return to the resource entrepreneurial ability; total revenue minus total cost.
    a. Thing  
    c. Undefined  
    b. Profit2  
    d. Undefined

41. Ability to compare the accounting information of different companies because they use the same accounting principles is known as _____.
    a. Comparability2  
    c. Undefined  
    b. Thing  
    d. Undefined

42. _____ generally refers to financial wealth, especially that used to start or maintain a business. In classical economics, _____ is one of four factors of production, the others being land and labor and entrepreneurship.
    a. Thing  
    c. Undefined  
    b. Capital2  
    d. Undefined

43. A _____ is a present obligation of the enterprise arizing from past events, the settlement of which is expected to result in an outflow from the enterprise of resources embodying economic benefits.
    a. Thing  
    c. Undefined  
    b. Liability2  
    d. Undefined

44. An examination of the financial reports to ensure that they represent what they claim and conform with generally accepted accounting principles is referred to as _____.

a. Audit2  
b. Thing  
c. Undefined  
d. Undefined

45. An item of property, such as land, capital, money, a share in ownership, or a claim on others for future payment, such as a bond or a bank deposit is an _____.
   a. Thing  
   b. Asset2  
   c. Undefined  
   d. Undefined

46. _____ refers to spending for the production and accumulation of capital and additions to inventories. In a financial sense, buying an asset with the expectation of making a return.
   a. Investment2  
   b. Thing  
   c. Undefined  
   d. Undefined

47. _____ refers to a financial statement that presents the revenues and expenses and resulting net income or net loss of a company for a specific period of time.
   a. Income statement2  
   b. Thing  
   c. Undefined  
   d. Undefined

48. _____ is the effort made by an ordinarily prudent or reasonable party to avoid harm to another party or himself. Failure to make this effort is considered negligence. Failure to make this effort is considered negligence.
   a. Thing  
   b. Due diligence2  
   c. Undefined  
   d. Undefined

49. A _____ refers to a layout accurate in size, color, scheme, and other necessary details to show how a final ad will look. For presentation only, never for reproduction.
   a. Thing  
   b. Comprehensive2  
   c. Undefined  
   d. Undefined

50. An _____ is a stock option for the company's own stock that is often offered to upper-level employees as part of the executive compenzation package, especially by American corporations. An _____ is identical to a call option on the company's stock, with some extra restrictions.
   a. Thing  
   b. Employee stock option2  
   c. Undefined  
   d. Undefined

51. The group of individuals elected by the stockholders of a corporation to oversee its operations is a _____.
   a. Board of directors2  
   b. Thing  
   c. Undefined  
   d. Undefined

52. _____ refers to restrictions state and federal laws place on business with regard to the conduct of its activities.
   a. Regulation2  
   b. Thing  
   c. Undefined  
   d. Undefined

53. _____ refers to an individual in the United States who have passed the Uniform _____ Examination and have met additional state education and experience requirements for certification as a _____.

## Chapter 2. Financial Reporting and Analysis

a. Thing
b. Certified Public Accountant2
c. Undefined
d. Undefined

54. With over 350,000 CPA members (in 2005), the _____ is the largest CPA professional organization in the United States of America. Approximately 40% of its members are engaged in the practice of public accounting, in areas such as auditing, accounting, taxation, general business consulting, business valuation, personal financial planning and business technology.
 a. Thing
 b. American Institute of Certified Public Accountants2
 c. Undefined
 d. Undefined

55. _____ refers to the private sector body given the primary responsibility to work out the detailed rules that become generally accepted accounting principles.
 a. Financial accounting standards board2
 b. Thing
 c. Undefined
 d. Undefined

56. _____ refer to concept statements issued by the FASB explaining and describing the type of information required from financial reporting.
 a. Statements of Financial Accounting2
 b. Thing
 c. Undefined
 d. Undefined

57. _____ refers to a set of standards that dictate accounting rules concerning financial reporting; establish generally accepted accounting principles.
 a. Thing
 b. Financial accounting Standards2
 c. Undefined
 d. Undefined

58. The role of the _____ is to issue accounting standards in the United Kingdom. It is recognized for that purpose under the Companies Act 1985. It took over the task of setting accounting standards from the Accounting Standards Committee (ASC) in 1990.
 a. Accounting Standards Board2
 b. Organization
 c. Undefined
 d. Undefined

59. The _____ is the former authoritative body of the American Institute of Certified Public Accountants (AICPA). It issued pronouncements on accounting principles until 1973. Of the 31 APB opinions, several were instrumental in improving the theory and practice of significant areas of accounting.
 a. Accounting Principles Board2
 b. Thing
 c. Undefined
 d. Undefined

60. A temporary team or committee formed to solve a specific short-term problem involving several departments is the _____.
 a. Thing
 b. Task force2
 c. Undefined
 d. Undefined

61. The households and business firms of the economy are referred to as _____.
 a. Private sector2
 b. Thing
 c. Undefined
 d. Undefined

62. A _____ is a proceeding before a court or other decision-making body or officer. A _____ is generally distinguished from a trial in that it is usually shorter and often less formal.
   a. Hearing2
   b. Thing
   c. Undefined
   d. Undefined

63. A signed, written order by which one party instructs another party to pay a specified sum to a third party, at sight or at a specific date is a _____.
   a. Thing
   b. Draft2
   c. Undefined
   d. Undefined

64. In finance and economics, _____ is the price paid by a borrower for the use of a lender's money. In other words, _____ is the amount of paid to "rent" money for a period of time.
   a. Thing
   b. Interest2
   c. Undefined
   d. Undefined

65. In banking and accountancy, the outstanding _____ is the amount of money owned, (or due), that remains in a deposit account (or a loan account) at a given date, after all past remittances, payments and withdrawal have been accounted for. It can be positive (then, in the _____ sheet of a firm, it is an asset) or negative (a liability).
   a. Balance2
   b. Thing
   c. Undefined
   d. Undefined

66. _____ refers to a claim on the borrower future income that is sold by the borrower to the lender. A _____ is a type of transferable interest representing financial value.
   a. Security2
   b. Thing
   c. Undefined
   d. Undefined

67. _____ refers to U.S. government agency that determines the financial statements that public companies must provide to stockholders and the measurement rules that they must use in producing those statements.
   a. Organization
   b. Securities and exchange commission2
   c. Undefined
   d. Undefined

68. _____ refers to a person who is authorized to vote the shares of another person. Also, the written authorization empowering a person to vote the shares of another person.
   a. Proxy2
   b. Thing
   c. Undefined
   d. Undefined

69. An organization that employs resources to produce a good or service for profit and owns and operates one or more plants is referred to as a _____.
   a. Firm2
   b. Thing
   c. Undefined
   d. Undefined

70. A type of influence process where a receiver accepts the position advocated by a source to obtain favorable outcomes or to avoid punishment is the _____.
   a. Compliance2
   b. Thing
   c. Undefined
   d. Undefined

## Chapter 2. Financial Reporting and Analysis

71. _____ in agency law, refers to an agent's ability to affect his principal's legal relations with third parties. Also used to refer to an actor's legal power or ability to do something. In addition, sometimes used to refer to a statute, case, or other legal source that justifies a particular result.
   a. Concept
   b. Authority2
   c. Undefined
   d. Undefined

72. _____ refers to the method under which income and expenses are determined for tax purposes. Important accounting methods include the cash basis and the accrual basis.
   a. Thing
   b. Accounting method2
   c. Undefined
   d. Undefined

73. _____ is a business magazine published by McGraw-Hill. It was first published in 1929 under the direction of Malcolm Muir, who was serving as president of the McGraw-Hill Publishing company at the time. It is considered to be the standard both in industry and among students.
   a. Business Week2
   b. Organization
   c. Undefined
   d. Undefined

74. _____ refers to the extent to which an economic variable, such as a price or an exchange rate, moves up and down over time.
   a. Volatility2
   b. Thing
   c. Undefined
   d. Undefined

75. The extent to which a source is perceived as having knowledge, skill, or experience relevant to a communication topic and can be trusted to give an unbiased opinion or present objective information on the issue is called _____.
   a. Thing
   b. Credibility2
   c. Undefined
   d. Undefined

76. In contract law a _____ is incorrect understanding by one or more parties to a contract and may be used as grounds to invalidate the agreement. Common law has identified three different types of _____ in contract: unilateral _____, mutual _____, and common _____.
   a. Thing
   b. Mistake2
   c. Undefined
   d. Undefined

77. _____ refers to collections of legal rules produced by the American Law Institute, covering certain subject matter areas. Although restatements are often persuasive to courts, they are not legally binding unless adopted by the highest court of a particular state.
   a. Thing
   b. Restatement2
   c. Undefined
   d. Undefined

78. A _____ is one issued by a CPA that means that for the most part, the company's financial statements are in compliance with GAAP, but the auditors have reservations about something in the statements or have other reasons not to give a fully unqualified opinion; reasons that a _____ is being issued are explained in the auditor's report.
   a. Thing
   b. Qualified opinion2
   c. Undefined
   d. Undefined

## Chapter 2. Financial Reporting and Analysis

79. _____ is the set of processes, customs, policies, laws and institutions affecting the way a corporation is directed, administered or controlled.
   a. Thing
   b. Corporate governance2
   c. Undefined
   d. Undefined

80. _____ in corporation law, a committee of the board that recommends and supervises the public accountant who audits the corporation's financial records.
   a. Audit committee2
   b. Thing
   c. Undefined
   d. Undefined

81. A long-lasting, sometimes permanent team in the organization structure created to deal with tasks that recur regularly is the _____.
   a. Thing
   b. Committee2
   c. Undefined
   d. Undefined

82. _____ is a company composed of what was formerly AT&T Technologies, which included Western Electric and Bell Labs. It was spun-off from AT&T on September 30, 1996. On April 2, 2006, they announced a merger with its French competitor, Alcatel. The combined company has revenues of approximately $25 billion U.S. based on 2005 calendar results.
   a. Lucent Technologies2
   b. Organization
   c. Undefined
   d. Undefined

83. The body of knowledge and techniques that can be used to combine economic resources to produce goods and services is called _____.
   a. Thing
   b. Technology2
   c. Undefined
   d. Undefined

84. An out-of-court settlement in which creditors agree to accept a fractional settlement on their original claim is referred to as _____.
   a. Composition2
   b. Thing
   c. Undefined
   d. Undefined

85. The assertion of a fact that is not in accord with the truth is _____. A contract can be rescinded on the ground of _____ when the assertion relates to a material fact or is made fraudulently and the other party actually and justifiably relies on the assertion.
   a. Thing
   b. Misrepresentation2
   c. Undefined
   d. Undefined

86. An _____ is an independent appraisal of operations, conducted under the direction of management, to assess the effectiveness of internal administrative and accounting controls and help ensure conformance with managerial policies.
   a. Internal audit2
   b. Thing
   c. Undefined
   d. Undefined

87. Tax _____ falls into two categories: civil and criminal. Under civil _____, the IRS may impose as a penalty of an amount equal to as much as 75 percent of the underpayment.

a. Thing
b. Fraud2
c. Undefined
d. Undefined

88. The process of bringing, maintaining, and defending a lawsuit is _____.
a. Thing
b. Litigation2
c. Undefined
d. Undefined

89. The sum of money recoverable by a plaintiff who has received a judgment in a civil case is called _____.
a. Thing
b. Damages2
c. Undefined
d. Undefined

90. Could refer to any good, but in trade a _____ is usually a raw material or primary product that enters into international trade, such as metals or basic agricultural products.
a. Thing
b. Commodity2
c. Undefined
d. Undefined

91. An organized marketplace in which common stocks are traded. In the United States, the largest _____ is the New York Stock Exchange, on which are traded the stocks of the largest U.S. companies.
a. Thing
b. Stock market2
c. Undefined
d. Undefined

92. A _____ is, as defined in economics, a social arrangement that allows buyers and sellers to discover information and carry out a voluntary exchange of goods or services.
a. Thing
b. Market2
c. Undefined
d. Undefined

93. The combination of two or more firms, generally of equal size and market power, to form an entirely new entity is a _____.
a. Thing
b. Consolidation2
c. Undefined
d. Undefined

94. A _____ functions as a form of shark repellent used to thwart hostile takeovers. Under implementation of this provision, a target company will acquire a troublesome firm in order to raise the acquisition price and make acquisition by other parties economically unattractive.
a. Safe harbor2
b. Thing
c. Undefined
d. Undefined

95. _____ specialize in information either to bring together two parties to a transaction or to buy in order to sell again.
a. Thing
b. Intermediaries2
c. Undefined
d. Undefined

96. A _____ is a business report produced by business research firms by their financial analysts. They are designed to dig out the important pieces of companies operational and financial reporting to paint a picture of the future of companies to assist debt and equity investing.

a. Thing  
b. Research report2  
c. Undefined  
d. Undefined  

97. Amounts of money put aside by corporations, nonprofit organizations, or unions to cover part of the financial needs of members when they retire is a _____.
a. Pension fund2  
b. Thing  
c. Undefined  
d. Undefined  

98. A _____ is a steady income given to a person (usually after retirement). Pensions are typically payments made in the form of a guaranteed annuity to a retired or disabled employee.
a. Thing  
b. Pension2  
c. Undefined  
d. Undefined  

99. Independent accounting entity with a self-balancing set of accounts segregated for the purposes of carrying on specific activities is referred to as a _____.
a. Thing  
b. Fund2  
c. Undefined  
d. Undefined  

100. _____ is the world's second-largest discount broker. Besides discount brokerage, the firm offers mutual funds, annuities, bond trading, and now mortgages through its _____ Bank.
a. Thing  
b. Charles Schwab2  
c. Undefined  
d. Undefined  

101. _____ refers to a recording as positive in the balance of payments, any transaction that gives rise to a payment into the country, such as an export, the sale of an asset, or borrowing from abroad.
a. Thing  
b. Credit2  
c. Undefined  
d. Undefined  

102. The _____ used by a firm or an economy are the labor, raw materials, electricity and other resources it uses to produce its outputs.
a. Inputs2  
b. Thing  
c. Undefined  
d. Undefined  

103. Forecast that predicts the cash inflows and outflows in future periods is a _____. It is a company's projected cash receipts and disbursements over a set time horizon.
a. Thing  
b. Cash flow forecast2  
c. Undefined  
d. Undefined  

104. _____ through its subsidiaries and affiliates, provides capital markets services, investment banking and advisory services, wealth management, asset management, insurance, banking and related products and services on a global basis. It is best known for its Global Private Client services and its strong sales force.
a. Merrill Lynch2  
b. Organization  
c. Undefined  
d. Undefined

## Chapter 2. Financial Reporting and Analysis

105. In finance, _____ refers to the amounts of cash being received and spent by a business during a defined period of time, sometimes tied to a specific project. Most of the time they are being used to determine gaps in the liquid position of a company.
   a. Cash flow2
   b. Thing
   c. Undefined
   d. Undefined

106. _____ refers to a debt instrument, issued by a borrower and promising a specified stream of payments to the purchaser, usually regular interest payments plus a final repayment of principal.
   a. Bond2
   b. Thing
   c. Undefined
   d. Undefined

107. A financial market in which long-term debt and equity instruments are traded is referred to as a _____. The _____ includes the stock market and the bond market.
   a. Capital market2
   b. Thing
   c. Undefined
   d. Undefined

108. The technical sophistication of the product and hence the amount of understanding required to use it is referred to as _____. It is the opposite of simplicity.
   a. Thing
   b. Complexity2
   c. Undefined
   d. Undefined

109. Converting the financial statements of foreign subsidiaries into the currency of the home country is a _____.
   a. Thing
   b. Currency translation2
   c. Undefined
   d. Undefined

110. A person to whom a debt or legal obligation is owed, and who has the right to enforce payment of that debt or obligation is referred to as _____.
   a. Thing
   b. Creditor2
   c. Undefined
   d. Undefined

111. A statement of the assets, liabilities, and net worth of a firm or individual at some given time often at the end of its "fiscal year," is referred to as a _____.
   a. Thing
   b. Balance sheet2
   c. Undefined
   d. Undefined

112. A _____ is a signed written agreement between two or more parties. Also referred to as a contract.
   a. Covenant2
   b. Thing
   c. Undefined
   d. Undefined

113. The process by which someone evaluates an employee's work behaviors by measurement and comparison with previously established standards, documents the results, and communicates the results to the employee is called _____.
   a. Thing
   b. Performance measurement2
   c. Undefined
   d. Undefined

114. _____ is the analysis of the accounts and the economic prospects of a firm.

a. Thing
b. Financial analysis2
c. Undefined
d. Undefined

115. Similar to a script in that a _____ can be a less than completely rational decision-making method. Involves the use of a pre-existing set of decision steps for any problem that presents itself.
a. Thing
b. Policy2
c. Undefined
d. Undefined

116. Assistance provided by countries and by international institutions such as the World Bank to developing countries in the form of monetary grants, loans at low interest rates, in kind, or a combination of these is called _____. _____ can also refer to assistance of any type rendered to benefit some group or individual.
a. Aid2
b. Thing
c. Undefined
d. Undefined

117. In accounting terminology, _____ describes the original cost of an asset at the time of purchase or payment as opposed to its market value
a. Thing
b. Historical cost2
c. Undefined
d. Undefined

118. _____ measures and reports financial and nonfinancial information relating to the cost of acquiring or consuming resources in an organization. It provides information for both management accounting and financial accounting.
a. Cost accounting2
b. Thing
c. Undefined
d. Undefined

119. _____ refers to recording revenues when earned and expenses when incurred, regardless of the timing of cash receipts or payments.
a. Thing
b. Accrual basis2
c. Undefined
d. Undefined

120. _____ is a U.S. business term for the amount of money that a company receives from its activities, mostly from sales of products and/or services to customers.
a. Revenue2
b. Thing
c. Undefined
d. Undefined

121. _____ is equal to the income that a firm has after subtracting costs and expenses from the total revenue. Expenses will typically include tax expense.
a. Net income2
b. Thing
c. Undefined
d. Undefined

122. _____ refers to portion of the assets remaining after the creditors' claims have been satisfied; also called equity or residual interest.
a. Thing
b. Net assets2
c. Undefined
d. Undefined

## Chapter 2. Financial Reporting and Analysis

123. _____ is the difference between the intrinsic value of a stock (i.e. value based on stock valuation and what the company is actually worth) and the price that the market sets on a stock (i.e. stock price is a matter of market participants' opinions and is different from the intrinsic value).
- a. Margin of safety2
- b. Thing
- c. Undefined
- d. Undefined

124. A deposit by a buyer in stocks with a seller or a stockbroker, as security to cover fluctuations in the market in reference to stocks that the buyer has purchased but for which he has not paid is a _____. Commodities are also traded on _____.
- a. Margin2
- b. Thing
- c. Undefined
- d. Undefined

125. _____ is an American stock investor, businessman and philanthropist. Nicknamed the "Oracle of Omaha" or the "Sage of Omaha", he has amassed an enormous fortune from astute investments, particularly through his company Berkshire Hathaway, in which he holds a greater than 38% stake.
- a. Warren Buffett2
- b. Person
- c. Undefined
- d. Undefined

126. Assets that have special rights but not physical substance are referred to as _____.
- a. Intangible assets2
- b. Thing
- c. Undefined
- d. Undefined

127. An intangible assets is defined as an asset that is not physical in nature. The most common types are trade secrets (e.g., customer lists and know-how), copyrights, patents, trademarks, and goodwill.
- a. Intangible asset2
- b. Thing
- c. Undefined
- d. Undefined

128. In agency law, one under whose direction an agent acts and for whose benefit that agent acts is a _____.
- a. Principal2
- b. Thing
- c. Undefined
- d. Undefined

129. Suppliers and financial institutions that lend money to companies is referred to as a _____.
- a. Lender2
- b. Thing
- c. Undefined
- d. Undefined

130. _____ refers to a rise in the value of a country's currency on the exchange market, relative either to a particular other currency or to a weighted average of other currencies. The currency is said to appreciate. Opposite of 'depreciation.' _____ can also refer to the increase in value of any asset.
- a. Thing
- b. Appreciation2
- c. Undefined
- d. Undefined

131. _____ refers to the capacity to turn assets into cash, or the amount of assets in a portfolio that have that capacity.
- a. Thing
- b. Liquidity2
- c. Undefined
- d. Undefined

## Chapter 2. Financial Reporting and Analysis

132. Amount of corporate profits paid out for each share of stock is referred to as _____.
 a. Dividend2
 b. Thing
 c. Undefined
 d. Undefined

133. Collecting information and providing feedback to employees about their behavior, communication style, or skills is an _____.
 a. Thing
 b. Assessment2
 c. Undefined
 d. Undefined

134. Other organizations in the same industry or type of business that provide a good or service to the same set of customers is referred to as a _____.
 a. Competitor2
 b. Thing
 c. Undefined
 d. Undefined

135. A _____ is a "promise" or an "agreement" that is enforced or recognized by the law. In the civil law, a _____ is considered to be part of the general law of obligations.
 a. Thing
 b. Contract2
 c. Undefined
 d. Undefined

136. In economics, a _____ is a mechanism which allows people to trade money for securities or commodities such as gold or other precious metals. In general, any commodity market might be considered to be a _____, if the usual purpose of traders is not the immediate consumption of the commodity, but rather as a means of delaying or accelerating consumption over time.
 a. Thing
 b. Financial market2
 c. Undefined
 d. Undefined

137. _____ refers to rebate of import duties when the imported good is re-exported or used as input to the production of an exported good.
 a. Thing
 b. Drawback2
 c. Undefined
 d. Undefined

138. a method of bookkeeping in which income is considered earned when received and expenses are not taken into account until paid is _____. Similarly, _____ does not generally recognise non-cash expenses such as depreciation.
 a. Event
 b. Cash Accounting2
 c. Undefined
 d. Undefined

139. Having a physical existence is referred to as the _____. Personal property other than real estate, such as cars, boats, stocks, or other assets.
 a. Tangible2
 b. Thing
 c. Undefined
 d. Undefined

140. Cash flow activities that include the cash effects of transactions that create revenues and expenses and thus enter into the determination of net income is an _____.

a. Thing
b. Operating activities2
c. Undefined
d. Undefined

141. Cash provided by operating activities adjusted for capital expenditures and dividends paid is referred to as _____.
a. Free cash flow2
b. Thing
c. Undefined
d. Undefined

142. In finance and economics, _____ or divestiture is the reduction of some kind of asset, for either financial or social goals. A _____ is the opposite of an investment.
a. Divestment2
b. Event
c. Undefined
d. Undefined

143. _____ refers to the act of asking an appellate court to overturn a decision after the trial court's final judgment has been entered.
a. Appeal2
b. Thing
c. Undefined
d. Undefined

144. A person in possession of a document of title or an instrument payable or indorsed to him, his order, or to bearer is a _____.
a. Holder2
b. Thing
c. Undefined
d. Undefined

145. A short-term investment with original maturities of three months or less that is readily convertible to cash and whose value is unlikely to change is a _____.
a. Cash equivalent2
b. Thing
c. Undefined
d. Undefined

146. The _____ is net income on the last line of a income statement.
a. Thing
b. Bottom line2
c. Undefined
d. Undefined

147. The dollar difference between total current assets and total current liabilities is called _____.
a. Working capital2
b. Thing
c. Undefined
d. Undefined

148. Systematic and rational allocation of the acquisition cost of an intangible asset over its useful life is referred to as _____.
a. Amortization2
b. Thing
c. Undefined
d. Undefined

149. _____ is an accounting and finance term for the method of attributing the cost of an asset across the useful life of the asset. _____ is a reduction in the value of a currency in floating exchange rate.
a. Depreciation2
b. Thing
c. Undefined
d. Undefined

## Chapter 2. Financial Reporting and Analysis

150. _____ refers to an accounting concept that establishes when expenses are recognized. Expenses are matched with the revenues they helped to generate and are recognized when those revenues are recognized.
   a. Matching2
   b. Thing
   c. Undefined
   d. Undefined

151. Cash flowing out of the business from all sources over a period of time is _____.
   a. Cash outflow2
   b. Thing
   c. Undefined
   d. Undefined

152. Cash coming into the company as the result of a previous investment is a _____.
   a. Thing
   b. Cash inflow2
   c. Undefined
   d. Undefined

153. A professional that provides expert advice in a particular field or area in which customers occassionaly require this type of knowledge is a _____.
   a. Consultant2
   b. Concept
   c. Undefined
   d. Undefined

154. The payment for the service of a unit of labor, per unit time. In trade theory, it is the only payment to labor, usually unskilled labor. In empirical work, _____ data may exclude other compenzation, which must be added to get the total cost of employment.
   a. Thing
   b. Wage2
   c. Undefined
   d. Undefined

155. Reports inflows and outflows of cash during the accounting period in the categories of operating, investing, and financing is a _____.
   a. Thing
   b. Statement of cash flow2
   c. Undefined
   d. Undefined

156. _____ refers to sum of the costs assigned to a product for a specific purpose. A concept used in applying the cost plus approach to product pricing in which only the costs of manufacturing the product are included in the cost amount to which the markup is added.
   a. Product cost2
   b. Thing
   c. Undefined
   d. Undefined

157. The creation of finished goods and services using the factors of _____: land, labor, capital, entrepreneurship, and knowledge.
   a. Thing
   b. Production2
   c. Undefined
   d. Undefined

158. _____ refers to the total costs of goods made or purchased and sold.
   a. Thing
   b. Cost of sales2
   c. Undefined
   d. Undefined

159. All costs in the income statement other than cost of goods sold are referred to as _____. Such costs consist of selling (marketing) and administrative expenses.

## Chapter 2. Financial Reporting and Analysis

a. Period costs2
b. Thing
c. Undefined
d. Undefined

160. The difference between the time a transaction occurs and the time the cash related to the transaction is exchanged is referred to as _____.
a. Timing differences2
b. Thing
c. Undefined
d. Undefined

161. Obligations to make future economic sacrifices, usually cash payments, are referred to as _____. Same as current liabilities.
a. Payables2
b. Thing
c. Undefined
d. Undefined

162. A _____ is a stretch of time when an individual is eligible to receive benefits. The duration of benefits refers to the number of weeks the benefits will continue as long as the individual remains eligible. It is based on the number of hours worked in the 52 weeks before the lay-off and on the regional unemployment rate.
a. Thing
b. Benefit period2
c. Undefined
d. Undefined

163. A substantial expenditure that is used by a company to acquire or upgrade physical assets such as equipment, property, industrial buildings, including those which improve the quality and life of an asset is referred to as a _____.
a. Capital expenditure2
b. Thing
c. Undefined
d. Undefined

164. Major investments in long-term assets such as land, buildings, equipment, or research and development are referred to as _____.
a. Thing
b. Capital expenditures2
c. Undefined
d. Undefined

165. _____ refers to cash inflows and outflows of activities related to the purchase and sale of assets in a firm not related to the firm's day-to-day operating activities. This is one of the three sections in the statement of cash flows.
a. Investing cash flows2
b. Thing
c. Undefined
d. Undefined

166. _____ refers to the final payment date of a loan or other financial instrument, after which point no further interest or principal need be paid.
a. Thing
b. Maturity2
c. Undefined
d. Undefined

167. _____ refers to the cash inflows and cash outflows from the general operating activities of the business; one of the three sections in the statement of cash flows.
a. Thing
b. Operating cash flows2
c. Undefined
d. Undefined

168. The interest rate that equates a future value or an annuity to a given present value is a _____.

a. Yield2  
b. Thing  
c. Undefined  
d. Undefined  

169. _____ is one of a series of accounting transactions dealing with the billing of customers which owe money to a person, company or organization for goods and services that have been provided to the customer. This is typically done in a one person organization by writing an invoice and mailing or delivering it to each customer.
a. Thing  
b. Accounts receivable2  
c. Undefined  
d. Undefined  

170. _____ is a business term that refers to the aggregate value of a firm's outstanding common shares. In essence, _____ reflects the total value of a firm's equity currently available on the market. This measure differs from equity value to the extent that a firm has outstanding stock options or other securities convertible to common shares. The size and growth of a firm's _____ is often one of the critical measurements of a public company's success or failure.
a. Market capitalization2  
b. Thing  
c. Undefined  
d. Undefined  

171. _____ is an international chain of discount department stores in the United States, Australia, and New Zealand. _____ merged with Sears in early 2005, creating the Sears Holdings Corporation.
a. Organization  
b. Kmart2  
c. Undefined  
d. Undefined  

172. The social science dealing with the use of scarce resources to obtain the maximum satisfaction of society's virtually unlimited economic wants is an _____.
a. Thing  
b. Economics2  
c. Undefined  
d. Undefined  

173. The process of eliminating managerial and non-managerial positions are called _____.
a. Downsizing2  
b. Thing  
c. Undefined  
d. Undefined  

174. _____ refers to any departure from the ideal of perfect competition that interferes with economic agents maximizing social welfare when they maximize their own.
a. Distortion2  
b. Thing  
c. Undefined  
d. Undefined  

175. _____ refers to a thing that was originally personal property and that has been actually or constructively affixed to the soil itself or to some structure legally a part of the land.
a. Fixture2  
b. Thing  
c. Undefined  
d. Undefined  

176. A _____ is a generic term for specific types of investments from which payoffs over time are derived from the performance of assets (such as commodities, shares or bonds), interest rates, exchange rates, or indices (such as a stock market index, consumer price index (CPI) or an index of weather conditions).
a. Derivative2  
b. Thing  
c. Undefined  
d. Undefined

## Chapter 2. Financial Reporting and Analysis

177. The value today of a stream of payments and/or receipts over time in the future and/or the past, converted to the present using an interest rate. If X t is the amount in period t and r the interest rate, then _____ at time t=0 is V = ?T /t.
    a. Thing
    b. Present value2
    c. Undefined
    d. Undefined

178. _____ refers to a period of time that permits an increase or decrease in current production volume with existing capacity, but one that is too short to permit enlargement of that capacity itself (eg, the building of new plants, training of additional workers, etc.).
    a. Thing
    b. Short run2
    c. Undefined
    d. Undefined

179. _____ refers to the time it takes for a company to purchase goods or services from suppliers, sell those goods and services to customers, and collect cash from customers.
    a. Thing
    b. Operating cycle2
    c. Undefined
    d. Undefined

180. _____ refers to the speed of the up and down movements of a fluctuating economic variable; that is, the number of times per unit of time that the variable completes a cycle of up and down movement.
    a. Thing
    b. Frequency2
    c. Undefined
    d. Undefined

181. In economic models, the _____ time frame assumes no fixed factors of production. Firms can enter or leave the marketplace, and the cost (and availability) of land, labor, raw materials, and capital goods can be assumed to vary.
    a. Long run2
    b. Thing
    c. Undefined
    d. Undefined

182. The _____ of an asset or group of assets is sometimes the price at which they were originally acquired, in many cases equal to purchase price.
    a. Thing
    b. Book value2
    c. Undefined
    d. Undefined

183. In finance, the _____ approach describes a method to value a project or an entire company. The DCF methods determine the present value of future cash flows by discounting them using the appropriate cost of capital.
    a. Discounted cash flow2
    b. Thing
    c. Undeflned
    d. Undefined

184. In finance, _____ occurs when a debtor has not met its legal obligations according to the debt contract, e.g. it has not made a scheduled payment, or violated a covenant (condition) of the debt contract.
    a. Default2
    b. Thing
    c. Undefined
    d. Undefined

185. A _____ occurs when a customer does not pay cash at the time of the sale but instead agrees to pay later. The sale occurs now, with payment from the customer to follow at a later time.
    a. Thing
    b. Credit sale2
    c. Undefined
    d. Undefined

186. Reduction in the selling price of goods extended to the buyer because the goods are defective or of lower quality than the buyer ordered and to encourage a buyer to keep merchandise that would otherwise be returned is the _____.
a. Thing
b. Allowance2
c. Undefined
d. Undefined

187. In accounting and finance, _____ is the portion of receivables that can no longer be collected, typically from accounts receivable or loans. _____ in accounting is considered an expense.
a. Thing
b. Bad debt2
c. Undefined
d. Undefined

188. Confidential information of a company, its products, or securities not generally available to the public gained from a source inside the company is called _____.
a. Thing
b. Inside information2
c. Undefined
d. Undefined

189. A contract for the possession and use of land or other property, including goods, on one side, and a recompense of rent or other income on the other is the _____.
a. Lease2
b. Thing
c. Undefined
d. Undefined

190. The amount of money a household can spend during a given period without increasing or decreasing its net assets. Wages, salaries, dividends, interest income, transfer payments, rents, and so forth are sources of _____.
a. Thing
b. Economic income2
c. Undefined
d. Undefined

191. _____ refers to the price of an asset agreed on between a willing buyer and a willing seller; the price an asset could demand if it is sold on the open market.
a. Thing
b. Market value2
c. Undefined
d. Undefined

192. A _____ is an annuity in which the periodic payments begin on a fixed date and continue indefinitely. Fixed coupon payments on permanently invested (irredeemable) sums of money are prime examples of perpetuities. Scholarships paid perpetually from an endowment fit the definition of _____.
a. Thing
b. Perpetuity2
c. Undefined
d. Undefined

193. A _____ is an underhand method used by companies to enhance the appearance of a company's future performance. The company writes off assets as much as possible to the profit and loss account in the current period in order ot show increase profits and return on investment in future periods.
a. Thing
b. Big bath2
c. Undefined
d. Undefined

194. That which involves playing down differences and finding areas of agreement are referred to as accommodation or _____.

## Chapter 2. Financial Reporting and Analysis

a. Thing
c. Undefined
b. Smoothing2
d. Undefined

195. Loan origination fees that may be deductible as interest by a buyer of property. A seller of property who pays _____ reduces the selling price by the amount of the _____ paid for the buyer.
a. Thing
c. Undefined
b. Points2
d. Undefined

196. _____ refers to the combination of two firms into a single firm.
a. Merger2
c. Undefined
b. Thing
d. Undefined

197. The Six Sigma quality system was developed at _____ even though it became most well known because of its use by General Electric. It was created by engineer Bill Smith, under the direction of Bob Galvin (son of founder Paul Galvin) when he was running the company.
a. Organization
c. Undefined
b. Motorola2
d. Undefined

198. The difference between the face value of a bond and its selling price, when a bond is sold for less than its face value it's referred to as a _____.
a. Thing
c. Undefined
b. Discount2
d. Undefined

199. _____ refers to government financial assistance to a domestic producer.
a. Subsidy2
c. Undefined
b. Thing
d. Undefined

200. _____ refers to the percentage cost of funds used for acquiring resources for an organization, typically a weighted average of the firms cost of equity and cost of debt.
a. Cost of capital2
c. Undefined
b. Place
d. Undefined

201. Government intervention to alter market structure or prevent abuse of market power is called _____.
a. Antitrust2
c. Undefined
b. Thing
d. Undefined

202. In finance, _____ is a profit or an increase in value of an investment such as a stock or bond. _____ is calculated by fair market value or the proceeds from the sale of the investment minus the sum of the purchase price and all costs associated with it.
a. Thing
c. Undefined
b. Gain2
d. Undefined

203. A group of workers organized to advance the interests of the group is called a _____.
a. Thing
c. Undefined
b. Labor union2
d. Undefined

## Chapter 2. Financial Reporting and Analysis

204. People's physical and mental talents and efforts that are used to help produce goods and services are called _____.
   a. Labor2
   b. Thing
   c. Undefined
   d. Undefined

205. A worker association that bargains with employers over wages and working conditions is called a _____.
   a. Thing
   b. Union2
   c. Undefined
   d. Undefined

206. _____ is an advertising technique. It uses less conventional methods than the usual specific channels of advertising to promote products, services, etc. than ATL (Above the line) strategy.
   a. Thing
   b. Below the line2
   c. Undefined
   d. Undefined

207. In throughput accounting, the cost accounting aspect of Theory of Constraints (TOC), _____ is the money spent turning inventory into throughput. In TOC, _____ is limited to costs that vary strictly with the quantity produced, like raw materials and purchased components.
   a. Operating expense2
   b. Thing
   c. Undefined
   d. Undefined

208. _____ refers to a contractual arrangement giving the lessee temporary use of the property with continued ownership of the property by the lessor. Accounted for as a rental.
   a. Operating lease2
   b. Thing
   c. Undefined
   d. Undefined

209. _____ is a financing technique that allows the corporation to separate credit origination and funding activities. The technique comes under the umbrella of structured finance as it applies to assets that typically are illiquid contracts.
   a. Thing
   b. Securitization2
   c. Undefined
   d. Undefined

210. A _____ is an individual or company (including a corporation) that legally owns one or more shares of stock in a joined stock company. The shareholders are the owners of a corporation. Companies listed at the stock market strive to enhance shareholder value.
   a. Stockholder2
   b. Thing
   c. Undefined
   d. Undefined

211. _____ refers to one who holds goods in trust for another or one who holds a position of trust and confidence.
   a. Thing
   b. Fiduciary2
   c. Undefined
   d. Undefined

212. _____ is a liability. It is recorded when an asset (e.g. receivable) is recorded, but the related income (i.e. revenue) will be earned only in the future.
   a. Deferred income2
   b. Thing
   c. Undefined
   d. Undefined

213. _____ refers to the final stage of the creative process where the validity or truthfulness of the insight is determined. The feedback portion of communication in which the receiver sends a message to the source indicating receipt of the message and the degree to which he or she understood the message.
   a. Verification2
   b. Concept
   c. Undefined
   d. Undefined

214. Standards for the methods and procedures that must be used to conduct audits are called _____.
   a. Generally accepted auditing standards2
   b. Thing
   c. Undefined
   d. Undefined

215. _____ are the tasks the internal auditor undertakes for collecting, analyzing, interpreting, and documenting information during an audit. They are the means to attain audit objectives.
   a. Thing
   b. Audit procedures2
   c. Undefined
   d. Undefined

216. In December of 1995, _____ became the first major North American retailer to accept independent monitoring of the working conditions in a contract factory producing its garments. _____ is the largest specialty retailer in the United States.
   a. Gap2
   b. Organization
   c. Undefined
   d. Undefined

217. A _____ is a legal statement which generally states that the person/group authoring the _____ is not responsible for any mishap in the event of using whatever object or information the _____ is attached to.
   a. Disclaimer2
   b. Thing
   c. Undefined
   d. Undefined

218. The _____ is an audit opinion for a set of financial statements issued by a certified public accountant that means that part of or all of the financial statements are not in compliance with GAAP and the auditors believe this noncompliance would be material to the average prudent investor.
   a. Adverse opinion2
   b. Thing
   c. Undefined
   d. Undefined

219. _____ of a project is the sum total of all projects products and their requirements or features.
   a. Scope2
   b. Thing
   c. Undefined
   d. Undefined

220. _____ is a term that is commonly applied in relation to the audit of the financial statements of an entity. The primary objective of such an audit is to provide an opinion as to whether or not the financial statements present fairly the financial position and results of the entity.
   a. Audit risk2
   b. Thing
   c. Undefined
   d. Undefined

221. _____ is a term in Corporate Finance used to indicate a condition when promises to creditors of a company are broken or honored with difficulty. Sometimes _____ can lead to bankruptcy. _____ is usually associated with some costs to the company and these are known as Costs of _____. A common example of a cost of _____ is bankrupty costs.

## Chapter 2. Financial Reporting and Analysis

a. Financial distress2  
b. Thing  
c. Undefined  
d. Undefined

222. _____ is used in marketing, as a measure of how much the public sees a product or its advertizing.
a. Thing  
b. Market visibility2  
c. Undefined  
d. Undefined

223. _____ refers to the way a corporation finances itself through some combination of equity sales, equity options, bonds, and loans. Optimal _____ refers to the particular combination that minimizes the cost of capital while maximizing the stock price.
a. Thing  
b. Capital structure2  
c. Undefined  
d. Undefined

224. _____ refers to concept that recognizes practical limits in financial reporting by allowing flexible handling of matters not considered material; information is considered material if the decisions of a reasonable person would be influenced by its omission or misstatement.
a. Thing  
b. Concept of materiality2  
c. Undefined  
d. Undefined

225. _____ refers to the constraint of determining whether an item is large enough to likely influence the decision of an investor or creditor.
a. Thing  
b. Materiality2  
c. Undefined  
d. Undefined

226. Formal agreements on remedies between all the parties to an antitrust case that must be approved by the courts. _____ can be signed before, during, or after a trial.
a. Thing  
b. Consent decrees2  
c. Undefined  
d. Undefined

227. _____ refers to the management and direction of the affairs of governments and institutions; a collective term for all policymaking officials of a government; the execution and implementation of public policy.
a. Administration2  
b. Thing  
c. Undefined  
d. Undefined

228. _____ is a court judgement in which both parties can resolve the case short of having a trial if they agree to work out the terms of the settlment subject to court approval.
a. Thing  
b. Consent decree2  
c. Undefined  
d. Undefined

229. The ultimate economic effect of a tax on the real incomes of producers or consumers. Thus a sales tax may be paid by a retailer, but it is likely that the _____ falls upon the consumer.
a. Thing  
b. Incidence2  
c. Undefined  
d. Undefined

230. _____ refers to paid, nonpersonal communication through various media by organizations and individuals who are in some way identified in the _____ message.

## Chapter 2. Financial Reporting and Analysis

a. Thing  
b. Advertising2  
c. Undefined  
d. Undefined

231. Promoting and selling products or services to customers, or prospective customers, is referred to as _____.
a. Thing  
b. Marketing2  
c. Undefined  
d. Undefined

232. The risk related to the inability of the firm to hold its competitive position and maintain stability and growth in earnings is _____.
a. Business risk2  
b. Thing  
c. Undefined  
d. Undefined

233. A cost that results from a discretionary management decision to spend a particular amount of money is called _____.
a. Discretionary cost2  
b. Thing  
c. Undefined  
d. Undefined

234. _____ refers to the want-satisfying power of a good or service; the satisfaction or pleasure a consumer obtains from the consumption of a good or service.
a. Utility2  
b. Thing  
c. Undefined  
d. Undefined

235. Notes that clarify information presented in the financial statements, as well as expand upon it where additional detail is needed are _____.
a. Thing  
b. Notes to the financial statements2  
c. Undefined  
d. Undefined

236. _____ is an American shoe company which has been making shoes since the early 20th century. The company's main turning point came in 1917 when the _____ All-Star basketball shoe was introduced. This was a real innovation at the time, considering the sport was only 25 years old.
a. Thing  
b. Converse2  
c. Undefined  
d. Undefined

237. _____ is an authority or agency in a country responsible for collecting _____ duties and for controlling the flow of people, animals and goods (including personal effects and hazardous items) in and out of the country.
a. Customs2  
b. Thing  
c. Undefined  
d. Undefined

238. The cost that a firm bears if it does not produce at all and that is independent of its output. The presence of a _____ tends to imply increasing returns to scale. Contrasts with variable cost.
a. Fixed cost2  
b. Thing  
c. Undefined  
d. Undefined

239. A collective term for all of the employees of an organization. _____ is also commonly used to refer to the _____ management function or the organizational unit responsible for administering _____ programs.

a. Concept  
b. Personnel2  
c. Undefined  
d. Undefined  

240. _____ refers to profits generated as a result of an inflationary economy, in which old inventory is sold at large profits because of increasing prices. This is particularly prevalent under First In, First Out accounting.
- a. Inventory profit2
- b. Thing
- c. Undefined
- d. Undefined

241. The overall level of prices in a country, as usually measured empirically by a price index, but often captured in theoretical models by a single variable is a _____.
- a. Thing
- b. Price level2
- c. Undefined
- d. Undefined

242. To be _____ is to act before a situation becomes a source of confrontation or crisis. It is the opposite of "retroactive," which refers to actions taken after an event.
- a. Proactive2
- b. Thing
- c. Undefined
- d. Undefined

243. _____ refers to the long-term movement of an economic variable, such as its average rate of increase or decrease over enough years to encompass several business cycles.
- a. Trend2
- b. Thing
- c. Undefined
- d. Undefined

244. _____ refers to an agency, commission, or board established by the Federal government or a state government to regulates businesses in the public interest.
- a. Thing
- b. Regulatory agency2
- c. Undefined
- d. Undefined

245. _____ refers to a financial institution, such as a bank or a life insurance company, which directs other people's money into such investments as government and corporate securities.
- a. Thing
- b. Financial intermediary2
- c. Undefined
- d. Undefined

246. _____ refers to annual profit of the corporation divided by the number of shares outstanding.
- a. Thing
- b. Earnings per share2
- c. Undefined
- d. Undefined

247. _____ refers to a statement provided to the shareholders that contains a balance sheet, an income statement, and a statement of changes in shareholder equity.
- a. Annual financial statement2
- b. Thing
- c. Undefined
- d. Undefined

248. A _____ is a 12-month period used for calculating annual ("yearly") financial reports in businesses and other organizations. In many jurisdictions, regulatory laws regarding accounting require such reports once per twelve months, but do not require that the twelve months constitute a calendar year (i.e. January to December).

## Chapter 2. Financial Reporting and Analysis

    a. Fiscal year2
    b. Thing
    c. Undefined
    d. Undefined

249. Large banks in key financial centers are referred to as _____.
    a. Money center banks2
    b. Thing
    c. Undefined
    d. Undefined

250. _____ is a term used to describe a delivery of nonconforming goods meant as a partial performance of a contract for the sale of goods, where a full performance is not possible.
    a. Accommodation2
    b. Thing
    c. Undefined
    d. Undefined

251. _____ is the branch of accounting that uses both past and future data in providing information that management uses in conducting daily operations in planning future operations, and in developing overall business strategies.
    a. Managerial Accounting2
    b. Thing
    c. Undefined
    d. Undefined

252. _____ is a concept used in finance and economics, defined as a rational and unbiased estimate of the potential market price of a good, service, or asset.
    a. Thing
    b. Fair value2
    c. Undefined
    d. Undefined

253. _____ is an economic concept with commonplace familiarity; it is the price that a good or service is offered at, or will fetch, in the marketplace; it is of interest mainly in the study of microeconomics.
    a. Market price2
    b. Thing
    c. Undefined
    d. Undefined

254. _____ refer to an equity security, representing a shareholder's ownership of a corporation. _____ are one of a finite number of equal portions in the capital of a company, entitling the owner to a proportion of distributed, non-reinvested profits known as dividends and to a portion of the value of the company in case of liquidation.
    a. Thing
    b. Shares2
    c. Undefined
    d. Undefined

255. There are several methods used for _____. They try to give an estimate of their fair value, by using fundamental economic criteria. This theoretical valuation has to be perfected with market criteria, as the final purpose is to determine potential market prices.
    a. Stock valuation2
    b. Thing
    c. Undefined
    d. Undefined

256. _____ occurs, among other instances, when one corporation acquires another in a merger or acquisition, a single corporation divides into two or more entities, or a corporation makes a substantial change in its capital structure.
    a. Reorganization2
    b. Thing
    c. Undefined
    d. Undefined

257. _____ refers to the amount by which expenses exceed revenues. The difference between income received and expenses, when expenses are greater.

a. Thing  
b. Net loss2  
c. Undefined  
d. Undefined  

258. _____ is either the cognitive process of transferring information from a particular subject to another particular subject (the target), or a linguistic expression corresponding to such a process. In a narrower sense, _____ is an inference or an argument from a particular to another particular, as opposed to deduction, induction, and abduction, where at least one of the premises or the conclusion is general.
a. Thing  
b. Analogy2  
c. Undefined  
d. Undefined  

259. From the early 1980s until the late 1990s, _____ was known for cutting its merchant fees (also known as a "discount rate") to fine merchants and restaurants if they only accepted _____ and no other credit or charge cards. This prompted competitors such as Visa and MasterCard to cry foul for a while, as the tactics "locked" restaurants into _____.
a. Organization  
b. American Express2  
c. Undefined  
d. Undefined  

260. _____ refers to money raized from within the firm or through the sale of ownership in the firm.
a. Equity capital2  
b. Thing  
c. Undefined  
d. Undefined  

261. As the word is applied to contracts, to terminate the contract as to future transactions or to annul the contract from the beginning is called _____.
a. Thing  
b. Rescind2  
c. Undefined  
d. Undefined  

262. A significant decline in economic activity. In the U.S., _____ is approximately defined as two successive quarters of falling GDP, as judged by NBER.
a. Recession2  
b. Thing  
c. Undefined  
d. Undefined  

263. Depreciation methods that recognize more depreciation expense in the early years of an asset's life and less in later years are referred to asan _____.
a. Thing  
b. Accelerated method2  
c. Undefined  
d. Undefined  

264. An increase in the overall price level of an economy, usually as measured by the CPI or by the implicit price deflator is called _____.
a. Thing  
b. Inflation2  
c. Undefined  
d. Undefined  

265. The _____ percentage shows how profitable a company's assets are in generating revenue.
a. Return on Assets2  
b. Thing  
c. Undefined  
d. Undefined

*Chapter 3. Analyzing Financing Activities*

1. _____ refers to a summary of all the transactions that have occurred over a particular period.
   a. Thing
   b. Financial statement3
   c. Undefined
   d. Undefined

2. _____ means the giving out of information, either voluntarily or to be in compliance with legal regulations or workplace rules.
   a. Thing
   b. Disclosure3
   c. Undefined
   d. Undefined

3. A contract for the possession and use of land or other property, including goods, on one side, and a recompense of rent or other income on the other is the _____.
   a. Thing
   b. Lease3
   c. Undefined
   d. Undefined

4. In finance, _____ is the process of estimating the market value of a financial asset or liability. They can be done on assets (for example, investments in marketable securities such as stocks, options, business enterprises, or intangible assets such as patents and trademarks) or on liabilities (e.g., Bonds issued by a company).
   a. Valuation3
   b. Event
   c. Undefined
   d. Undefined

5. An organization that employs resources to produce a good or service for profit and owns and operates one or more plants is referred to as a _____.
   a. Thing
   b. Firm3
   c. Undefined
   d. Undefined

6. _____ refers to potential liability that does not currently exist but is probable and reasonably estimable, such as lawsuits and tax disputes, is referred to as a _____.
   a. Contingent liability3
   b. Thing
   c. Undefined
   d. Undefined

7. A _____ is a present obligation of the enterprise arizing from past events, the settlement of which is expected to result in an outflow from the enterprise of resources embodying economic benefits.
   a. Thing
   b. Liability3
   c. Undefined
   d. Undefined

8. _____ is the name given to the set of legal principles, in countries following the English common law tradition, which supplement strict rules of law where their application would operate harshly, so as to achieve what is sometimes referred to as "natural justice."
   a. Thing
   b. Equity3
   c. Undefined
   d. Undefined

9. The total amount of physical capital that has been accumulated, usually in a country is _____. Also refers to the total issued capital of a firm, including ordinary and preferred shares.
   a. Capital stock3
   b. Thing
   c. Undefined
   d. Undefined

## Chapter 3. Analyzing Financing Activities

10. _____ generally refers to financial wealth, especially that used to start or maintain a business. In classical economics, _____ is one of four factors of production, the others being land and labor and entrepreneurship.
    a. Thing
    b. Capital3
    c. Undefined
    d. Undefined

11. In financial terminology, _____ is the capital raized by a corporation, through the issuance and sale of shares.
    a. Stock3
    b. Thing
    c. Undefined
    d. Undefined

12. Cumulative earnings of a company that are not distributed to the owners and are reinvested in the business are called _____.
    a. Retained earnings3
    b. Thing
    c. Undefined
    d. Undefined

13. _____ in economics, the manner in which total output and income is distributed among individuals or factors.
    a. Thing
    b. Distribution3
    c. Undefined
    d. Undefined

14. Amount of corporate profits paid out for each share of stock is referred to as _____.
    a. Dividend3
    b. Thing
    c. Undefined
    d. Undefined

15. A _____ is an individual or company (including a corporation) that legally owns one or more shares of stock in a joined stock company. The shareholders are the owners of a corporation. Companies listed at the stock market strive to enhance shareholder value.
    a. Stockholder3
    b. Thing
    c. Undefined
    d. Undefined

16. _____ Corportaion's global reputation was undermined by persistent rumours of bribery and political pressure to secure contracts in Central America, South America, Africa, and the Philippines. Especially controversial was its $3 billion contract with the Maharashtra State Electricity Board in India, where it is alleged that _____ officials used political connections within the Clinton and Bush administrations to exert pressure on the board.
    a. Enron3
    b. Thing
    c. Undefined
    d. Undefined

17. _____ refers to the shortening of the time for the performance of a contract or the payment of a note by the operation of some provision in the contract or note itself.
    a. Thing
    b. Acceleration3
    c. Undefined
    d. Undefined

18. _____ is a business term that refers to the aggregate value of a firm's outstanding common shares. In essence, _____ reflects the total value of a firm's equity currently available on the market. This measure differs from equity value to the extent that a firm has outstanding stock options or other securities convertible to common shares. The size and growth of a firm's _____ is often one of the critical measurements of a public company's success or failure.

## Chapter 3. Analyzing Financing Activities

a. Market capitalization3  
b. Thing  
c. Undefined  
d. Undefined

19. A _____ is, as defined in economics, a social arrangement that allows buyers and sellers to discover information and carry out a voluntary exchange of goods or services.
   a. Market3  
   b. Thing  
   c. Undefined  
   d. Undefined

20. _____ refers to spending for the production and accumulation of capital and additions to inventories. In a financial sense, buying an asset with the expectation of making a return.
   a. Thing  
   b. Investment3  
   c. Undefined  
   d. Undefined

21. _____ refers to a recording as positive in the balance of payments, any transaction that gives rise to a payment into the country, such as an export, the sale of an asset, or borrowing from abroad.
   a. Thing  
   b. Credit3  
   c. Undefined  
   d. Undefined

22. _____ refers to a debt instrument, issued by a borrower and promising a specified stream of payments to the purchaser, usually regular interest payments plus a final repayment of principal.
   a. Thing  
   b. Bond3  
   c. Undefined  
   d. Undefined

23. Independent accounting entity with a self-balancing set of accounts segregated for the purposes of carrying on specific activities is referred to as a _____.
   a. Fund3  
   b. Thing  
   c. Undefined  
   d. Undefined

24. A defense that relieves a seller of product liability if the user abnormally misused the product is called _____. Products must be designed to protect against foreseeable _____.
   a. Misuse3  
   b. Thing  
   c. Undefined  
   d. Undefined

25. When debt owed by a corporation to the shareholders becomes too large in relation to the corporation's capital structure, the IRS may contend that the corporation is _____.
   a. Thing  
   b. Thinly capitalized3  
   c. Undefined  
   d. Undefined

26. One of the original Seven Sisters, Royal Dutch/_____ is the world's third-largest oil company by revenue, and a major player in the petrochemical industry and the solar energy business. _____ has six core businesses: Exploration and Production, Gas and Power, Downstream, Chemicals, Renewables, and Trading/Shipping, and operates in more than 140 countries.
   a. Organization  
   b. Shell3  
   c. Undefined  
   d. Undefined

# Chapter 3. Analyzing Financing Activities

27. An item of property, such as land, capital, money, a share in ownership, or a claim on others for future payment, such as a bond or a bank deposit is an _____.
    a. Thing
    b. Asset3
    c. Undefined
    d. Undefined

28. A _____ is a legal and financial term. It means a party to a contract. Any legal entity can be a _____.
    a. Counterparty3
    b. Thing
    c. Undefined
    d. Undefined

29. A technique for avoiding a risk by making a counteracting transaction is referred to as _____.
    a. Hedging3
    b. Thing
    c. Undefined
    d. Undefined

30. An _____ is prepared by corporate management that presents financial information including financial statements, footnotes, and the management discussion and analysis.
    a. Thing
    b. Annual report3
    c. Undefined
    d. Undefined

31. A system that collects and processes financial information about an organization and reports that information to decision makers is referred to as _____.
    a. Accounting3
    b. Thing
    c. Undefined
    d. Undefined

32. A person in possession of a document of title or an instrument payable or indorsed to him, his order, or to bearer is a _____.
    a. Thing
    b. Holder3
    c. Undefined
    d. Undefined

33. _____ refers to a "non tangible product" that is not embodied in a physical good and that typically effects some change in another product, person, or institution. Contrasts with good.
    a. Thing
    b. Service3
    c. Undefined
    d. Undefined

34. Cash flow activities that include obtaining cash from issuing debt and repaying the amounts borrowed and obtaining cash from stockholders and paying dividends is referred to as _____.
    a. Financing activities3
    b. Thing
    c. Undefined
    d. Undefined

35. A standardized method or technique that is performed repetitively, often on different materials resulting in different finished goods is called an _____.
    a. Thing
    b. Operation3
    c. Undefined
    d. Undefined

36. A person to whom a debt or legal obligation is owed, and who has the right to enforce payment of that debt or obligation is referred to as _____.

*Chapter 3. Analyzing Financing Activities*  75

    a. Creditor3
    b. Thing
    c. Undefined
    d. Undefined

37. _____ refers to portion of the assets remaining after the creditors' claims have been satisfied; also called equity or residual interest.
    a. Net assets3
    b. Thing
    c. Undefined
    d. Undefined

38. _____ payments can refer to an ongoing stream of payments in respect of the completion of past achievements.
    a. Thing
    b. Residual3
    c. Undefined
    d. Undefined

39. A _____ is type of bond that can be converted into shares of stock in the issuing company, usually at some pre-announced ratio.
    a. Thing
    b. Convertible bond3
    c. Undefined
    d. Undefined

40. _____ refers to a claim on the borrower future income that is sold by the borrower to the lender. A _____ is a type of transferable interest representing financial value.
    a. Thing
    b. Security3
    c. Undefined
    d. Undefined

41. _____ refers to a debt that can reasonably be expected to be paid from existing current assets or through the creation of other current liabilities, within one year or the operating cycle, whichever is longer.
    a. Thing
    b. Current liability3
    c. Undefined
    d. Undefined

42. A _____ is an asset on the balance sheet which is expected to be sold or otherwise used up in the near future, usually within one year.
    a. Current asset3
    b. Thing
    c. Undefined
    d. Undefined

43. _____ refers to the time it takes for a company to purchase goods or services from suppliers, sell those goods and services to customers, and collect cash from customers.
    a. Thing
    b. Operating cycle3
    c. Undefined
    d. Undefined

44. The value today of a stream of payments and/or receipts over time in the future and/or the past, converted to the present using an interest rate. If X t is the amount in period t and r the interest rate, then _____ at time t=0 is V = ?T /t.
    a. Thing
    b. Present value3
    c. Undefined
    d. Undefined

45. Cash flowing out of the business from all sources over a period of time is _____.
    a. Thing
    b. Cash outflow3
    c. Undefined
    d. Undefined

## Chapter 3. Analyzing Financing Activities

46. _____ refers to the final payment date of a loan or other financial instrument, after which point no further interest or principal need be paid.
   a. Maturity3
   b. Thing
   c. Undefined
   d. Undefined

47. _____ refer to representation of ownership rights to the corporation.
   a. Thing
   b. Equity securities3
   c. Undefined
   d. Undefined

48. A statement of the assets, liabilities, and net worth of a firm or individual at some given time often at the end of its "fiscal year," is referred to as a _____.
   a. Balance sheet3
   b. Thing
   c. Undefined
   d. Undefined

49. In banking and accountancy, the outstanding _____ is the amount of money owned, (or due), that remains in a deposit account (or a loan account) at a given date, after all past remittances, payments and withdrawal have been accounted for. It can be positive (then, in the _____ sheet of a firm, it is an asset) or negative (a liability).
   a. Balance3
   b. Thing
   c. Undefined
   d. Undefined

50. _____ is the analysis of the accounts and the economic prospects of a firm.
   a. Thing
   b. Financial analysis3
   c. Undefined
   d. Undefined

51. A _____ is a signed written agreement between two or more parties. Also referred to as a contract.
   a. Covenant3
   b. Thing
   c. Undefined
   d. Undefined

52. _____ is the practice of making the sale of one good (the _____ good) to the de facto or de jure customer conditional on the purchase of a second distinctive good.
   a. Tying3
   b. Thing
   c. Undefined
   d. Undefined

53. _____ is the total assets minus total liabilities of an individual or company
   a. Net worth3
   b. Thing
   c. Undefined
   d. Undefined

54. A group of firms that produce identical or similar products is an _____. It is also used specifically to refer to an area of economic production focused on manufacturing which involves large amounts of capital investment before any profit can be realized, also called "heavy _____".
   a. Thing
   b. Industry3
   c. Undefined
   d. Undefined

55. In finance, _____ occurs when a debtor has not met its legal obligations according to the debt contract, e.g. it has not made a scheduled payment, or violated a covenant (condition) of the debt contract.

## Chapter 3. Analyzing Financing Activities

a. Default3  
b. Thing  
c. Undefined  
d. Undefined  

56. _____ is the corporate management term for the act of partially dismantling and reorganizing a company for the purpose of making it more efficient and therefore more profitable.
a. Restructuring3  
b. Thing  
c. Undefined  
d. Undefined  

57. In finance and economics, _____ is the reduction of some kind of asset, for either financial or social goals. A divestment is the opposite of an investment.
a. Thing  
b. Divestiture3  
c. Undefined  
d. Undefined  

58. Suppliers and financial institutions that lend money to companies is referred to as a _____.
a. Thing  
b. Lender3  
c. Undefined  
d. Undefined  

59. _____ refers to obligations that are not paid within 1 year.
a. Noncurrent liabilities3  
b. Thing  
c. Undefined  
d. Undefined  

60. Collecting information and providing feedback to employees about their behavior, communication style, or skills is an _____.
a. Thing  
b. Assessment3  
c. Undefined  
d. Undefined  

61. The rate of return on bonds, loans, or deposits. When one speaks of 'the' _____, it is usually in a model where there is only one.
a. Thing  
b. Interest rate3  
c. Undefined  
d. Undefined  

62. The date on which the final payment on a bond is due from the bond issuer to the investor is a _____.
a. Thing  
b. Maturity date3  
c. Undefined  
d. Undefined  

63. _____ refers to any distinct act of dominion wrongfully exerted over another's personal property in denial of or inconsistent with his rights therein. That tort committed by a person who deals with chattels not belonging to him in a manner that is inconsistent with the ownership of the lawful owner.
a. Thing  
b. Conversion3  
c. Undefined  
d. Undefined  

64. Generally, a legal right to engage in conduct that would otherwise result in legal liability is a _____. Privileges are commonly classified as absolute or conditional. Occasionally, _____ is also used to denote a legal right to refrain from particular behavior.

a. Privilege3  
b. Thing  
c. Undefined  
d. Undefined

65. In finance and economics, _____ is the price paid by a borrower for the use of a lender's money. In other words, _____ is the amount of paid to "rent" money for a period of time.
a. Thing  
b. Interest3  
c. Undefined  
d. Undefined

66. Remuneration paid to the owners of technology, patents, or trade names for the use of same name are called _____.
a. Thing  
b. Royalties3  
c. Undefined  
d. Undefined

67. In finance, a _____ is a bond that is rated below investment grade. These bonds have a higher risk of defaulting, but typically pay high yields in order to make them attractive to investors.
a. Thing  
b. Junk bond3  
c. Undefined  
d. Undefined

68. _____ refers to the extent to which an economic variable, such as a price or an exchange rate, moves up and down over time.
a. Thing  
b. Volatility3  
c. Undefined  
d. Undefined

69. In agency law, one under whose direction an agent acts and for whose benefit that agent acts is a _____.
a. Principal3  
b. Thing  
c. Undefined  
d. Undefined

70. A _____ is a "promise" or an "agreement" that is enforced or recognized by the law. In the civil law, a _____ is considered to be part of the general law of obligations.
a. Thing  
b. Contract3  
c. Undefined  
d. Undefined

71. In finance, a _____ is "attached" to a bond, either physically (as with old bonds) or electronically. Each _____ represents a predetermined payment promized to the bond-holder in return for his or her loan of money to the bond-issuer. .
a. Coupon3  
b. Concept  
c. Undefined  
d. Undefined

72. A _____ is a comparison of the money earned (or lost) on an investment to the amount of money invested.
a. Thing  
b. Rate of return3  
c. Undefined  
d. Undefined

73. The difference between the face value of a bond and its selling price, when a bond is sold for less than its face value it's referred to as a _____.
a. Discount3  
b. Thing  
c. Undefined  
d. Undefined

*Chapter 3. Analyzing Financing Activities* 79

74. _____ refers to the fee charged by an insurance company for an insurance policy. The rate of losses must be relatively predictable: In order to set the _____ (prices) insurers must be able to estimate them accurately.
   a. Premium3
   b. Thing
   c. Undefined
   d. Undefined

75. The company that borrows money from investors by issuing bonds is referred to as _____. They are legally responsible for the obligations of the issue and for reporting financial conditions, material developments and any other operational activities as required by the regulations of their jurisdictions.
   a. Issuer3
   b. Thing
   c. Undefined
   d. Undefined

76. The interest rate that equates a future value or an annuity to a given present value is a _____.
   a. Thing
   b. Yield3
   c. Undefined
   d. Undefined

77. _____ refers to a loan backed by something valuable, such as property.
   a. Thing
   b. Secured loan3
   c. Undefined
   d. Undefined

78. _____ refers to the long-term movement of an economic variable, such as its average rate of increase or decrease over enough years to encompass several business cycles.
   a. Trend3
   b. Thing
   c. Undefined
   d. Undefined

79. A company's purchase of the property and obligations of another company is an _____.
   a. Acquisition3
   b. Thing
   c. Undefined
   d. Undefined

80. An _____ is any factor (financial or non-financial) that provides a motive for a particular course of action, or counts as a reason for preferring one choice to the alternatives.
   a. Thing
   b. Incentive3
   c. Undefined
   d. Undefined

81. In accounting, an _____ represents an event in which an asset is used up or a liability is incurred. In terms of the accounting equation, expenses reduce owners' equity.
   a. Thing
   b. Expense3
   c. Undefined
   d. Undefined

82. Tangible property held for sale in the normal course of business or used in producing goods or services for sale is an _____.
   a. Thing
   b. Inventory3
   c. Undefined
   d. Undefined

83. _____ characterizes the process of leading and directing all or part of an organization, often a business, through the deployment and manipulation of resources. Early twentieth-century _____ writer Mary Parker Follett defined _____ as "the art of getting things done through people."

## Chapter 3. Analyzing Financing Activities

a. Thing
b. Management3
c. Undefined
d. Undefined

84. _____ refers to a report detailing a future stock offering containing a set of financial statements; required by the SEC from a company that wishes to make an initial public offering of its stock.
a. Prospectus3
b. Thing
c. Undefined
d. Undefined

85. _____ is Japan's second largest car company after Toyota. _____ is among the top three Asian rivals of the "big three" in the US.
a. Organization
b. Nissan3
c. Undefined
d. Undefined

86. _____ refer to people in the organization who actually use the product or service purchased by the buying center.
a. Thing
b. Users3
c. Undefined
d. Undefined

87. _____ is one of a series of accounting transactions dealing with the billing of customers which owe money to a person, company or organization for goods and services that have been provided to the customer. This is typically done in a one person organization by writing an invoice and mailing or delivering it to each customer.
a. Thing
b. Accounts receivable3
c. Undefined
d. Undefined

88. Reduction in the selling price of goods extended to the buyer because the goods are defective or of lower quality than the buyer ordered and to encourage a buyer to keep merchandise that would otherwise be returned is the _____.
a. Allowance3
b. Thing
c. Undefined
d. Undefined

89. Contra-asset account containing the estimated uncollectible accounts receivable is an _____. Also called allowance for bad debts or allowance for uncollectible accounts.
a. Allowance for doubtful accounts3
b. Thing
c. Undefined
d. Undefined

90. The dollar difference between total current assets and total current liabilities is called _____.
a. Thing
b. Working capital3
c. Undefined
d. Undefined

91. _____ refers to denial of the right to import or export, applying to particular products and/or particular countries. Includes embargo.
a. Thing
b. Prohibition3
c. Undefined
d. Undefined

92. _____ is a financial condition experienced by a person or business entity when their assets no longer exceed their liabilities or when the person or entity can no longer meet its debt obligations when they come due.

a. Thing
b. Insolvency3
c. Undefined
d. Undefined

93. A type of influence process where a receiver accepts the position advocated by a source to obtain favorable outcomes or to avoid punishment is the _____.
a. Thing
b. Compliance3
c. Undefined
d. Undefined

94. _____ is the difference between the intrinsic value of a stock (i.e. value based on stock valuation and what the company is actually worth) and the price that the market sets on a stock (i.e. stock price is a matter of market participants' opinions and is different from the intrinsic value).
a. Margin of safety3
b. Thing
c. Undefined
d. Undefined

95. A deposit by a buyer in stocks with a seller or a stockbroker, as security to cover fluctuations in the market in reference to stocks that the buyer has purchased but for which he has not paid is a _____. Commodities are also traded on _____.
a. Margin3
b. Thing
c. Undefined
d. Undefined

96. One who rents property from another. In the case of real estate, the _____ is also known as the tenant.
a. Lessee3
b. Thing
c. Undefined
d. Undefined

97. The person who transfers the right of possession and use of goods under the lease is referred to as _____.
a. Thing
b. Lessor3
c. Undefined
d. Undefined

98. The ending of a corporation that occurs only after the winding-up of the corporation's affairs, the liquidation of its assets, and the distribution of the proceeds to the claimants are referred to as a _____.
a. Termination3
b. Thing
c. Undefined
d. Undefined

99. _____ refers to a contractual arrangement giving the lessee temporary use of the property with continued ownership of the property by the lessor. Accounted for as a rental.
a. Operating lease3
b. Thing
c. Undefined
d. Undefined

100. A type of lease whose characteristics make it similar to a debt-financed purchase and that is consequently accounted for in that fashion is called _____. A _____ is usually used to finance equipment for the major part of its useful life, and there is a reasonable assurance that the lessee will obtain ownership of the equipment by the end of the lease term.
a. Capital lease3
b. Thing
c. Undefined
d. Undefined

101. _____ is a U.S. business term for the amount of money that a company receives from its activities, mostly from sales of products and/or services to customers.

## Chapter 3. Analyzing Financing Activities

a. Revenue3  
b. Thing  
c. Undefined  
d. Undefined

102. _____ refers to a person or tool with a primary function of information analysis, generally with a more limited, practical and short term set of goals than a researcher.
a. Person  
b. Analyst3  
c. Undefined  
d. Undefined

103. _____ refers to payments of income to those who supply the economy with capital.
a. Interest income3  
b. Thing  
c. Undefined  
d. Undefined

104. Refers to part of a transaction that involves an activity other than the exchange of cash. Providing a service or delivering goods would be considered the _____ of a transaction.
a. Economic substance3  
b. Thing  
c. Undefined  
d. Undefined

105. A provision of the corporate income tax that reduces a firm's tax when it buys new capital goods is referred to as _____.
a. Investment tax credit3  
b. Thing  
c. Undefined  
d. Undefined

106. _____ is a concept used in finance and economics, defined as a rational and unbiased estimate of the potential market price of a good, service, or asset.
a. Thing  
b. Fair value3  
c. Undefined  
d. Undefined

107. Allows a firm to reduce the taxes paid to the home government by the amount of taxes paid to the foreign government is referred to as _____.
a. Thing  
b. Tax credit3  
c. Undefined  
d. Undefined

108. The date and time on which coverage under an insurance policy takes effect is _____. Also refers to the date at which a stock or mutual fund was first traded.
a. Inception3  
b. Thing  
c. Undefined  
d. Undefined

109. Assets defined in the broadest legal sense. _____ includes the unrealized receivables of a cash basis taxpayer, but not services rendered.
a. Property3  
b. Thing  
c. Undefined  
d. Undefined

110. A contract that gives the purchaser the _____ to buy or sell the underlying financial instrument at a specified price, called the exercise price or strike price, within a specific period of time.

a. Option3  
c. Undefined  
b. Thing  
d. Undefined

111. A _____ refers to a layout accurate in size, color, scheme, and other necessary details to show how a final ad will look. For presentation only, never for reproduction.
   a. Thing
   b. Comprehensive3
   c. Undefined
   d. Undefined

112. _____ is an accounting and finance term for the method of attributing the cost of an asset across the useful life of the asset. _____ is a reduction in the value of a currency in floating exchange rate.
   a. Depreciation3
   b. Thing
   c. Undefined
   d. Undefined

113. _____ refers to a system by which individuals can reduce their exposure to risk of large losses by spreading the risks among a large number of persons.
   a. Thing
   b. Insurance3
   c. Undefined
   d. Undefined

114. Similar to a script in that a _____ can be a less than completely rational decision-making method. Involves the use of a pre-existing set of decision steps for any problem that presents itself.
   a. Policy3
   b. Thing
   c. Undefined
   d. Undefined

115. _____ refers to a financial statement that presents the revenues and expenses and resulting net income or net loss of a company for a specific period of time.
   a. Income statement3
   b. Thing
   c. Undefined
   d. Undefined

116. In accounting, the _____ of an asset is its remaining value after depreciation. The estimated value of an asset at the end of its useful life.
   a. Thing
   b. Salvage value3
   c. Undefined
   d. Undefined

117. A nation's currency Is said to _____ when exchange rates change so that a unit of its currency can buy fewer units of foreign currency.
   a. Depreciate3
   b. Thing
   c. Undefined
   d. Undefined

118. _____ refers to a note payable issued for property, such as a house, usually repaid in equal installments consisting of part principle and part interest, over a specified period.
   a. Mortgage3
   b. Thing
   c. Undefined
   d. Undefined

119. _____ refers to the method under which income and expenses are determined for tax purposes. Important accounting methods include the cash basis and the accrual basis.

a. Accounting method3  
b. Thing  
c. Undefined  
d. Undefined

120. Systematic and rational allocation of the acquisition cost of an intangible asset over its useful life is referred to as _____.

a. Amortization3  
b. Thing  
c. Undefined  
d. Undefined

121. In finance, _____ refers to the amounts of cash being received and spent by a business during a defined period of time, sometimes tied to a specific project. Most of the time they are being used to determine gaps in the liquid position of a company.

a. Cash flow3  
b. Thing  
c. Undefined  
d. Undefined

122. _____ is the largest specialty retailer of consumer electronics, personal computers and related goods in North America. The company's subsidiaries include Geek Squad, Magnolia Audio Video, and Future Shop in Canada, which together operate over 700 stores in the United States and Canada. _____ is noted for being staffed with non-commissioned sales associates.

a. Best Buy3  
b. Thing  
c. Undefined  
d. Undefined

123. An _____ is the totality of the legal rights, interests, entitlements and obligations attaching to property. In the context of wills and probate, it refers to the totality of the property which the deceased owned or in which some interest was held.

a. Estate3  
b. Thing  
c. Undefined  
d. Undefined

124. _____ is area on a piece of property or part of a building that is available for use to all owners or tenants. Examples include: hallways, swimming pools, parking garage, and cummunity centers.

a. Thing  
b. Common area3  
c. Undefined  
d. Undefined

125. Regarding the structure of tariffs. In the context of a trade war, _____ refers to the increase in tariffs that occurs as countries retaliate again and again.

a. Thing  
b. Escalation3  
c. Undefined  
d. Undefined

126. A _____ is a ratio of two numbers of reported levels or flows of a company. It may be two financial flows categories divided by each other (profit margin, profit/revenue). It may be a level divided by a financial flow (price/earnings). It may be a flow divided by a level (return on equity or earnings/equity). The numerator or denominator may itself be a ratio (PEG ratio).

a. Thing  
b. Financial ratio3  
c. Undefined  
d. Undefined

127. A _____ is a cost incurred in making an economic exchange. For example, most people, when buying or selling a stock, must pay a commission to their broker; that commission is a _____ of doing the stock deal.

## Chapter 3. Analyzing Financing Activities

a. Thing
c. Undefined

b. Transaction cost3
d. Undefined

128. In finance, _____ is a profit or an increase in value of an investment such as a stock or bond. _____ is calculated by fair market value or the proceeds from the sale of the investment minus the sum of the purchase price and all costs associated with it.

a. Gain3
c. Undefined

b. Thing
d. Undefined

129. A _____ is a 12-month period used for calculating annual ("yearly") financial reports in businesses and other organizations. In many jurisdictions, regulatory laws regarding accounting require such reports once per twelve months, but do not require that the twelve months constitute a calendar year (i.e. January to December).

a. Fiscal year3
c. Undefined

b. Thing
d. Undefined

130. An out-of-court settlement in which creditors agree to accept a fractional settlement on their original claim is referred to as _____.

a. Composition3
c. Undefined

b. Thing
d. Undefined

131. Notes that clarify information presented in the financial statements, as well as expand upon it where additional detail is needed are _____.

a. Notes to the financial statements3
c. Undefined

b. Thing
d. Undefined

132. The social science dealing with the use of scarce resources to obtain the maximum satisfaction of society's virtually unlimited economic wants is an _____.

a. Thing
c. Undefined

b. Economics3
d. Undefined

133. The _____ measures the size of a company's after-tax income, excluding non-cash depreciation expenses, as compared to the firm's total debt obligations. It is used to gauge a company's ability to meet long term obligations.

a. Solvency ratio3
c. Undefined

b. Thing
d. Undefined

134. The ability of a company to pay interest as it comes due and to repay the face value of debt at maturity is called _____.

a. Solvency3
c. Undefined

b. Thing
d. Undefined

135. In throughput accounting, the cost accounting aspect of Theory of Constraints (TOC), _____ is the money spent turning inventory into throughput. In TOC, _____ is limited to costs that vary strictly with the quantity produced, like raw materials and purchased components.

a. Operating expense3
c. Undefined

b. Thing
d. Undefined

136. The cost a business incurs to borrow money. With respect to bonds payable, the _____ is calculated by multiplying the market rate of interest by the carrying value of the bonds on the date of the payment.
    a. Thing
    b. Interest expense3
    c. Undefined
    d. Undefined

137. Total revenues from operation minus cost of goods sold and operating costs are called _____.
    a. Operating income3
    b. Thing
    c. Undefined
    d. Undefined

138. An examination before a competent tribunal, according to the law of the land, of the facts or law put in issue in a cause, for the purpose of determining such issue is a _____. When the court hears and determines any issue of fact or law for the purpose of determining the rights of the parties, it may be considered a _____.
    a. Trial3
    b. Thing
    c. Undefined
    d. Undefined

139. _____ refers to a person who is authorized to vote the shares of another person. Also, the written authorization empowering a person to vote the shares of another person.
    a. Proxy3
    b. Thing
    c. Undefined
    d. Undefined

140. _____ is one of the constituents of a leasing calculus or operation. It describes the future value of a good in terms of percentage of depreciation of its initial value.
    a. Thing
    b. Residual value3
    c. Undefined
    d. Undefined

141. _____ is an airline based in Tempe, Arizona, owned by _____ Group, Inc.. As of May 2006, the combined airline is the fifth largest airline in the United States and has a fleet of 358 mainline jet aircraft and 295 express aircraft connecting 237 destinations in North America, Central America, the Caribbean, Hawaii, and Europe.
    a. US airways3
    b. Organization
    c. Undefined
    d. Undefined

142. The _____ is a comparison of a firm's current assets to its current liabilities. The _____ is an indication of a firm's market liquidity and ability to meet short-term debt obligations.
    a. Thing
    b. Current ratio3
    c. Undefined
    d. Undefined

143. _____ refers to net income before interest and taxes, divided by interest expense; describes a company's ability to make interest payments on its debt.
    a. Times interest earned3
    b. Thing
    c. Undefined
    d. Undefined

144. The _____ percentage shows how profitable a company's assets are in generating revenue.
    a. Return on Assets3
    b. Thing
    c. Undefined
    d. Undefined

## Chapter 3. Analyzing Financing Activities

145. The common stock or ownership capital of the firm is _____. _____ may be supplied through retained earnings or the sale of new common stock.
    a. Common equity3
    b. Thing
    c. Undefined
    d. Undefined

146. _____ - earnings before extraordinary items, less preferred-share dividends, divided by average common shareholders' equity. Shows the rate of return on the investment for the company's common shareholders, the only providers of capital who do not have a fixed return.
    a. Thing
    b. Return on common Equity3
    c. Undefined
    d. Undefined

147. The _____ is a financial ratio debt divided by shareholders' equity. The two components are often taken from the firm's balance sheet, but they might also be calulated as market values if both the companiy's debt and equity are publicly traded. It is used to calculate a company's "financial leverage" and indicates what proportion of equity and debt the company is using to finance its assets.
    a. Debt to equity ratio3
    b. Thing
    c. Undefined
    d. Undefined

148. A measure of a company's solvency, calculated by dividing income before interest expense and taxes by interest expense is a _____.
    a. Times interest earned ratio3
    b. Concept
    c. Undefined
    d. Undefined

149. Net profit after taxes per dollar of equity capital is referred to as _____.
    a. Return on equity3
    b. Thing
    c. Undefined
    d. Undefined

150. _____ in a financial context refers to the rate at which a provider of goods cycles through its average inventory. _____ in a human resources context refers to the characteristic of a given company or industry, relative to rate at which an employer gains and loses staff.
    a. Thing
    b. Turnover3
    c. Undefined
    d. Undefined

151. A measure of the amount of debt used in the capital structure of the firm is the _____.
    a. Thing
    b. Financial leverage3
    c. Undefined
    d. Undefined

152. _____ is using given resources in such a way that the potential positive or negative outcome is magnified. In finance, this generally refers to borrowing.
    a. Thing
    b. Leverage3
    c. Undefined
    d. Undefined

153. Bundle of legal rights over the use to which a resource is put and over the use made of any income that may be derived from that resource are referred to as _____.

a. Property rights3  
b. Thing  
c. Undefined  
d. Undefined

154. A _____ is a steady income given to a person (usually after retirement). Pensions are typically payments made in the form of a guaranteed annuity to a retired or disabled employee.
a. Pension3  
b. Thing  
c. Undefined  
d. Undefined

155. A _____ is a term used in marketing and broadcasting, to describe a _____ grouping or a market segment.
a. Demographic3  
b. Thing  
c. Undefined  
d. Undefined

156. Amounts of money put aside by corporations, nonprofit organizations, or unions to cover part of the financial needs of members when they retire is a _____.
a. Thing  
b. Pension fund3  
c. Undefined  
d. Undefined

157. An independent party appointed to represent the bondholders is referred to as a _____.
a. Trustee3  
b. Thing  
c. Undefined  
d. Undefined

158. In business organization law, the cash or property contributed to a business by its owners is referred to as _____.
a. Contribution3  
b. Thing  
c. Undefined  
d. Undefined

159. A pension plan in which benefits are set in advance is referred to as _____.
a. Defined benefit plan3  
b. Thing  
c. Undefined  
d. Undefined

160. A pension plan in which benefits are determined by the contributions into the plan and their earnings is called _____.
a. Defined contribution plan3  
b. Thing  
c. Undefined  
d. Undefined

161. The payment for the service of a unit of labor, per unit time. In trade theory, it is the only payment to labor, usually unskilled labor. In empirical work, _____ data may exclude other compenzation, which must be added to get the total cost of employment.
a. Wage3  
b. Thing  
c. Undefined  
d. Undefined

162. _____ in contract law, a basic requirement for an enforceable agreement under traditional contract principles, defined in this text as legal value, bargained for and given in exchange for an act or promise. In corporation law, cash or property contributed to a corporation in exchange for shares, or a promise to contribute such cash or property.

## Chapter 3. Analyzing Financing Activities

a. Thing  
c. Undefined  
b. Consideration3  
d. Undefined  

163. The _____ of 1974 is a United States federal statute enacted to deal with widespread concerns about the funding and vesting of defined benefit pension plans.
   a. Employee Retirement Income Security Act3
   b. Thing
   c. Undefined
   d. Undefined

164. _____ refers to the rate, per year, at which future values are diminished to make them comparable to values in the present. Can be either subjective or objective .
   a. Discount rate3
   b. Thing
   c. Undefined
   d. Undefined

165. _____ refers to the price of an asset agreed on between a willing buyer and a willing seller; the price an asset could demand if it is sold on the open market.
   a. Thing
   b. Market value3
   c. Undefined
   d. Undefined

166. The acquisition of an increasing quantity of something. The _____ of factors, especially capital, is a primary mechanism for economic growth.
   a. Accumulation3
   b. Thing
   c. Undefined
   d. Undefined

167. In law, a _____ is an agreement such that one party takes ownership of a piece of property from another under the understanding that the ownership will revert to the second party when an agreed event occurs.
   a. Thing
   b. Reversion3
   c. Undefined
   d. Undefined

168. _____ refers to the negotiation of labor contracts between labor unions and firms or government entities.
   a. Collective bargaining3
   b. Thing
   c. Undefined
   d. Undefined

169. _____ is the process whereby interested parties resolve disputes, agree upon courses of action, bargain for individual or collective advantage, and/or attempt to craft outcomes which serve their mutual interests.
   a. Thing
   b. Negotiation3
   c. Undefined
   d. Undefined

170. People's physical and mental talents and efforts that are used to help produce goods and services are called _____.
   a. Thing
   b. Labor3
   c. Undefined
   d. Undefined

171. _____ refers to consisting of virtually the same elements as portfolio income, a measure by which to justify a deduction for interest on investment indebtedness. Income derived from investments.

a. Thing
b. Investment income3
c. Undefined
d. Undefined

172. _____ refers to a rise in the value of a country's currency on the exchange market, relative either to a particular other currency or to a weighted average of other currencies. The currency is said to appreciate. Opposite of 'depreciation.' _____ can also refer to the increase in value of any asset.
a. Appreciation3
b. Thing
c. Undefined
d. Undefined

173. Reports inflows and outflows of cash during the accounting period in the categories of operating, investing, and financing is a _____.
a. Statement of cash flow3
b. Thing
c. Undefined
d. Undefined

174. Method of accounting that records the effects of accounting events in the period in which such events occur regardless of when cash is exchanged is _____.
a. Thing
b. Accrual accounting3
c. Undefined
d. Undefined

175. An _____ is an accounting event in which the transaction is recognized when the action takes place, instead of when cash is disbursed or received.
a. Accrual3
b. Thing
c. Undefined
d. Undefined

176. That which involves playing down differences and finding areas of agreement are referred to as accommodation or _____.
a. Smoothing3
b. Thing
c. Undefined
d. Undefined

177. A financial market in which long-term debt and equity instruments are traded is referred to as a _____. The _____ includes the stock market and the bond market.
a. Capital market3
b. Thing
c. Undefined
d. Undefined

178. _____ refers to a period of time that permits an increase or decrease in current production volume with existing capacity, but one that is too short to permit enlargement of that capacity itself (eg, the building of new plants, training of additional workers, etc.).
a. Short run3
b. Thing
c. Undefined
d. Undefined

179. In economic models, the _____ time frame assumes no fixed factors of production. Firms can enter or leave the marketplace, and the cost (and availability) of land, labor, raw materials, and capital goods can be assumed to vary.
a. Long run3
b. Thing
c. Undefined
d. Undefined

## Chapter 3. Analyzing Financing Activities

180. In economics, a _____ is a mechanism which allows people to trade money for securities or commodities such as gold or other precious metals. In general, any commodity market might be considered to be a _____, if the usual purpose of traders is not the immediate consumption of the commodity, but rather as a means of delaying or accelerating consumption over time.
   a. Thing
   b. Financial market3
   c. Undefined
   d. Undefined

181. _____ refers to the return on an asset expected over the next period.
   a. Thing
   b. Expected return3
   c. Undefined
   d. Undefined

182. Deferred is any account where the asset or liability is not realized until a future date, e.g. annuities, charges, taxes, income, etc. The deferred item may be carried, dependent on type of _____, as either an asset or liability.
   a. Deferral3
   b. Thing
   c. Undefined
   d. Undefined

183. _____ refers to a thing that was originally personal property and that has been actually or constructively affixed to the soil itself or to some structure legally a part of the land.
   a. Thing
   b. Fixture3
   c. Undefined
   d. Undefined

184. An approximate measure of the liability of a pension plan, vested and non-vested, in the event of a termination at the date the calculation is performed is the _____.
   a. Accumulated Benefit Obligation3
   b. Thing
   c. Undefined
   d. Undefined

185. The dollar sum of costs that an insured individual must pay before the insurer begins to pay is called _____.
   a. Deductible3
   b. Thing
   c. Undefined
   d. Undefined

186. The body of knowledge and techniques that can be used to combine economic resources to produce goods and services is called _____.
   a. Technology3
   b. Thing
   c. Undefined
   d. Undefined

187. In corporation law, a corporation's acceptance of a pre-incorporation contract by action of its board of directors, by which the corporation becomes liable on the contract, is referred to as _____.
   a. Adoption3
   b. Concept
   c. Undefined
   d. Undefined

188. _____ is a bookkeeping method that recognizes revenue and expenses at the time of cash receipt or payment. It is the opposite of Accrual Basis.
   a. Thing
   b. Cash basis3
   c. Undefined
   d. Undefined

189. _____ refers to the combining of two or more things into a single category. Data on international trade necessarily aggregate goods and services into manageable groups.
   a. Aggregation3
   b. Thing
   c. Undefined
   d. Undefined

190. _____ refers to any departure from the ideal of perfect competition that interferes with economic agents maximizing social welfare when they maximize their own.
   a. Distortion3
   b. Thing
   c. Undefined
   d. Undefined

191. _____ refers to payments made or incomes forgone to obtain and retain the services of a resource.
   a. Economic cost3
   b. Thing
   c. Undefined
   d. Undefined

192. _____ refers to recording as negative in the balance of payments, any transaction that gives rise to a payment out of the country, such as an import, the purchase of an asset, or lending to foreigners. Opposite of credit.
   a. Debit3
   b. Thing
   c. Undefined
   d. Undefined

193. _____ are those assets usually in service over one year such as buildings, equipment, and long-term investments. These often receive favorable tax treatment over current assets. Tangible long-term assets are usually referred to as fixed assets.
   a. Thing
   b. Noncurrent assets3
   c. Undefined
   d. Undefined

194. The total array of money, incentives, benefits, perquisites, and awards provided by the organization to an employee is the _____.
   a. Thing
   b. Compensation package3
   c. Undefined
   d. Undefined

195. The cost of something in terms of opportunity foregone. The _____ to a country of producing a unit more of a good, such as for export or to replace an import, is the quantity of some other good that could have been produced instead.
   a. Opportunity cost3
   b. Thing
   c. Undefined
   d. Undefined

196. _____ refers to usually the first stage in the creative process. It includes education and formal training.
   a. Preparation3
   b. Thing
   c. Undefined
   d. Undefined

197. An organized marketplace in which common stocks are traded. In the United States, the largest _____ is the New York Stock Exchange, on which are traded the stocks of the largest U.S. companies.
   a. Stock market3
   b. Thing
   c. Undefined
   d. Undefined

198. Movements in a stock portfolio's value that are attributable to macroeconomic forces affecting all firms in an economy, rather than factors specific to an individual firm are referred to as _____.

*Chapter 3. Analyzing Financing Activities*

a. Thing
c. Undefined
b. Systematic risk3
d. Undefined

199. A _____ is the measure of the extent to which two economic or statistical variables move together, normalized so that its values range from -1 to +1. It is defined as the covariance of the two variables divided by the square root of the product of their variances.
a. Correlation3
c. Undefined
b. Thing
d. Undefined

200. A what-if technique that managers use to examine how a result will change if the original predicted data are not achieved or if an underlying assumption changes is _____.
a. Thing
c. Undefined
b. Sensitivity analysis3
d. Undefined

201. _____ refers to the increase in profit a firm anticipates it will obtain by purchasing capital ; expressed as a percentage of the total cost of the investment activity.
a. Expected rate of return3
c. Undefined
b. Thing
d. Undefined

202. _____ refers to the return to the resource entrepreneurial ability; total revenue minus total cost.
a. Profit3
c. Undefined
b. Thing
d. Undefined

203. A worker association that bargains with employers over wages and working conditions is called a _____.
a. Union3
c. Undefined
b. Thing
d. Undefined

204. _____ is the act of removing from control the owner of an item of property. The term is used to both refer to acts by a government or by any group of people.
a. Thing
c. Undefined
b. Expropriation3
d. Undefined

205. The process of bringing, maintaining, and defending a lawsuit is _____.
a. Thing
c. Undefined
b. Litigation3
d. Undefined

206. An obligation of a company to replace defective goods or correct any deficiencies in performance or quality of a product is called a _____.
a. Thing
c. Undefined
b. Warranty3
d. Undefined

207. _____ is an American manufacturer of televisions headquartered in Lincolnshire, Illinois. It was the inventor of the modern remote control, and it introduced HDTV in North America.
a. Organization
c. Undefined
b. Zenith3
d. Undefined

## Chapter 3. Analyzing Financing Activities

208. A _____ refers to a financial statement of a parent company and its subsidiaries that has been combined into a single set of financial statements as if the companies were one.
   a. Thing
   b. Consolidated financial statement3
   c. Undefined
   d. Undefined

209. Marketers tend to define _____ as making repeat purchases. Some argue that it should be defined attitudinally as a strongly positive feeling about the brand.
   a. Customer loyalty3
   b. Thing
   c. Undefined
   d. Undefined

210. Promoting and selling products or services to customers, or prospective customers, is referred to as _____.
   a. Thing
   b. Marketing3
   c. Undefined
   d. Undefined

211. Marketers tend to define customer _____ as making repeat purchases. Some argue that it should be defined attitudinally as a strongly positive feeling about the brand.
   a. Thing
   b. Loyalty3
   c. Undefined
   d. Undefined

212. The ultimate economic effect of a tax on the real incomes of producers or consumers. Thus a sales tax may be paid by a retailer, but it is likely that the _____ falls upon the consumer.
   a. Thing
   b. Incidence3
   c. Undefined
   d. Undefined

213. Loan origination fees that may be deductible as interest by a buyer of property. A seller of property who pays _____ reduces the selling price by the amount of the _____ paid for the buyer.
   a. Thing
   b. Points3
   c. Undefined
   d. Undefined

214. _____ refers to the speed of the up and down movements of a fluctuating economic variable; that is, the number of times per unit of time that the variable completes a cycle of up and down movement.
   a. Frequency3
   b. Thing
   c. Undefined
   d. Undefined

215. Formal or legal documents in writing, such as contracts, deeds, wills, bonds, leases, and mortgages is referred to as a _____.
   a. Thing
   b. Financial instrument3
   c. Undefined
   d. Undefined

216. _____ refers to an economic variable that is controlled by policy makers and can be used to influence other variables, called targets. Examples are monetary and fiscal policies used to achieve external and internal balance.
   a. Thing
   b. Instrument3
   c. Undefined
   d. Undefined

217. A partnership in which some of the partners are limited partners. At least one of the partners in a _____ must be a general partner.

a. Limited partnership3  
b. Thing  
c. Undefined  
d. Undefined  

218. _____ refers to an undertaking by two parties for a specific purpose and duration, taking any of several legal forms.
a. Thing  
b. Joint venture3  
c. Undefined  
d. Undefined  

219. In the common law, a _____ is a type of business entity in which partners share with each other the profits or losses of the business undertaking in which they have all invested.
a. Thing  
b. Partnership3  
c. Undefined  
d. Undefined  

220. An arrangement in which shareholders of independent firms agree to give up their stock in exchange for _____ certificates that entitle them to a share of the _____'s common profits.
a. Trust3  
b. Thing  
c. Undefined  
d. Undefined  

221. _____ refers to the entity that has a controlling influence over another company. It may have its own operations, or it may have been set up solely for the purpose of owning the Subject Company.
a. Parent company3  
b. Thing  
c. Undefined  
d. Undefined  

222. Other organizations in the same industry or type of business that provide a good or service to the same set of customers is referred to as a _____.
a. Thing  
b. Competitor3  
c. Undefined  
d. Undefined  

223. The payments made by a borrower on their debt, usually including both interest payments and partial repayment of principal, are called _____.
a. Debt service3  
b. Thing  
c. Undefined  
d. Undefined  

224. A _____ refers to a role in the buying center with formal authority and responsibility to select the supplier and negotiate the terms of the contract.
a. Thing  
b. Buyer3  
c. Undefined  
d. Undefined  

225. The _____ is a court's determination of a matter of law based on the issue presented in the particular case. In other words: under this law, with these facts, this result.
a. Thing  
b. Holding3  
c. Undefined  
d. Undefined  

226. The process of using inventory such as raw materials as collateral for a loan is _____. Lenders may require additional collateral and may require an appraisal by a national appraisal firm acceptable to the lender. Depending on the type of inventory, the lender's advance rate can range from 35% to 80% of the orderly liquidation value of the inventory.

a. Thing
b. Inventory financing3
c. Undefined
d. Undefined

227. A company that is controlled by another company or corporation is a _____.
a. Subsidiary3
b. Thing
c. Undefined
d. Undefined

228. _____ is a specific area of finance dealing with the financial decisions corporations make and the tools as well as analyses used to make these decisions. The discipline as a whole may be divided among long-term and short-term decisions and techniques with the primary goal being the enhancing of corporate value by ensuring that return on capital exceeds cost of capital, without taking excessive financial risks.
a. Thing
b. Corporate finance3
c. Undefined
d. Undefined

229. _____ is a legally declared inability or impairment of ability of an individual or organization to pay their creditors.
a. Thing
b. Bankruptcy3
c. Undefined
d. Undefined

230. _____ generally refers to the buying and holding of shares of stock on a stock market by individuals and funds in anticipation of income from dividends and capital gain as the value of the stock rises.
a. Equity investment3
b. Thing
c. Undefined
d. Undefined

231. A _____ is where borrowers come together with lenders to determine conditions of exchange such as interest rates and the duration of a loan.
a. Thing
b. Credit market3
c. Undefined
d. Undefined

232. In finance, a _____ is a collection of investments held by an institution or a private individual. Holding but not always a _____ is part of an investment and risk-limiting strategy called diversification. By owning several assets, certain types of risk (in particular specific risk) can be reduced.
a. Thing
b. Portfolio3
c. Undefined
d. Undefined

233. _____ in the most basic sense of the word refers to any kind of lending to consumers. However, in the United States financial services industry, the term "_____" often refers to a particular type of business, sub prime branch lending (that is lending to people with bad credit).
a. Thing
b. Consumer finance3
c. Undefined
d. Undefined

234. A _____ is a generic term for specific types of investments from which payoffs over time are derived from the performance of assets (such as commodities, shares or bonds), interest rates, exchange rates, or indices (such as a stock market index, consumer price index (CPI) or an index of weather conditions).
a. Derivative3
b. Thing
c. Undefined
d. Undefined

## Chapter 3. Analyzing Financing Activities

235. _____ refers to a contract that has not been fully performed. With court approval, executory contracts may be rejected by a debtor in bankruptcy.
   a. Thing
   b. Executory contract3
   c. Undefined
   d. Undefined

236. Production of goods primarily by the application of labor and capital to raw materials and other intermediate inputs, in contrast to agriculture, mining, forestry, fishing, and services a _____.
   a. Manufacturing3
   b. Thing
   c. Undefined
   d. Undefined

237. The combination of two or more firms, generally of equal size and market power, to form an entirely new entity is a _____.
   a. Consolidation3
   b. Thing
   c. Undefined
   d. Undefined

238. A measure of how efficiently a company uses its assets to generate sales, an _____ is computed as net sales divided by average total assets.
   a. Asset turnover ratio3
   b. Thing
   c. Undefined
   d. Undefined

239. _____ refers to a bank's capital divided by its assets.
   a. Thing
   b. Leverage ratio3
   c. Undefined
   d. Undefined

240. _____ is a financing technique that allows the corporation to separate credit origination and funding activities. The technique comes under the umbrella of structured finance as it applies to assets that typically are illiquid contracts.
   a. Thing
   b. Securitization3
   c. Undefined
   d. Undefined

241. Cash coming into the company as the result of a previous investment is a _____.
   a. Thing
   b. Cash inflow3
   c. Undefined
   d. Undefined

242. _____ refers to the sale of securities directly to a financial institution by a corporation. This eliminates the middleman and reduces the cost of issue to the corporation.
   a. Concept
   b. Private placement3
   c. Undefined
   d. Undefined

243. The sum of fixed cost and variable cost is referred to as _____.
   a. Thing
   b. Total cost3
   c. Undefined
   d. Undefined

244. _____ manages an online auction and shopping website, where people buy and sell goods and services worldwide.

a. Organization
b. EBay3
c. Undefined
d. Undefined

245. The _____ Bank was formed by the merger of the Chase National Bank and the Bank of the Manhattan Company in 1955.
a. Organization
b. Chase Manhattan3
c. Undefined
d. Undefined

246. A person who makes economic decisions for another economic actor. A hired manager operates as an _____ for a firm's owner.
a. Agent3
b. Thing
c. Undefined
d. Undefined

247. A transfer of property or some right or interest is referred to as _____.
a. Thing
b. Assignment3
c. Undefined
d. Undefined

248. Property that is pledged to the lender to guarantee payment in the event that the borrower is unable to make debt payments is called _____.
a. Thing
b. Collateral3
c. Undefined
d. Undefined

249. _____ is the branch of accountancy concerned with the preparation of financial statements for external decision makers, such as stockholders, suppliers, banks and government agencies. The fundamental need for _____ is to reduce principal-agent problem by measuring and monitoring agents' performance.
a. Financial accounting3
b. Thing
c. Undefined
d. Undefined

250. _____ refers to a set of standards that dictate accounting rules concerning financial reporting; establish generally accepted accounting principles.
a. Thing
b. Financial accounting Standards3
c. Undefined
d. Undefined

251. The process of researching and developing new financial products and services that would meet customer needs and prove profitable is called _____.
a. Financial engineering3
b. Thing
c. Undefined
d. Undefined

252. _____ refers to a concept that describes a company being so open to other companies working with it that the once-solid barriers between them become see-through and electronic information is shared as if the companies were one.
a. Transparency3
b. Thing
c. Undefined
d. Undefined

253. _____ refers to the basic, normal, voting stock issued by a corporation; called residual equity because it ranks after preferred stock for dividend and liquidation distributions.

## Chapter 3. Analyzing Financing Activities

a. Thing
b. Common stock3
c. Undefined
d. Undefined

254. _____ refers to a process of offsetting risk. In the foreign exchange market, hedgers use the forward market to cover a transaction or open position and thereby reduce exchange risk. The term applies most commonly to trade.
a. Hedge3
b. Thing
c. Undefined
d. Undefined

255. _____, assist public and private corporations in raising funds in the capital markets (both equity and debt), as well as in providing strategic advisory services for mergers, acquisitions and other types of financial transactions. They also act as intermediaries in trading for clients. _____ differ from commercial banks, which take deposits and make commercial and retail loans.
a. Thing
b. Investment banks3
c. Undefined
d. Undefined

256. An undertaking by one person to be answerable for the payment of some debt, or the due performance of some contract or duty by another person, who remains liable to pay or perform the same is called _____.
a. Guaranty3
b. Thing
c. Undefined
d. Undefined

257. _____ refers to collections of legal rules produced by the American Law Institute, covering certain subject matter areas. Although restatements are often persuasive to courts, they are not legally binding unless adopted by the highest court of a particular state.
a. Restatement3
b. Thing
c. Undefined
d. Undefined

258. Under the Uniform Commercial Code, one who regularly deals in goods of the kind sold in the contract at issue, or holds himself out as having special knowledge or skill relevant to such goods, or who makes the sale through an agent who regularly deals in such goods or claims such knowledge or skill is referred to as _____.
a. Thing
b. Merchant3
c. Undefined
d. Undefined

259. _____ through its subsidiaries and affiliates, provides capital markets services, investment banking and advisory services, wealth management, asset management, insurance, banking and related products and services on a global basis. It is best known for its Global Private Client services and its strong sales force.
a. Organization
b. Merrill Lynch3
c. Undefined
d. Undefined

260. _____ refers to a financial organization that specializes in selling primary offerings of securities. Investment bankers can also perform other financial functions, such as advising clients, negotiating mergers and takeovers, and selling secondary offerings.
a. Investment banker3
b. Thing
c. Undefined
d. Undefined

261. An owner of a limited partnership who has no right to manage the business but who possesses liability limited to his capital contribution to the business is referred to as _____.

a. Limited partner3     b. Thing
c. Undefined     d. Undefined

262. _____ refers to an obligation in the form of a written promissory note. It is a balance sheet term referring to a company's outstanding bank loans.
a. Notes payable3     b. Thing
c. Undefined     d. Undefined

263. Method of accounting for investments in marketable equity securities; is required when the investor owns percent to percent of the investee company. The amount of investments carried under the _____ represents a measure of the book value of the investee rather than the cost or market value of the investment security.
a. Thing     b. Equity method3
c. Undefined     d. Undefined

264. _____ refers to a liability that results from the execution of a legal document called a note that describes technical terms, including interest charges, maturity date, collateral, and so on.
a. Thing     b. Note payable3
c. Undefined     d. Undefined

265. A _____ is a security that entitles the holder to buy or sell a certain additional quantity of an underlying security at an agreed-upon price, at the holder's discretion.
a. Thing     b. Warrant3
c. Undefined     d. Undefined

266. _____ refer to an equity security, representing a shareholder's ownership of a corporation. _____ are one of a finite number of equal portions in the capital of a company, entitling the owner to a proportion of distributed, non-reinvested profits known as dividends and to a portion of the value of the company in case of liquidation.
a. Shares3     b. Thing
c. Undefined     d. Undefined

267. _____ refers to written promises that require another party to pay the business under specified conditions.
a. Notes receivable3     b. Thing
c. Undefined     d. Undefined

268. A note having no date for repayment, but due on demand of the lender is a _____.
a. Demand note3     b. Thing
c. Undefined     d. Undefined

269. a _____ outstanding is defined as the gross nominal or notional value of all deals concluded and not yet settled on the reporting date. For contracts with variable nominal or notional principal amounts, the basis for reporting is the nominal or notional principal amounts at the time of reporting.
a. Notional amount3     b. Thing
c. Undefined     d. Undefined

270. A _____ is an individual or company (including a corporation) that legally owns one or more shares of stock in a joined stock company.

## Chapter 3. Analyzing Financing Activities

    a. Shareholder3
    b. Thing
    c. Undefined
    d. Undefined

271. _____ refers to a process whereby the assets of a business are converted to money. The conversion may be coerced by a legal process to pay off the debt of the business, or to satisfy any other business obligation that the business has not voluntarily satisfied.
    a. Liquidation3
    b. Thing
    c. Undefined
    d. Undefined

272. Securities giving their holders the power to exchange those securities for other securities without paying any additional consideration are _____.
    a. Thing
    b. Convertible securities3
    c. Undefined
    d. Undefined

273. A _____ is a security that can be converted into another security, for example, a bond that under certain terms can be converted into equity.
    a. Thing
    b. Convertible security3
    c. Undefined
    d. Undefined

274. A _____ is a specific type of option that uses the stock itself as an underlying instrument to determine the option's pay-off and therefore its value.
    a. Stock option3
    b. Thing
    c. Undefined
    d. Undefined

275. The act of a debtor in paying or securing one or more of his creditors in a manner more favorable to them than to other creditors or to the exclusion of such other creditors is a _____. In the absence of statute, a _____ is perfectly good, but to be legal it must be bona fide, and not a mere subterfuge of the debtor to secure a future benefit to himself or to prevent the application of his property to his debts.
    a. Thing
    b. Preference3
    c. Undefined
    d. Undefined

276. _____ refers to pro rata distributions of stock or stock rights on common stock. They are usually issued in proportion to shares owned.
    a. Thing
    b. Stock dividend3
    c. Undefined
    d. Undefined

277. The consumer's appraisal of the product or brand on important attributes is called _____.
    a. Evaluation3
    b. Thing
    c. Undefined
    d. Undefined

278. The trade of things of value between buyer and seller so that each is better off after the trade is called the _____.
    a. Thing
    b. Exchange3
    c. Undefined
    d. Undefined

279. _____ is a phrase used to mean that no bargaining is allowed over the price of a good or, less commonly, a service.

## Chapter 3. Analyzing Financing Activities

a. Thing
b. Fixed price3
c. Undefined
d. Undefined

280. Like profit sharing, _____ are based on the total organization's performance, but are measured in terms of stock price.
a. Employee Stock Ownership Plans3
b. Thing
c. Undefined
d. Undefined

281. _____ is a qualified employee-benefit plan in which employees are entitled and encouraged to invest in shares of the company's stock and often at a favorable price. The employer's contributions are tax deductible for the employer and tax deferred for the employee.
a. Employee stock ownership plan3
b. Thing
c. Undefined
d. Undefined

282. _____ refers to the combination of two firms into a single firm.
a. Thing
b. Merger3
c. Undefined
d. Undefined

283. Total shareholders' equity divided by the number of outstanding common shares is referred to as _____.
a. Thing
b. Book value per share3
c. Undefined
d. Undefined

284. The _____ of an asset or group of assets is sometimes the price at which they were originally acquired, in many cases equal to purchase price.
a. Book value3
b. Thing
c. Undefined
d. Undefined

285. _____ is the value of funds or other consideration contributed to a company in return for an ownership interest. For instance, _____ increases when a person invests money in a company and received a stock certificate recognizing their right to share in the profits and losses of a company and increases or decreases in the equity value of the company.
a. Contributed capital3
b. Thing
c. Undefined
d. Undefined

286. Stock that has specified rights over common stock is a _____.
a. Thing
b. Preferred stock3
c. Undefined
d. Undefined

287. An arbitrary dollar amount assigned to shares by the board of directors, representing the minimum amount of consideration for which the corporation may issue the shares and the portion of consideration that must be allocated to the stated capital account is the _____.
a. Thing
b. Stated value3
c. Undefined
d. Undefined

288. A _____ in property law is a future interest created in a transferee that is capable of becoming possessory upon the natural termination of a prior estate created by the same instrument.

## Chapter 3. Analyzing Financing Activities

a. Remainder3  
b. Thing  
c. Undefined  
d. Undefined

289. The amount of contributed capital less the par value of the stock is _____.
a. Capital in excess of par3  
b. Thing  
c. Undefined  
d. Undefined

290. Corporate stock that has been reacquired by the corporation is _____. It is stock which is bought back by the issuing company. It reduces the number of outstanding stocks on the open market ("open market" including insiders holdings).
a. Thing  
b. Treasury stock3  
c. Undefined  
d. Undefined

291. At equality refers to _____. Two currencies are said to be '_____' if they are trading one-for-one.
a. At par3  
b. Thing  
c. Undefined  
d. Undefined

292. In 2000 _____ and Time Warner announced plans to merge, and the deal was approved by the Federal Trade Commission on January 11, 2001. This merger was primarily a product of the Internet mania of the late-1990s, known as the Internet bubble. The deal is known as one of the worst corporate mergers in history, destroying over $200 billion in shareholder value.
a. Organization  
b. America Online3  
c. Undefined  
d. Undefined

293. _____ is the world's largest media company with major Internet, publishing, film, telecommunications and television divisions.
a. Thing  
b. Time Warner3  
c. Undefined  
d. Undefined

294. A _____ price is a price offered by a buyer when he/she buys a good. In the context of stock trading on a stock exchange, the _____ price is the highest price a buyer of a stock is willing to pay for a share of that given stock.
a. Thing  
b. Bid3  
c. Undefined  
d. Undefined

295. The central value of a pegged exchange rate, around which the actual rate is permitted to fluctuate within set bounds is a _____.
a. Thing  
b. Par value3  
c. Undefined  
d. Undefined

296. _____ refer to shareholders who have dividend and liquidation preferences over other classes of shareholders, usually common shareholders. _____ get paid before common shareholders.
a. Preferred shareholders3  
b. Thing  
c. Undefined  
d. Undefined

297. _____ refer to shareholders who claim the residual profits and assets of a corporation, and usually have the exclusive power and right to elect the directors of the corporation.

## Chapter 3. Analyzing Financing Activities

a. Thing
b. Common shareholders3
c. Undefined
d. Undefined

298. _____ refers to bonds and some preferred stock, in which a call allows the corporation to retire securities before maturity by forcing the bondholders to sell bonds back to it at a set price. The call provisions are included in the bond indenture.
a. Call provision3
b. Thing
c. Undefined
d. Undefined

299. The _____ is the amount over par value an issuer must pay to redeem a callable bond on a call date.
a. Call premium3
b. Thing
c. Undefined
d. Undefined

300. _____ is equal to the income that a firm has after subtracting costs and expenses from the total revenue. Expenses will typically include tax expense.
a. Net income3
b. Thing
c. Undefined
d. Undefined

301. _____ was the United States' second largest long distance phone company (AT&T was the largest). _____ grew largely by acquiring other telecommunications companies, most notably MCI Communications. It also owned the Tier 1 ISP UUNET, a major part of the Internet backbone.
a. Organization
b. WorldCom3
c. Undefined
d. Undefined

302. A _____ is a business report produced by business research firms by their financial analysts. They are designed to dig out the important pieces of companies operational and financial reporting to paint a picture of the future of companies to assist debt and equity investing.
a. Research report3
b. Thing
c. Undefined
d. Undefined

303. _____ refers to a company's accumulation of earnings since it began, reduced by any distributions to stockholders or owners; commonly called retained earnings.
a. Thing
b. Earned capital3
c. Undefined
d. Undefined

304. A pro rata distribution of cash to stockholders of corporate stock is called a _____.
a. Cash dividend3
b. Thing
c. Undefined
d. Undefined

305. _____ is a distribution of something other than cash and is generally treated in the same manner as a cash distribution, measured by the fair market value of the property on the date of distribution.
a. Property dividend3
b. Thing
c. Undefined
d. Undefined

## Chapter 3. Analyzing Financing Activities

306. Referring to a payment made with goods instead of money is an _____. An expression relating to the insurer's right in many Property contracts to replace damaged objects with new or equivalent (_____) material, rather than to pay a cash benefit.
   a. In kind3
   b. Thing
   c. Undefined
   d. Undefined

307. Proportionate is referred to as _____. A method of equally and proportionately allocating money, profits or liabilities by percentage.
   a. Thing
   b. Pro rata3
   c. Undefined
   d. Undefined

308. The _____ is one of two primary components of the balance of payments. It tracks the movement of funds for investments and loans into and out of a country.
   a. Capital account3
   b. Thing
   c. Undefined
   d. Undefined

309. Amount debited or credited directly to retained earnings to correct an accounting error of a prior period is called _____.
   a. Thing
   b. Prior period adjustment3
   c. Undefined
   d. Undefined

310. A privacy tort that consists of using a person's name or likeness for commercial gain without the person's permission is an _____.
   a. Appropriation3
   b. Thing
   c. Undefined
   d. Undefined

311. A circumstances that makes a portion of retained earnings currently unavailable for dividends is referred to as a _____.
   a. Thing
   b. Retained earnings restriction3
   c. Undefined
   d. Undefined

312. Bond contract that specifies the stated rate of interest and the face value of the bond as well as other contractual provisions is called the _____. A company's _____ will cover all bonds issued by that company and also list all bond covenants
   a. Bond indenture3
   b. Thing
   c. Undefined
   d. Undefined

313. A bond contract that specifies the legal provisions of a bond issue is called an _____.
   a. Thing
   b. Indenture3
   c. Undefined
   d. Undefined

314. A _____ is a legal obligation imposed in a deed by the seller upon the buyer of real estate to do or not to do something.
   a. Restrictive covenant3
   b. Thing
   c. Undefined
   d. Undefined

## Chapter 3. Analyzing Financing Activities

315. Having a physical existence is referred to as the _____. Personal property other than real estate, such as cars, boats, stocks, or other assets.
   a. Tangible3
   b. Thing
   c. Undefined
   d. Undefined

316. The _____ is a term used to describe the value of an entity's assets less the value of its liabilities. The term is commonly used in relation to collective investment schemes.
   a. Net asset value3
   b. Thing
   c. Undefined
   d. Undefined

317. _____ refers to the ownership interest in the firm. It may be represented by new shares or retained earnings. The same as net worth.
   a. Common stock equity3
   b. Thing
   c. Undefined
   d. Undefined

318. Assets that have special rights but not physical substance are referred to as _____.
   a. Thing
   b. Intangible assets3
   c. Undefined
   d. Undefined

319. An intangible assets is defined as an asset that is not physical in nature. The most common types are trade secrets (e.g., customer lists and know-how), copyrights, patents, trademarks, and goodwill.
   a. Intangible asset3
   b. Thing
   c. Undefined
   d. Undefined

320. Stock that permits the corporation to buy back preferred stock at some future date is called _____.
   a. Thing
   b. Redeemable preferred stock3
   c. Undefined
   d. Undefined

321. Dividends on cumulative preferred stock that have not been declared in prior years are called _____.
   a. Thing
   b. Dividends in arrears3
   c. Undefined
   d. Undefined

322. A transaction where a corporation buys back its own stock from a specified shareholder is a _____.
   a. Stock redemption3
   b. Thing
   c. Undefined
   d. Undefined

323. _____ refers to money raized from within the firm or through the sale of ownership in the firm.
   a. Equity capital3
   b. Thing
   c. Undefined
   d. Undefined

324. _____ refers to the amount recognized as an expense in one period resulting from the periodic recognition of the used portion of the cost of a long-term tangible asset over its life.
   a. Thing
   b. Depreciation expense3
   c. Undefined
   d. Undefined

## Chapter 3. Analyzing Financing Activities

325. _____ is income received but not yet earned. Normally, such income is taxed when received, even for accrual basis taxpayers.
   a. Unearned income3
   b. Thing
   c. Undefined
   d. Undefined

326. A liability created when a business receives payment for goods or services before the goods are delivered or the services are rendered is referred to as _____.
   a. Thing
   b. Unearned revenue3
   c. Undefined
   d. Undefined

327. Net sales less cost of goods sold is called _____.
   a. Thing
   b. Gross profit3
   c. Undefined
   d. Undefined

328. In 1876, Thomas Alva Edison opened a new laboratory in Menlo Park, New Jersey. Out of the laboratory was to come perhaps the most famous invention of all—a successful development of the incandescent electric lamp. By 1890, Edison had organized his various businesses into the Edison _____ Company.
   a. Organization
   b. General Electric3
   c. Undefined
   d. Undefined

329. A legal entity chartered by a state or the Federal government that is distinct and separate from the individuals who own it is a _____. This separation gives the _____ unique powers which other legal entities lack.
   a. Corporation3
   b. Organization
   c. Undefined
   d. Undefined

330. _____ refers to an out-of-court settlement in which creditors agree to allow the firm more time to meet its financial obligations. A new repayment schedule will be developed, subject to the acceptance of creditors.
   a. Extension3
   b. Thing
   c. Undefined
   d. Undefined

331. _____ was founded in 1906 as "The Haloid Company" manufacturing photographic paper and equipment. The company came to prominence in 1959 with the introduction of the first plain paper photocopier using the process of xerography (electrophotography) developed by Chester Carlson, the _____ 914.
   a. Xerox3
   b. Organization
   c. Undefined
   d. Undefined

332. _____ refers to a corporate action that increases the shares in a public company. The price of the shares are adjusted such that the before and after market capitalization of the company remains the same and dilution does not occur.
   a. Thing
   b. Stock split3
   c. Undefined
   d. Undefined

333. Type of security acquired by loaning assets is called a _____.
   a. Thing
   b. Debt security3
   c. Undefined
   d. Undefined

## Chapter 3. Analyzing Financing Activities

334. In contract law a _____ is incorrect understanding by one or more parties to a contract and may be used as grounds to invalidate the agreement. Common law has identified three different types of _____ in contract: unilateral _____, mutual _____, and common _____.
    a. Mistake3
    b. Thing
    c. Undefined
    d. Undefined

335. The rate that a bank charges its most creditworthy customers is referred to as the _____.
    a. Prime rate3
    b. Thing
    c. Undefined
    d. Undefined

336. Usually, the decision made by a jury and reported to the judge on the matters or questions submitted to it at trial is a _____. In some situations, however, the judge may be the party issuing a _____.
    a. Thing
    b. Verdict3
    c. Undefined
    d. Undefined

337. From or in one's own country. A _____ producer is one that produces inside the home country. A _____ price is the price inside the home country. Opposite of 'foreign' or 'world.'.
    a. Domestic3
    b. Thing
    c. Undefined
    d. Undefined

338. Previously outstanding shares repurchased by a corporation that are not canceled or restored to unissued status are _____.
    a. Treasury shares3
    b. Person
    c. Undefined
    d. Undefined

339. _____ is an asset with an artificially-inflated value. The term is most commonly used to refer to a form of securities fraud common under older corporate laws that placed a heavy emphasis upon the par value of stock.
    a. Thing
    b. Watered stock3
    c. Undefined
    d. Undefined

340. _____ refers to the way a corporation finances itself through some combination of equity sales, equity options, bonds, and loans. Optimal _____ refers to the particular combination that minimizes the cost of capital while maximizing the stock price.
    a. Capital structure3
    b. Thing
    c. Undefined
    d. Undefined

341. In finance, _____ is the interest that has accumulated since the principal investment, or since the previous interest payment if there has been one already. For a financial instrument such as a bond, interest is calculated and paid in set intervals.
    a. Thing
    b. Accrued interest3
    c. Undefined
    d. Undefined

342. Book of original entry, in which transactions are recorded in a general ledger system, is referred to as a _____.
    a. Thing
    b. Journal3
    c. Undefined
    d. Undefined

## Chapter 3. Analyzing Financing Activities

343. The length of service of a productive facility or piece of equipment is its _____. The period of time during which an asset will have economic value and be usable.
    a. Thing
    b. Useful life3
    c. Undefined
    d. Undefined

344. A contract to make regular payments to a person for life or for a fixed period is an _____.
    a. Thing
    b. Annuity3
    c. Undefined
    d. Undefined

345. _____ is the professional fees and registration fees associated with the issuance of bonds. It is considered a long-term asset which is reported on a balance sheet under the classification of other asset.
    a. Bond issue cost3
    b. Thing
    c. Undefined
    d. Undefined

346. _____ refers to a document authorizing its holder to purchase a stated number of shares of stock at a stated price, usually for a stated period of time; may be freely traded.
    a. Stock warrant3
    b. Thing
    c. Undefined
    d. Undefined

347. The nominal or par value of an instrument as expressed on its face is referred to as the _____.
    a. Face value3
    b. Thing
    c. Undefined
    d. Undefined

348. Total number of shares of stock that are owned by stockholders on any particular date is referred to as _____.
    a. Outstanding shares3
    b. Thing
    c. Undefined
    d. Undefined

349. An administrative agency created by Congress in 1970 to coordinate the implementation and enforcement of the federal environmental protection laws is referred to as the _____ or EPA.
    a. Organization
    b. Environmental protection agency3
    c. Undefined
    d. Undefined

350. _____ is an airline of the United States. Based in Houston, Texas, it is the 6th largest airline in the U.S. and the 8th largest in the world. Continental's tagline, since 1998, has been Work Hard, Fly Right.
    a. Organization
    b. Continental Airlines3
    c. Undefined
    d. Undefined

351. A marketing-oriented strategy whereby a service retailer sets its prices on the basis of the prices charged by competitors is _____.
    a. Competitive Pricing3
    b. Thing
    c. Undefined
    d. Undefined

352. The relative proportion of an organization's fixed, variable, and mixed costs is referred to as _____.
    a. Thing
    b. Cost structure3
    c. Undefined
    d. Undefined

## Chapter 3. Analyzing Financing Activities

353. The income, expenditures, and resources that affect the cost of running a business and household are called an _____.

a. Thing
b. Economy3
c. Undefined
d. Undefined

354. Effects that fixed costs have on changes in operating income as changes occur in units sold and hence in contribution margin are called _____.

a. Operating leverage3
b. Thing
c. Undefined
d. Undefined

355. The cost that a firm bears if it does not produce at all and that is independent of its output. The presence of a _____ tends to imply increasing returns to scale. Contrasts with variable cost.

a. Thing
b. Fixed cost3
c. Undefined
d. Undefined

356. That fraction of an industry's output accounted for by an individual firm or group of firms is called _____.

a. Thing
b. Market share3
c. Undefined
d. Undefined

357. A decline in a stock market or economic cycle is a _____.

a. Thing
b. Downturn3
c. Undefined
d. Undefined

358. A _____ is something measured by a number; it is used to analyze what happens to other things when the size of that number changes.

a. Variable3
b. Thing
c. Undefined
d. Undefined

359. _____ developed from a conglomeration of about 82 small airlines through a series of corporate acquisitions and reorganizations: initially, the name American Airways was used as a common brand by a number of independent air carriers. _____ is the largest airline in the world in terms of total passengers transported and fleet size, and the second-largest airline in the world.

a. American Airlines3
b. Organization
c. Undefined
d. Undefined

360. _____ is a major airline of the United States headquartered in unincorporated Elk Grove Township, Illinois, near Chicago's O'Hare International Airport, the airline's largest traffic hub, with 650 daily departures. On February 1, 2006, it emerged from Chapter 11 bankruptcy protection under which it had operated since December 9, 2002, the largest and longest airline bankruptcy case in history.

a. Thing
b. United airlines3
c. Undefined
d. Undefined

361. _____ refers to the return a businessperson gets on the money he and other owners invest in the firm; for example, a business that earned $100 on a $1,000 investment would have a ROI of 10 percent: 100 divided by 1000.

*Chapter 3. Analyzing Financing Activities* 111

a. Thing  
b. Return on investment3  
c. Undefined  
d. Undefined

362. _____ refers to the capacity to turn assets into cash, or the amount of assets in a portfolio that have that capacity.
a. Liquidity3  
b. Thing  
c. Undefined  
d. Undefined

363. The percentage of an additional dollar of earnings that goes to taxes is referred to as the _____.
a. Marginal tax rate3  
b. Thing  
c. Undefined  
d. Undefined

364. A _____ is the party who initiates a lawsuit (also known as an action) before a court. By doing so, the _____ seeks a legal remedy, and if successful, the court will issue judgment in favour of the _____ and make the appropriate court order.
a. Thing  
b. Plaintiff3  
c. Undefined  
d. Undefined

365. _____ refers to the economic well being of an individual, group, or economy. For individuals, it is conceptualized by a utility function. For groups, including countries and the world, it is a tricky philosophical concept, since individuals fare differently.
a. Thing  
b. Welfare3  
c. Undefined  
d. Undefined

366. In law, a _____ is an equitable procedural device used in litigation to determine the rights of and remedies, if any, for large numbers of people whose cases involve common questions of law and fact. Traditionally, they have been used to litigate antitrust and securities lawsuits, as well as school desegregation cases, but more recently have been used for a wide range of legal disputes that involve a large number of injured parties.
a. Thing  
b. Class action3  
c. Undefined  
d. Undefined

367. The sum of money recoverable by a plaintiff who has received a judgment in a civil case is called _____.
a. Thing  
b. Damages3  
c. Undefined  
d. Undefined

368. Characterized by rizing output, falling unemployment, rizing profits, and increasing economic activity following a decline is a _____.
a. Recovery3  
b. Thing  
c. Undefined  
d. Undefined

369. Local television stations that are associated with a major network are called _____. _____ agree to preempt time during specified hours for programming provided by the network and carry the advertising contained in the program.
a. Thing  
b. Affiliates3  
c. Undefined  
d. Undefined

370. A body of lay persons, selected by lot, or by some other fair and impartial means, to ascertain, under the guidance of the judge, the truth in questions of fact arising either in civil litigation or a criminal process is referred to as _____.
   a. Jury3
   b. Thing
   c. Undefined
   d. Undefined

371. _____ refers to the act of asking an appellate court to overturn a decision after the trial court's final judgment has been entered.
   a. Appeal3
   b. Thing
   c. Undefined
   d. Undefined

372. The name of a writ by which a jury is summoned is the _____. Summoning persons to court to act as jurors.
   a. Venire3
   b. Thing
   c. Undefined
   d. Undefined

373. Assistance provided by countries and by international institutions such as the World Bank to developing countries in the form of monetary grants, loans at low interest rates, in kind, or a combination of these is called _____. _____ can also refer to assistance of any type rendered to benefit some group or individual.
   a. Thing
   b. Aid3
   c. Undefined
   d. Undefined

374. _____ refers to paid, nonpersonal communication through various media by organizations and individuals who are in some way identified in the _____ message.
   a. Thing
   b. Advertising3
   c. Undefined
   d. Undefined

375. An increase in the overall price level of an economy, usually as measured by the CPI or by the implicit price deflator is called _____.
   a. Inflation3
   b. Thing
   c. Undefined
   d. Undefined

376. _____ refers to the rejection for employment, placement, or promotion of a significantly higher percentage of a protected class, when compared with a non-protected class.
   a. Adverse impact3
   b. Thing
   c. Undefined
   d. Undefined

377. Possession of a lower cost of production or operation than a competing firm or country is _____.
   a. Thing
   b. Cost advantage3
   c. Undefined
   d. Undefined

378. _____, is the world's largest commercial tobacco company by sales. _____ was begun by a London tobacconist of the same name. He was one of the first people to sell hand-rolled cigarettes in the 1860s, selling them under the brand names Oxford and Cambridge Blues, following the adoption of cigarette smoking by British soldiers returning from the Crimean War.
   a. Philip Morris3
   b. Organization
   c. Undefined
   d. Undefined

## Chapter 4. Analyzing Investing Activities 113

1. _____ characterizes the process of leading and directing all or part of an organization, often a business, through the deployment and manipulation of resources. Early twentieth-century _____ writer Mary Parker Follett defined _____ as "the art of getting things done through people."
   - a. Thing
   - b. Management4
   - c. Undefined
   - d. Undefined

2. _____ is a financing technique that allows the corporation to separate credit origination and funding activities. The technique comes under the umbrella of structured finance as it applies to assets that typically are illiquid contracts.
   - a. Thing
   - b. Securitization4
   - c. Undefined
   - d. Undefined

3. Reduction in the selling price of goods extended to the buyer because the goods are defective or of lower quality than the buyer ordered and to encourage a buyer to keep merchandise that would otherwise be returned is the _____.
   - a. Allowance4
   - b. Thing
   - c. Undefined
   - d. Undefined

4. In accounting and finance, _____ is the portion of receivables that can no longer be collected, typically from accounts receivable or loans. _____ in accounting is considered an expense.
   - a. Thing
   - b. Bad debt4
   - c. Undefined
   - d. Undefined

5. Tangible property held for sale in the normal course of business or used in producing goods or services for sale is an _____.
   - a. Inventory4
   - b. Thing
   - c. Undefined
   - d. Undefined

6. _____ refers to a summary of all the transactions that have occurred over a particular period.
   - a. Thing
   - b. Financial statement4
   - c. Undefined
   - d. Undefined

7. _____ means the giving out of information, either voluntarily or to be in compliance with legal regulations or workplace rules.
   - a. Disclosure4
   - b. Thing
   - c. Undefined
   - d. Undefined

8. _____ refers to spending for the production and accumulation of capital and additions to inventories. In a financial sense, buying an asset with the expectation of making a return.
   - a. Investment4
   - b. Thing
   - c. Undefined
   - d. Undefined

9. _____ refers to a claim on the borrower future income that is sold by the borrower to the lender. A _____ is a type of transferable interest representing financial value.
   - a. Security4
   - b. Thing
   - c. Undefined
   - d. Undefined

## Chapter 4. Analyzing Investing Activities

10. A _____ is a generic term for specific types of investments from which payoffs over time are derived from the performance of assets (such as commodities, shares or bonds), interest rates, exchange rates, or indices (such as a stock market index, consumer price index (CPI) or an index of weather conditions).
    a. Derivative4
    b. Thing
    c. Undefined
    d. Undefined

11. An item of property, such as land, capital, money, a share in ownership, or a claim on others for future payment, such as a bond or a bank deposit is an _____.
    a. Thing
    b. Asset4
    c. Undefined
    d. Undefined

12. _____ refers to the process of assigning costs in a cost pool to the appropriate cost objects.
    a. Thing
    b. Cost allocation4
    c. Undefined
    d. Undefined

13. In finance, _____ is the process of estimating the market value of a financial asset or liability. They can be done on assets (for example, investments in marketable securities such as stocks, options, business enterprises, or intangible assets such as patents and trademarks) or on liabilities (e.g., Bonds issued by a company).
    a. Valuation4
    b. Event
    c. Undefined
    d. Undefined

14. Assets that have special rights but not physical substance are referred to as _____.
    a. Intangible assets4
    b. Thing
    c. Undefined
    d. Undefined

15. An intangible assets is defined as an asset that is not physical in nature. The most common types are trade secrets (e.g., customer lists and know-how), copyrights, patents, trademarks, and goodwill.
    a. Thing
    b. Intangible asset4
    c. Undefined
    d. Undefined

16. In economics, a _____ is a mechanism which allows people to trade money for securities or commodities such as gold or other precious metals. In general, any commodity market might be considered to be a _____, if the usual purpose of traders is not the immediate consumption of the commodity, but rather as a means of delaying or accelerating consumption over time.
    a. Thing
    b. Financial market4
    c. Undefined
    d. Undefined

17. A _____ is, as defined in economics, a social arrangement that allows buyers and sellers to discover information and carry out a voluntary exchange of goods or services.
    a. Market4
    b. Thing
    c. Undefined
    d. Undefined

18. _____ refers to the amount at which property would change hands between a willing buyer and a willing seller, neither being under any compulsion to buy or to sell, and both having reasonable knowledge of the relevant facts.

a. Fair market value4  
b. Thing  
c. Undefined  
d. Undefined

19. A statement of the assets, liabilities, and net worth of a firm or individual at some given time often at the end of its "fiscal year," is referred to as a _____.
   a. Thing
   b. Balance sheet4
   c. Undefined
   d. Undefined

20. _____ refers to the price of an asset agreed on between a willing buyer and a willing seller; the price an asset could demand if it is sold on the open market.
   a. Market value4
   b. Thing
   c. Undefined
   d. Undefined

21. In banking and accountancy, the outstanding _____ is the amount of money owned, (or due), that remains in a deposit account (or a loan account) at a given date, after all past remittances, payments and withdrawal have been accounted for. It can be positive (then, in the _____ sheet of a firm, it is an asset) or negative (a liability).
   a. Balance4
   b. Thing
   c. Undefined
   d. Undefined

22. A _____ is a "promise" or an "agreement" that is enforced or recognized by the law. In the civil law, a _____ is considered to be part of the general law of obligations.
   a. Thing
   b. Contract4
   c. Undefined
   d. Undefined

23. A _____ refers to a layout accurate in size, color, scheme, and other necessary details to show how a final ad will look. For presentation only, never for reproduction.
   a. Comprehensive4
   b. Thing
   c. Undefined
   d. Undefined

24. The consumer's appraisal of the product or brand on important attributes is called _____.
   a. Thing
   b. Evaluation4
   c. Undefined
   d. Undefined

25. In finance, _____ is a profit or an increase in value of an investment such as a stock or bond. _____ is calculated by fair market value or the proceeds from the sale of the investment minus the sum of the purchase price and all costs associated with it.
   a. Gain4
   b. Thing
   c. Undefined
   d. Undefined

26. A _____ is a present obligation of the enterprise arizing from past events, the settlement of which is expected to result in an outflow from the enterprise of resources embodying economic benefits.
   a. Liability4
   b. Thing
   c. Undefined
   d. Undefined

27. _____ refers to a form of risk that refers to the possibility of experiencing a drop in revenue or an increase in cost in an international transaction due to a change in foreign exchange rates. Importers, exporters, investors, and multinational firms alike are exposed to this risk.
- a. Thing
- b. Foreign exchange risk4
- c. Undefined
- d. Undefined

28. In finance, _____ means currencies, such as U.S. Dollars and Euros. These are traded on _____ markets.
- a. Foreign exchange4
- b. Thing
- c. Undefined
- d. Undefined

29. The trade of things of value between buyer and seller so that each is better off after the trade is called the _____.
- a. Thing
- b. Exchange4
- c. Undefined
- d. Undefined

30. The common currency of a subset of the countries of the EU, adopted January 1, 1999 is called _____.
- a. Thing
- b. Euro4
- c. Undefined
- d. Undefined

31. a _____ outstanding is defined as the gross nominal or notional value of all deals concluded and not yet settled on the reporting date. For contracts with variable nominal or notional principal amounts, the basis for reporting is the nominal or notional principal amounts at the time of reporting.
- a. Notional amount4
- b. Thing
- c. Undefined
- d. Undefined

32. _____ refers to the extent to which an economic variable, such as a price or an exchange rate, moves up and down over time.
- a. Thing
- b. Volatility4
- c. Undefined
- d. Undefined

33. In finance, _____ refers to the amounts of cash being received and spent by a business during a defined period of time, sometimes tied to a specific project. Most of the time they are being used to determine gaps in the liquid position of a company.
- a. Thing
- b. Cash flow4
- c. Undefined
- d. Undefined

34. In finance and economics, _____ is the price paid by a borrower for the use of a lender's money. In other words, _____ is the amount of paid to "rent" money for a period of time.
- a. Thing
- b. Interest4
- c. Undefined
- d. Undefined

35. A technique for avoiding a risk by making a counteracting transaction is referred to as _____.
- a. Thing
- b. Hedging4
- c. Undefined
- d. Undefined

36. A company's purchase of the property and obligations of another company is an _____.

## Chapter 4. Analyzing Investing Activities

a. Acquisition4
b. Thing
c. Undefined
d. Undefined

37. _____ refers to a process of offsetting risk. In the foreign exchange market, hedgers use the forward market to cover a transaction or open position and thereby reduce exchange risk. The term applies most commonly to trade.
a. Thing
b. Hedge4
c. Undefined
d. Undefined

38. _____ refers to cash flow activities that include purchasing and disposing of investments and productive long-lived assets using cash and lending money and collecting on those loans.
a. Thing
b. Investing activities4
c. Undefined
d. Undefined

39. An out-of-court settlement in which creditors agree to accept a fractional settlement on their original claim is referred to as _____.
a. Composition4
b. Thing
c. Undefined
d. Undefined

40. An _____ is prepared by corporate management that presents financial information including financial statements, footnotes, and the management discussion and analysis.
a. Thing
b. Annual report4
c. Undefined
d. Undefined

41. A _____ is an asset on the balance sheet which is expected to be sold or otherwise used up in the near future, usually within one year.
a. Current asset4
b. Thing
c. Undefined
d. Undefined

42. _____ refer to securities that are readily traded in the secondary securities market.
a. Marketable securities4
b. Thing
c. Undefined
d. Undefined

43. A short-term investment with original maturities of three months or less that is readily convertible to cash and whose value is unlikely to change is a _____.
a. Thing
b. Cash equivalent4
c. Undefined
d. Undefined

44. In accounting, an _____ represents an event in which an asset is used up or a liability is incurred. In terms of the accounting equation, expenses reduce owners' equity.
a. Thing
b. Expense4
c. Undefined
d. Undefined

45. Assets defined in the broadest legal sense. _____ includes the unrealized receivables of a cash basis taxpayer, but not services rendered.

a. Property4  
b. Thing  
c. Undefined  
d. Undefined  

46. _____ refer to monetary claims or obligations by one party against another party. Examples are bonds, mortgages, bank loans, and equities.
   a. Financial assets4  
   b. Thing  
   c. Undefined  
   d. Undefined  

47. Cash flow activities that include the cash effects of transactions that create revenues and expenses and thus enter into the determination of net income is an _____.
   a. Thing  
   b. Operating activities4  
   c. Undefined  
   d. Undefined  

48. _____ refers to the time it takes for a company to purchase goods or services from suppliers, sell those goods and services to customers, and collect cash from customers.
   a. Operating cycle4  
   b. Thing  
   c. Undefined  
   d. Undefined  

49. _____ refers to a debt that can reasonably be expected to be paid from existing current assets or through the creation of other current liabilities, within one year or the operating cycle, whichever is longer.
   a. Current liability4  
   b. Thing  
   c. Undefined  
   d. Undefined  

50. The dollar difference between total current assets and total current liabilities is called _____.
   a. Thing  
   b. Working capital4  
   c. Undefined  
   d. Undefined  

51. _____ generally refers to financial wealth, especially that used to start or maintain a business. In classical economics, _____ is one of four factors of production, the others being land and labor and entrepreneurship.
   a. Capital4  
   b. Thing  
   c. Undefined  
   d. Undefined  

52. The planning, coordinating, and controlling activities related to the flow of inventory into, through, and out of an organization is referred to as _____.
   a. Inventory management4  
   b. Thing  
   c. Undefined  
   d. Undefined  

53. _____ arises from situations in which a party interested in trading an asset cannot do it because nobody in the market wants to trade that asset. _____ becomes particularly important to parties who are about to hold or currently hold an asset, since it affects their ability to trade.
   a. Thing  
   b. Liquidity risk4  
   c. Undefined  
   d. Undefined  

54. _____ refers to the capacity to turn assets into cash, or the amount of assets in a portfolio that have that capacity.

a. Liquidity4  
b. Thing  
c. Undefined  
d. Undefined  

55. _____ refers to the financing and management of the current assets of the firm. The financial manager determines the mix between temporary and permanent 'current assets' and the nature of the financing arrangement.
   a. Thing  
   b. Working capital management4  
   c. Undefined  
   d. Undefined  

56. A means of measuring the profitability of the firm's products, customer groups, sales territories, channels of distribution, and order sizes is called _____.
   a. Thing  
   b. Profitability analysis4  
   c. Undefined  
   d. Undefined  

57. _____ refers to a recording as positive in the balance of payments, any transaction that gives rise to a payment into the country, such as an export, the sale of an asset, or borrowing from abroad.
   a. Thing  
   b. Credit4  
   c. Undefined  
   d. Undefined  

58. _____ are the most liquid asset found within the asset portion of a company's balance sheet. Cash "equivalents" are typically comprized of assets that are readily convertible into cash such as money market accounts, short-term government bonds and commercial paper.
   a. Cash and cash equivalents4  
   b. Thing  
   c. Undefined  
   d. Undefined  

59. Independent accounting entity with a self-balancing set of accounts segregated for the purposes of carrying on specific activities is referred to as a _____.
   a. Fund4  
   b. Thing  
   c. Undefined  
   d. Undefined  

60. The rate of return on bonds, loans, or deposits. When one speaks of 'the' _____, it is usually in a model where there is only one.
   a. Interest rate4  
   b. Thing  
   c. Undefined  
   d. Undefined  

61. _____ refers to the final payment date of a loan or other financial instrument, after which point no further interest or principal need be paid.
   a. Maturity4  
   b. Thing  
   c. Undefined  
   d. Undefined  

62. Other organizations in the same industry or type of business that provide a good or service to the same set of customers is referred to as a _____.
   a. Competitor4  
   b. Thing  
   c. Undefined  
   d. Undefined  

63. _____ refers to an economic variable that is controlled by policy makers and can be used to influence other variables, called targets. Examples are monetary and fiscal policies used to achieve external and internal balance.

a. Instrument4  
b. Thing  
c. Undefined  
d. Undefined

64. _____, formerly PC's Limited, was founded on the principle that by selling personal computer systems directly to customers, PC's Limited could best understand their needs and provide the most effective computing solutions to meet those needs.
   a. Dell Computer4  
   b. Thing  
   c. Undefined  
   d. Undefined

65. A group of firms that produce identical or similar products is an _____. It is also used specifically to refer to an area of economic production focused on manufacturing which involves large amounts of capital investment before any profit can be realized, also called "heavy _____".
   a. Industry4  
   b. Thing  
   c. Undefined  
   d. Undefined

66. _____ refer to a bank requirement that business customers maintain a minimum average balance. The required amount is usually computed as a percentage of customer loans outstanding or as a percentage of the future loans to which the bank has committed itself.
   a. Compensating balances4  
   b. Thing  
   c. Undefined  
   d. Undefined

67. A required minimum amount of funds that a firm receiving a loan must keep in a checking account at the lending bank is called _____.
   a. Thing  
   b. Compensating balance4  
   c. Undefined  
   d. Undefined

68. Property that is pledged to the lender to guarantee payment in the event that the borrower is unable to make debt payments is called _____.
   a. Collateral4  
   b. Thing  
   c. Undefined  
   d. Undefined

69. A contract for the possession and use of land or other property, including goods, on one side, and a recompense of rent or other income on the other is the _____.
   a. Lease4  
   b. Thing  
   c. Undefined  
   d. Undefined

70. _____ refers to a "non tangible product" that is not embodied in a physical good and that typically effects some change in another product, person, or institution. Contrasts with good.
   a. Service4  
   b. Thing  
   c. Undefined  
   d. Undefined

71. _____ is one of a series of accounting transactions dealing with the billing of customers which owe money to a person, company or organization for goods and services that have been provided to the customer. This is typically done in a one person organization by writing an invoice and mailing or delivering it to each customer.

## Chapter 4. Analyzing Investing Activities

a. Accounts receivable4  
c. Undefined  
b. Thing  
d. Undefined

72. _____ refers to written promises that require another party to pay the business under specified conditions.
   a. Notes receivable4
   b. Thing
   c. Undefined
   d. Undefined

73. The income, expenditures, and resources that affect the cost of running a business and household are called an _____.
   a. Thing
   b. Economy4
   c. Undefined
   d. Undefined

74. _____ is equal to the income that a firm has after subtracting costs and expenses from the total revenue. Expenses will typically include tax expense.
   a. Net income4
   b. Thing
   c. Undefined
   d. Undefined

75. The expected sales price less selling costs is referred to as _____. Gross receivables less allowance for doubtful accounts, representing the expected collectibility of those receivables.
   a. Net realizable value4
   b. Thing
   c. Undefined
   d. Undefined

76. _____ refers to the amount of accounts receivable that is expected to go uncollected. It is called a contra-asset because it is deducted from the asset, accounts receivable. Also called allowance for doubtful accounts or allowance for bad debts.
   a. Allowance for uncollectible accounts4
   b. Thing
   c. Undefined
   d. Undefined

77. Similar to a script in that a _____ can be a less than completely rational decision-making method. Involves the use of a pre-existing set of decision steps for any problem that presents itself.
   a. Policy4
   b. Thing
   c. Undefined
   d. Undefined

78. In throughput accounting, the cost accounting aspect of Theory of Constraints (TOC), _____ is the money spent turning inventory into throughput. In TOC, _____ is limited to costs that vary strictly with the quantity produced, like raw materials and purchased components.
   a. Thing
   b. Operating expense4
   c. Undefined
   d. Undefined

79. _____ refers to certified public accountant licensed to perform audits who is not an employee and does not have ownership or interest in the company being audited.
   a. Thing
   b. Independent auditor4
   c. Undefined
   d. Undefined

80. An examination of the financial reports to ensure that they represent what they claim and conform with generally accepted accounting principles is referred to as _____.

a. Audit4 b. Thing
c. Undefined d. Undefined

81. A system that collects and processes financial information about an organization and reports that information to decision makers is referred to as _____.
a. Thing b. Accounting4
c. Undefined d. Undefined

82. Generally, a legal right to engage in conduct that would otherwise result in legal liability is a _____. Privileges are commonly classified as absolute or conditional. Occasionally, _____ is also used to denote a legal right to refrain from particular behavior.
a. Thing b. Privilege4
c. Undefined d. Undefined

83. A _____ is a property interest created by agreement or by operation of law over assets to secure the performance of an obligation (usually but not always the payment of a debt) which gives the beneficiary of the _____ certain preferential rights in relation to the assets.
a. Security interest4 b. Thing
c. Undefined d. Undefined

84. People who link buyers with sellers by buying and selling securities at stated prices are referred to as a _____.
a. Thing b. Dealer4
c. Undefined d. Undefined

85. _____ refers to an agreement that creates or provides a security interest or lien on personal property. A term used in the UCC including a wide range of transactions in the nature of chattel mortgages, conditional sales, and so on.
a. Thing b. Security agreement4
c. Undefined d. Undefined

86. A _____ refers to a role in the buying center with formal authority and responsibility to select the supplier and negotiate the terms of the contract.
a. Buyer4 b. Thing
c. Undefined d. Undefined

87. An arrangement in which shareholders of independent firms agree to give up their stock in exchange for _____ certificates that entitle them to a share of the _____'s common profits.
a. Trust4 b. Thing
c. Undefined d. Undefined

88. _____ refers to a debt instrument, issued by a borrower and promising a specified stream of payments to the purchaser, usually regular interest payments plus a final repayment of principal.
a. Bond4 b. Thing
c. Undefined d. Undefined

## Chapter 4. Analyzing Investing Activities

89. _____ in the most basic sense of the word refers to any kind of lending to consumers. However, in the United States financial services industry, the term "_____" often refers to a particular type of business, sub prime branch lending (that is lending to people with bad credit).
   a. Thing
   b. Consumer finance4
   c. Undefined
   d. Undefined

90. In finance, a _____ is a collection of investments held by an institution or a private individual. Holding but not always a _____ is part of an investment and risk-limiting strategy called diversification. By owning several assets, certain types of risk (in particular specific risk) can be reduced.
   a. Portfolio4
   b. Thing
   c. Undefined
   d. Undefined

91. Before the _____ catalog, farmers typically bought supplies (often at very high prices) from local general stores. _____ took advantage of this by publishing his catalog with clearly stated prices, so that consumers could know what he was selling and at what price, and order and obtain them conveniently. The catalog business soon grew quickly.
   a. Sears4
   b. Organization
   c. Undefined
   d. Undefined

92. The combination of two or more firms, generally of equal size and market power, to form an entirely new entity is a _____.
   a. Thing
   b. Consolidation4
   c. Undefined
   d. Undefined

93. Suppliers and financial institutions that lend money to companies is referred to as a _____.
   a. Lender4
   b. Thing
   c. Undefined
   d. Undefined

94. An _____ is the part of a contractually due sum that is paid in advance, while the balance will only follow after receipt on the counterpart in goods or services.
   a. Advance payment4
   b. Thing
   c. Undefined
   d. Undefined

95. _____ are those activities involved in the running of a business for the purpose of producing value for the stakeholders. The outcome of _____ is the harvesting of value from assets owned by a business.
   a. Business operations4
   b. Thing
   c. Undefined
   d. Undefined

96. A standardized method or technique that is performed repetitively, often on different materials resulting in different finished goods is called an _____.
   a. Operation4
   b. Thing
   c. Undefined
   d. Undefined

97. _____ refers to the assignment of income for various tax purposes. A multistate corporation's nonbusiness income usually is distributed to the state where the nonbusiness assets are located; it is not apportioned with the rest of the entity's income.

a. Thing
b. Allocate4
c. Undefined
d. Undefined

98. _____ refers to the cost of all inventory on hand and available to be sold during the accounting period; includes the cost of beginning inventory and the cost of the purchases made during the period.
a. Thing
b. Cost of goods available for sale4
c. Undefined
d. Undefined

99. In accounting, the _____ describes the direct expenses incurred in producing a particular good for sale, including the actual cost of materials that comprise the good, and direct labor expense in putting the good in salable condition.
a. Thing
b. Cost of goods sold4
c. Undefined
d. Undefined

100. _____ refers to a financial statement that presents the revenues and expenses and resulting net income or net loss of a company for a specific period of time.
a. Income statement4
b. Thing
c. Undefined
d. Undefined

101. _____ is a U.S. business term for the amount of money that a company receives from its activities, mostly from sales of products and/or services to customers.
a. Thing
b. Revenue4
c. Undefined
d. Undefined

102. A contract that gives the purchaser the _____ to buy or sell the underlying financial instrument at a specified price, called the exercise price or strike price, within a specific period of time.
a. Thing
b. Option4
c. Undefined
d. Undefined

103. Net sales less cost of goods sold is called _____.
a. Thing
b. Gross profit4
c. Undefined
d. Undefined

104. _____ refers to the return to the resource entrepreneurial ability; total revenue minus total cost.
a. Thing
b. Profit4
c. Undefined
d. Undefined

105. _____ is an economic concept with commonplace familiarity; it is the price that a good or service is offered at, or will fetch, in the marketplace; it is of interest mainly in the study of microeconomics.
a. Market price4
b. Thing
c. Undefined
d. Undefined

106. Net cash equivalent amount paid or to be paid for the asset is an _____. e expense undertaken to acquire new business. The concept applies to both agents and companies. The largest portion of an insurer's _____ is agent's or sales representative's commission or bonus.

## Chapter 4. Analyzing Investing Activities

a. Acquisition cost4
b. Thing
c. Undefined
d. Undefined

107. The current purchase price of replacing a property damaged or lost with similar property is the _____.
a. Thing
b. Replacement cost4
c. Undefined
d. Undefined

108. In Economics, a firm is said to be making an _____ when its revenue exceeds the total opportunity cost of its inputs. It is said to be making an accounting profit if its revenues exceed the total price the firm pays for those inputs. This is sometimes referred to as producer's surplus.
a. Thing
b. Economic profit4
c. Undefined
d. Undefined

109. The _____ is a court's determination of a matter of law based on the issue presented in the particular case. In other words: under this law, with these facts, this result.
a. Holding4
b. Thing
c. Undefined
d. Undefined

110. An increase in the overall price level of an economy, usually as measured by the CPI or by the implicit price deflator is called _____.
a. Thing
b. Inflation4
c. Undefined
d. Undefined

111. _____ in a financial context refers to the rate at which a provider of goods cycles through its average inventory. _____ in a human resources context refers to the characteristic of a given company or industry, relative to rate at which an employer gains and loses staff.
a. Thing
b. Turnover4
c. Undefined
d. Undefined

112. _____, in the field of loss prevention, are systems designed to introduce technical barriers to shoplifting.
a. Thing
b. Inventory control4
c. Undefined
d. Undefined

113. Production of goods primarily by the application of labor and capital to raw materials and other intermediate inputs, in contrast to agriculture, mining, forestry, fishing, and services a _____.
a. Manufacturing4
b. Thing
c. Undefined
d. Undefined

114. The percentage increase in the price level per year is an _____. Alternatively, the _____ is the rate of decrease in the purchasing power of money.
a. Thing
b. Inflation rate4
c. Undefined
d. Undefined

115. Inventory on hand at the end of the accounting period, shown on the balance sheet in the current assets section is called _____.

## Chapter 4. Analyzing Investing Activities

    a. Thing  
    c. Undefined  
    b. Ending inventory4  
    d. Undefined

116. Damages made certain by the prior agreement of the parties are called _____.
    a. Liquidated4  
    c. Undefined  
    b. Thing  
    d. Undefined

117. Completed products awaiting sale are called _____. An item considered a finished good in a supplying plant might be considered a component or raw material in a receiving plant.
    a. Finished goods4  
    c. Undefined  
    b. Thing  
    d. Undefined

118. _____ refers to a good that has not been transformed by production; a primary product.
    a. Raw material4  
    c. Undefined  
    b. Thing  
    d. Undefined

119. _____ refers to goods held for resale in the ordinary course of business.
    a. Thing  
    c. Undefined  
    b. Merchandise inventory4  
    d. Undefined

120. In corporation law, a corporation's acceptance of a pre-incorporation contract by action of its board of directors, by which the corporation becomes liable on the contract, is referred to as _____.
    a. Concept  
    c. Undefined  
    b. Adoption4  
    d. Undefined

121. _____ is the amount by which a company's inventory account balance under FIFO would exceed its inventory account balance under LIFO for the same physical inventory.
    a. LIFO reserve4  
    c. Undefined  
    b. Thing  
    d. Undefined

122. _____ is an increase in the market value of money which is equivalent to a decrease in the general price level, over a period of time. The term is also used to refer to a decrease in the size of the money supply
    a. Thing  
    c. Undefined  
    b. Deflation4  
    d. Undefined

123. _____ is the expected or anticipated increase in the price level in the future.
    a. Thing  
    c. Undefined  
    b. Anticipated inflation4  
    d. Undefined

124. An _____ is all executive, organizational, and clerical costs associated with the general management of an organization rather than with manufacturing, marketing, or selling
    a. Administrative cost4  
    c. Undefined  
    b. Thing  
    d. Undefined

125. The value today of a stream of payments and/or receipts over time in the future and/or the past, converted to the present using an interest rate. If X t is the amount in period t and r the interest rate, then _____ at time t=0 is V = ?T /t.

a. Thing
c. Undefined
b. Present value4
d. Undefined

126. _____ is the value of anything expressed in money of the day with the effects of inflation removed.
a. Real value4
c. Undefined
b. Thing
d. Undefined

127. _____ refers to a process whereby the assets of a business are converted to money. The conversion may be coerced by a legal process to pay off the debt of the business, or to satisfy any other business obligation that the business has not voluntarily satisfied.
a. Thing
c. Undefined
b. Liquidation4
d. Undefined

128. A legal entity chartered by a state or the Federal government that is distinct and separate from the individuals who own it is a _____. This separation gives the _____ unique powers which other legal entities lack.
a. Corporation4
c. Undefined
b. Organization
d. Undefined

129. Asset measure based on the cost of purchasing an asset today identical to the one currently held, or the cost of purchasing an asset that provides services like the one currently held, if an identical one cannot be purchased is a _____.
a. Current cost4
c. Undefined
b. Thing
d. Undefined

130. _____ refers to a person or tool with a primary function of information analysis, generally with a more limited, practical and short term set of goals than a researcher.
a. Person
c. Undefined
b. Analyst4
d. Undefined

131. _____ refers to collections of legal rules produced by the American Law Institute, covering certain subject matter areas. Although restatements are often persuasive to courts, they are not legally binding unless adopted by the highest court of a particular state.
a. Thing
c. Undefined
b. Restatement4
d. Undefined

132. _____ refers to the method under which income and expenses are determined for tax purposes. Important accounting methods include the cash basis and the accrual basis.
a. Accounting method4
c. Undefined
b. Thing
d. Undefined

133. Deferred is any account where the asset or liability is not realized until a future date, e.g. annuities, charges, taxes, income, etc. The deferred item may be carried, dependent on type of _____, as either an asset or liability.
a. Thing
c. Undefined
b. Deferral4
d. Undefined

134. Goods on hand at the beginning of the inventory period are referred to as _____.

a. Beginning inventory4  
b. Thing  
c. Undefined  
d. Undefined

135. An organization that employs resources to produce a good or service for profit and owns and operates one or more plants is referred to as a _____.
   a. Firm4  
   b. Thing  
   c. Undefined  
   d. Undefined

136. A group of products that are physically similar or are intended for a similar market are called the _____.
   a. Thing  
   b. Product line4  
   c. Undefined  
   d. Undefined

137. The creation of finished goods and services using the factors of _____: land, labor, capital, entrepreneurship, and knowledge.
   a. Thing  
   b. Production4  
   c. Undefined  
   d. Undefined

138. The earnings of employees who work directly on the products being manufactured are _____.
   a. Thing  
   b. Direct labor4  
   c. Undefined  
   d. Undefined

139. People's physical and mental talents and efforts that are used to help produce goods and services are called _____.
   a. Labor4  
   b. Thing  
   c. Undefined  
   d. Undefined

140. _____ refers to a cost that cannot be traced to a particular department.
   a. Thing  
   b. Indirect cost4  
   c. Undefined  
   d. Undefined

141. _____ is an accounting and finance term for the method of attributing the cost of an asset across the useful life of the asset. _____ is a reduction in the value of a currency in floating exchange rate.
   a. Depreciation4  
   b. Thing  
   c. Undefined  
   d. Undefined

142. _____ refers to the want-satisfying power of a good or service; the satisfaction or pleasure a consumer obtains from the consumption of a good or service.
   a. Thing  
   b. Utility4  
   c. Undefined  
   d. Undefined

143. The payment for the service of a unit of labor, per unit time. In trade theory, it is the only payment to labor, usually unskilled labor. In empirical work, _____ data may exclude other compenzation, which must be added to get the total cost of employment.
   a. Thing  
   b. Wage4  
   c. Undefined  
   d. Undefined

## Chapter 4. Analyzing Investing Activities

144. A _____ would be used to reduce the number of motions in performing a task in order to increase productivity. The best known experiment involved bricklaying.
   a. Time and motion study4
   b. Thing
   c. Undefined
   d. Undefined

145. An _____ is a manufacturing process in which interchangeable parts are added to a product in a sequential manner to create a finished product.
   a. Thing
   b. Assembly line4
   c. Undefined
   d. Undefined

146. _____ refers to sum of the costs assigned to a product for a specific purpose. A concept used in applying the cost plus approach to product pricing in which only the costs of manufacturing the product are included in the cost amount to which the markup is added.
   a. Product cost4
   b. Thing
   c. Undefined
   d. Undefined

147. An expenses of operating a business over and above the direct costs of producing a product is an _____. They can include utilities (eg, electricity, telephone), advertizing and marketing, and any other costs not billed directly to the client or included in the price of the product.
   a. Thing
   b. Overhead cost4
   c. Undefined
   d. Undefined

148. _____ has recently added self checkout registers at most of its stores in North America. These automated kiosks allow the customer to scan the barcode of the item they wish to purchase, then insert money to pay for the items, and receive any change automatically. The customer no longer needs to interact with a store employee during checkout.
   a. Organization
   b. Home Depot4
   c. Undefined
   d. Undefined

149. The Six Sigma quality system was developed at _____ even though it became most well known because of its use by General Electric. It was created by engineer Bill Smith, under the direction of Bob Galvin (son of founder Paul Galvin) when he was running the company.
   a. Organization
   b. Motorola4
   c. Undefined
   d. Undefined

150. Valuation method departing from the cost principle that recognizes a loss when replacement cost or net realizable value drops below cost is called _____.
   a. Thing
   b. Lower of cost4
   c. Undefined
   d. Undefined

151. _____ is an accounting method used to establish the dollar amount at which assets are recorded on a savings association's books. The amount established is the lower of the cost of the asset or the current market value.
   a. Thing
   b. Lower of Cost or Market4
   c. Undefined
   d. Undefined

152. Characterized by rizing output, falling unemployment, rizing profits, and increasing economic activity following a decline is a _____.

## Chapter 4. Analyzing Investing Activities

a. Recovery4  
c. Undefined  
b. Thing  
d. Undefined

153. The current cost to replace an inventory item is a _____.
   a. Thing
   b. Current replacement cost4
   c. Undefined
   d. Undefined

154. _____ is the sale of assets when an entity is being liquidated.
   a. Realization4
   b. Thing
   c. Undefined
   d. Undefined

155. _____ is equal to total cost divided by the number of goods produced (Quantity-Q). It is also equal to the sum of average variable costs (total variable costs divided by Q) plus average fixed costs (total fixed costs divided by Q).
   a. Average cost4
   b. Thing
   c. Undefined
   d. Undefined

156. A good that is used in conjunction with another good is a _____. For example, cameras and film would _____ eachother.
   a. Thing
   b. Complement4
   c. Undefined
   d. Undefined

157. A _____ is a comparison of the money earned (or lost) on an investment to the amount of money invested.
   a. Rate of return4
   b. Thing
   c. Undefined
   d. Undefined

158. A person who makes economic decisions for another economic actor. A hired manager operates as an _____ for a firm's owner.
   a. Agent4
   b. Thing
   c. Undefined
   d. Undefined

159. _____ is an ambiguous phrase that expresses the relationship between gross profit and sales revenue as _____ = Revenue - costs of good sold.
   a. Gross margin4
   b. Thing
   c. Undefined
   d. Undefined

160. A deposit by a buyer in stocks with a seller or a stockbroker, as security to cover fluctuations in the market in reference to stocks that the buyer has purchased but for which he has not paid is a _____. Commodities are also traded on _____.
   a. Thing
   b. Margin4
   c. Undefined
   d. Undefined

161. _____ is the name given to the set of legal principles, in countries following the English common law tradition, which supplement strict rules of law where their application would operate harshly, so as to achieve what is sometimes referred to as "natural justice."

a. Equity4  
b. Thing  
c. Undefined  
d. Undefined  

162. A _____ is a bond issued by a national government denominated in the country's own currency. Bonds issued by national governments in foreign currencies are normally referred to as sovereign bonds.
a. Thing  
b. Government bond4  
c. Undefined  
d. Undefined  

163. _____ refer to securities issued by state and local government units. The income from these securities is exempt from federal income taxes.
a. Municipal securities4  
b. Thing  
c. Undefined  
d. Undefined  

164. A _____ is a bond issued by a corporation, as the name suggests. The term is usually applied to longer term debt instruments, generally with a maturity date falling at least 12 months after their issue date (the term "commercial paper" being sometimes used for instruments with a shorter maturity).
a. Thing  
b. Corporate bond4  
c. Undefined  
d. Undefined  

165. Type of security acquired by loaning assets is called a _____.
a. Thing  
b. Debt security4  
c. Undefined  
d. Undefined  

166. A person to whom a debt or legal obligation is owed, and who has the right to enforce payment of that debt or obligation is referred to as _____.
a. Creditor4  
b. Thing  
c. Undefined  
d. Undefined  

167. _____ refer to representation of ownership rights to the corporation.
a. Equity securities4  
b. Thing  
c. Undefined  
d. Undefined  

168. Stock that has specified rights over common stock is a _____.
a. Preferred stock4  
b. Thing  
c. Undefined  
d. Undefined  

169. _____ refers to the basic, normal, voting stock issued by a corporation; called residual equity because it ranks after preferred stock for dividend and liquidation distributions.
a. Common stock4  
b. Thing  
c. Undefined  
d. Undefined  

170. In financial terminology, _____ is the capital raized by a corporation, through the issuance and sale of shares.
a. Thing  
b. Stock4  
c. Undefined  
d. Undefined

171. _____ are those assets usually in service over one year such as buildings, equipment, and long-term investments. These often receive favorable tax treatment over current assets. Tangible long-term assets are usually referred to as fixed assets.
- a. Thing
- b. Noncurrent assets4
- c. Undefined
- d. Undefined

172. _____ is a concept used in finance and economics, defined as a rational and unbiased estimate of the potential market price of a good, service, or asset.
- a. Fair value4
- b. Thing
- c. Undefined
- d. Undefined

173. In accounting terminology, _____ describes the original cost of an asset at the time of purchase or payment as opposed to its market value
- a. Thing
- b. Historical cost4
- c. Undefined
- d. Undefined

174. All investments in stocks or bonds that are held primarily for the purpose of active trading in the near future are called _____.
- a. Trading securities4
- b. Thing
- c. Undefined
- d. Undefined

175. _____ refers to payments of income to those who supply the economy with capital.
- a. Thing
- b. Interest income4
- c. Undefined
- d. Undefined

176. Systematic and rational allocation of the acquisition cost of an intangible asset over its useful life is referred to as _____.
- a. Amortization4
- b. Thing
- c. Undefined
- d. Undefined

177. The difference between the face value of a bond and its selling price, when a bond is sold for less than its face value it's referred to as a _____.
- a. Thing
- b. Discount4
- c. Undefined
- d. Undefined

178. _____ refers to the fee charged by an insurance company for an insurance policy. The rate of losses must be relatively predictable: In order to set the _____ (prices) insurers must be able to estimate them accurately.
- a. Thing
- b. Premium4
- c. Undefined
- d. Undefined

179. In finance and economics, _____ is the reduction of some kind of asset, for either financial or social goals. A divestment is the opposite of an investment.
- a. Thing
- b. Divestiture4
- c. Undefined
- d. Undefined

180. _____ refers to the combination of two firms into a single firm.

a. Thing
c. Undefined
b. Merger4
d. Undefined

181. _____ refers to a rise in the value of a country's currency on the exchange market, relative either to a particular other currency or to a weighted average of other currencies. The currency is said to appreciate. Opposite of 'depreciation.' _____ can also refer to the increase in value of any asset.
a. Appreciation4
c. Undefined
b. Thing
d. Undefined

182. A company that is controlled by another company or corporation is a _____.
a. Thing
c. Undefined
b. Subsidiary4
d. Undefined

183. Amount of corporate profits paid out for each share of stock is referred to as _____.
a. Thing
c. Undefined
b. Dividend4
d. Undefined

184. Stock that permits the corporation to buy back preferred stock at some future date is called _____.
a. Thing
c. Undefined
b. Redeemable preferred stock4
d. Undefined

185. _____ refer to an equity security, representing a shareholder's ownership of a corporation. _____ are one of a finite number of equal portions in the capital of a company, entitling the owner to a proportion of distributed, non-reinvested profits known as dividends and to a portion of the value of the company in case of liquidation.
a. Thing
c. Undefined
b. Shares4
d. Undefined

186. Method of accounting for investments in marketable equity securities; is required when the investor owns percent to percent of the investee company. The amount of investments carried under the _____ represents a measure of the book value of the investee rather than the cost or market value of the investment security.
a. Thing
c. Undefined
b. Equity method4
d. Undefined

187. A firm has a _____ in another business entity when it owns more than 50 percent of that entity's voting stock.
a. Controlling interest4
c. Undefined
b. Thing
d. Undefined

188. A corporation whose purpose or function is to own or otherwise hold the shares of other corporations either for investment or control is called _____.
a. Holding company4
c. Undefined
b. Thing
d. Undefined

189. A management function that involves determining whether or not an organization is progressing toward its goals and objectives, and taking corrective action if it is not is called _____.

a. Controlling4  
b. Thing  
c. Undefined  
d. Undefined

190. A _____ refers to a financial statement of a parent company and its subsidiaries that has been combined into a single set of financial statements as if the companies were one.
    a. Thing
    b. Consolidated financial statement4
    c. Undefined
    d. Undefined

191. _____ is a multinational computer technology corporation with 2004 global annual sales of US$39.79 billion and 71,553 employees in 102 countries and regions as of July 2006. It develops, manufactures, licenses, and supports a wide range of software products for computing devices.
    a. Microsoft4
    b. Organization
    c. Undefined
    d. Undefined

192. _____ refers to net income plus unrealized gain or loss on securities, minimum pension liability adjustment, and foreign currency translation adjustment.
    a. Comprehensive income4
    b. Thing
    c. Undefined
    d. Undefined

193. Inventory method that allocates costs between cost of goods sold and ending inventory using the cost of the specific goods sold or retained in the business is referred to as _____. If the units in the ending inventory can be identified as coming from a specific purchase, the _____ method may be used to price the inventory.
    a. Thing
    b. Specific identification4
    c. Undefined
    d. Undefined

194. _____ refers to consisting of virtually the same elements as portfolio income, a measure by which to justify a deduction for interest on investment indebtedness. Income derived from investments.
    a. Investment income4
    b. Thing
    c. Undefined
    d. Undefined

195. An _____ is an aggregate of investments, such as stocks, bonds, real estate, arts or even fine wines. What distinguishes an _____ from net worth is that some asset classes are not considered investments.
    a. Investment portfolio4
    b. Thing
    c. Undefined
    d. Undefined

196. A _____ is a 12-month period used for calculating annual ("yearly") financial reports in businesses and other organizations. In many jurisdictions, regulatory laws regarding accounting require such reports once per twelve months, but do not require that the twelve months constitute a calendar year (i.e. January to December).
    a. Thing
    b. Fiscal year4
    c. Undefined
    d. Undefined

197. _____ refers to the return a businessperson gets on the money he and other owners invest in the firm; for example, a business that earned $100 on a $1,000 investment would have a ROI of 10 percent: 100 divided by 1000.
    a. Thing
    b. Return on investment4
    c. Undefined
    d. Undefined

198. _____ generally refers to the buying and holding of shares of stock on a stock market by individuals and funds in anticipation of income from dividends and capital gain as the value of the stock rises.
   a. Thing
   b. Equity investment4
   c. Undefined
   d. Undefined

199. _____ refers to the gain in value that the owner of an asset experiences when the price of the asset rises, including when the currency in which the asset is denominated appreciates.
   a. Capital gain4
   b. Thing
   c. Undefined
   d. Undefined

200. _____ refers to any departure from the ideal of perfect competition that interferes with economic agents maximizing social welfare when they maximize their own.
   a. Thing
   b. Distortion4
   c. Undefined
   d. Undefined

201. The extent to which a source is perceived as having knowledge, skill, or experience relevant to a communication topic and can be trusted to give an unbiased opinion or present objective information on the issue is called _____.
   a. Credibility4
   b. Thing
   c. Undefined
   d. Undefined

202. _____ is the risk that the value of an investment will decrease due to moves in market factors.
   a. Market risk4
   b. Thing
   c. Undefined
   d. Undefined

203. _____ is the aggregate amount of any material good that can be called into being at a certain price point; it comprises one half of the equation of _____ and demand. In classical economic theory, a curve representing _____ is one of the factors that produce price.
   a. Supply4
   b. Thing
   c. Undefined
   d. Undefined

204. A _____ is type of bond that can be converted into shares of stock in the issuing company, usually at some pre-announced ratio.
   a. Thing
   b. Convertible bond4
   c. Undefined
   d. Undefined

205. _____ is a form of risk that arises from the change in price of one currency against another. Whenever investors or companies have assets or business operations across national borders, they face _____ if their positions are not hedged.
   a. Thing
   b. Currency risk4
   c. Undefined
   d. Undefined

206. _____ refers to a note payable issued for property, such as a house, usually repaid in equal installments consisting of part principle and part interest, over a specified period.
   a. Thing
   b. Mortgage4
   c. Undefined
   d. Undefined

## Chapter 4. Analyzing Investing Activities

207. An _____ is the totality of the legal rights, interests, entitlements and obligations attaching to property. In the context of wills and probate, it refers to the totality of the property which the deceased owned or in which some interest was held.
   a. Thing
   b. Estate4
   c. Undefined
   d. Undefined

208. _____ refers to a system by which individuals can reduce their exposure to risk of large losses by spreading the risks among a large number of persons.
   a. Thing
   b. Insurance4
   c. Undefined
   d. Undefined

209. Formal or legal documents in writing, such as contracts, deeds, wills, bonds, leases, and mortgages is referred to as a _____.
   a. Thing
   b. Financial instrument4
   c. Undefined
   d. Undefined

210. _____ refer to contracts for the sale and future delivery of stocks or commodities, wherein either party may waive delivery, and receive or pay, as the case may be, the difference in market price at the time set for delivery.
   a. Futures4
   b. Thing
   c. Undefined
   d. Undefined

211. In finance a _____ is a derivative, where two counterparties exchange one stream of cash flows against another stream. These streams are called the legs of the _____. The cash flows are calculated over a notional principal amount. Swaps are often used to hedge certain risks, for instance interest rate risk. Another use is speculation.
   a. Swap4
   b. Thing
   c. Undefined
   d. Undefined

212. The rate between two currencies that specifies how much one country's currency is worth expressed in terms of the other country's currency is the _____.
   a. Currency exchange rate4
   b. Thing
   c. Undefined
   d. Undefined

213. _____ refers to the price at which one country's currency trades for another, typically on the exchange market.
   a. Thing
   b. Exchange rate4
   c. Undefined
   d. Undefined

214. Could refer to any good, but in trade a _____ is usually a raw material or primary product that enters into international trade, such as metals or basic agricultural products.
   a. Thing
   b. Commodity4
   c. Undefined
   d. Undefined

215. A _____ is something measured by a number; it is used to analyze what happens to other things when the size of that number changes.
   a. Thing
   b. Variable4
   c. Undefined
   d. Undefined

## Chapter 4. Analyzing Investing Activities

216. A _____ is a legal and financial term. It means a party to a contract. Any legal entity can be a _____.
 a. Counterparty4
 b. Thing
 c. Undefined
 d. Undefined

217. A _____ acts as an agent that provides financial services for its clients. Financial institutions generally fall under financial regulation from a government authority.
 a. Thing
 b. Financial institution4
 c. Undefined
 d. Undefined

218. In finance, a _____ is a standardized contract, traded on a futures exchange, to buy or sell a certain underlying instrument at a certain date in the future, at a pre-set price. The
 a. Futures contract4
 b. Thing
 c. Undefined
 d. Undefined

219. A person in possession of a document of title or an instrument payable or indorsed to him, his order, or to bearer is a _____.
 a. Thing
 b. Holder4
 c. Undefined
 d. Undefined

220. The payment to holders of bonds payable, calculated by multiplying the stated rate on the face of the bond by the par, or face, value of the bond. If bonds are issued at a discount or premium, the _____ does not equal the interest expense.
 a. Interest payment4
 b. Thing
 c. Undefined
 d. Undefined

221. _____ refers to the exchange of a set of payments in one currency for a set of payments in another currency.
 a. Thing
 b. Currency swap4
 c. Undefined
 d. Undefined

222. _____ refers to an option contract that provides the right to buy a security at a specified price within a certain time period.
 a. Thing
 b. Call option4
 c. Undefined
 d. Undefined

223. An option contract that provides the right to sell a security at a specified price within a specified period of time is a _____.
 a. Put option4
 b. Thing
 c. Undefined
 d. Undefined

224. An option that can be exercized only at the expiration date of the contract is referred to as _____.
 a. European option4
 b. Thing
 c. Undefined
 d. Undefined

225. The nominal or par value of an instrument as expressed on its face is referred to as the _____.
 a. Face value4
 b. Thing
 c. Undefined
 d. Undefined

## Chapter 4. Analyzing Investing Activities

226. A _____ is an individual or company (including a corporation) that legally owns one or more shares of stock in a joined stock company. The shareholders are the owners of a corporation. Companies listed at the stock market strive to enhance shareholder value.
- a. Thing
- b. Stockholder4
- c. Undefined
- d. Undefined

227. The cost a business incurs to borrow money. With respect to bonds payable, the _____ is calculated by multiplying the market rate of interest by the carrying value of the bonds on the date of the payment.
- a. Thing
- b. Interest expense4
- c. Undefined
- d. Undefined

228. _____ refers to that portion of the effect of price on quantity demanded that reflects the change in real income due to the price change.
- a. Thing
- b. Income effect4
- c. Undefined
- d. Undefined

229. In economics, _____ refers to an activity of spending which increases the availability of fixed capital goods or means of production. It is the total spending on new fixed investment minus replacement investment, which simply replaces depreciated capital goods.
- a. Net investment4
- b. Thing
- c. Undefined
- d. Undefined

230. In agency law, one under whose direction an agent acts and for whose benefit that agent acts is a _____.
- a. Principal4
- b. Thing
- c. Undefined
- d. Undefined

231. _____ refers to the calculation of the total liabilities divided by the total liabilities plus capital. This results in the measurment of the debt level of the business (leverage).
- a. Thing
- b. Debt ratio4
- c. Undefined
- d. Undefined

232. Gross sales less sales returns and allowances and sales discounts are referred to as _____.
- a. Thing
- b. Net sales4
- c. Undefined
- d. Undefined

233. A form on which items or services needed by a business firm are specified and then communicated to the vendor is a _____.
- a. Purchase order4
- b. Place
- c. Undefined
- d. Undefined

234. Interest rate that fluctuates from period to period over the life of the loan is the _____. These rates are most often tied to the prime rate of a particular lending institution, the Consumer Price Index, Federal Funds rates or other money market measurements.
- a. Thing
- b. Variable interest rate4
- c. Undefined
- d. Undefined

## Chapter 4. Analyzing Investing Activities

235. The _____ unit cost of the goods available for sale for both cost of goods sold and ending inventory.
a. Weighted average4
b. Thing
c. Undefined
d. Undefined

236. _____ refers to the currency of the economic environment in which the taxpayer carries on most of its activities, and in which the taxpayer transacts most of its business.
a. Thing
b. Functional currency4
c. Undefined
d. Undefined

237. Obligations to make future economic sacrifices, usually cash payments, are referred to as _____. Same as current liabilities.
a. Thing
b. Payables4
c. Undefined
d. Undefined

238. The purchase or sale of an asset in hopes that its price will rise or fall respectively, in order to make a profit is called _____.
a. Speculation4
b. Thing
c. Undefined
d. Undefined

239. _____ refers to an organization's strategy; the ways an organization will attempt to fulfill its mission and achieve its long-term goals.
a. Strategic choice4
b. Thing
c. Undefined
d. Undefined

240. _____ is a measure of profitability. It is calculated using a formula and written as a percentage or a number. _____ = Net income before tax and interest / Revenue.
a. Profit margin4
b. Thing
c. Undefined
d. Undefined

241. _____ refers to all the techniques sellers use to motivate people to buy products or services. An attempt by marketers to inform people about products and to persuade them to participate in an exchange.
a. Promotion4
b. Thing
c. Undefined
d. Undefined

242. Total revenues from operation minus cost of goods sold and operating costs are called _____.
a. Operating income4
b. Thing
c. Undefined
d. Undefined

243. _____ of the evidence means that evidence, in the judgment of the juror, is entitled to the greatest weight, appears to be more credible, has greater force, and overcomes not only the opposing presumptions, but also the opposing evidence.
a. Thing
b. Preponderance4
c. Undefined
d. Undefined

244. _____ refers to a legal standard whereby a bare majority of the evidence is sufficient to justify a ruling.

a. Thing
c. Undefined
b. Preponderance of evidence4
d. Undefined

245. _____, also known as property, plant, and equipment (PP&E), is a term used in accountancy for assets and property which cannot easily be converted into cash. This can be compared with current assets such as cash or bank accounts, which are described as liquid assets. In most cases, only tangible assets are referred to as fixed.
a. Fixed asset4
c. Undefined
b. Thing
d. Undefined

246. Having a physical existence is referred to as the _____. Personal property other than real estate, such as cars, boats, stocks, or other assets.
a. Thing
c. Undefined
b. Tangible4
d. Undefined

247. A distinctive word, name, symbol, device, or combination thereof, which enables consumers to identify favored products or services and which may find protection under state or federal law is a _____.
a. Thing
c. Undefined
b. Trademark4
d. Undefined

248. The legal right to the proceeds from and control over the use of a created product, such a written work, audio, video, film, or software is a _____. This right generally extends over the life of the author plus fifty years.
a. Thing
c. Undefined
b. Copyright4
d. Undefined

249. _____ is an important accounting concept that describes the value of a business entity not directly attributable to its tangible assets and liabilities.
a. Goodwill4
c. Undefined
b. Thing
d. Undefined

250. The legal right to the proceeds from and control over the use of an invented product or process, granted for a fixed period of time, usually 20 years. _____ is one form of intellectual property that is subject of the TRIPS agreement.
a. Patent4
c. Undefined
b. Thing
d. Undefined

251. Method of accounting that records the effects of accounting events in the period in which such events occur regardless of when cash is exchanged is _____.
a. Thing
c. Undefined
b. Accrual accounting4
d. Undefined

252. An _____ is an accounting event in which the transaction is recognized when the action takes place, instead of when cash is disbursed or received.
a. Accrual4
c. Undefined
b. Thing
d. Undefined

## Chapter 4. Analyzing Investing Activities

253. A _____ is a stretch of time when an individual is eligible to receive benefits. The duration of benefits refers to the number of weeks the benefits will continue as long as the individual remains eligible. It is based on the number of hours worked in the 52 weeks before the lay-off and on the regional unemployment rate.
   a. Thing
   b. Benefit period4
   c. Undefined
   d. Undefined

254. The _____ of an asset or group of assets is sometimes the price at which they were originally acquired, in many cases equal to purchase price.
   a. Thing
   b. Book value4
   c. Undefined
   d. Undefined

255. _____ means a rise of a price of goods or products. This term is specially used as _____ of a currency, where it means a rise of currency to the relation with a foreign currency in a fixed exchange rate.
   a. Revaluation4
   b. Thing
   c. Undefined
   d. Undefined

256. The body of knowledge and techniques that can be used to combine economic resources to produce goods and services is called _____.
   a. Technology4
   b. Thing
   c. Undefined
   d. Undefined

257. _____ makes an organization worth more than its balance sheet value. For many years, _____ and goodwill meant the same thing. Today, _____ management is far broader. It seeks to explain how knowledge, collaboration, and process-engagement create decisions and actions that lead to cost allocations, productivity, and finally financial performance.
   a. Intellectual capital4
   b. Thing
   c. Undefined
   d. Undefined

258. The interest rate that equates a future value or an annuity to a given present value is a _____.
   a. Thing
   b. Yield4
   c. Undefined
   d. Undefined

259. The length of service of a productive facility or piece of equipment is its _____. The period of time during which an asset will have economic value and be usable.
   a. Useful life4
   b. Thing
   c. Undefined
   d. Undefined

260. A transfer of property or some right or interest is referred to as _____.
   a. Assignment4
   b. Thing
   c. Undefined
   d. Undefined

261. In accounting, the _____ of an asset is its remaining value after depreciation. The estimated value of an asset at the end of its useful life.
   a. Thing
   b. Salvage value4
   c. Undefined
   d. Undefined

## Chapter 4. Analyzing Investing Activities

262. _____ refers to the total depreciation that has been reported as depreciation expense for the entire life of a long-term tangible asset. It is a contra-asset account.
    a. Thing
    b. Accumulated depreciation4
    c. Undefined
    d. Undefined

263. A substantial expenditure that is used by a company to acquire or upgrade physical assets such as equipment, property, industrial buildings, including those which improve the quality and life of an asset is referred to as a _____.
    a. Thing
    b. Capital expenditure4
    c. Undefined
    d. Undefined

264. Major investments in long-term assets such as land, buildings, equipment, or research and development are referred to as _____.
    a. Capital expenditures4
    b. Thing
    c. Undefined
    d. Undefined

265. The _____ measures the size of a company's after-tax income, excluding non-cash depreciation expenses, as compared to the firm's total debt obligations. It is used to gauge a company's ability to meet long term obligations.
    a. Solvency ratio4
    b. Thing
    c. Undefined
    d. Undefined

266. The ability of a company to pay interest as it comes due and to repay the face value of debt at maturity is called _____.
    a. Thing
    b. Solvency4
    c. Undefined
    d. Undefined

267. _____ refers to the cash inflows and cash outflows from the general operating activities of the business; one of the three sections in the statement of cash flows.
    a. Thing
    b. Operating cash flows4
    c. Undefined
    d. Undefined

268. Cash flowing out of the business from all sources over a period of time is _____.
    a. Cash outflow4
    b. Thing
    c. Undefined
    d. Undefined

269. In accounting, a _____ is an asset that is recorded as property that creates more property, e.g. a factory that creates shoes, or a forest that yields a quantity of wood.
    a. Capital asset4
    b. Thing
    c. Undefined
    d. Undefined

270. _____ refers to the long-term movement of an economic variable, such as its average rate of increase or decrease over enough years to encompass several business cycles.
    a. Thing
    b. Trend4
    c. Undefined
    d. Undefined

271. A principle that holds that it is unethical to charge a higher price for a commodity than the cost of purchasing, producing or acquiring, and bringing it to market is the _____.

## Chapter 4. Analyzing Investing Activities

a. Thing
c. Undefined
b. Cost principle4
d. Undefined

272. _____ refers to usually the first stage in the creative process. It includes education and formal training.
a. Thing
c. Undefined
b. Preparation4
d. Undefined

273. In Keynesian economics _____ refers to personal _____ expenditure, i.e., the purchase of currently produced goods and services out of income, out of savings (net worth), or from borrowed funds. It refers to that part of disposable income that does not go to saving.
a. Consumption4
c. Undefined
b. Thing
d. Undefined

274. Cash flow activities that include obtaining cash from issuing debt and repaying the amounts borrowed and obtaining cash from stockholders and paying dividends is referred to as _____.
a. Financing activities4
c. Undefined
b. Thing
d. Undefined

275. _____ refers to the speed of the up and down movements of a fluctuating economic variable; that is, the number of times per unit of time that the variable completes a cycle of up and down movement.
a. Frequency4
c. Undefined
b. Thing
d. Undefined

276. Forces that affect the availability, production, and distribution of a society's resources among competing users are referred to as _____.
a. Thing
c. Undefined
b. Economic forces4
d. Undefined

277. _____ refers to the amount recognized as an expense in one period resulting from the periodic recognition of the used portion of the cost of a long-term tangible asset over its life.
a. Depreciation expense4
c. Undefined
b. Thing
d. Undefined

278. Depreciation methods that recognize more depreciation expense in the early years of an asset's life and less in later years are referred to asan _____.
a. Accelerated method4
c. Undefined
b. Thing
d. Undefined

279. Methods that result in higher depreciation expense in the early years of an asset's life, and lower expense in the later years are referred to as _____.
a. Thing
c. Undefined
b. Accelerated depreciation4
d. Undefined

## Chapter 4. Analyzing Investing Activities

280. During its life, _____ was one of the largest shipbuilding companies in the world and was one of the most powerful symbols of American manufacturing leadership. It was the second largest steel producer in the United States, but following its 2001 bankruptcy, the company was dissolved and the remaining assets sold to International Steel Group in 2003.
    a. Bethlehem Steel4
    b. Thing
    c. Undefined
    d. Undefined

281. An accounting principle explaining that when doubt exists between two reporting alternatives, _____ holds that the user of the information should select the alternative with the least favorable impact on owner's equity.
    a. Conservatism principle4
    b. Thing
    c. Undefined
    d. Undefined

282. _____ refer to people in the organization who actually use the product or service purchased by the buying center.
    a. Users4
    b. Thing
    c. Undefined
    d. Undefined

283. A _____ is an underhand method used by companies to enhance the appearance of a company's future performance. The company writes off assets as much as possible to the profit and loss account in the current period in order ot show increase profits and return on investment in future periods.
    a. Big bath4
    b. Thing
    c. Undefined
    d. Undefined

284. The discussion by counsel for the respective parties of their contentions on the law and the facts of the case being tried in order to aid the jury in arriving at a correct and just conclusion is called _____.
    a. Thing
    b. Argument4
    c. Undefined
    d. Undefined

285. A _____ is a security that entitles the holder to buy or sell a certain additional quantity of an underlying security at an agreed-upon price, at the holder's discretion.
    a. Warrant4
    b. Thing
    c. Undefined
    d. Undefined

286. A firm that produces an essential good or service, has obtained from a government the right to be the sole supplier of the good or service in the area, and is regulated by that government to prevent the abuse of its monopoly power is a _____.
    a. Event
    b. Public utility4
    c. Undefined
    d. Undefined

287. _____ is defined as excess of actual cost over budget. _____ is typically calculated in one of two ways. Either as a percentage, namely actual cost minus budgeted cost, in percent of budgeted cost. Or as a ratio, viz. actual cost divided by budgeted cost.
    a. Cost overrun4
    b. Thing
    c. Undefined
    d. Undefined

288. The lessening or complete removal of government regulations on an industry, especially concerning the price that firms are allowed to charge and leaving price to be determined by market forces a _____.

## Chapter 4. Analyzing Investing Activities

a. Deregulation4
b. Thing
c. Undefined
d. Undefined

289. _____ refers to assets used to operate the business; frequently called long-term assets. They are property such as land, livestock, and trees that produce income.
a. Thing
b. Productive assets4
c. Undefined
d. Undefined

290. _____ refers to the shortening of the time for the performance of a contract or the payment of a note by the operation of some provision in the contract or note itself.
a. Thing
b. Acceleration4
c. Undefined
d. Undefined

291. _____ is an accounting term, meaning future tax liability or asset, resulting from temporary differences between book (accounting) value of assets and liabilities, and their tax value.
a. Deferred tax4
b. Thing
c. Undefined
d. Undefined

292. _____ refers to the function in a firm that searches for quality material resources, finds the best suppliers, and negotiates the best price for goods and services.
a. Thing
b. Purchasing4
c. Undefined
d. Undefined

293. _____ refers to paid, nonpersonal communication through various media by organizations and individuals who are in some way identified in the _____ message.
a. Thing
b. Advertising4
c. Undefined
d. Undefined

294. A contractual right to sell certain products or services, use certain trademarks, or perform activities in a geographical region is called a _____.
a. Thing
b. Franchise4
c. Undefined
d. Undefined

295. To provide for the payment of a debt by creating a sinking fund or paying in installments is to _____.
a. Thing
b. Amortize4
c. Undefined
d. Undefined

296. _____ refers to the allocation of the cost of an asset over several accounting periods. Also, to expense a cost, that is, put it on the income statement as an expense.
a. Writing off4
b. Thing
c. Undefined
d. Undefined

297. _____ refers to portion of the assets remaining after the creditors' claims have been satisfied; also called equity or residual interest.

## Chapter 4. Analyzing Investing Activities

    a. Thing                                                b. Net assets4
    c. Undefined                                       d. Undefined

298. _____ is a form of property tenure where one party buys the right to occupy land or a building for a given length of time. A lease is a legal estate _____ estate that can be bought and sold on the open market and differs from a tenancy where a property is let on a periodic basis such as weekly or monthly.
    a. Leasehold4                                 b. Thing
    c. Undefined                                   d. Undefined

299. A _____ is a proceeding before a court or other decision-making body or officer. A _____ is generally distinguished from a trial in that it is usually shorter and often less formal.
    a. Thing                                          b. Hearing4
    c. Undefined                                d. Undefined

300. Loan origination fees that may be deductible as interest by a buyer of property. A seller of property who pays _____ reduces the selling price by the amount of the _____ paid for the buyer.
    a. Points4                                      b. Thing
    c. Undefined                                d. Undefined

301. The amount of money a household can spend during a given period without increasing or decreasing its net assets. Wages, salaries, dividends, interest income, transfer payments, rents, and so forth are sources of _____.
    a. Thing                                          b. Economic income4
    c. Undefined                             d. Undefined

302. A name, symbol, or design that identifies the goods or services of one seller or group of sellers and distinguishes them from the goods and services of competitors is a _____.
    a. Thing                                       b. Brand4
    c. Undefined                          d. Undefined

303. _____ refers to the return on an asset expected over the next period.
    a. Expected return4                b. Thing
    c. Undefined                      d. Undefined

304. _____ refers to the percentage cost of funds used for acquiring resources for an organization, typically a weighted average of the firms cost of equity and cost of debt.
    a. Cost of capital4                  b. Place
    c. Undefined                        d. Undefined

305. A _____ is a corporation or mutual organization which provides facilities for stock brokers and traders, to trade company stocks and other securities.
    a. Thing                                          b. Stock exchange4
    c. Undefined                              d. Undefined

306. _____ refers to the individuals within the firm, and to the portion of the firm's organization that deals with hiring, firing, training, and other personnel issues.

a. Thing
b. Human resources4
c. Undefined
d. Undefined

307. Cash coming into the company as the result of a previous investment is a _____.
a. Thing
b. Cash inflow4
c. Undefined
d. Undefined

308. In December of 1995, _____ became the first major North American retailer to accept independent monitoring of the working conditions in a contract factory producing its garments. _____ is the largest specialty retailer in the United States.
a. Gap4
b. Organization
c. Undefined
d. Undefined

309. _____ are shares that give the stockholder the right to vote on matters of corporate policy making as well as who will compose the members of the board of directors.
a. Thing
b. Voting shares4
c. Undefined
d. Undefined

310. Assets that have physical substance that cannot easily be converted into cash are referd to as a _____.
a. Thing
b. Tangible asset4
c. Undefined
d. Undefined

311. In the trial of a case the formal remonstrance made by counsel to something that has been said or done, in order to obtain the court's ruling thereon is an _____.
a. Thing
b. Objection4
c. Undefined
d. Undefined

312. A _____ occurs when a customer does not pay cash at the time of the sale but instead agrees to pay later. The sale occurs now, with payment from the customer to follow at a later time.
a. Credit sale4
b. Thing
c. Undefined
d. Undefined

313. _____ refers to a method that bases bad debt expense on an estimate of uncollectible accounts
a. Allowance method4
b. Thing
c. Undefined
d. Undefined

314. _____ refers to the payment made by a firm to obtain and retain entrepreneurial ability; the minimum income entrepreneurial ability must receive to induce it to perform entrepreneurial functions for a firm.
a. Thing
b. Normal profit4
c. Undefined
d. Undefined

315. The flow of inventory costs from the balance sheet to the income statement is an _____.
a. Thing
b. Inventory cost flow4
c. Undefined
d. Undefined

316. _____ refers to a method of inventory accounting that refers to First In, First Out.

## Chapter 4. Analyzing Investing Activities

a. Thing
b. Fifo method4
c. Undefined
d. Undefined

317. _____ is a phrase used to mean that no bargaining is allowed over the price of a good or, less commonly, a service.
a. Thing
b. Fixed price4
c. Undefined
d. Undefined

318. Cumulative earnings of a company that are not distributed to the owners and are reinvested in the business are called _____.
a. Retained earnings4
b. Thing
c. Undefined
d. Undefined

319. The use of resources for the deliberate discovery of new information and ways of doing things, together with the application of that information in inventing new products or processes is referred to as _____.
a. Research and development4
b. Thing
c. Undefined
d. Undefined

320. A _____ in property law is a future interest created in a transferee that is capable of becoming possessory upon the natural termination of a prior estate created by the same instrument.
a. Thing
b. Remainder4
c. Undefined
d. Undefined

321. The cost of something in terms of opportunity foregone. The _____ to a country of producing a unit more of a good, such as for export or to replace an import, is the quantity of some other good that could have been produced instead.
a. Opportunity cost4
b. Thing
c. Undefined
d. Undefined

322. The sum of fixed cost and variable cost is referred to as _____.
a. Thing
b. Total cost4
c. Undefined
d. Undefined

323. A nation's currency is said to _____ when exchange rates change so that a unit of its currency can buy fewer units of foreign currency.
a. Thing
b. Depreciate4
c. Undefined
d. Undefined

324. The _____ percentage shows how profitable a company's assets are in generating revenue.
a. Thing
b. Return on Assets4
c. Undefined
d. Undefined

325. Promoting and selling products or services to customers, or prospective customers, is referred to as _____.
a. Marketing4
b. Thing
c. Undefined
d. Undefined

## Chapter 4. Analyzing Investing Activities

326. _____ refers to unauthorized use of another's patent. A patent holder may recover damages and other remedies against a patent infringer.
- a. Thing
- b. Patent infringement4
- c. Undefined
- d. Undefined

327. _____ refers to a court order directing a person or organization not to perform a certain act because the act would do irreparable damage to some other person or persons; a restraining order.
- a. Injunction4
- b. Thing
- c. Undefined
- d. Undefined

328. The sum of money recoverable by a plaintiff who has received a judgment in a civil case is called _____.
- a. Thing
- b. Damages4
- c. Undefined
- d. Undefined

329. _____ in economics, the manner in which total output and income is distributed among individuals or factors.
- a. Thing
- b. Distribution4
- c. Undefined
- d. Undefined

330. The owner of intellectual property or informational rights who transfers rights in the property or information to the licensee is called _____.
- a. Licensor4
- b. Thing
- c. Undefined
- d. Undefined

331. _____ is a form of strategic alliance which involves the sale of a right to use certain proprietary knowledge (so called intellectual property) in a defined way.
- a. Licensing4
- b. Thing
- c. Undefined
- d. Undefined

332. _____ refers to cost computed by dividing some amount of total costs by the related number of units. Also called average cost.
- a. Thing
- b. Unit cost4
- c. Undefined
- d. Undefined

333. The _____ is a comparison of a firm's current assets to its current liabilities. The _____ is an indication of a firm's market liquidity and ability to meet short-term debt obligations.
- a. Thing
- b. Current ratio4
- c. Undefined
- d. Undefined

334. _____ is an accounting term which is commonly used in business. It is equal to the gross revenue for a given time period minus associated expenses.
- a. Net profit4
- b. Thing
- c. Undefined
- d. Undefined

335. _____ refers to a ratio that measures the number of times on average the inventory sold during the period; computed by dividing cost of goods sold by the average inventory during the period.

## Chapter 4. Analyzing Investing Activities

a. Thing
c. Undefined
b. Inventory turnover ratio4
d. Undefined

336. _____ refers to a written statement-also called an accountant's certificate, accountant's opinion, or audit report-prepared by an independent accountant or auditor after an audit.
a. Financial report4
c. Undefined
b. Thing
d. Undefined

337. A decline in a stock market or economic cycle is a _____.
a. Downturn4
c. Undefined
b. Thing
d. Undefined

338. A _____ is an individual or company (including a corporation) that legally owns one or more shares of stock in a joined stock company.
a. Thing
c. Undefined
b. Shareholder4
d. Undefined

339. _____ is using given resources in such a way that the potential positive or negative outcome is magnified. In finance, this generally refers to borrowing.
a. Thing
c. Undefined
b. Leverage4
d. Undefined

340. _____ relates to the likelihood that changes in the business environment will occur that reduce the profitability of doing business in a country. These changes can adversely affect operating profits as well as the value of assets.
a. Thing
c. Undefined
b. Country risk4
d. Undefined

341. A _____ refers to previously recorded assets, liabilities, revenues, or expenses that need to be adjusted at the end of the period to reflect earned revenues or incurred expenses.
a. Thing
c. Undefined
b. Deferred revenue4
d. Undefined

342. The _____ is a key variable in a derivatives contract between two parties. Where the contract requires delivery of the underlying instrument, the trade will be at the _____, regardless of the spot price of the underlying at that time.
a. Thing
c. Undefined
b. Strike price4
d. Undefined

343. The withholding of labor services by an organized group of workers is referred to as a _____.
a. Thing
c. Undefined
b. Strike4
d. Undefined

344. Repriced and settled in the margin account at the end of every trading day to reflect any change in the value of the futures contract is called _____.
a. Thing
c. Undefined
b. Marked to market4
d. Undefined

*Chapter 4. Analyzing Investing Activities*  151

345. _____ refers to the institution in a country that is normally responsible for managing the supply of the country's money and the value of its currency on the foreign exchange market.
   a. Central Bank4
   b. Thing
   c. Undefined
   d. Undefined

346. _____ refers to the amount by which expenses exceed revenues. The difference between income received and expenses, when expenses are greater.
   a. Net loss4
   b. Thing
   c. Undefined
   d. Undefined

347. The social science dealing with the use of scarce resources to obtain the maximum satisfaction of society's virtually unlimited economic wants is an _____.
   a. Economics4
   b. Thing
   c. Undefined
   d. Undefined

## Chapter 5. Analyzing Investing Activities: Special Topics

1. A system that collects and processes financial information about an organization and reports that information to decision makers is referred to as _____.
   - a. Thing
   - b. Accounting5
   - c. Undefined
   - d. Undefined

2. _____ is an important accounting concept that describes the value of a business entity not directly attributable to its tangible assets and liabilities.
   - a. Thing
   - b. Goodwill5
   - c. Undefined
   - d. Undefined

3. Converting the financial statements of foreign subsidiaries into the currency of the home country is a _____.
   - a. Currency translation5
   - b. Thing
   - c. Undefined
   - d. Undefined

4. _____ means the giving out of information, either voluntarily or to be in compliance with legal regulations or workplace rules.
   - a. Disclosure5
   - b. Thing
   - c. Undefined
   - d. Undefined

5. In finance, _____ is a profit or an increase in value of an investment such as a stock or bond. _____ is calculated by fair market value or the proceeds from the sale of the investment minus the sum of the purchase price and all costs associated with it.
   - a. Gain5
   - b. Thing
   - c. Undefined
   - d. Undefined

6. A _____ is a large company that consists of divisions of often seemingly unrelated businesses.
   - a. Thing
   - b. Conglomerate5
   - c. Undefined
   - d. Undefined

7. _____ is the world's largest media company with major Internet, publishing, film, telecommunications and television divisions.
   - a. Thing
   - b. Time Warner5
   - c. Undefined
   - d. Undefined

8. _____ refers to the combination of two firms into a single firm.
   - a. Merger5
   - b. Thing
   - c. Undefined
   - d. Undefined

9. _____ refers to the total number of dollars received by a firm from the sale of a product; equal to the total expenditures for the product produced by the firm; equal to the quantity sold multiplied by the price at which it is sold.
   - a. Thing
   - b. Total revenue5
   - c. Undefined
   - d. Undefined

10. _____ is a U.S. business term for the amount of money that a company receives from its activities, mostly from sales of products and/or services to customers.

## Chapter 5. Analyzing Investing Activities: Special Topics

a. Thing
c. Undefined

b. Revenue5
d. Undefined

11. In accounting, an _____ represents an event in which an asset is used up or a liability is incurred. In terms of the accounting equation, expenses reduce owners' equity.
a. Expense5
c. Undefined

b. Thing
d. Undefined

12. _____ refers to collections of legal rules produced by the American Law Institute, covering certain subject matter areas. Although restatements are often persuasive to courts, they are not legally binding unless adopted by the highest court of a particular state.
a. Restatement5
c. Undefined

b. Thing
d. Undefined

13. A company's purchase of the property and obligations of another company is an _____.
a. Thing
c. Undefined

b. Acquisition5
d. Undefined

14. The _____ of an asset or group of assets is sometimes the price at which they were originally acquired, in many cases equal to purchase price.
a. Book value5
c. Undefined

b. Thing
d. Undefined

15. A _____ is, as defined in economics, a social arrangement that allows buyers and sellers to discover information and carry out a voluntary exchange of goods or services.
a. Thing
c. Undefined

b. Market5
d. Undefined

16. A contract that gives the purchaser the _____ to buy or sell the underlying financial instrument at a specified price, called the exercise price or strike price, within a specific period of time.
a. Option5
c. Undefined

b. Thing
d. Undefined

17. An item of property, such as land, capital, money, a share in ownership, or a claim on others for future payment, such as a bond or a bank deposit is an _____.
a. Thing
c. Undefined

b. Asset5
d. Undefined

18. _____ characterizes the process of leading and directing all or part of an organization, often a business, through the deployment and manipulation of resources. Early twentieth-century _____ writer Mary Parker Follett defined _____ as "the art of getting things done through people."
a. Thing
c. Undefined

b. Management5
d. Undefined

19. _____ refers to spending for the production and accumulation of capital and additions to inventories. In a financial sense, buying an asset with the expectation of making a return.

a. Thing  
b. Investment5  
c. Undefined  
d. Undefined

20. A standardized method or technique that is performed repetitively, often on different materials resulting in different finished goods is called an _____.
   a. Thing  
   b. Operation5  
   c. Undefined  
   d. Undefined

21. In finance, _____ refers to the amounts of cash being received and spent by a business during a defined period of time, sometimes tied to a specific project. Most of the time they are being used to determine gaps in the liquid position of a company.
   a. Cash flow5  
   b. Thing  
   c. Undefined  
   d. Undefined

22. _____ refers to a person or tool with a primary function of information analysis, generally with a more limited, practical and short term set of goals than a researcher.
   a. Person  
   b. Analyst5  
   c. Undefined  
   d. Undefined

23. There are several methods used for _____. They try to give an estimate of their fair value, by using fundamental economic criteria. This theoretical valuation has to be perfected with market criteria, as the final purpose is to determine potential market prices.
   a. Stock valuation5  
   b. Thing  
   c. Undefined  
   d. Undefined

24. In finance, _____ is the process of estimating the market value of a financial asset or liability. They can be done on assets (for example, investments in marketable securities such as stocks, options, business enterprises, or intangible assets such as patents and trademarks) or on liabilities (e.g., Bonds issued by a company).
   a. Valuation5  
   b. Event  
   c. Undefined  
   d. Undefined

25. In financial terminology, _____ is the capital raized by a corporation, through the issuance and sale of shares.
   a. Stock5  
   b. Thing  
   c. Undefined  
   d. Undefined

26. In finance a _____ is a derivative, where two counterparties exchange one stream of cash flows against another stream. These streams are called the legs of the _____. The cash flows are calculated over a notional principal amount. Swaps are often used to hedge certain risks, for instance interest rate risk. Another use is speculation.
   a. Thing  
   b. Swap5  
   c. Undefined  
   d. Undefined

27. Investing in a collection of assets whose returns do not always move together, with the result that overall risk is lower than for individual assets is referred to as _____.
   a. Thing  
   b. Diversification5  
   c. Undefined  
   d. Undefined

## Chapter 5. Analyzing Investing Activities: Special Topics

28. _____ refers to a corporation that owns a controlling interest of another corporation, called a subsidiary corporation.
    a. Parent corporation5
    b. Thing
    c. Undefined
    d. Undefined

29. _____ refer to representation of ownership rights to the corporation.
    a. Thing
    b. Equity securities5
    c. Undefined
    d. Undefined

30. A _____ is a legal construct through which the law allows a group of natural persons to act as if it were an individual for certain purposes. The most common purposes are lawsuits, property ownership, and contracts.
    a. Legal entity5
    b. Thing
    c. Undefined
    d. Undefined

31. A legal entity chartered by a state or the Federal government that is distinct and separate from the individuals who own it is a _____. This separation gives the _____ unique powers which other legal entities lack.
    a. Organization
    b. Corporation5
    c. Undefined
    d. Undefined

32. A company that is controlled by another company or corporation is a _____.
    a. Thing
    b. Subsidiary5
    c. Undefined
    d. Undefined

33. _____ refers to a claim on the borrower future income that is sold by the borrower to the lender. A _____ is a type of transferable interest representing financial value.
    a. Security5
    b. Thing
    c. Undefined
    d. Undefined

34. _____ is the name given to the set of legal principles, in countries following the English common law tradition, which supplement strict rules of law where their application would operate harshly, so as to achieve what is sometimes referred to as "natural justice."
    a. Thing
    b. Equity5
    c. Undefined
    d. Undefined

35. Local television stations that are associated with a major network are called _____. _____ agree to preempt time during specified hours for programming provided by the network and carry the advertising contained in the program.
    a. Thing
    b. Affiliates5
    c. Undefined
    d. Undefined

36. _____ refers to a summary of all the transactions that have occurred over a particular period.
    a. Financial statement5
    b. Thing
    c. Undefined
    d. Undefined

37. _____ refers to the entity that has a controlling influence over another company. It may have its own operations, or it may have been set up solely for the purpose of owning the Subject Company.

a. Parent company5  
b. Thing  
c. Undefined  
d. Undefined  

38. Method of accounting for investments in marketable equity securities; is required when the investor owns percent to percent of the investee company. The amount of investments carried under the _____ represents a measure of the book value of the investee rather than the cost or market value of the investment security.
    a. Thing  
    b. Equity method5  
    c. Undefined  
    d. Undefined  

39. A _____ refers to a financial statement of a parent company and its subsidiaries that has been combined into a single set of financial statements as if the companies were one.
    a. Consolidated financial statement5  
    b. Thing  
    c. Undefined  
    d. Undefined  

40. Refers to part of a transaction that involves an activity other than the exchange of cash. Providing a service or delivering goods would be considered the _____ of a transaction.
    a. Economic substance5  
    b. Thing  
    c. Undefined  
    d. Undefined  

41. _____ refers to a term used to signify that which may be assumed without proof, or taken for granted. It is asserted as a self-evident result of human reason and experience.
    a. Thing  
    b. Presumption5  
    c. Undefined  
    d. Undefined  

42. In finance and economics, _____ is the price paid by a borrower for the use of a lender's money. In other words, _____ is the amount of paid to "rent" money for a period of time.
    a. Thing  
    b. Interest5  
    c. Undefined  
    d. Undefined  

43. A subsidiary in which the firm owns 100 percent of the stock is a _____.
    a. Thing  
    b. Wholly owned subsidiary5  
    c. Undefined  
    d. Undefined  

44. _____ refers to the amount at which property would change hands between a willing buyer and a willing seller, neither being under any compulsion to buy or to sell, and both having reasonable knowledge of the relevant facts.
    a. Thing  
    b. Fair market value5  
    c. Undefined  
    d. Undefined  

45. The combination of two or more firms, generally of equal size and market power, to form an entirely new entity is a _____.
    a. Consolidation5  
    b. Thing  
    c. Undefined  
    d. Undefined  

46. A statement of the assets, liabilities, and net worth of a firm or individual at some given time often at the end of its "fiscal year," is referred to as a _____.

## Chapter 5. Analyzing Investing Activities: Special Topics 157

a. Thing
b. Balance sheet5
c. Undefined
d. Undefined

47. _____ refers to the price of an asset agreed on between a willing buyer and a willing seller; the price an asset could demand if it is sold on the open market.
a. Thing
b. Market value5
c. Undefined
d. Undefined

48. In banking and accountancy, the outstanding _____ is the amount of money owned, (or due), that remains in a deposit account (or a loan account) at a given date, after all past remittances, payments and withdrawal have been accounted for. It can be positive (then, in the _____ sheet of a firm, it is an asset) or negative (a liability).
a. Thing
b. Balance5
c. Undefined
d. Undefined

49. _____ refers to a financial statement that presents the revenues and expenses and resulting net income or net loss of a company for a specific period of time.
a. Income statement5
b. Thing
c. Undefined
d. Undefined

50. _____ refers to a system by which individuals can reduce their exposure to risk of large losses by spreading the risks among a large number of persons.
a. Insurance5
b. Thing
c. Undefined
d. Undefined

51. _____ refers to a recording as positive in the balance of payments, any transaction that gives rise to a payment into the country, such as an export, the sale of an asset, or borrowing from abroad.
a. Credit5
b. Thing
c. Undefined
d. Undefined

52. _____ refers to measures that are important to monitoring and tracking the effectiveness of a company's operations.
a. Thing
b. Operating results5
c. Undefined
d. Undefined

53. A _____ is a present obligation of the enterprise arizing from past events, the settlement of which is expected to result in an outflow from the enterprise of resources embodying economic benefits.
a. Thing
b. Liability5
c. Undefined
d. Undefined

54. That aspect of management concerned with the comparison of actual versus planned performance as well as the development and implementation of procedures to correct substandard performance is called _____.
a. Management control5
b. Thing
c. Undefined
d. Undefined

55. _____ refers to any distinct act of dominion wrongfully exerted over another's personal property in denial of or inconsistent with his rights therein. That tort committed by a person who deals with chattels not belonging to him in a manner that is inconsistent with the ownership of the lawful owner.
- a. Conversion5
- b. Thing
- c. Undefined
- d. Undefined

56. Similar to a script in that a _____ can be a less than completely rational decision-making method. Involves the use of a pre-existing set of decision steps for any problem that presents itself.
- a. Policy5
- b. Thing
- c. Undefined
- d. Undefined

57. A signed, written order by which one party instructs another party to pay a specified sum to a third party, at sight or at a specific date is a _____.
- a. Draft5
- b. Thing
- c. Undefined
- d. Undefined

58. Securities giving their holders the power to exchange those securities for other securities without paying any additional consideration are _____.
- a. Thing
- b. Convertible securities5
- c. Undefined
- d. Undefined

59. A _____ is a security that can be converted into another security, for example, a bond that under certain terms can be converted into equity.
- a. Convertible security5
- b. Thing
- c. Undefined
- d. Undefined

60. A person in possession of a document of title or an instrument payable or indorsed to him, his order, or to bearer is a _____.
- a. Holder5
- b. Thing
- c. Undefined
- d. Undefined

61. A partnership in which some of the partners are limited partners. At least one of the partners in a _____ must be a general partner.
- a. Limited partnership5
- b. Thing
- c. Undefined
- d. Undefined

62. An owner who has unlimited liability and is active in managing the firm is a _____. The individual or firm that organizes and manages the limited partnership. For example a hedge fund.
- a. General partner5
- b. Thing
- c. Undefined
- d. Undefined

63. In the common law, a _____ is a type of business entity in which partners share with each other the profits or losses of the business undertaking in which they have all invested.
- a. Thing
- b. Partnership5
- c. Undefined
- d. Undefined

## Chapter 5. Analyzing Investing Activities: Special Topics

64. _____ refers to the return to the resource entrepreneurial ability; total revenue minus total cost.
   a. Profit5
   b. Thing
   c. Undefined
   d. Undefined

65. _____ refers to an undertaking by two parties for a specific purpose and duration, taking any of several legal forms.
   a. Joint venture5
   b. Thing
   c. Undefined
   d. Undefined

66. _____ refers to restrictions state and federal laws place on business with regard to the conduct of its activities.
   a. Regulation5
   b. Thing
   c. Undefined
   d. Undefined

67. Corporate _____ occurs when corporations interact congruently. A corporate _____ refers to a financial benefit that a corporation expects to realize when it merges with or acquires another corporation.
   a. Synergy5
   b. Thing
   c. Undefined
   d. Undefined

68. A _____ is an individual or company (including a corporation) that legally owns one or more shares of stock in a joined stock company. The shareholders are the owners of a corporation. Companies listed at the stock market strive to enhance shareholder value.
   a. Thing
   b. Stockholder5
   c. Undefined
   d. Undefined

69. Assets defined in the broadest legal sense. _____ includes the unrealized receivables of a cash basis taxpayer, but not services rendered.
   a. Thing
   b. Property5
   c. Undefined
   d. Undefined

70. Loan origination fees that may be deductible as interest by a buyer of property. A seller of property who pays _____ reduces the selling price by the amount of the _____ paid for the buyer.
   a. Thing
   b. Points5
   c. Undefined
   d. Undefined

71. A _____ is the set of feasible allocations in an economy that cannot be improved upon by subset of the set of the economy's consumers (a coalition). In construction, when the force in an element is within a certain center section, the _____, the element will only be under compression.
   a. Thing
   b. Core5
   c. Undefined
   d. Undefined

72. The _____ is the amount by which expenditure exceed revenue.
   a. Deficit5
   b. Thing
   c. Undefined
   d. Undefined

73. _____ refers to consisting of virtually the same elements as portfolio income, a measure by which to justify a deduction for interest on investment indebtedness. Income derived from investments.

## Chapter 5. Analyzing Investing Activities: Special Topics

a. Investment income5  
b. Thing  
c. Undefined  
d. Undefined

74. _____ in contract law, a basic requirement for an enforceable agreement under traditional contract principles, defined in this text as legal value, bargained for and given in exchange for an act or promise. In corporation law, cash or property contributed to a corporation in exchange for shares, or a promise to contribute such cash or property.
a. Thing  
b. Consideration5  
c. Undefined  
d. Undefined

75. _____ refers to cash flow activities that include purchasing and disposing of investments and productive long-lived assets using cash and lending money and collecting on those loans.
a. Thing  
b. Investing activities5  
c. Undefined  
d. Undefined

76. _____ in agency law, refers to an agent's ability to affect his principal's legal relations with third parties. Also used to refer to an actor's legal power or ability to do something. In addition, sometimes used to refer to a statute, case, or other legal source that justifies a particular result.
a. Concept  
b. Authority5  
c. Undefined  
d. Undefined

77. Amount of corporate profits paid out for each share of stock is referred to as _____.
a. Thing  
b. Dividend5  
c. Undefined  
d. Undefined

78. Refers to the many different actions of people, subgroups, and whole countries that have the potential to affect the financial status of a firm is called _____.
a. Political risk5  
b. Thing  
c. Undefined  
d. Undefined

79. _____ generally refers to financial wealth, especially that used to start or maintain a business. In classical economics, _____ is one of four factors of production, the others being land and labor and entrepreneurship.
a. Thing  
b. Capital5  
c. Undefined  
d. Undefined

80. A measure of the amount of debt used in the capital structure of the firm is the _____.
a. Financial leverage5  
b. Thing  
c. Undefined  
d. Undefined

81. _____ is using given resources in such a way that the potential positive or negative outcome is magnified. In finance, this generally refers to borrowing.
a. Leverage5  
b. Thing  
c. Undefined  
d. Undefined

82. The accountant's concept of income is generally based upon the realization principle. Financial _____ may differ from taxable income. Differences are included in a reconciliation of taxable and _____ on Schedule M-1 of Form 1120.

| a. Thing | b. Accounting income5 |
| c. Undefined | d. Undefined |

83. _____ occurs, among other instances, when one corporation acquires another in a merger or acquisition, a single corporation divides into two or more entities, or a corporation makes a substantial change in its capital structure.
| a. Reorganization5 | b. Thing |
| c. Undefined | d. Undefined |

84. _____ is the corporate management term for the act of partially dismantling and reorganizing a company for the purpose of making it more efficient and therefore more profitable.
| a. Restructuring5 | b. Thing |
| c. Undefined | d. Undefined |

85. An _____ is any factor (financial or non-financial) that provides a motive for a particular course of action, or counts as a reason for preferring one choice to the alternatives.
| a. Thing | b. Incentive5 |
| c. Undefined | d. Undefined |

86. In economics, returns to scale and _____ are related terms that describe what happens as the scale of production increases. They are different terms and not to be used interchangeably.
| a. Economies of scale5 | b. Thing |
| c. Undefined | d. Undefined |

87. Individuals and firms involved in the process of making a product or service available for use or consumption by consumers or industrial users is a _____.
| a. Thing | b. Marketing channel5 |
| c. Undefined | d. Undefined |

88. That fraction of an industry's output accounted for by an individual firm or group of firms is called _____.
| a. Market share5 | b. Thing |
| c. Undefined | d. Undefined |

89. The body of knowledge and techniques that can be used to combine economic resources to produce goods and services is called _____.
| a. Technology5 | b. Thing |
| c. Undefined | d. Undefined |

90. Promoting and selling products or services to customers, or prospective customers, is referred to as _____.
| a. Marketing5 | b. Thing |
| c. Undefined | d. Undefined |

91. The income, expenditures, and resources that affect the cost of running a business and household are called an _____.
| a. Economy5 | b. Thing |
| c. Undefined | d. Undefined |

92. _____, in communications (sometimes called communications _____), refers to the medium used to convey information from a sender (or transmitter) to a receiver.
   a. Channel5
   b. Thing
   c. Undefined
   d. Undefined

93. _____ refers to a location, often decentralized, that a firm uses to store, consolidate, age, or mix stock; house product-recall programs; or ease tax burdens.
   a. Thing
   b. Warehouse5
   c. Undefined
   d. Undefined

94. A long-lasting, sometimes permanent team in the organization structure created to deal with tasks that recur regularly is the _____.
   a. Committee5
   b. Thing
   c. Undefined
   d. Undefined

95. _____ refer to shareholders who claim the residual profits and assets of a corporation, and usually have the exclusive power and right to elect the directors of the corporation.
   a. Thing
   b. Common shareholders5
   c. Undefined
   d. Undefined

96. A _____ is an individual or company (including a corporation) that legally owns one or more shares of stock in a joined stock company.
   a. Thing
   b. Shareholder5
   c. Undefined
   d. Undefined

97. _____ is the branch of accountancy concerned with the preparation of financial statements for external decision makers, such as stockholders, suppliers, banks and government agencies. The fundamental need for _____ is to reduce principal-agent problem by measuring and monitoring agents' performance.
   a. Thing
   b. Financial accounting5
   c. Undefined
   d. Undefined

98. Assets that have special rights but not physical substance are referred to as _____.
   a. Intangible assets5
   b. Thing
   c. Undefined
   d. Undefined

99. An intangible assets is defined as an asset that is not physical in nature. The most common types are trade secrets (e.g., customer lists and know-how), copyrights, patents, trademarks, and goodwill.
   a. Thing
   b. Intangible asset5
   c. Undefined
   d. Undefined

100. _____ refers to the private sector body given the primary responsibility to work out the detailed rules that become generally accepted accounting principles.
   a. Financial accounting standards board5
   b. Thing
   c. Undefined
   d. Undefined

## Chapter 5. Analyzing Investing Activities: Special Topics

101. _____ refers to a set of standards that dictate accounting rules concerning financial reporting; establish generally accepted accounting principles.
- a. Thing
- b. Financial accounting Standards5
- c. Undefined
- d. Undefined

102. The role of the _____ is to issue accounting standards in the United Kingdom. It is recognized for that purpose under the Companies Act 1985. It took over the task of setting accounting standards from the Accounting Standards Committee (ASC) in 1990.
- a. Accounting Standards Board5
- b. Organization
- c. Undefined
- d. Undefined

103. Having a physical existence is referred to as the _____. Personal property other than real estate, such as cars, boats, stocks, or other assets.
- a. Tangible5
- b. Thing
- c. Undefined
- d. Undefined

104. _____ is a concept used in finance and economics, defined as a rational and unbiased estimate of the potential market price of a good, service, or asset.
- a. Fair value5
- b. Thing
- c. Undefined
- d. Undefined

105. _____ refers to the basic, normal, voting stock issued by a corporation; called residual equity because it ranks after preferred stock for dividend and liquidation distributions.
- a. Thing
- b. Common stock5
- c. Undefined
- d. Undefined

106. The central value of a pegged exchange rate, around which the actual rate is permitted to fluctuate within set bounds is a _____.
- a. Par value5
- b. Thing
- c. Undefined
- d. Undefined

107. _____ refer to an equity security, representing a shareholder's ownership of a corporation. _____ are one of a finite number of equal portions in the capital of a company, entitling the owner to a proportion of distributed, non-reinvested profits known as dividends and to a portion of the value of the company in case of liquidation.
- a. Thing
- b. Shares5
- c. Undefined
- d. Undefined

108. _____ is a measure of the position of a company or product on a market.
- a. Market position5
- b. Thing
- c. Undefined
- d. Undefined

109. _____ is an economic concept with commonplace familiarity; it is the price that a good or service is offered at, or will fetch, in the marketplace; it is of interest mainly in the study of microeconomics.
- a. Thing
- b. Market price5
- c. Undefined
- d. Undefined

110. A distinctive word, name, symbol, device, or combination thereof, which enables consumers to identify favored products or services and which may find protection under state or federal law is a _____.
   a. Thing
   b. Trademark5
   c. Undefined
   d. Undefined

111. _____ refers to the method under which income and expenses are determined for tax purposes. Important accounting methods include the cash basis and the accrual basis.
   a. Accounting method5
   b. Thing
   c. Undefined
   d. Undefined

112. _____ refers to a summary of all the data in the account ledgers to show whether the figures are correct and balanced.
   a. Thing
   b. Trial balance5
   c. Undefined
   d. Undefined

113. An examination before a competent tribunal, according to the law of the land, of the facts or law put in issue in a cause, for the purpose of determining such issue is a _____. When the court hears and determines any issue of fact or law for the purpose of determining the rights of the parties, it may be considered a _____.
   a. Thing
   b. Trial5
   c. Undefined
   d. Undefined

114. _____ refers to portion of the assets remaining after the creditors' claims have been satisfied; also called equity or residual interest.
   a. Net assets5
   b. Thing
   c. Undefined
   d. Undefined

115. Systematic and rational allocation of the acquisition cost of an intangible asset over its useful life is referred to as _____.
   a. Amortization5
   b. Thing
   c. Undefined
   d. Undefined

116. _____ is an accounting and finance term for the method of attributing the cost of an asset across the useful life of the asset. _____ is a reduction in the value of a currency in floating exchange rate.
   a. Depreciation5
   b. Thing
   c. Undefined
   d. Undefined

117. _____ refers to the amount recognized as an expense in one period resulting from the periodic recognition of the used portion of the cost of a long-term tangible asset over its life.
   a. Thing
   b. Depreciation expense5
   c. Undefined
   d. Undefined

118. Cash provided by operating activities adjusted for capital expenditures and dividends paid is referred to as _____.
   a. Thing
   b. Free cash flow5
   c. Undefined
   d. Undefined

## Chapter 5. Analyzing Investing Activities: Special Topics

119. The sum of fixed cost and variable cost is referred to as _____.
   a. Total cost5
   b. Thing
   c. Undefined
   d. Undefined

120. The value today of a stream of payments and/or receipts over time in the future and/or the past, converted to the present using an interest rate. If X t is the amount in period t and r the interest rate, then _____ at time t=0 is V = ?T /t.
   a. Present value5
   b. Thing
   c. Undefined
   d. Undefined

121. The rate of return on bonds, loans, or deposits. When one speaks of 'the' _____, it is usually in a model where there is only one.
   a. Interest rate5
   b. Thing
   c. Undefined
   d. Undefined

122. Type of security acquired by loaning assets is called a _____.
   a. Thing
   b. Debt security5
   c. Undefined
   d. Undefined

123. The difference between the face value of a bond and its selling price, when a bond is sold for less than its face value it's referred to as a _____.
   a. Thing
   b. Discount5
   c. Undefined
   d. Undefined

124. _____ refers to the fee charged by an insurance company for an insurance policy. The rate of losses must be relatively predictable: In order to set the _____ (prices) insurers must be able to estimate them accurately.
   a. Premium5
   b. Thing
   c. Undefined
   d. Undefined

125. Stock that has specified rights over common stock is a _____.
   a. Preferred stock5
   b. Thing
   c. Undefined
   d. Undefined

126. The trade of things of value between buyer and seller so that each is better off after the trade is called the _____.
   a. Exchange5
   b. Thing
   c. Undefined
   d. Undefined

127. _____ is the process whereby interested parties resolve disputes, agree upon courses of action, bargain for individual or collective advantage, and/or attempt to craft outcomes which serve their mutual interests.
   a. Negotiation5
   b. Thing
   c. Undefined
   d. Undefined

128. _____ refers to the assignment of income for various tax purposes. A multistate corporation's nonbusiness income usually is distributed to the state where the nonbusiness assets are located; it is not apportioned with the rest of the entity's income.

a. Thing  
b. Allocate5  
c. Undefined  
d. Undefined  

129. Assets that have physical substance that cannot easily be converted into cash are referd to as a _____.
a. Thing  
b. Tangible asset5  
c. Undefined  
d. Undefined  

130. A _____ is a "promise" or an "agreement" that is enforced or recognized by the law. In the civil law, a _____ is considered to be part of the general law of obligations.
a. Thing  
b. Contract5  
c. Undefined  
d. Undefined  

131. An arrangement whereby someone with a good idea for a business sells the rights to use the business name and sell a product or service to others in a given territory is a _____.
a. Thing  
b. Franchise agreement5  
c. Undefined  
d. Undefined  

132. _____ refers to paid, nonpersonal communication through various media by organizations and individuals who are in some way identified in the _____ message.
a. Thing  
b. Advertising5  
c. Undefined  
d. Undefined  

133. _____ is a form of strategic alliance which involves the sale of a right to use certain proprietary knowledge (so called intellectual property) in a defined way.
a. Thing  
b. Licensing5  
c. Undefined  
d. Undefined  

134. A contractual right to sell certain products or services, use certain trademarks, or perform activities in a geographical region is called a _____.
a. Thing  
b. Franchise5  
c. Undefined  
d. Undefined  

135. A contract for the possession and use of land or other property, including goods, on one side, and a recompense of rent or other income on the other is the _____.
a. Thing  
b. Lease5  
c. Undefined  
d. Undefined  

136. _____ refers to a secret formula, pattern, process, program, device, method, technique, or compilation of information that is used in its owner's business and affords that owner a competitive advantage. Trade secrets are protected by state law.
a. Thing  
b. Trade secret5  
c. Undefined  
d. Undefined  

137. The legal right to the proceeds from and control over the use of an invented product or process, granted for a fixed period of time, usually 20 years. _____ is one form of intellectual property that is subject of the TRIPS agreement.

## Chapter 5. Analyzing Investing Activities: Special Topics

a. Patent5  
b. Thing  
c. Undefined  
d. Undefined  

138. The length of service of a productive facility or piece of equipment is its _____. The period of time during which an asset will have economic value and be usable.
a. Useful life5  
b. Thing  
c. Undefined  
d. Undefined  

139. _____ refer to securities that are readily traded in the secondary securities market.
a. Marketable securities5  
b. Thing  
c. Undefined  
d. Undefined  

140. _____ are those assets usually in service over one year such as buildings, equipment, and long-term investments. These often receive favorable tax treatment over current assets. Tangible long-term assets are usually referred to as fixed assets.
a. Noncurrent assets5  
b. Thing  
c. Undefined  
d. Undefined  

141. Capable of being lawfully assigned or transferred to another is the _____.
a. Assignable5  
b. Thing  
c. Undefined  
d. Undefined  

142. A _____ in the sphere of Intellectual Property Rights (IPR) is a document, contract or agreement giving permission or the 'right' to a legally-definable entity to do something (such as manufacture a product or to use a service), or to apply something (such as a trademark), with the objective of achieving commercial gain.
a. Thing  
b. License5  
c. Undefined  
d. Undefined  

143. A name, symbol, or design that identifies the goods or services of one seller or group of sellers and distinguishes them from the goods and services of competitors is a _____.
a. Brand5  
b. Thing  
c. Undefined  
d. Undefined  

144. The use of resources for the deliberate discovery of new information and ways of doing things, together with the application of that information in inventing new products or processes Is referred to as _____.
a. Thing  
b. Research and development5  
c. Undefined  
d. Undefined  

145. _____ refers to the long-term movement of an economic variable, such as its average rate of increase or decrease over enough years to encompass several business cycles.
a. Trend5  
b. Thing  
c. Undefined  
d. Undefined  

146. In its most extensive meaning, it is a charge on property for the payment or discharge of a debt or duty is referred to as _____.

a. Thing  
c. Undefined  
b. Lien5  
d. Undefined  

147. A person to whom a debt or legal obligation is owed, and who has the right to enforce payment of that debt or obligation is referred to as _____.
   a. Thing  
   c. Undefined  
   b. Creditor5  
   d. Undefined  

148. In finance, _____ occurs when a debtor has not met its legal obligations according to the debt contract, e.g. it has not made a scheduled payment, or violated a covenant (condition) of the debt contract.
   a. Thing  
   c. Undefined  
   b. Default5  
   d. Undefined  

149. _____ is the difference between the intrinsic value of a stock (i.e. value based on stock valuation and what the company is actually worth) and the price that the market sets on a stock (i.e. stock price is a matter of market participants' opinions and is different from the intrinsic value).
   a. Thing  
   c. Undefined  
   b. Margin of safety5  
   d. Undefined  

150. A deposit by a buyer in stocks with a seller or a stockbroker, as security to cover fluctuations in the market in reference to stocks that the buyer has purchased but for which he has not paid is a _____. Commodities are also traded on _____.
   a. Margin5  
   c. Undefined  
   b. Thing  
   d. Undefined  

151. Firms in the process of becoming publicly traded companies will issue shares of stock using an _____, which is merely the process of selling stock for the first time to interested investors.
   a. Thing  
   c. Undefined  
   b. Initial public offering5  
   d. Undefined  

152. The _____ is a court's determination of a matter of law based on the issue presented in the particular case. In other words: under this law, with these facts, this result.
   a. Holding5  
   c. Undefined  
   b. Thing  
   d. Undefined  

153. Cumulative earnings of a company that are not distributed to the owners and are reinvested in the business are called _____.
   a. Thing  
   c. Undefined  
   b. Retained earnings5  
   d. Undefined  

154. _____ is equal to the income that a firm has after subtracting costs and expenses from the total revenue. Expenses will typically include tax expense.
   a. Net income5  
   c. Undefined  
   b. Thing  
   d. Undefined

## Chapter 5. Analyzing Investing Activities: Special Topics

155. _____ refers to the total revenues or sales mentioned in the income statement. This refers to the fact that the total revenues collected by a company appears at the top of the income statement. This is in contrast to the net profit that is calculated after subtracting the net expenses. Since this forms the last line of the income statement, it is generally referred to the bottom line.
- a. Thing
- b. Top line5
- c. Undefined
- d. Undefined

156. _____ refers to the total amount owed by the Federal government to the owners of government securities; equal to the sum of past government budget deficits less government budget surpluses.
- a. Thing
- b. Public debt5
- c. Undefined
- d. Undefined

157. _____ refers to a debt that can reasonably be expected to be paid from existing current assets or through the creation of other current liabilities, within one year or the operating cycle, whichever is longer.
- a. Current liability5
- b. Thing
- c. Undefined
- d. Undefined

158. A _____ is an asset on the balance sheet which is expected to be sold or otherwise used up in the near future, usually within one year.
- a. Current asset5
- b. Thing
- c. Undefined
- d. Undefined

159. _____ refers to the combining of two or more things into a single category. Data on international trade necessarily aggregate goods and services into manageable groups.
- a. Aggregation5
- b. Thing
- c. Undefined
- d. Undefined

160. An _____ is prepared by corporate management that presents financial information including financial statements, footnotes, and the management discussion and analysis.
- a. Thing
- b. Annual report5
- c. Undefined
- d. Undefined

161. _____ originated with the Mr. Potato Head toy. Mr. Potato Head was the invention of George Lerner in the late 1940s. The idea was originally sold to a breakfast cereal manufacturer so that the separate parts could be distributed as cereal package premiums.
- a. Hasbro5
- b. Thing
- c. Undefined
- d. Undefined

162. _____ (NYSE: AA) is the world's leading producer of alumina, primary and fabricated aluminum, with operations in 43 countries. (It is followed in this by a former subsidiary, Alcan, the second-leading producer.)
- a. Organization
- b. Alcoa5
- c. Undefined
- d. Undefined

163. _____ payments can refer to an ongoing stream of payments in respect of the completion of past achievements.

## Chapter 5. Analyzing Investing Activities: Special Topics

a. Thing
b. Residual5
c. Undefined
d. Undefined

164. _____ is an American stock investor, businessman and philanthropist. Nicknamed the "Oracle of Omaha" or the "Sage of Omaha", he has amassed an enormous fortune from astute investments, particularly through his company Berkshire Hathaway, in which he holds a greater than 38% stake.
a. Warren Buffett5
b. Person
c. Undefined
d. Undefined

165. A _____ is an underhand method used by companies to enhance the appearance of a company's future performance. The company writes off assets as much as possible to the profit and loss account in the current period in order ot show increase profits and return on investment in future periods.
a. Thing
b. Big bath5
c. Undefined
d. Undefined

166. A market in which no buyer or seller has market power is called a _____.
a. Thing
b. Competitive market5
c. Undefined
d. Undefined

167. The consumer's appraisal of the product or brand on important attributes is called _____.
a. Thing
b. Evaluation5
c. Undefined
d. Undefined

168. A _____ acts as an agent that provides financial services for its clients. Financial institutions generally fall under financial regulation from a government authority.
a. Thing
b. Financial institution5
c. Undefined
d. Undefined

169. In 2000 Philip Morris Companies acquired _____; that acquisition was approved by the Federal Trade Commission subject to the divestiture of products in five areas: three Jell-O and Royal brands types of products (dry-mix gelatin dessert, dry-mix pudding, no-bake desserts), intense mints (such as Altoids), and baking powder. Kraft later purchased the company.
a. Organization
b. Nabisco5
c. Undefined
d. Undefined

170. _____ is the term used to describe income received based on the production of those others who have become members of one's organization.
a. Residual income5
b. Thing
c. Undefined
d. Undefined

171. _____ indicates that a party, or proprietor, exercises private ownership, control or use over an item of property, usually to the exclusion of other parties. Where a party, holds or claims _____ interests in relation to certain types of property (eg. a creative literary work, or software), that property may also be the subject of intellectual property law (eg. copyright or patents).

a. Thing
b. Proprietary5
c. Undefined
d. Undefined

172. _____ refers to the standard framework of guidelines for financial accounting. It includes the standards, conventions, and rules accountants follow in recording and summarizing transactions, and in the preparation of financial statements.
a. Thing
b. Generally accepted accounting principles5
c. Undefined
d. Undefined

173. _____, is the world's largest commercial tobacco company by sales. _____ was begun by a London tobacconist of the same name. He was one of the first people to sell hand-rolled cigarettes in the 1860s, selling them under the brand names Oxford and Cambridge Blues, following the adoption of cigarette smoking by British soldiers returning from the Crimean War.
a. Organization
b. Philip Morris5
c. Undefined
d. Undefined

174. In accounting terminology, _____ describes the original cost of an asset at the time of purchase or payment as opposed to its market value
a. Thing
b. Historical cost5
c. Undefined
d. Undefined

175. _____, also known as property, plant, and equipment (PP&E), is a term used in accountancy for assets and property which cannot easily be converted into cash. This can be compared with current assets such as cash or bank accounts, which are described as liquid assets. In most cases, only tangible assets are referred to as fixed.
a. Fixed asset5
b. Thing
c. Undefined
d. Undefined

176. The interest rate that equates a future value or an annuity to a given present value is a _____.
a. Thing
b. Yield5
c. Undefined
d. Undefined

177. In accounting, the _____ describes the direct expenses incurred in producing a particular good for sale, including the actual cost of materials that comprise the good, and direct labor expense in putting the good in salable condition.
a. Cost of goods sold5
b. Thing
c. Undefined
d. Undefined

178. Tangible property held for sale in the normal course of business or used in producing goods or services for sale is an _____.
a. Inventory5
b. Thing
c. Undefined
d. Undefined

179. _____ refers to the return a businessperson gets on the money he and other owners invest in the firm; for example, a business that earned $100 on a $1,000 investment would have a ROI of 10 percent: 100 divided by 1000.

a. Return on investment5  
b. Thing  
c. Undefined  
d. Undefined

180. An _____ is a company offering debit and credit card acceptance services for merchants. Often the company is partially or wholly owned by a bank, sometimes a bank itself offers acquiring services.
a. Thing  
b. Acquirer5  
c. Undefined  
d. Undefined

181. A _____ refers to a role in the buying center with formal authority and responsibility to select the supplier and negotiate the terms of the contract.
a. Thing  
b. Buyer5  
c. Undefined  
d. Undefined

182. A _____ is a ratio of two numbers of reported levels or flows of a company. It may be two financial flows categories divided by each other (profit margin, profit/revenue). It may be a level divided by a financial flow (price/earnings). It may be a flow divided by a level (return on equity or earnings/equity). The numerator or denominator may itself be a ratio (PEG ratio).
a. Thing  
b. Financial ratio5  
c. Undefined  
d. Undefined

183. _____ refers to the regional and economic differences in a country, province, state, or continent
a. Thing  
b. Disparity5  
c. Undefined  
d. Undefined

184. _____ refers to the final payment date of a loan or other financial instrument, after which point no further interest or principal need be paid.
a. Thing  
b. Maturity5  
c. Undefined  
d. Undefined

185. _____ refers to annual profit of the corporation divided by the number of shares outstanding.
a. Thing  
b. Earnings per share5  
c. Undefined  
d. Undefined

186. The universal label that political actors wrap around the policies and programs that they advocate is referred to as _____.
a. Public interest5  
b. Thing  
c. Undefined  
d. Undefined

187. A _____ is a steady income given to a person (usually after retirement). Pensions are typically payments made in the form of a guaranteed annuity to a retired or disabled employee.
a. Pension5  
b. Thing  
c. Undefined  
d. Undefined

188. In finance, _____ means currencies, such as U.S. Dollars and Euros. These are traded on _____ markets.

## Chapter 5. Analyzing Investing Activities: Special Topics

a. Thing
c. Undefined
b. Foreign exchange5
d. Undefined

189. _____ is an American electronic stock exchange. It was founded in 1971 by the National Association of Securities Dealers who divested it in a series of sales in 2000 and 2001.
a. NASDAQ5
c. Undefined
b. Thing
d. Undefined

190. The _____ represents the external conditions under which people are engaged in, and benefit from, economic activity. It includes aspects of economic status, paid employment, and finances.
a. Economic environment5
c. Undefined
b. Thing
d. Undefined

191. _____ refers to a written statement-also called an accountant's certificate, accountant's opinion, or audit report- prepared by an independent accountant or auditor after an audit.
a. Financial report5
c. Undefined
b. Thing
d. Undefined

192. _____ refers to system of rules that regulate behavior and the processes by which the laws of a country are enforced and through which redress of grievances is obtained.
a. Thing
c. Undefined
b. Legal system5
d. Undefined

193. _____ refers to the minimum amount a depository institution must keep on deposit with the Federal Reserve Bank in its district or must hold as vault cash. _____ is expressed as a percent of demand deposits.
a. Legal reserve5
c. Undefined
b. Thing
d. Undefined

194. _____ refers to pro rata distributions of stock or stock rights on common stock. They are usually issued in proportion to shares owned.
a. Thing
c. Undefined
b. Stock dividend5
d. Undefined

195. _____ refers to a method of financial recording for mergers, in which the financial statements of the firms are combined, subject to minor adjustments, and goodwill is not created.
a. Thing
c. Undefined
b. Pooling of interests5
d. Undefined

196. _____ refers to the legal requirement that anyone seeking to challenge a particular action in court must demonstrate that such action substantially affects his legitimate interests before he will be entitled to bring suit.
a. Standing5
c. Undefined
b. Thing
d. Undefined

197. The extent to which a source is perceived as having knowledge, skill, or experience relevant to a communication topic and can be trusted to give an unbiased opinion or present objective information on the issue is called _____.

a. Credibility5  b. Thing
c. Undefined  d. Undefined

198. An organization that employs resources to produce a good or service for profit and owns and operates one or more plants is referred to as a _____.
a. Thing  b. Firm5
c. Undefined  d. Undefined

199. A _____ is an employee of an organization with some of the powers and responsibilities of management, occupying a role between true manager and a regular employee. A _____ position is typically the first step towards being promoted into a management role.
a. Supervisor5  b. Thing
c. Undefined  d. Undefined

200. _____ refers to a debt instrument, issued by a borrower and promising a specified stream of payments to the purchaser, usually regular interest payments plus a final repayment of principal.
a. Bond5  b. Thing
c. Undefined  d. Undefined

201. A company owned in a foreign country by another company is referred to as _____.
a. Thing  b. Foreign subsidiary5
c. Undefined  d. Undefined

202. _____ refers to translating assets valued in a foreign currency into the home currency using the exchange rate that existed when the assets were originally purchased.
a. Thing  b. Temporal method5
c. Undefined  d. Undefined

203. _____ refers to the currency of the economic environment in which the taxpayer carries on most of its activities, and in which the taxpayer transacts most of its business.
a. Functional currency5  b. Thing
c. Undefined  d. Undefined

204. Using the exchange rate at the balance sheet date to translate the financial statements of a foreign subsidiary into the home currency is referred to as _____.
a. Current rate method5  b. Thing
c. Undefined  d. Undefined

205. The percentage increase in the price level per year is an _____. Alternatively, the _____ is the rate of decrease in the purchasing power of money.
a. Thing  b. Inflation rate5
c. Undefined  d. Undefined

206. An increase in the overall price level of an economy, usually as measured by the CPI or by the implicit price deflator is called _____.

a. Thing
b. Inflation5
c. Undefined
d. Undefined

207. _____ refers to net income plus unrealized gain or loss on securities, minimum pension liability adjustment, and foreign currency translation adjustment.
a. Thing
b. Comprehensive income5
c. Undefined
d. Undefined

208. A _____ refers to a layout accurate in size, color, scheme, and other necessary details to show how a final ad will look. For presentation only, never for reproduction.
a. Thing
b. Comprehensive5
c. Undefined
d. Undefined

209. Firms that own production facilities in two or more countries and produce and sell their products globally are referred to as _____.
a. Multinational corporations5
b. Thing
c. Undefined
d. Undefined

210. An organization that manufactures and markets products in many different countries and has multinational stock ownership and multinational management is referred to as _____.
a. Multinational corporation5
b. Thing
c. Undefined
d. Undefined

211. _____ refers to the price at which one country's currency trades for another, typically on the exchange market.
a. Exchange rate5
b. Thing
c. Undefined
d. Undefined

212. The _____ unit cost of the goods available for sale for both cost of goods sold and ending inventory.
a. Weighted average5
b. Thing
c. Undefined
d. Undefined

213. _____ refers to a process whereby the assets of a business are converted to money. The conversion may be coerced by a legal process to pay off the debt of the business, or to satisfy any other business obligation that the business has not voluntarily satisfied.
a. Thing
b. Liquidation5
c. Undefined
d. Undefined

214. _____ is one of a series of accounting transactions dealing with the billing of customers which owe money to a person, company or organization for goods and services that have been provided to the customer. This is typically done in a one person organization by writing an invoice and mailing or delivering it to each customer.
a. Thing
b. Accounts receivable5
c. Undefined
d. Undefined

215. Obligations to make future economic sacrifices, usually cash payments, are referred to as _____. Same as current liabilities.

a. Thing
b. Payables5
c. Undefined
d. Undefined

216. In throughput accounting, the cost accounting aspect of Theory of Constraints (TOC), _____ is the money spent turning inventory into throughput. In TOC, _____ is limited to costs that vary strictly with the quantity produced, like raw materials and purchased components.
a. Thing
b. Operating expense5
c. Undefined
d. Undefined

217. _____ refers to the price paid in one's own money to acquire 1 unit of a foreign currency; the rate at which the money of one nation is exchanged for the money of another nation.
a. Thing
b. Rate of exchange5
c. Undefined
d. Undefined

218. The total amount of physical capital that has been accumulated, usually in a country is _____. Also refers to the total issued capital of a firm, including ordinary and preferred shares.
a. Thing
b. Capital stock5
c. Undefined
d. Undefined

219. The term _____ is commonly used to describe business and market activity in industrializing or emerging regions of the world. It is sometimes loosely used as a replacement for emerging economies, but really signifies a business phenomenon that is not fully described by or constrained to geography or economic strength; such countries are considered to be in a transitional phase between developing and developed status.
a. Thing
b. Emerging markets5
c. Undefined
d. Undefined

220. The term _____ is commonly used to describe business and market activity in industrializing or emerging regions of the world.
a. Emerging market5
b. Thing
c. Undefined
d. Undefined

221. _____ was founded in Germany on January 22, 1870 as a specialist bank for foreign trade. Major projects in its first decades included the Northern Pacific Railroad in the United States (1883) and the Baghdad Railway (1888). It also financed bond offerings of the steel concern Krupp (1885) and introduced the chemical company Bayer on the Berlin stock market.
a. Organization
b. Deutsche Bank5
c. Undefined
d. Undefined

222. In economics, _____ refers to an activity of spending which increases the availability of fixed capital goods or means of production. It is the total spending on new fixed investment minus replacement investment, which simply replaces depreciated capital goods.
a. Net investment5
b. Thing
c. Undefined
d. Undefined

223. The technical sophistication of the product and hence the amount of understanding required to use it is referred to as _____. It is the opposite of simplicity.

## Chapter 5. Analyzing Investing Activities: Special Topics

a. Complexity5
c. Undefined

b. Thing
d. Undefined

224. _____ measures and reports financial and nonfinancial information relating to the cost of acquiring or consuming resources in an organization. It provides information for both management accounting and financial accounting.
a. Thing
c. Undefined

b. Cost accounting5
d. Undefined

225. _____ refers to an out-of-court settlement in which creditors agree to allow the firm more time to meet its financial obligations. A new repayment schedule will be developed, subject to the acceptance of creditors.
a. Extension5
c. Undefined

b. Thing
d. Undefined

226. _____ refers to a process of offsetting risk. In the foreign exchange market, hedgers use the forward market to cover a transaction or open position and thereby reduce exchange risk. The term applies most commonly to trade.
a. Hedge5
c. Undefined

b. Thing
d. Undefined

227. _____ refers to a very rapid rise in the price level; an extremely high rate of inflation.
a. Thing
c. Undefined

b. Hyperinflation5
d. Undefined

228. Total shareholders' equity divided by the number of outstanding common shares is referred to as _____.
a. Thing
c. Undefined

b. Book value per share5
d. Undefined

229. _____ refers to money raized from within the firm or through the sale of ownership in the firm.
a. Thing
c. Undefined

b. Equity capital5
d. Undefined

230. A _____ is a signed written agreement between two or more parties. Also referred to as a contract.
a. Thing
c. Undefined

b. Covenant5
d. Undefined

231. A management function that involves determining whether or not an organization is progressing toward its goals and objectives, and taking corrective action if it is not is called _____.
a. Controlling5
c. Undefined

b. Thing
d. Undefined

232. The _____ measures the size of a company's after-tax income, excluding non-cash depreciation expenses, as compared to the firm's total debt obligations. It is used to gauge a company's ability to meet long term obligations.
a. Thing
c. Undefined

b. Solvency ratio5
d. Undefined

233. The ability of a company to pay interest as it comes due and to repay the face value of debt at maturity is called _____.

a. Solvency5  
b. Thing  
c. Undefined  
d. Undefined

234. _____ refers to a financial organization that specializes in selling primary offerings of securities. Investment bankers can also perform other financial functions, such as advising clients, negotiating mergers and takeovers, and selling secondary offerings.
a. Investment banker5  
b. Thing  
c. Undefined  
d. Undefined

235. _____ refers to rating of bonds according to risk by Standard & Poor's and Moody's Investor Service. A bond that is rated A by Moody's has the lowest risk, while a bond with a C rating has the highest risk. Coupon rates are greatly influenced by a corporation's bond rating.
a. Bond ratings5  
b. Thing  
c. Undefined  
d. Undefined

236. An examination of the financial reports to ensure that they represent what they claim and conform with generally accepted accounting principles is referred to as _____.
a. Audit5  
b. Thing  
c. Undefined  
d. Undefined

237. A firm has a _____ in another business entity when it owns more than 50 percent of that entity's voting stock.
a. Thing  
b. Controlling interest5  
c. Undefined  
d. Undefined

238. A _____ is a stretch of time when an individual is eligible to receive benefits. The duration of benefits refers to the number of weeks the benefits will continue as long as the individual remains eligible. It is based on the number of hours worked in the 52 weeks before the lay-off and on the regional unemployment rate.
a. Benefit period5  
b. Thing  
c. Undefined  
d. Undefined

239. Book of original entry, in which transactions are recorded in a general ledger system, is referred to as a _____.
a. Journal5  
b. Thing  
c. Undefined  
d. Undefined

240. A _____ is a 12-month period used for calculating annual ("yearly") financial reports in businesses and other organizations. In many jurisdictions, regulatory laws regarding accounting require such reports once per twelve months, but do not require that the twelve months constitute a calendar year (i.e. January to December).
a. Fiscal year5  
b. Thing  
c. Undefined  
d. Undefined

241. _____ refers to usually the first stage in the creative process. It includes education and formal training.
a. Preparation5  
b. Thing  
c. Undefined  
d. Undefined

242. Reduction in the selling price of goods extended to the buyer because the goods are defective or of lower quality than the buyer ordered and to encourage a buyer to keep merchandise that would otherwise be returned is the _____.

## Chapter 5. Analyzing Investing Activities: Special Topics

a. Allowance5  
b. Thing  
c. Undefined  
d. Undefined  

243. The common currency of a subset of the countries of the EU, adopted January 1, 1999 is called _____.
a. Euro5  
b. Thing  
c. Undefined  
d. Undefined  

244. Ending inventory and cost of goods sold determined at the end of the accounting period based on a physical inventory count is referred to as _____.
a. Thing  
b. Periodic inventory system5  
c. Undefined  
d. Undefined  

245. _____ refers to a liability that results from the execution of a legal document called a note that describes technical terms, including interest charges, maturity date, collateral, and so on.
a. Note payable5  
b. Thing  
c. Undefined  
d. Undefined  

246. _____ refers to the rate at which the currency is traded for immediate delivery. It is the existing cash price.
a. Thing  
b. Spot rate5  
c. Undefined  
d. Undefined  

247. _____ is the aggregate amount of any material good that can be called into being at a certain price point; it comprises one half of the equation of _____ and demand. In classical economic theory, a curve representing _____ is one of the factors that produce price.
a. Thing  
b. Supply5  
c. Undefined  
d. Undefined  

248. _____ refers to a projection of future asset, liability, and stockholders' equity levels. Notes payable or cash is used as a plug or balancing figure for the statement.
a. Pro forma balance sheet5  
b. Thing  
c. Undefined  
d. Undefined  

249. Economic _____ refers to reducing barriers among countries to transactions and to movements of goods, capital, and labor, including harmonization of laws, regulations, and standards. Integrated markets theoretically function as a unified market.
a. Integration5  
b. Thing  
c. Undefined  
d. Undefined  

250. _____, which refers to the aggregated operational strategies of single business firm or that of an SBU in a diversified corporation refers to the way in which a firm competes in its chosen arenas.
a. Thing  
b. Business strategy5  
c. Undefined  
d. Undefined  

251. _____ refers to a "non tangible product" that is not embodied in a physical good and that typically effects some change in another product, person, or institution. Contrasts with good.

a. Thing
b. Service5
c. Undefined
d. Undefined

252. Net cash equivalent amount paid or to be paid for the asset is an _____. e expense undertaken to acquire new business. The concept applies to both agents and companies. The largest portion of an insurer's _____ is agent's or sales representative's commission or bonus.
a. Thing
b. Acquisition cost5
c. Undefined
d. Undefined

253. A _____ refers to a product created as a result of project work.
a. Thing
b. Deliverable5
c. Undefined
d. Undefined

254. _____ refers to another name for a business organization. Other similar terms are business firm, sometimes simply business, sometimes simply firm, as well as company, and entity.
a. Thing
b. Enterprise5
c. Undefined
d. Undefined

255. A _____ is built to test the function of a new design before starting production of a product.
a. Prototype5
b. Thing
c. Undefined
d. Undefined

256. A _____ is an area where the sellers of a product and its close rivals compete for the business of a common group of buyers.
a. Relevant market5
b. Thing
c. Undefined
d. Undefined

257. Other organizations in the same industry or type of business that provide a good or service to the same set of customers is referred to as a _____.
a. Thing
b. Competitor5
c. Undefined
d. Undefined

258. _____ refers to the final stage of the creative process where the validity or truthfulness of the insight is determined. The feedback portion of communication in which the receiver sends a message to the source indicating receipt of the message and the degree to which he or she understood the message.
a. Verification5
b. Concept
c. Undefined
d. Undefined

259. An iterative approach to design in which a series of mock-ups or models are developed until the customer and the designer come to agreement as to the final design is called _____.
a. Prototyping5
b. Thing
c. Undefined
d. Undefined

260. _____ refers to a requirement that an importer or exporter achieve some level of performance, in terms of exporting, domestic content, etc., in order to obtain an import or export license.

*Chapter 5. Analyzing Investing Activities: Special Topics*  181

a. Performance requirement5
b. Thing
c. Undefined
d. Undefined

261. _____ refers to used to describe a product characteristic, it means a good fit with other products used by the consumer or with the consumer's lifestyle. Used in a technical context, it means the ability of systems to work together.
a. Compatibility5
b. Thing
c. Undefined
d. Undefined

262. _____ is capital provided by outside investors for financing of new, growing or struggling businesses. _____ investments generally are high risk investments but offer the potential for above average returns.
a. Venture capital5
b. Thing
c. Undefined
d. Undefined

263. _____ refers to the rate, per year, at which future values are diminished to make them comparable to values in the present. Can be either subjective or objective .
a. Discount rate5
b. Thing
c. Undefined
d. Undefined

264. _____ is a business magazine published by McGraw-Hill. It was first published in 1929 under the direction of Malcolm Muir, who was serving as president of the McGraw-Hill Publishing company at the time. It is considered to be the standard both in industry and among students.
a. Business Week5
b. Organization
c. Undefined
d. Undefined

265. An _____ is a statement of a fact by a party in a pleading, which the party claims it will prove. Allegations remain assertions without proof, only claims until they are proved.
a. Allegation5
b. Thing
c. Undefined
d. Undefined

## Chapter 6. Analyzing Operating Activities

1. _____ refer to gains and losses that are both unusual in nature and infrequent in occurrence; they are reported net of tax on the income statement.
   a. Thing
   b. Extraordinary items6
   c. Undefined
   d. Undefined

2. _____ is the corporate management term for the act of partially dismantling and reorganizing a company for the purpose of making it more efficient and therefore more profitable.
   a. Restructuring6
   b. Thing
   c. Undefined
   d. Undefined

3. A system that collects and processes financial information about an organization and reports that information to decision makers is referred to as _____.
   a. Accounting6
   b. Thing
   c. Undefined
   d. Undefined

4. _____ refers to a summary of all the transactions that have occurred over a particular period.
   a. Thing
   b. Financial statement6
   c. Undefined
   d. Undefined

5. _____ is a U.S. business term for the amount of money that a company receives from its activities, mostly from sales of products and/or services to customers.
   a. Revenue6
   b. Thing
   c. Undefined
   d. Undefined

6. In accounting, an _____ represents an event in which an asset is used up or a liability is incurred. In terms of the accounting equation, expenses reduce owners' equity.
   a. Expense6
   b. Thing
   c. Undefined
   d. Undefined

7. An _____ is a stock option for the company's own stock that is often offered to upper-level employees as part of the executive compenzation package, especially by American corporations. An _____ is identical to a call option on the company's stock, with some extra restrictions.
   a. Thing
   b. Employee stock option6
   c. Undefined
   d. Undefined

8. A _____ is a specific type of option that uses the stock itself as an underlying instrument to determine the option's pay-off and therefore its value.
   a. Thing
   b. Stock option6
   c. Undefined
   d. Undefined

9. _____ means the giving out of information, either voluntarily or to be in compliance with legal regulations or workplace rules.
   a. Disclosure6
   b. Thing
   c. Undefined
   d. Undefined

10. In finance and economics, _____ is the price paid by a borrower for the use of a lender's money. In other words, _____ is the amount of paid to "rent" money for a period of time.

a. Thing
b. Interest6
c. Undefined
d. Undefined

11. A contract that gives the purchaser the _____ to buy or sell the underlying financial instrument at a specified price, called the exercise price or strike price, within a specific period of time.
a. Thing
b. Option6
c. Undefined
d. Undefined

12. In financial terminology, _____ is the capital raized by a corporation, through the issuance and sale of shares.
a. Thing
b. Stock6
c. Undefined
d. Undefined

13. _____ characterizes the process of leading and directing all or part of an organization, often a business, through the deployment and manipulation of resources. Early twentieth-century _____ writer Mary Parker Follett defined _____ as "the art of getting things done through people."
a. Management6
b. Thing
c. Undefined
d. Undefined

14. In banking and accountancy, the outstanding _____ is the amount of money owned, (or due), that remains in a deposit account (or a loan account) at a given date, after all past remittances, payments and withdrawal have been accounted for. It can be positive (then, in the _____ sheet of a firm, it is an asset) or negative (a liability).
a. Balance6
b. Thing
c. Undefined
d. Undefined

15. _____ refers to spending for the production and accumulation of capital and additions to inventories. In a financial sense, buying an asset with the expectation of making a return.
a. Investment6
b. Thing
c. Undefined
d. Undefined

16. _____ refers to a person or tool with a primary function of information analysis, generally with a more limited, practical and short term set of goals than a researcher.
a. Analyst6
b. Person
c. Undefined
d. Undefined

17. A rising stock market. A _____ exists when stock prices are strong and rising and Investors are optimistic about future market performance.
a. Thing
b. Bull market6
c. Undefined
d. Undefined

18. A _____ is, as defined in economics, a social arrangement that allows buyers and sellers to discover information and carry out a voluntary exchange of goods or services.
a. Market6
b. Thing
c. Undefined
d. Undefined

## Chapter 6. Analyzing Operating Activities

19. In throughput accounting, the cost accounting aspect of Theory of Constraints (TOC), _____ is the money spent turning inventory into throughput. In TOC, _____ is limited to costs that vary strictly with the quantity produced, like raw materials and purchased components.
    a. Thing
    b. Operating expense6
    c. Undefined
    d. Undefined

20. Cash flow activities that include the cash effects of transactions that create revenues and expenses and thus enter into the determination of net income is an _____.
    a. Operating activities6
    b. Thing
    c. Undefined
    d. Undefined

21. _____ refers to recording revenues when earned and expenses when incurred, regardless of the timing of cash receipts or payments.
    a. Thing
    b. Accrual basis6
    c. Undefined
    d. Undefined

22. An _____ is an accounting event in which the transaction is recognized when the action takes place, instead of when cash is disbursed or received.
    a. Accrual6
    b. Thing
    c. Undefined
    d. Undefined

23. _____ refers to a financial statement that presents the revenues and expenses and resulting net income or net loss of a company for a specific period of time.
    a. Thing
    b. Income statement6
    c. Undefined
    d. Undefined

24. _____ is equal to the income that a firm has after subtracting costs and expenses from the total revenue. Expenses will typically include tax expense.
    a. Thing
    b. Net income6
    c. Undefined
    d. Undefined

25. In finance, _____ is a profit or an increase in value of an investment such as a stock or bond. _____ is calculated by fair market value or the proceeds from the sale of the investment minus the sum of the purchase price and all costs associated with it.
    a. Thing
    b. Gain6
    c. Undefined
    d. Undefined

26. The _____ is net income on the last line of a income statement.
    a. Thing
    b. Bottom line6
    c. Undefined
    d. Undefined

27. _____ refers to the return to the resource entrepreneurial ability; total revenue minus total cost.
    a. Thing
    b. Profit6
    c. Undefined
    d. Undefined

## Chapter 6. Analyzing Operating Activities

28. In economics, a _____ is a mechanism which allows people to trade money for securities or commodities such as gold or other precious metals. In general, any commodity market might be considered to be a _____, if the usual purpose of traders is not the immediate consumption of the commodity, but rather as a means of delaying or accelerating consumption over time.
    a. Thing
    b. Financial market6
    c. Undefined
    d. Undefined

29. The amount of money a household can spend during a given period without increasing or decreasing its net assets. Wages, salaries, dividends, interest income, transfer payments, rents, and so forth are sources of _____.
    a. Thing
    b. Economic income6
    c. Undefined
    d. Undefined

30. Cash provided by operating activities adjusted for capital expenditures and dividends paid is referred to as _____.
    a. Thing
    b. Free cash flow6
    c. Undefined
    d. Undefined

31. In finance, _____ refers to the amounts of cash being received and spent by a business during a defined period of time, sometimes tied to a specific project. Most of the time they are being used to determine gaps in the liquid position of a company.
    a. Thing
    b. Cash flow6
    c. Undefined
    d. Undefined

32. _____ refers to the payments received by those who supply land to the economy.
    a. Rental income6
    b. Thing
    c. Undefined
    d. Undefined

33. In accounting, the _____ of an asset is its remaining value after depreciation. The estimated value of an asset at the end of its useful life.
    a. Thing
    b. Salvage value6
    c. Undefined
    d. Undefined

34. _____ is an accounting and finance term for the method of attributing the cost of an asset across the useful life of the asset. _____ is a reduction in the value of a currency in floating exchange rate.
    a. Depreciation6
    b. Thing
    c. Undefined
    d. Undefined

35. The length of service of a productive facility or piece of equipment is its _____. The period of time during which an asset will have economic value and be usable.
    a. Thing
    b. Useful life6
    c. Undefined
    d. Undefined

36. The accountant's concept of income is generally based upon the realization principle. Financial _____ may differ from taxable income. Differences are included in a reconciliation of taxable and _____ on Schedule M-1 of Form 1120.
    a. Thing
    b. Accounting income6
    c. Undefined
    d. Undefined

## Chapter 6. Analyzing Operating Activities

37. _____ is a concept used in finance and economics, defined as a rational and unbiased estimate of the potential market price of a good, service, or asset.
    a. Thing
    b. Fair value6
    c. Undefined
    d. Undefined

38. _____ refers to portion of the assets remaining after the creditors' claims have been satisfied; also called equity or residual interest.
    a. Thing
    b. Net assets6
    c. Undefined
    d. Undefined

39. An item of property, such as land, capital, money, a share in ownership, or a claim on others for future payment, such as a bond or a bank deposit is an _____.
    a. Thing
    b. Asset6
    c. Undefined
    d. Undefined

40. The _____ is a court's determination of a matter of law based on the issue presented in the particular case. In other words: under this law, with these facts, this result.
    a. Thing
    b. Holding6
    c. Undefined
    d. Undefined

41. For a publicly traded company, _____ is the part of its capitalization that is equity as opposed to long-term debt. In the case of only one type of stock, this would roughly be the number of outstanding shares times current shareprice.
    a. Thing
    b. Shareholder value6
    c. Undefined
    d. Undefined

42. A _____ is an individual or company (including a corporation) that legally owns one or more shares of stock in a joined stock company.
    a. Thing
    b. Shareholder6
    c. Undefined
    d. Undefined

43. A _____ refers to a layout accurate in size, color, scheme, and other necessary details to show how a final ad will look. For presentation only, never for reproduction.
    a. Comprehensive6
    b. Thing
    c. Undefined
    d. Undefined

44. _____ is an economic concept with commonplace familiarity; it is the price that a good or service is offered at, or will fetch, in the marketplace; it is of interest mainly in the study of microeconomics.
    a. Thing
    b. Market price6
    c. Undefined
    d. Undefined

45. _____ is a security or stock valuation method that uses financial and economic analysis to predict the movement of security prices such as Bond prices, but more commonly stock prices. The fundamental information that is analyzed can include a company's financial reports, and non-finanical information such as estimates of the growth of demand for competing products, industry comparisons, analysis of the effects of new regulations or demographic changes, and economy-wide changes.

## Chapter 6. Analyzing Operating Activities

a. Thing
c. Undefined
b. Fundamental analysis6
d. Undefined

46. _____ is an American stock investor, businessman and philanthropist. Nicknamed the "Oracle of Omaha" or the "Sage of Omaha", he has amassed an enormous fortune from astute investments, particularly through his company Berkshire Hathaway, in which he holds a greater than 38% stake.
a. Warren Buffett6
c. Undefined
b. Person
d. Undefined

47. An experienced employee who supervises, coaches, and guides lower-level employees by introducing them to the right people and generally being their organizational sponsor is a _____.
a. Mentor6
c. Undefined
b. Person
d. Undefined

48. Method of accounting that records the effects of accounting events in the period in which such events occur regardless of when cash is exchanged is _____.
a. Accrual accounting6
c. Undefined
b. Thing
d. Undefined

49. _____ refers to an accounting concept that establishes when expenses are recognized. Expenses are matched with the revenues they helped to generate and are recognized when those revenues are recognized.
a. Thing
c. Undefined
b. Matching6
d. Undefined

50. A _____ refers to a role in the buying center with formal authority and responsibility to select the supplier and negotiate the terms of the contract.
a. Thing
c. Undefined
b. Buyer6
d. Undefined

51. The interest rate that equates a future value or an annuity to a given present value is a _____.
a. Thing
c. Undefined
b. Yield6
d. Undefined

52. The value today of a stream of payments and/or receipts over time in the future and/or the past, converted to the present using an interest rate. If X t is the amount in period t and r the interest rate, then _____ at time t=0 is V = ?T /t.
a. Thing
c. Undefined
b. Present value6
d. Undefined

53. _____ refer to securities that are readily traded in the secondary securities market.
a. Thing
c. Undefined
b. Marketable securities6
d. Undefined

54. _____ refers to a claim on the borrower future income that is sold by the borrower to the lender. A _____ is a type of transferable interest representing financial value.

a. Thing
b. Security6
c. Undefined
d. Undefined

55. A _____ is a steady income given to a person (usually after retirement). Pensions are typically payments made in the form of a guaranteed annuity to a retired or disabled employee.
a. Pension6
b. Thing
c. Undefined
d. Undefined

56. In accounting terminology, _____ describes the original cost of an asset at the time of purchase or payment as opposed to its market value
a. Thing
b. Historical cost6
c. Undefined
d. Undefined

57. _____ refers to the total costs of goods made or purchased and sold.
a. Thing
b. Cost of sales6
c. Undefined
d. Undefined

58. Asset measure based on the cost of purchasing an asset today identical to the one currently held, or the cost of purchasing an asset that provides services like the one currently held, if an identical one cannot be purchased is a _____.
a. Thing
b. Current cost6
c. Undefined
d. Undefined

59. _____, also known as property, plant, and equipment (PP&E), is a term used in accountancy for assets and property which cannot easily be converted into cash. This can be compared with current assets such as cash or bank accounts, which are described as liquid assets. In most cases, only tangible assets are referred to as fixed.
a. Fixed asset6
b. Thing
c. Undefined
d. Undefined

60. Tangible property held for sale in the normal course of business or used in producing goods or services for sale is an _____.
a. Inventory6
b. Thing
c. Undefined
d. Undefined

61. _____ refers to any departure from the ideal of perfect competition that interferes with economic agents maximizing social welfare when they maximize their own.
a. Thing
b. Distortion6
c. Undefined
d. Undefined

62. _____ is the analysis of the accounts and the economic prospects of a firm.
a. Financial analysis6
b. Thing
c. Undefined
d. Undefined

63. In finance, the _____ of a stock is used to measure how cheap or expensive share prices are. It is probably the single most consistent red flag to excessive optimism and over-investment.

## Chapter 6. Analyzing Operating Activities

a. Thing  
c. Undefined  
b. P/E ratio6  
d. Undefined  

64. A _____ describes a business that functions without the intention or threat of liquidation for the foreseeable future. Accountants and auditors may be required to evaluate and disclose whether a company is no longer a _____, or is at risk of ceasing to be one.
   a. Going concern6  
   c. Undefined  
   b. Thing  
   d. Undefined  

65. An advertising effectiveness measure of print ads that allows the advertiser to assess the impact of an ad in a single issue of a magazine over time and/or across alternative magazines is called the _____.
   a. Recognition method6  
   c. Undefined  
   b. Thing  
   d. Undefined  

66. _____ are those activities involved in the running of a business for the purpose of producing value for the stakeholders. The outcome of _____ is the harvesting of value from assets owned by a business.
   a. Business operations6  
   c. Undefined  
   b. Thing  
   d. Undefined  

67. A standardized method or technique that is performed repetitively, often on different materials resulting in different finished goods is called an _____.
   a. Operation6  
   c. Undefined  
   b. Thing  
   d. Undefined  

68. Deferred is any account where the asset or liability is not realized until a future date, e.g. annuities, charges, taxes, income, etc. The deferred item may be carried, dependent on type of _____, as either an asset or liability.
   a. Thing  
   c. Undefined  
   b. Deferral6  
   d. Undefined  

69. Total revenues from operation minus cost of goods sold and operating costs are called _____.
   a. Thing  
   c. Undefined  
   b. Operating income6  
   d. Undefined  

70. Cash flow activities that include obtaining cash from issuing debt and repaying the amounts borrowed and obtaining cash from stockholders and paying dividends is referred to as _____.
   a. Financing activities6  
   c. Undefined  
   b. Thing  
   d. Undefined  

71. _____ refers to net income plus unrealized gain or loss on securities, minimum pension liability adjustment, and foreign currency translation adjustment.
   a. Thing  
   c. Undefined  
   b. Comprehensive income6  
   d. Undefined  

72. _____ is the name given to the set of legal principles, in countries following the English common law tradition, which supplement strict rules of law where their application would operate harshly, so as to achieve what is sometimes referred to as "natural justice."

## Chapter 6. Analyzing Operating Activities

a. Equity6  
c. Undefined  
b. Thing  
d. Undefined

73. Amount of corporate profits paid out for each share of stock is referred to as _____.
a. Dividend6  
c. Undefined  
b. Thing  
d. Undefined

74. _____ refers to a person who is authorized to vote the shares of another person. Also, the written authorization empowering a person to vote the shares of another person.
a. Thing  
c. Undefined  
b. Proxy6  
d. Undefined

75. _____ refers to financial results from the disposal of a major segment of the business and are reported net of income tax effects.
a. Discontinued operations6  
c. Undefined  
b. Thing  
d. Undefined

76. A _____ is the set of feasible allocations in an economy that cannot be improved upon by subset of the set of the economy's consumers (a coalition). In construction, when the force in an element is within a certain center section, the _____, the element will only be under compression.
a. Core6  
c. Undefined  
b. Thing  
d. Undefined

77. _____ refer to people in the organization who actually use the product or service purchased by the buying center.
a. Users6  
c. Undefined  
b. Thing  
d. Undefined

78. _____ is a specific area of finance dealing with the financial decisions corporations make and the tools as well as analyses used to make these decisions. The discipline as a whole may be divided among long-term and short-term decisions and techniques with the primary goal being the enhancing of corporate value by ensuring that return on capital exceeds cost of capital, without taking excessive financial risks.
a. Corporate finance6  
c. Undefined  
b. Thing  
d. Undefined

79. _____ of a project is the sum total of all projects products and their requirements or features.
a. Thing  
c. Undefined  
b. Scope6  
d. Undefined

80. A statement of the assets, liabilities, and net worth of a firm or individual at some given time often at the end of its "fiscal year," is referred to as a _____.
a. Thing  
c. Undefined  
b. Balance sheet6  
d. Undefined

81. _____ refers to the extent to which an economic variable, such as a price or an exchange rate, moves up and down over time.

## Chapter 6. Analyzing Operating Activities

a. Thing
b. Volatility6
c. Undefined
d. Undefined

82. A _____ is a present obligation of the enterprise arizing from past events, the settlement of which is expected to result in an outflow from the enterprise of resources embodying economic benefits.
a. Liability6
b. Thing
c. Undefined
d. Undefined

83. A _____ acts as an agent that provides financial services for its clients. Financial institutions generally fall under financial regulation from a government authority.
a. Financial institution6
b. Thing
c. Undefined
d. Undefined

84. In finance, _____ is the process of estimating the market value of a financial asset or liability. They can be done on assets (for example, investments in marketable securities such as stocks, options, business enterprises, or intangible assets such as patents and trademarks) or on liabilities (e.g., Bonds issued by a company).
a. Event
b. Valuation6
c. Undefined
d. Undefined

85. A _____ is a bond issued by a corporation, as the name suggests. The term is usually applied to longer term debt instruments, generally with a maturity date falling at least 12 months after their issue date (the term "commercial paper" being sometimes used for instruments with a shorter maturity).
a. Corporate bond6
b. Thing
c. Undefined
d. Undefined

86. The rate of return on bonds, loans, or deposits. When one speaks of 'the' _____, it is usually in a model where there is only one.
a. Thing
b. Interest rate6
c. Undefined
d. Undefined

87. _____ refers to a debt instrument, issued by a borrower and promising a specified stream of payments to the purchaser, usually regular interest payments plus a final repayment of principal.
a. Bond6
b. Thing
c. Undefined
d. Undefined

88. _____ refers to a thing that was originally personal property and that has been actually or constructively affixed to the soil itself or to some structure legally a part of the land.
a. Thing
b. Fixture6
c. Undefined
d. Undefined

89. _____ in law, is the relinquishment of an interest, claim, privilege or possession. This broad meaning has a number of applications in different branches of law.
a. Abandonment6
b. Thing
c. Undefined
d. Undefined

## Chapter 6. Analyzing Operating Activities

90. Assets defined in the broadest legal sense. _____ includes the unrealized receivables of a cash basis taxpayer, but not services rendered.
    a. Thing
    b. Property6
    c. Undefined
    d. Undefined

91. Other organizations in the same industry or type of business that provide a good or service to the same set of customers is referred to as a _____.
    a. Thing
    b. Competitor6
    c. Undefined
    d. Undefined

92. The withholding of labor services by an organized group of workers is referred to as a _____.
    a. Thing
    b. Strike6
    c. Undefined
    d. Undefined

93. A _____ is a "promise" or an "agreement" that is enforced or recognized by the law. In the civil law, a _____ is considered to be part of the general law of obligations.
    a. Contract6
    b. Thing
    c. Undefined
    d. Undefined

94. _____ refers to a good that has not been transformed by production; a primary product.
    a. Raw material6
    b. Thing
    c. Undefined
    d. Undefined

95. _____ is the aggregate amount of any material good that can be called into being at a certain price point; it comprises one half of the equation of _____ and demand. In classical economic theory, a curve representing _____ is one of the factors that produce price.
    a. Thing
    b. Supply6
    c. Undefined
    d. Undefined

96. A group of products that are physically similar or are intended for a similar market are called the _____.
    a. Thing
    b. Product line6
    c. Undefined
    d. Undefined

97. _____ refers to the speed of the up and down movements of a fluctuating economic variable; that is, the number of times per unit of time that the variable completes a cycle of up and down movement.
    a. Thing
    b. Frequency6
    c. Undefined
    d. Undefined

98. A company that is controlled by another company or corporation is a _____.
    a. Subsidiary6
    b. Thing
    c. Undefined
    d. Undefined

99. An _____ is prepared by corporate management that presents financial information including financial statements, footnotes, and the management discussion and analysis.

## Chapter 6. Analyzing Operating Activities

a. Thing
c. Undefined
b. Annual report6
d. Undefined

100. Occurring across time, or across different periods of time are _____. _____ choice is essentially the question of whether you consume something now or in the future,this is a form of delayed gratification.
   a. Thing
   c. Undefined
   b. Intertemporal6
   d. Undefined

101. _____ refers to the method under which income and expenses are determined for tax purposes. Important accounting methods include the cash basis and the accrual basis.
   a. Accounting method6
   c. Undefined
   b. Thing
   d. Undefined

102. The particular business or other organization for which a financial statement is prepared is referred to as the _____.
   a. Thing
   c. Undefined
   b. Reporting entity6
   d. Undefined

103. _____ refers to a term used to signify that which may be assumed without proof, or taken for granted. It is asserted as a self-evident result of human reason and experience.
   a. Presumption6
   c. Undefined
   b. Thing
   d. Undefined

104. _____ refers to usually the first stage in the creative process. It includes education and formal training.
   a. Thing
   c. Undefined
   b. Preparation6
   d. Undefined

105. _____ refers to another name for a business organization. Other similar terms are business firm, sometimes simply business, sometimes simply firm, as well as company, and entity.
   a. Thing
   c. Undefined
   b. Enterprise6
   d. Undefined

106. Cumulative earnings of a company that are not distributed to the owners and are reinvested in the business are called _____.
   a. Retained earnings6
   c. Undefined
   b. Thing
   d. Undefined

107. _____ refers to annual profit of the corporation divided by the number of shares outstanding.
   a. Thing
   c. Undefined
   b. Earnings per share6
   d. Undefined

108. An obligation of a company to replace defective goods or correct any deficiencies in performance or quality of a product is called a _____.
   a. Warranty6
   c. Undefined
   b. Thing
   d. Undefined

## Chapter 6. Analyzing Operating Activities

109. A _____ refers to a financial statement of a parent company and its subsidiaries that has been combined into a single set of financial statements as if the companies were one.
    a. Consolidated financial statement6
    b. Thing
    c. Undefined
    d. Undefined

110. The combination of two or more firms, generally of equal size and market power, to form an entirely new entity is a _____.
    a. Consolidation6
    b. Thing
    c. Undefined
    d. Undefined

111. Similar to a script in that a _____ can be a less than completely rational decision-making method. Involves the use of a pre-existing set of decision steps for any problem that presents itself.
    a. Policy6
    b. Thing
    c. Undefined
    d. Undefined

112. In contract law a _____ is incorrect understanding by one or more parties to a contract and may be used as grounds to invalidate the agreement. Common law has identified three different types of _____ in contract: unilateral _____, mutual _____, and common _____.
    a. Thing
    b. Mistake6
    c. Undefined
    d. Undefined

113. The social science dealing with the use of scarce resources to obtain the maximum satisfaction of society's virtually unlimited economic wants is an _____.
    a. Thing
    b. Economics6
    c. Undefined
    d. Undefined

114. In corporation law, a corporation's acceptance of a pre-incorporation contract by action of its board of directors, by which the corporation becomes liable on the contract, is referred to as _____.
    a. Adoption6
    b. Concept
    c. Undefined
    d. Undefined

115. _____ refers to the fee charged by an insurance company for an insurance policy. The rate of losses must be relatively predictable: In order to set the _____ (prices) insurers must be able to estimate them accurately.
    a. Thing
    b. Premium6
    c. Undefined
    d. Undefined

116. _____ is an important accounting concept that describes the value of a business entity not directly attributable to its tangible assets and liabilities.
    a. Thing
    b. Goodwill6
    c. Undefined
    d. Undefined

117. _____, which refers to the aggregated operational strategies of single business firm or that of an SBU in a diversified corporation refers to the way in which a firm competes in its chosen arenas.
    a. Business strategy6
    b. Thing
    c. Undefined
    d. Undefined

## Chapter 6. Analyzing Operating Activities

118. _____ occurs, among other instances, when one corporation acquires another in a merger or acquisition, a single corporation divides into two or more entities, or a corporation makes a substantial change in its capital structure.
   a. Thing
   b. Reorganization6
   c. Undefined
   d. Undefined

119. _____ refers to the price of an asset agreed on between a willing buyer and a willing seller; the price an asset could demand if it is sold on the open market.
   a. Market value6
   b. Thing
   c. Undefined
   d. Undefined

120. The _____ of an asset or group of assets is sometimes the price at which they were originally acquired, in many cases equal to purchase price.
   a. Thing
   b. Book value6
   c. Undefined
   d. Undefined

121. Valuation method departing from the cost principle that recognizes a loss when replacement cost or net realizable value drops below cost is called _____.
   a. Lower of cost6
   b. Thing
   c. Undefined
   d. Undefined

122. A _____ is a secondary or incidental product deriving from a manufacturing process or chemical reaction, and is not the primary product or service being produced.
   a. Thing
   b. Byproduct6
   c. Undefined
   d. Undefined

123. _____ is an accounting method used to establish the dollar amount at which assets are recorded on a savings association's books. The amount established is the lower of the cost of the asset or the current market value.
   a. Lower of Cost or Market6
   b. Thing
   c. Undefined
   d. Undefined

124. _____ refers to the allocation of the cost of an asset over several accounting periods. Also, to expense a cost, that is, put it on the income statement as an expense.
   a. Writing off6
   b. Thing
   c. Undefined
   d. Undefined

125. The lowest level of the company which contains the set of functions that carry a product through its life span from concept through manufacture, distribution, sales and service is a _____.
   a. Business unit6
   b. Thing
   c. Undefined
   d. Undefined

126. _____ means the reduction of expenditures in order to become financially stable. It is a tactical concept similar to downsizing.
   a. Thing
   b. Retrenchment6
   c. Undefined
   d. Undefined

## Chapter 6. Analyzing Operating Activities

127. The ending of a corporation that occurs only after the winding-up of the corporation's affairs, the liquidation of its assets, and the distribution of the proceeds to the claimants are referred to as a _____.
    a. Termination6
    b. Thing
    c. Undefined
    d. Undefined

128. In finance and economics, _____ or divestiture is the reduction of some kind of asset, for either financial or social goals. A _____ is the opposite of an investment.
    a. Event
    b. Divestment6
    c. Undefined
    d. Undefined

129. The body of knowledge and techniques that can be used to combine economic resources to produce goods and services is called _____.
    a. Technology6
    b. Thing
    c. Undefined
    d. Undefined

130. A contract for the possession and use of land or other property, including goods, on one side, and a recompense of rent or other income on the other is the _____.
    a. Thing
    b. Lease6
    c. Undefined
    d. Undefined

131. The process of bringing, maintaining, and defending a lawsuit is _____.
    a. Thing
    b. Litigation6
    c. Undefined
    d. Undefined

132. Having a physical existence is referred to as the _____. Personal property other than real estate, such as cars, boats, stocks, or other assets.
    a. Thing
    b. Tangible6
    c. Undefined
    d. Undefined

133. _____ refers to the long-term movement of an economic variable, such as its average rate of increase or decrease over enough years to encompass several business cycles.
    a. Trend6
    b. Thing
    c. Undefined
    d. Undefined

134. The sum of fixed cost and variable cost is referred to as _____.
    a. Thing
    b. Total cost6
    c. Undefined
    d. Undefined

135. _____ is widely respected as a financial advisor to some of the most important companies, largest governments, and wealthiest families in the world. It is a primary dealer in the U.S. Treasury securities market. It offers its clients mergers & acquisitions advisory, provides underwriting services, engages in proprietary trading, invests in private equity deals, and also manages the wealth of affluent individuals and families.
    a. Thing
    b. Goldman Sachs6
    c. Undefined
    d. Undefined

## Chapter 6. Analyzing Operating Activities

136. In statistics and signal processing, a _____ is a sequence of data points, measured typically at successive times, spaced at (often uniform) time intervals. Analysts throughout the economy will use these to aid in the management of their corresponding businesses.
 a. Time series6
 b. Thing
 c. Undefined
 d. Undefined

137. The legal right to the proceeds from and control over the use of an invented product or process, granted for a fixed period of time, usually 20 years. _____ is one form of intellectual property that is subject of the TRIPS agreement.
 a. Patent6
 b. Thing
 c. Undefined
 d. Undefined

138. _____ refers to the amount recognized as an expense in one period resulting from the periodic recognition of the used portion of the cost of a long-term tangible asset over its life.
 a. Depreciation expense6
 b. Thing
 c. Undefined
 d. Undefined

139. _____ refers to a written statement-also called an accountant's certificate, accountant's opinion, or audit report- prepared by an independent accountant or auditor after an audit.
 a. Financial report6
 b. Thing
 c. Undefined
 d. Undefined

140. Cash flowing out of the business from all sources over a period of time is _____.
 a. Cash outflow6
 b. Thing
 c. Undefined
 d. Undefined

141. A _____ is a stretch of time when an individual is eligible to receive benefits. The duration of benefits refers to the number of weeks the benefits will continue as long as the individual remains eligible. It is based on the number of hours worked in the 52 weeks before the lay-off and on the regional unemployment rate.
 a. Benefit period6
 b. Thing
 c. Undefined
 d. Undefined

142. A _____ in property law is a future interest created in a transferee that is capable of becoming possessory upon the natural termination of a prior estate created by the same instrument.
 a. Remainder6
 b. Thing
 c. Undefined
 d. Undefined

143. _____ refers to the assignment of income for various tax purposes. A multistate corporation's nonbusiness income usually is distributed to the state where the nonbusiness assets are located; it is not apportioned with the rest of the entity's income.
 a. Allocate6
 b. Thing
 c. Undefined
 d. Undefined

144. To provide for the payment of a debt by creating a sinking fund or paying in installments is to _____.
 a. Thing
 b. Amortize6
 c. Undefined
 d. Undefined

## Chapter 6. Analyzing Operating Activities

145. _____ is the sale of assets when an entity is being liquidated.
   a. Realization6
   b. Thing
   c. Undefined
   d. Undefined

146. A _____ occurs when a customer does not pay cash at the time of the sale but instead agrees to pay later. The sale occurs now, with payment from the customer to follow at a later time.
   a. Credit sale6
   b. Thing
   c. Undefined
   d. Undefined

147. _____, in general, refers to the recalling or voiding of a prior action. In contract law, the withdrawal of an offer by the offeror prior to effective acceptance by the offeree.
   a. Thing
   b. Revocation6
   c. Undefined
   d. Undefined

148. _____ refers to a recording as positive in the balance of payments, any transaction that gives rise to a payment into the country, such as an export, the sale of an asset, or borrowing from abroad.
   a. Credit6
   b. Thing
   c. Undefined
   d. Undefined

149. Refers to part of a transaction that involves an activity other than the exchange of cash. Providing a service or delivering goods would be considered the _____ of a transaction.
   a. Economic substance6
   b. Thing
   c. Undefined
   d. Undefined

150. A contractual right to sell certain products or services, use certain trademarks, or perform activities in a geographical region is called a _____.
   a. Thing
   b. Franchise6
   c. Undefined
   d. Undefined

151. The sale of goods and services to consumers for their own use is a _____.
   a. Retail sale6
   b. Thing
   c. Undefined
   d. Undefined

152. A company that develops a product concept and sells others the rights to make and sell the products is referred to as a _____.
   a. Thing
   b. Franchisor6
   c. Undefined
   d. Undefined

153. _____ refers to a "non tangible product" that is not embodied in a physical good and that typically effects some change in another product, person, or institution. Contrasts with good.
   a. Thing
   b. Service6
   c. Undefined
   d. Undefined

154. A _____ in the sphere of Intellectual Property Rights (IPR) is a document, contract or agreement giving permission or the 'right' to a legally-definable entity to do something (such as manufacture a product or to use a service), or to apply something (such as a trademark), with the objective of achieving commercial gain.

## Chapter 6. Analyzing Operating Activities

a. License6  
c. Undefined  
b. Thing  
d. Undefined

155. _____ refers to a debt that can reasonably be expected to be paid from existing current assets or through the creation of other current liabilities, within one year or the operating cycle, whichever is longer.
   a. Thing
   b. Current liability6
   c. Undefined
   d. Undefined

156. A person lawfully on land in possession of another for purposes unconnected with the business interests of the possessor is referred to as the _____.
   a. Licensee6
   b. Thing
   c. Undefined
   d. Undefined

157. A company's purchase of the property and obligations of another company is an _____.
   a. Acquisition6
   b. Thing
   c. Undefined
   d. Undefined

158. _____ specializes in the design, manufacturing, and installation of automotive systems and nonresidential climate control systems. Its Controls Group also has a prominent facilities management division. It was founded in 1885 by professor Warren S. Johnson, inventor of the first electric room thermostat.
   a. Organization
   b. Johnson Controls6
   c. Undefined
   d. Undefined

159. Net sales less cost of goods sold is called _____.
   a. Thing
   b. Gross profit6
   c. Undefined
   d. Undefined

160. _____ is one of a series of accounting transactions dealing with the billing of customers which owe money to a person, company or organization for goods and services that have been provided to the customer. This is typically done in a one person organization by writing an invoice and mailing or delivering it to each customer.
   a. Thing
   b. Accounts receivable6
   c. Undefined
   d. Undefined

161. An _____ is any factor (financial or non financial) that provides a motive for a particular course of action, or counts as a reason for preferring one choice to the alternatives.
   a. Thing
   b. Incentive6
   c. Undefined
   d. Undefined

162. A legal entity chartered by a state or the Federal government that is distinct and separate from the individuals who own it is a _____. This separation gives the _____ unique powers which other legal entities lack.
   a. Corporation6
   b. Organization
   c. Undefined
   d. Undefined

163. _____ refers to an agency, commission, or board established by the Federal government or a state government to regulates businesses in the public interest.

## Chapter 6. Analyzing Operating Activities

a. Thing
c. Undefined
b. Regulatory agency6
d. Undefined

164. _____ refers to potential liability that does not currently exist but is probable and reasonably estimable, such as lawsuits and tax disputes, is referred to as a _____.
a. Contingent liability6
c. Undefined
b. Thing
d. Undefined

165. When debt owed by a corporation to the shareholders becomes too large in relation to the corporation's capital structure, the IRS may contend that the corporation is _____.
a. Thing
c. Undefined
b. Thinly capitalized6
d. Undefined

166. _____ refers to money raized from within the firm or through the sale of ownership in the firm.
a. Equity capital6
c. Undefined
b. Thing
d. Undefined

167. _____ refers to the function in a firm that searches for quality material resources, finds the best suppliers, and negotiates the best price for goods and services.
a. Purchasing6
c. Undefined
b. Thing
d. Undefined

168. _____ generally refers to financial wealth, especially that used to start or maintain a business. In classical economics, _____ is one of four factors of production, the others being land and labor and entrepreneurship.
a. Thing
c. Undefined
b. Capital6
d. Undefined

169. _____ refers to the cash inflows and cash outflows from the general operating activities of the business; one of the three sections in the statement of cash flows.
a. Operating cash flows6
c. Undefined
b. Thing
d. Undefined

170. The payments made by a borrower on their debt, usually including both interest payments and partial repayment of principal, are called _____.
a. Debt service6
c. Undefined
b. Thing
d. Undefined

171. Independent accounting entity with a self-balancing set of accounts segregated for the purposes of carrying on specific activities is referred to as a _____.
a. Thing
c. Undefined
b. Fund6
d. Undefined

172. Movement of funds related to the company's operations, reported on the cash flow statement of a company's annual report are _____.

## Chapter 6. Analyzing Operating Activities

a. Cash flows from operating activities6
b. Thing
c. Undefined
d. Undefined

173. A _____ refers to previously recorded assets, liabilities, revenues, or expenses that need to be adjusted at the end of the period to reflect earned revenues or incurred expenses.
a. Deferred revenue6
b. Thing
c. Undefined
d. Undefined

174. Notes that clarify information presented in the financial statements, as well as expand upon it where additional detail is needed are _____.
a. Thing
b. Notes to the financial statements6
c. Undefined
d. Undefined

175. The creation of finished goods and services using the factors of _____: land, labor, capital, entrepreneurship, and knowledge.
a. Production6
b. Thing
c. Undefined
d. Undefined

176. The technical sophistication of the product and hence the amount of understanding required to use it is referred to as _____. It is the opposite of simplicity.
a. Thing
b. Complexity6
c. Undefined
d. Undefined

177. Assets that have special rights but not physical substance are referred to as _____.
a. Thing
b. Intangible assets6
c. Undefined
d. Undefined

178. An intangible assets is defined as an asset that is not physical in nature. The most common types are trade secrets (e.g., customer lists and know-how), copyrights, patents, trademarks, and goodwill.
a. Thing
b. Intangible asset6
c. Undefined
d. Undefined

179. _____ refers to cash flow activities that include purchasing and disposing of investments and productive long-lived assets using cash and lending money and collecting on those loans.
a. Thing
b. Investing activities6
c. Undefined
d. Undefined

180. The use of resources for the deliberate discovery of new information and ways of doing things, together with the application of that information in inventing new products or processes is referred to as _____.
a. Thing
b. Research and development6
c. Undefined
d. Undefined

181. _____ refers to an offer that terminates when a stated time period expires. If no time is stated, an offer terminates after a reasonable time.

a. Lapse of time6  
b. Thing  
c. Undefined  
d. Undefined  

182. The consumer's appraisal of the product or brand on important attributes is called _____.  
a. Evaluation6  
b. Thing  
c. Undefined  
d. Undefined  

183. Assets that have physical substance that cannot easily be converted into cash are referd to as a _____.  
a. Tangible asset6  
b. Thing  
c. Undefined  
d. Undefined  

184. _____ measures what money is worth at a specified time in the future assuming a certain interest rate. This is used in time value of money calculations.  
a. Future value6  
b. Thing  
c. Undefined  
d. Undefined  

185. Systematic and rational allocation of the acquisition cost of an intangible asset over its useful life is referred to as _____.  
a. Thing  
b. Amortization6  
c. Undefined  
d. Undefined  

186. A collective term for all of the employees of an organization. _____ is also commonly used to refer to the _____ management function or the organizational unit responsible for administering _____ programs.  
a. Personnel6  
b. Concept  
c. Undefined  
d. Undefined  

187. An _____ is all executive, organizational, and clerical costs associated with the general management of an organization rather than with manufacturing, marketing, or selling  
a. Administrative cost6  
b. Thing  
c. Undefined  
d. Undefined  

188. _____ refers to a cost that cannot be traced to a particular department.  
a. Thing  
b. Indirect cost6  
c. Undefined  
d. Undefined  

189. _____ is a multinational computer technology corporation with 2004 global annual sales of US$39.79 billion and 71,553 employees in 102 countries and regions as of July 2006. It develops, manufactures, licenses, and supports a wide range of software products for computing devices.  
a. Microsoft6  
b. Organization  
c. Undefined  
d. Undefined  

190. _____ refers to certified public accountant licensed to perform audits who is not an employee and does not have ownership or interest in the company being audited.  
a. Independent auditor6  
b. Thing  
c. Undefined  
d. Undefined

## Chapter 6. Analyzing Operating Activities

191. Suppliers and financial institutions that lend money to companies is referred to as a _____.
 a. Thing
 b. Lender6
 c. Undefined
 d. Undefined

192. Promoting and selling products or services to customers, or prospective customers, is referred to as _____.
 a. Marketing6
 b. Thing
 c. Undefined
 d. Undefined

193. _____ in economics, the manner in which total output and income is distributed among individuals or factors.
 a. Distribution6
 b. Thing
 c. Undefined
 d. Undefined

194. A group of firms that produce identical or similar products is an _____. It is also used specifically to refer to an area of economic production focused on manufacturing which involves large amounts of capital investment before any profit can be realized, also called "heavy _____".
 a. Thing
 b. Industry6
 c. Undefined
 d. Undefined

195. Production of goods primarily by the application of labor and capital to raw materials and other intermediate inputs, in contrast to agriculture, mining, forestry, fishing, and services a _____.
 a. Thing
 b. Manufacturing6
 c. Undefined
 d. Undefined

196. _____ refers to measures that are important to monitoring and tracking the effectiveness of a company's operations.
 a. Operating results6
 b. Thing
 c. Undefined
 d. Undefined

197. _____ is defined as not having sufficient resources to produce enough to fulfill unlimited subjective wants. Alternatively, _____ implies that not all of society's goals can be attained at the same time, so that trade-offs one good against others are made.
 a. Scarcity6
 b. Thing
 c. Undefined
 d. Undefined

198. The payment for the service of a unit of labor, per unit time. In trade theory, it is the only payment to labor, usually unskilled labor. In empirical work, _____ data may exclude other compenzation, which must be added to get the total cost of employment.
 a. Wage6
 b. Thing
 c. Undefined
 d. Undefined

199. The rewards other than wages that employees receive from their employers and that include pensions, medical and dental insurance, paid vacations, and sick leaves are referred to as _____.
 a. Thing
 b. Fringe benefits6
 c. Undefined
 d. Undefined

# Chapter 6. Analyzing Operating Activities

200. Benefits such as sick-leave pay, vacation pay, pension plans, and health plans that represent additional compenzation to employees beyond base wages is a _____.
   a. Thing
   b. Fringe benefit6
   c. Undefined
   d. Undefined

201. A compenzation plan in which payments are based on a measure of organization performance and do not become part of the employees' base salary is _____.
   a. Thing
   b. Profit sharing6
   c. Undefined
   d. Undefined

202. _____ refers to a system by which individuals can reduce their exposure to risk of large losses by spreading the risks among a large number of persons.
   a. Thing
   b. Insurance6
   c. Undefined
   d. Undefined

203. _____ refers to an intergovernmental transfer of funds . Since the New Deal, state and local governments have become increasingly dependent upon federal grants for an almost infinite variety of programs.
   a. Thing
   b. Grant6
   c. Undefined
   d. Undefined

204. _____ refers to a rise in the value of a country's currency on the exchange market, relative either to a particular other currency or to a weighted average of other currencies. The currency is said to appreciate. Opposite of 'depreciation.' _____ can also refer to the increase in value of any asset.
   a. Thing
   b. Appreciation6
   c. Undefined
   d. Undefined

205. A _____ is an asset that conveys to the holder the power to purchase corporate stock at a specified price, often for a limited period of time. A _____ received may be taxed as a distribution of earnings and profits.
   a. Stock right6
   b. Thing
   c. Undefined
   d. Undefined

206. _____ refer to an equity security, representing a shareholder's ownership of a corporation. _____ are one of a finite number of equal portions in the capital of a company, entitling the owner to a proportion of distributed, non-reinvested profits known as dividends and to a portion of the value of the company in case of liquidation.
   a. Shares6
   b. Thing
   c. Undefined
   d. Undefined

207. _____ is a kind of compenzation to employee with an Employee Stock Option. _____ requires the company to pay cash for the difference between the grant price and the market price of the company stock on the exercise date.
   a. Thing
   b. Stock Appreciation Right6
   c. Undefined
   d. Undefined

208. _____ refers to the amount at which property would change hands between a willing buyer and a willing seller, neither being under any compulsion to buy or to sell, and both having reasonable knowledge of the relevant facts.

## Chapter 6. Analyzing Operating Activities

a. Fair market value6  
b. Thing  
c. Undefined  
d. Undefined

209. _____ refers to the basic, normal, voting stock issued by a corporation; called residual equity because it ranks after preferred stock for dividend and liquidation distributions.
a. Thing  
b. Common stock6  
c. Undefined  
d. Undefined

210. _____ refers to a process whereby the assets of a business are converted to money. The conversion may be coerced by a legal process to pay off the debt of the business, or to satisfy any other business obligation that the business has not voluntarily satisfied.
a. Liquidation6  
b. Thing  
c. Undefined  
d. Undefined

211. _____ refers to any distinct act of dominion wrongfully exerted over another's personal property in denial of or inconsistent with his rights therein. That tort committed by a person who deals with chattels not belonging to him in a manner that is inconsistent with the ownership of the lawful owner.
a. Conversion6  
b. Thing  
c. Undefined  
d. Undefined

212. A task established for an employee that provides the comparative basis for performance appraisal is a _____.
a. Performance target6  
b. Thing  
c. Undefined  
d. Undefined

213. In some contexts, the word bears the same import as the word evidence, but in most connections it has a much narrower meaning. _____ are the words heard from the witness in court, and evidence is what the jury considers it worth.
a. Testimony6  
b. Thing  
c. Undefined  
d. Undefined

214. _____ refers to the price at which the purchaser of an option has the right to buy or sell the underlying financial instrument. Also known as the strike price.
a. Thing  
b. Exercise price6  
c. Undefined  
d. Undefined

215. The discussion by counsel for the respective parties of their contentions on the law and the facts of the case being tried in order to aid the jury in arriving at a correct and just conclusion is called _____.
a. Thing  
b. Argument6  
c. Undefined  
d. Undefined

216. _____ refers to as applied to a warrant, this represents the market value of common stock minus the exercise price. The difference is then multiplied by the number of shares each warrant entitles the holder to purchase.
a. Thing  
b. Intrinsic value6  
c. Undefined  
d. Undefined

## Chapter 6. Analyzing Operating Activities

217. _____ refers to the percentage cost of funds used for acquiring resources for an organization, typically a weighted average of the firms cost of equity and cost of debt.
    a. Place
    b. Cost of capital6
    c. Undefined
    d. Undefined

218. _____ refers to the monetary income a firm sacrifices when it uses a resource it owns rather than supplying the resource in the market; equal to what the resource could have earned in the best-paying alternative employment.
    a. Thing
    b. Implicit cost6
    c. Undefined
    d. Undefined

219. _____ occurs when additional shares of stock are sold without creating an immediate increase in income. The result is a decline in earnings per share until earnings can be generated from the funds raized.
    a. Dilution of earnings per share6
    b. Thing
    c. Undefined
    d. Undefined

220. EPS adjusted for all potential dilution from the issuance of any new shares of common stock arising from convertible bonds, convertible preferred stock, warrants, or any other options outstanding is referred to as the _____.
    a. Diluted earnings per share6
    b. Thing
    c. Undefined
    d. Undefined

221. Corporate stock that has been reacquired by the corporation is _____. It is stock which is bought back by the issuing company. It reduces the number of outstanding stocks on the open market ("open market" including insiders holdings).
    a. Thing
    b. Treasury stock6
    c. Undefined
    d. Undefined

222. A person in possession of a document of title or an instrument payable or indorsed to him, his order, or to bearer is a _____.
    a. Thing
    b. Holder6
    c. Undefined
    d. Undefined

223. _____ occurs when the interaction is moderately important to meeting goals and the goals are neither completely compatible nor completely incompatible.
    a. Thing
    b. Compromise6
    c. Undefined
    d. Undefined

224. _____ in a financial context refers to the rate at which a provider of goods cycles through its average inventory. _____ in a human resources context refers to the characteristic of a given company or industry, relative to rate at which an employer gains and loses staff.
    a. Turnover6
    b. Thing
    c. Undefined
    d. Undefined

225. In economic models, the _____ time frame assumes no fixed factors of production. Firms can enter or leave the marketplace, and the cost (and availability) of land, labor, raw materials, and capital goods can be assumed to vary.

## Chapter 6. Analyzing Operating Activities

a. Thing
c. Undefined
b. Long run6
d. Undefined

226. _____ refers to a measure of income that usually excludes items that a company thinks are unusual or nonrecurring; forecast income.
a. Thing
c. Undefined
b. Pro forma income6
d. Undefined

227. _____ is the world's largest pharmaceutical company based in New York City. It produces the number-one selling drug Lipitor (atorvastatin, used to lower blood cholesterol).
a. Organization
c. Undefined
b. Pfizer6
d. Undefined

228. A contract remedy whereby the defendant is ordered to perform according to the terms of his contract is referred to as _____.
a. Specific performance6
c. Undefined
b. Thing
d. Undefined

229. _____ refers to the maximum total sales of a product that a firm expects to sell during a specified time period under specified environmental conditions and its own marketing efforts.
a. Thing
c. Undefined
b. Sales forecast6
d. Undefined

230. _____ in contract law, a basic requirement for an enforceable agreement under traditional contract principles, defined in this text as legal value, bargained for and given in exchange for an act or promise. In corporation law, cash or property contributed to a corporation in exchange for shares, or a promise to contribute such cash or property.
a. Thing
c. Undefined
b. Consideration6
d. Undefined

231. _____ refers to the manner in which an economy distributes its resources among the potential uses so as to produce a particular set of final goods.
a. Resource allocation6
c. Undefined
b. Thing
d. Undefined

232. In agency law, one under whose direction an agent acts and for whose benefit that agent acts Is a _____.
a. Principal6
c. Undefined
b. Thing
d. Undefined

233. The cost a business incurs to borrow money. With respect to bonds payable, the _____ is calculated by multiplying the market rate of interest by the carrying value of the bonds on the date of the payment.
a. Interest expense6
c. Undefined
b. Thing
d. Undefined

234. In many ways, _____ differs from its main competitor, having three times as many employees, larger revenues, but a smaller net profit.

a. Thing  
c. Undefined  
b. PepsiCo6  
d. Undefined

235. Because _____ creates goods for a wide range of sports, they have competition from every sports and sports fashion brand there is. _____ has no direct competitors because there is no single brand which can compete directly with their range of sports and non-sports oriented gear, except for Reebok.
a. Thing  
c. Undefined  
b. Nike6  
d. Undefined

236. A _____ is something measured by a number; it is used to analyze what happens to other things when the size of that number changes.
a. Thing  
c. Undefined  
b. Variable6  
d. Undefined

237. Obtaining financing by borrowing money is _____.
a. Thing  
c. Undefined  
b. Debt financing6  
d. Undefined

238. The difference between the face value of a bond and its selling price, when a bond is sold for less than its face value it's referred to as a _____.
a. Thing  
c. Undefined  
b. Discount6  
d. Undefined

239. A _____ is a security that entitles the holder to buy or sell a certain additional quantity of an underlying security at an agreed-upon price, at the holder's discretion.
a. Warrant6  
c. Undefined  
b. Thing  
d. Undefined

240. _____ refers to a document authorizing its holder to purchase a stated number of shares of stock at a stated price, usually for a stated period of time; may be freely traded.
a. Thing  
c. Undefined  
b. Stock warrant6  
d. Undefined

241. Net cash equivalent amount paid or to be paid for the asset is an _____. e expense undertaken to acquire new business. The concept applies to both agents and companies. The largest portion of an insurer's _____ is agent's or sales representative's commission or bonus.
a. Acquisition cost6  
c. Undefined  
b. Thing  
d. Undefined

242. In bonds, notes or other fixed income securities, the stated percentage rate of interest, usually paid twice a year is the _____.
a. Thing  
c. Undefined  
b. Coupon rate6  
d. Undefined

## Chapter 6. Analyzing Operating Activities

243. Generally, a legal right to engage in conduct that would otherwise result in legal liability is a _____. Privileges are commonly classified as absolute or conditional. Occasionally, _____ is also used to denote a legal right to refrain from particular behavior.
   a. Privilege6
   b. Thing
   c. Undefined
   d. Undefined

244. In finance, a _____ is "attached" to a bond, either physically (as with old bonds) or electronically. Each _____ represents a predetermined payment promized to the bond-holder in return for his or her loan of money to the bond-issuer. .
   a. Concept
   b. Coupon6
   c. Undefined
   d. Undefined

245. Interest expenditures included in the cost of a self-constructed asset is _____.
   a. Capitalized interest6
   b. Thing
   c. Undefined
   d. Undefined

246. _____ is the result of computing current and deferred tax payable using the asset-liability method in which the balance sheet is seen as primary and the income statement as secondary.
   a. Thing
   b. Tax expense6
   c. Undefined
   d. Undefined

247. Taxes not paid until future years because of the difference in accounting methods selected for financial statements and methods required for tax purposes are _____.
   a. Deferred tax liability6
   b. Thing
   c. Undefined
   d. Undefined

248. _____ is an accounting term, meaning future tax liability or asset, resulting from temporary differences between book (accounting) value of assets and liabilities, and their tax value.
   a. Thing
   b. Deferred tax6
   c. Undefined
   d. Undefined

249. The dollar sum of costs that an insured individual must pay before the insurer begins to pay is called _____.
   a. Deductible6
   b. Thing
   c. Undefined
   d. Undefined

250. Allows a firm to reduce the taxes paid to the home government by the amount of taxes paid to the foreign government is referred to as _____.
   a. Thing
   b. Tax credit6
   c. Undefined
   d. Undefined

251. Reduction in the selling price of goods extended to the buyer because the goods are defective or of lower quality than the buyer ordered and to encourage a buyer to keep merchandise that would otherwise be returned is the _____.
   a. Allowance6
   b. Thing
   c. Undefined
   d. Undefined

## Chapter 6. Analyzing Operating Activities

252. _____ refers to the entity that has a controlling influence over another company. It may have its own operations, or it may have been set up solely for the purpose of owning the Subject Company.
   a. Thing
   b. Parent company6
   c. Undefined
   d. Undefined

253. _____ refers to restrictions state and federal laws place on business with regard to the conduct of its activities.
   a. Regulation6
   b. Thing
   c. Undefined
   d. Undefined

254. _____ is a bookkeeping method that recognizes revenue and expenses at the time of cash receipt or payment. It is the opposite of Accrual Basis.
   a. Thing
   b. Cash basis6
   c. Undefined
   d. Undefined

255. _____ in agency law, refers to an agent's ability to affect his principal's legal relations with third parties. Also used to refer to an actor's legal power or ability to do something. In addition, sometimes used to refer to a statute, case, or other legal source that justifies a particular result.
   a. Concept
   b. Authority6
   c. Undefined
   d. Undefined

256. Proportionate is referred to as _____. A method of equally and proportionately allocating money, profits or liabilities by percentage.
   a. Pro rata6
   b. Thing
   c. Undefined
   d. Undefined

257. _____ refers to the regional and economic differences in a country, province, state, or continent
   a. Thing
   b. Disparity6
   c. Undefined
   d. Undefined

258. Methods that result in higher depreciation expense in the early years of an asset's life, and lower expense in the later years are referred to as _____.
   a. Accelerated depreciation6
   b. Thing
   c. Undefined
   d. Undefined

259. A company owned in a foreign country by another company is referred to as _____.
   a. Foreign subsidiary6
   b. Thing
   c. Undefined
   d. Undefined

260. A _____ is a 12-month period used for calculating annual ("yearly") financial reports in businesses and other organizations. In many jurisdictions, regulatory laws regarding accounting require such reports once per twelve months, but do not require that the twelve months constitute a calendar year (i.e. January to December).
   a. Fiscal year6
   b. Thing
   c. Undefined
   d. Undefined

261. A nation's currency is said to _____ when exchange rates change so that a unit of its currency can buy fewer units of foreign currency.

a. Depreciate6  
b. Thing  
c. Undefined  
d. Undefined

262. _____ is the concept that the value of money varies depending on the timing of the cash flows, given any interest rate greater than zero.
a. Concept  
b. Time value of money6  
c. Undefined  
d. Undefined

263. _____ refers to the quantity of goods and services for which a unit of money can be exchanged; the purchasing power of a unit of money; the reciprocal of the price level.
a. Thing  
b. Value of money6  
c. Undefined  
d. Undefined

264. _____ is the branch of accountancy concerned with the preparation of financial statements for external decision makers, such as stockholders, suppliers, banks and government agencies. The fundamental need for _____ is to reduce principal-agent problem by measuring and monitoring agents' performance.
a. Thing  
b. Financial accounting6  
c. Undefined  
d. Undefined

265. _____ refers to the gain in value that the owner of an asset experiences when the price of the asset rises, including when the currency in which the asset is denominated appreciates.
a. Thing  
b. Capital gain6  
c. Undefined  
d. Undefined

266. _____ refer to the typical tax shelter generated large losses in the early years of the activity. Investors would offset these losses against other types of income and, therefore, avoid paying income taxes on this income.
a. Tax shelters6  
b. Thing  
c. Undefined  
d. Undefined

267. A provision of the corporate income tax that reduces a firm's tax when it buys new capital goods is referred to as _____.
a. Thing  
b. Investment tax credit6  
c. Undefined  
d. Undefined

268. The _____ is the amount of income tax an individual or firm pays divided by the individual or firm's total taxable income. This ratio is usually expressed as a percentage.
a. Effective tax rate6  
b. Thing  
c. Undefined  
d. Undefined

269. _____ is a liability. It is recorded when an asset (e.g. receivable) is recorded, but the related income (i.e. revenue) will be earned only in the future.
a. Thing  
b. Deferred income6  
c. Undefined  
d. Undefined

270. A type of influence process where a receiver accepts the position advocated by a source to obtain favorable outcomes or to avoid punishment is the _____.

a. Thing  
c. Undefined  
b. Compliance6  
d. Undefined  

271. _____ refers to the amount by which expenses exceed revenues. The difference between income received and expenses, when expenses are greater.
   a. Net loss6  
   c. Undefined  
   b. Thing  
   d. Undefined  

272. _____ refers to the way a corporation finances itself through some combination of equity sales, equity options, bonds, and loans. Optimal _____ refers to the particular combination that minimizes the cost of capital while maximizing the stock price.
   a. Thing  
   c. Undefined  
   b. Capital structure6  
   d. Undefined  

273. An organization that employs resources to produce a good or service for profit and owns and operates one or more plants is referred to as a _____.
   a. Thing  
   c. Undefined  
   b. Firm6  
   d. Undefined  

274. Securities giving their holders the power to exchange those securities for other securities without paying any additional consideration are _____.
   a. Convertible securities6  
   c. Undefined  
   b. Thing  
   d. Undefined  

275. A _____ is a security that can be converted into another security, for example, a bond that under certain terms can be converted into equity.
   a. Convertible security6  
   c. Undefined  
   b. Thing  
   d. Undefined  

276. Earnings per share unadjusted for dilution are _____.
   a. Basic earnings per share6  
   c. Undefined  
   b. Thing  
   d. Undefined  

277. Stock that has specified rights over common stock is a _____.
   a. Thing  
   c. Undefined  
   b. Preferred stock6  
   d. Undefined  

278. A _____ is type of bond that can be converted into shares of stock in the issuing company, usually at some pre-announced ratio.
   a. Convertible bond6  
   c. Undefined  
   b. Thing  
   d. Undefined  

279. At equality refers to _____. Two currencies are said to be '_____' if they are trading one-for-one.
   a. Thing  
   c. Undefined  
   b. At par6  
   d. Undefined

## Chapter 6. Analyzing Operating Activities

280. The percentage of an additional dollar of earnings that goes to taxes is referred to as the _____.
    a. Thing
    b. Marginal tax rate6
    c. Undefined
    d. Undefined

281. _____ indicates that a party, or proprietor, exercises private ownership, control or use over an item of property, usually to the exclusion of other parties. Where a party, holds or claims _____ interests in relation to certain types of property (eg. a creative literary work, or software), that property may also be the subject of intellectual property law (eg. copyright or patents).
    a. Proprietary6
    b. Thing
    c. Undefined
    d. Undefined

282. Collecting information and providing feedback to employees about their behavior, communication style, or skills is an _____.
    a. Assessment6
    b. Thing
    c. Undefined
    d. Undefined

283. _____ refers to the total number of dollars received by a firm from the sale of a product; equal to the total expenditures for the product produced by the firm; equal to the quantity sold multiplied by the price at which it is sold.
    a. Total revenue6
    b. Thing
    c. Undefined
    d. Undefined

284. _____ can mean a retail shop, a checkout counter in a shop, or a variable location where a transaction occurs.
    a. Thing
    b. Point of Sale6
    c. Undefined
    d. Undefined

285. _____ refers to collections of legal rules produced by the American Law Institute, covering certain subject matter areas. Although restatements are often persuasive to courts, they are not legally binding unless adopted by the highest court of a particular state.
    a. Restatement6
    b. Thing
    c. Undefined
    d. Undefined

286. In finance, _____ occurs when a debtor has not met its legal obligations according to the debt contract, e.g. it has not made a scheduled payment, or violated a covenant (condition) of the debt contract.
    a. Thing
    b. Default6
    c. Undefined
    d. Undefined

287. _____ refers to all the techniques sellers use to motivate people to buy products or services. An attempt by marketers to inform people about products and to persuade them to participate in an exchange.
    a. Thing
    b. Promotion6
    c. Undefined
    d. Undefined

288. Converting the financial statements of foreign subsidiaries into the currency of the home country is a _____.
    a. Thing
    b. Currency translation6
    c. Undefined
    d. Undefined

289. The _____ percentage shows how profitable a company's assets are in generating revenue.

a. Thing  
c. Undefined  
b. Return on Assets6  
d. Undefined

290. _____ refers to the return on an asset expected over the next period.
a. Thing  
c. Undefined  
b. Expected return6  
d. Undefined

291. Amounts of money put aside by corporations, nonprofit organizations, or unions to cover part of the financial needs of members when they retire is a _____.
a. Thing  
c. Undefined  
b. Pension fund6  
d. Undefined

292. The expense associated with uncollectible accounts is _____. When it is a significant amount, the _____ is estimated with the allowance method.
a. Thing  
c. Undefined  
b. Bad debt expense6  
d. Undefined

293. In accounting and finance, _____ is the portion of receivables that can no longer be collected, typically from accounts receivable or loans. _____ in accounting is considered an expense.
a. Bad debt6  
c. Undefined  
b. Thing  
d. Undefined

294. Reduction of sales revenues for return of or allowances for unsatisfactory goods are _____.
a. Sales returns and allowances6  
c. Undefined  
b. Thing  
d. Undefined

295. _____ refers to paid, nonpersonal communication through various media by organizations and individuals who are in some way identified in the _____ message.
a. Thing  
c. Undefined  
b. Advertising6  
d. Undefined

296. The group of individuals elected by the stockholders of a corporation to oversee its operations is a _____.
a. Thing  
c. Undefined  
b. Board of directors6  
d. Undefined

297. The central value of a pegged exchange rate, around which the actual rate is permitted to fluctuate within set bounds is a _____.
a. Thing  
c. Undefined  
b. Par value6  
d. Undefined

298. A publicity tool consisting of an announcement regarding changes in the company or the product line is called a _____.
a. Thing  
c. Undefined  
b. News release6  
d. Undefined

## Chapter 6. Analyzing Operating Activities

299. Characterized by rizing output, falling unemployment, rizing profits, and increasing economic activity following a decline is a _____.
   a. Recovery6
   b. Thing
   c. Undefined
   d. Undefined

300. _____ refers to pro rata distributions of stock or stock rights on common stock. They are usually issued in proportion to shares owned.
   a. Thing
   b. Stock dividend6
   c. Undefined
   d. Undefined

301. A _____ is a long-term debt instrument used by governments and large companies to obtain funds. It is similar to a bond except the securitization conditions are different.
   a. Debenture6
   b. Thing
   c. Undefined
   d. Undefined

302. _____ refers to the combination of two firms into a single firm.
   a. Thing
   b. Merger6
   c. Undefined
   d. Undefined

303. An _____ is the totality of the legal rights, interests, entitlements and obligations attaching to property. In the context of wills and probate, it refers to the totality of the property which the deceased owned or in which some interest was held.
   a. Thing
   b. Estate6
   c. Undefined
   d. Undefined

304. A name, symbol, or design that identifies the goods or services of one seller or group of sellers and distinguishes them from the goods and services of competitors is a _____.
   a. Brand6
   b. Thing
   c. Undefined
   d. Undefined

305. Tax _____ falls into two categories: civil and criminal. Under civil _____, the IRS may impose as a penalty of an amount equal to as much as 75 percent of the underpayment.
   a. Thing
   b. Fraud6
   c. Undcfincd
   d. Undefined

306. A short-term immediate decision that, in its totality, leads to the achievement of strategic goals is called a _____.
   a. Tactic6
   b. Thing
   c. Undefined
   d. Undefined

307. _____ refers to a business that is independently owned and operated, is not dominant in its field of operation, and meets certain standards of size in terms of employees or annual receipts.
   a. Thing
   b. Small business6
   c. Undefined
   d. Undefined

308. _____ refers to that part of the production process that puts together components.

## Chapter 6. Analyzing Operating Activities

a. Concept
c. Undefined
b. Assembly process6
d. Undefined

309. A detailed written statement that describes the nature of the business, the target market, the advantages the business will have in relation to competition, and the resources and qualifications of the owner is referred to as a _____.
a. Business plan6
c. Undefined
b. Thing
d. Undefined

310. Designed to facilitate the timely movement of goods and represent a very important part of a supply chain is a _____.
a. Thing
c. Undefined
b. Distribution center6
d. Undefined

311. _____ refers to the flow of goods, services, and information from the initial sources of materials and services to the delivery of products to consumers.
a. Supply chain6
c. Undefined
b. Thing
d. Undefined

312. That fraction of an industry's output accounted for by an individual firm or group of firms is called _____.
a. Thing
c. Undefined
b. Market share6
d. Undefined

313. A _____ is an individual or company (including a corporation) that legally owns one or more shares of stock in a joined stock company. The shareholders are the owners of a corporation. Companies listed at the stock market strive to enhance shareholder value.
a. Stockholder6
c. Undefined
b. Thing
d. Undefined

314. In business and engineering, new _____ is the complete process of bringing a new product to market. There are two parallel aspects to this process : one involves product engineering ; the other marketing analysis. Marketers see new _____ as the first stage in product life cycle management, engineers as part of Product Lifecycle Management.
a. Product development6
c. Undefined
b. Thing
d. Undefined

315. Changing the position an offering occupies in a consumer's mind relative to competitive offerings and so expanding or otherwise altering its potential market is called _____.
a. Repositioning6
c. Undefined
b. Thing
d. Undefined

316. _____, in communications (sometimes called communications _____), refers to the medium used to convey information from a sender (or transmitter) to a receiver.
a. Thing
c. Undefined
b. Channel6
d. Undefined

317. A _____ is directly responsible for managing the day-to-day operations (and profitability) of a company.

## Chapter 6. Analyzing Operating Activities

a. Management team6
b. Thing
c. Undefined
d. Undefined

318. A _____ is a type of philanthropic organization set up by either individuals or institutions as a legal entity (either as a corporation or trust) with the purpose of distributing grants to support causes in line with the goals of the _____.
a. Thing
b. Foundation6
c. Undefined
d. Undefined

319. After-tax operating income minus the weighted average cost of capital multiplied by total assets minus current liabilities is called _____.
a. Thing
b. Economic value added6
c. Undefined
d. Undefined

320. The value of output minus the value of all intermediate inputs, representing therefore the contribution of, and payments to, primary factors of production a _____.
a. Value added6
b. Thing
c. Undefined
d. Undefined

321. The dollar difference between total current assets and total current liabilities is called _____.
a. Working capital6
b. Thing
c. Undefined
d. Undefined

322. _____ refers to the total output of goods and services in a given period of time divided by work hours.
a. Productivity6
b. Thing
c. Undefined
d. Undefined

323. A transfer of property or some right or interest is referred to as _____.
a. Thing
b. Assignment6
c. Undefined
d. Undefined

324. The finalization of a real estate sales transaction that passes title to the property from the seller to the buyer is referred to as a _____. _____ is a sales term which refers to the process of making a sale. It refers to reaching the final step, which may be an exchange of money or acquiring a signature.
a. Thing
b. Closing6
c. Undefined
d. Undefined

325. Expenses that have been incurred by the end of the current accounting period but that will not be paid until a future accounting period are _____.
a. Thing
b. Accrued expenses6
c. Undefined
d. Undefined

326. Previously outstanding shares repurchased by a corporation that are not canceled or restored to unissued status are _____.
a. Person
b. Treasury shares6
c. Undefined
d. Undefined

## Chapter 6. Analyzing Operating Activities

327. In accrual basis accounting, _____ is a liability resulting from an expense for which no invoice or other official document is available yet.
   a. Accrued expense6
   b. Thing
   c. Undefined
   d. Undefined

328. From or in one's own country. A _____ producer is one that produces inside the home country. A _____ price is the price inside the home country. Opposite of 'foreign' or 'world.'.
   a. Thing
   b. Domestic6
   c. Undefined
   d. Undefined

329. A _____ is a type of business loan that leaves the lender the option of taking stock in the company instead of repayment.In theory, the market price of a _____ should never drop below its intrinsic value.
   a. Thing
   b. Convertible debenture6
   c. Undefined
   d. Undefined

330. Short-term obligations of the federal government are _____. They are like zero coupon bonds in that they do not pay interest prior to maturity; instead they are sold at a discount of the par value to create a positive yield to maturity.
   a. Thing
   b. Treasury bills6
   c. Undefined
   d. Undefined

331. A _____ is a method by which an organization sets aside money over time to retire its indebtedness. More specifically, it is a fund into which money can be deposited, so that over time its preferred stock, debentures or stocks can be retired.
   a. Thing
   b. Sinking fund6
   c. Undefined
   d. Undefined

332. A pro rata distribution of cash to stockholders of corporate stock is called a _____.
   a. Cash dividend6
   b. Thing
   c. Undefined
   d. Undefined

## Chapter 7. Cash Flow Analysis

1. In finance, _____ refers to the amounts of cash being received and spent by a business during a defined period of time, sometimes tied to a specific project. Most of the time they are being used to determine gaps in the liquid position of a company.
   - a. Thing
   - b. Cash flow7
   - c. Undefined
   - d. Undefined

2. Reports inflows and outflows of cash during the accounting period in the categories of operating, investing, and financing is a _____.
   - a. Statement of cash flow7
   - b. Thing
   - c. Undefined
   - d. Undefined

3. _____ refers to usually the first stage in the creative process. It includes education and formal training.
   - a. Thing
   - b. Preparation7
   - c. Undefined
   - d. Undefined

4. Cash flow activities that include the cash effects of transactions that create revenues and expenses and thus enter into the determination of net income is an _____.
   - a. Thing
   - b. Operating activities7
   - c. Undefined
   - d. Undefined

5. Movement of funds related to the company's operations, reported on the cash flow statement of a company's annual report are _____.
   - a. Cash flows from operating activities7
   - b. Thing
   - c. Undefined
   - d. Undefined

6. _____ refers to cash flow activities that include purchasing and disposing of investments and productive long-lived assets using cash and lending money and collecting on those loans.
   - a. Investing activities7
   - b. Thing
   - c. Undefined
   - d. Undefined

7. Cash flowing out of the business from all sources over a period of time is _____.
   - a. Thing
   - b. Cash outflow7
   - c. Undefined
   - d. Undefined

8. _____ is a United States retailer and pharmacy chain, operating nearly 3,400 stores in 28 states and the District of Columbia. _____ is a major contributor to the Children's Miracle Network. It was named the third largest drugstore in the United States by 1981; shortly thereafter, 1983 marked a sales milestone of $1 billion.
   - a. Rite Aid7
   - b. Organization
   - c. Undefined
   - d. Undefined

9. Assistance provided by countries and by international institutions such as the World Bank to developing countries in the form of monetary grants, loans at low interest rates, in kind, or a combination of these is called _____. _____ can also refer to assistance of any type rendered to benefit some group or individual.
   - a. Aid7
   - b. Thing
   - c. Undefined
   - d. Undefined

10. _____ refers to paid, nonpersonal communication through various media by organizations and individuals who are in some way identified in the _____ message.
   a. Advertising7
   b. Thing
   c. Undefined
   d. Undefined

11. Tangible property held for sale in the normal course of business or used in producing goods or services for sale is an _____.
   a. Thing
   b. Inventory7
   c. Undefined
   d. Undefined

12. _____ refers to the basic, normal, voting stock issued by a corporation; called residual equity because it ranks after preferred stock for dividend and liquidation distributions.
   a. Common stock7
   b. Thing
   c. Undefined
   d. Undefined

13. _____ refers to a recording as positive in the balance of payments, any transaction that gives rise to a payment into the country, such as an export, the sale of an asset, or borrowing from abroad.
   a. Thing
   b. Credit7
   c. Undefined
   d. Undefined

14. In financial terminology, _____ is the capital raized by a corporation, through the issuance and sale of shares.
   a. Stock7
   b. Thing
   c. Undefined
   d. Undefined

15. Cash coming into the company as the result of a previous investment is a _____.
   a. Thing
   b. Cash inflow7
   c. Undefined
   d. Undefined

16. _____ refers to spending for the production and accumulation of capital and additions to inventories. In a financial sense, buying an asset with the expectation of making a return.
   a. Thing
   b. Investment7
   c. Undefined
   d. Undefined

17. A _____ is a present obligation of the enterprise arizing from past events, the settlement of which is expected to result in an outflow from the enterprise of resources embodying economic benefits.
   a. Thing
   b. Liability7
   c. Undefined
   d. Undefined

18. The trade of things of value between buyer and seller so that each is better off after the trade is called the _____.
   a. Exchange7
   b. Thing
   c. Undefined
   d. Undefined

19. A person in possession of a document of title or an instrument payable or indorsed to him, his order, or to bearer is a _____.

## Chapter 7. Cash Flow Analysis

a. Thing
b. Holder7
c. Undefined
d. Undefined

20. A contract for the possession and use of land or other property, including goods, on one side, and a recompense of rent or other income on the other is the _____.
a. Lease7
b. Thing
c. Undefined
d. Undefined

21. _____ refers to a debt instrument, issued by a borrower and promising a specified stream of payments to the purchaser, usually regular interest payments plus a final repayment of principal.
a. Bond7
b. Thing
c. Undefined
d. Undefined

22. _____ refers to a "non tangible product" that is not embodied in a physical good and that typically effects some change in another product, person, or institution. Contrasts with good.
a. Thing
b. Service7
c. Undefined
d. Undefined

23. _____ is a business magazine published by McGraw-Hill. It was first published in 1929 under the direction of Malcolm Muir, who was serving as president of the McGraw-Hill Publishing company at the time. It is considered to be the standard both in industry and among students.
a. Business Week7
b. Organization
c. Undefined
d. Undefined

24. In accounting, an _____ represents an event in which an asset is used up or a liability is incurred. In terms of the accounting equation, expenses reduce owners' equity.
a. Thing
b. Expense7
c. Undefined
d. Undefined

25. _____ refers to the cash inflows and cash outflows from the general operating activities of the business; one of the three sections in the statement of cash flows.
a. Thing
b. Operating cash flows7
c. Undefined
d. Undefined

26. _____ is a bookkeeping method that recognizes revenue and expenses at the time of cash receipt or payment. It is the opposite of Accrual Basis.
a. Thing
b. Cash basis7
c. Undefined
d. Undefined

27. _____ is equal to the income that a firm has after subtracting costs and expenses from the total revenue. Expenses will typically include tax expense.
a. Net income7
b. Thing
c. Undefined
d. Undefined

28. A standardized method or technique that is performed repetitively, often on different materials resulting in different finished goods is called an _____.

a. Operation7  
b. Thing  
c. Undefined  
d. Undefined

29. An _____ is an accounting event in which the transaction is recognized when the action takes place, instead of when cash is disbursed or received.
    a. Thing
    b. Accrual7
    c. Undefined
    d. Undefined

30. The amount of earnings attributable to higher sales or lower costs rather than artificial profits created by accounting anomalies such as inflation of inventory is the _____.
    a. Quality of earnings7
    b. Thing
    c. Undefined
    d. Undefined

31. Cash flow activities that include obtaining cash from issuing debt and repaying the amounts borrowed and obtaining cash from stockholders and paying dividends is referred to as _____.
    a. Thing
    b. Financing activities7
    c. Undefined
    d. Undefined

32. _____ refers to the capacity to turn assets into cash, or the amount of assets in a portfolio that have that capacity.
    a. Thing
    b. Liquidity7
    c. Undefined
    d. Undefined

33. An item of property, such as land, capital, money, a share in ownership, or a claim on others for future payment, such as a bond or a bank deposit is an _____.
    a. Asset7
    b. Thing
    c. Undefined
    d. Undefined

34. _____ refers to the time it takes for a company to purchase goods or services from suppliers, sell those goods and services to customers, and collect cash from customers.
    a. Thing
    b. Operating cycle7
    c. Undefined
    d. Undefined

35. A _____ occurs when a customer does not pay cash at the time of the sale but instead agrees to pay later. The sale occurs now, with payment from the customer to follow at a later time.
    a. Credit sale7
    b. Thing
    c. Undefined
    d. Undefined

36. _____ refers to any distinct act of dominion wrongfully exerted over another's personal property in denial of or inconsistent with his rights therein. That tort committed by a person who deals with chattels not belonging to him in a manner that is inconsistent with the ownership of the lawful owner.
    a. Thing
    b. Conversion7
    c. Undefined
    d. Undefined

37. The interest rate that equates a future value or an annuity to a given present value is a _____.

a. Yield7  
b. Thing  
c. Undefined  
d. Undefined

38. _____ refers to giving workers the education and tools they need to assume their new decision-making powers.
a. Thing  
b. Enabling7  
c. Undefined  
d. Undefined

39. Amount of corporate profits paid out for each share of stock is referred to as _____.
a. Thing  
b. Dividend7  
c. Undefined  
d. Undefined

40. The ability of a company to pay interest as it comes due and to repay the face value of debt at maturity is called _____.
a. Thing  
b. Solvency7  
c. Undefined  
d. Undefined

41. _____ refers to a financial statement that presents the revenues and expenses and resulting net income or net loss of a company for a specific period of time.
a. Income statement7  
b. Thing  
c. Undefined  
d. Undefined

42. A statement of the assets, liabilities, and net worth of a firm or individual at some given time often at the end of its "fiscal year," is referred to as a _____.
a. Balance sheet7  
b. Thing  
c. Undefined  
d. Undefined

43. In banking and accountancy, the outstanding _____ is the amount of money owned, (or due), that remains in a deposit account (or a loan account) at a given date, after all past remittances, payments and withdrawal have been accounted for. It can be positive (then, in the _____ sheet of a firm, it is an asset) or negative (a liability).
a. Thing  
b. Balance7  
c. Undefined  
d. Undefined

44. Two or more balance sheets from the same company for consecutive accounting periods, shown together to reflect the company's financial situation over time are refrred to as _____.
a. Comparative balance sheets7  
b. Thing  
c. Undefined  
d. Undefined

45. _____ refers to a summary of all the transactions that have occurred over a particular period.
a. Thing  
b. Financial statement7  
c. Undefined  
d. Undefined

46. _____ refer to people in the organization who actually use the product or service purchased by the buying center.
a. Thing  
b. Users7  
c. Undefined  
d. Undefined

47. A system that collects and processes financial information about an organization and reports that information to decision makers is referred to as _____.
   a. Thing
   b. Accounting7
   c. Undefined
   d. Undefined

48. _____ is a U.S. business term for the amount of money that a company receives from its activities, mostly from sales of products and/or services to customers.
   a. Thing
   b. Revenue7
   c. Undefined
   d. Undefined

49. Expenses that have been incurred by the end of the current accounting period but that will not be paid until a future accounting period are _____.
   a. Thing
   b. Accrued expenses7
   c. Undefined
   d. Undefined

50. The dollar difference between total current assets and total current liabilities is called _____.
   a. Thing
   b. Working capital7
   c. Undefined
   d. Undefined

51. The _____ is one of two primary components of the balance of payments. It tracks the movement of funds for investments and loans into and out of a country.
   a. Thing
   b. Capital account7
   c. Undefined
   d. Undefined

52. In accrual basis accounting, _____ is a liability resulting from an expense for which no invoice or other official document is available yet.
   a. Accrued expense7
   b. Thing
   c. Undefined
   d. Undefined

53. Obligations to make future economic sacrifices, usually cash payments, are referred to as _____. Same as current liabilities.
   a. Payables7
   b. Thing
   c. Undefined
   d. Undefined

54. _____ generally refers to financial wealth, especially that used to start or maintain a business. In classical economics, _____ is one of four factors of production, the others being land and labor and entrepreneurship.
   a. Thing
   b. Capital7
   c. Undefined
   d. Undefined

55. In agency law, one under whose direction an agent acts and for whose benefit that agent acts is a _____.
   a. Principal7
   b. Thing
   c. Undefined
   d. Undefined

56. Independent accounting entity with a self-balancing set of accounts segregated for the purposes of carrying on specific activities is referred to as a _____.

a. Thing  
b. Fund7  
c. Undefined  
d. Undefined

57. A _____ is a financial report that shows incoming and outgoing money during a particular period (often monthly or quarterly). The statement shows how changes in balance sheet and income accounts affected cash and cash equivalents and breaks the analysis down according to operating, investing, and financing activities.
   a. Cash flow statement7  
   b. Thing  
   c. Undefined  
   d. Undefined

58. The method of presenting the operating activities section of the statement of cash flow statement reports components of cash flows from operating activities as gross receipts and gross payments is called _____.
   a. Concept  
   b. Direct method7  
   c. Undefined  
   d. Undefined

59. The method of presenting the operating activities section of the statement of cash flows that adjusts net income to compute cash flows from operating activities is referred to as _____.
   a. Indirect method7  
   b. Thing  
   c. Undefined  
   d. Undefined

60. _____ means the giving out of information, either voluntarily or to be in compliance with legal regulations or workplace rules.
   a. Disclosure7  
   b. Thing  
   c. Undefined  
   d. Undefined

61. _____ refers to the return to the resource entrepreneurial ability; total revenue minus total cost.
   a. Thing  
   b. Profit7  
   c. Undefined  
   d. Undefined

62. A _____ is an asset on the balance sheet which is expected to be sold or otherwise used up in the near future, usually within one year.
   a. Current asset7  
   b. Thing  
   c. Undefined  
   d. Undefined

63. Systematic and rational allocation of the acquisition cost of an intangible asset over its useful life is referred to as _____.
   a. Amortization7  
   b. Thing  
   c. Undefined  
   d. Undefined

64. _____ is an accounting and finance term for the method of attributing the cost of an asset across the useful life of the asset. _____ is a reduction in the value of a currency in floating exchange rate.
   a. Depreciation7  
   b. Thing  
   c. Undefined  
   d. Undefined

65. In finance, _____ is a profit or an increase in value of an investment such as a stock or bond. _____ is calculated by fair market value or the proceeds from the sale of the investment minus the sum of the purchase price and all costs associated with it.

a. Gain7
b. Thing
c. Undefined
d. Undefined

66. Movement of funds related to the company's investments, reported on the cash flow statement of a company's annual report are _____.
a. Event
b. Cash flows from investing activities7
c. Undefined
d. Undefined

67. The _____ of an asset or group of assets is sometimes the price at which they were originally acquired, in many cases equal to purchase price.
a. Thing
b. Book value7
c. Undefined
d. Undefined

68. A _____ in property law is a future interest created in a transferee that is capable of becoming possessory upon the natural termination of a prior estate created by the same instrument.
a. Thing
b. Remainder7
c. Undefined
d. Undefined

69. Book of original entry, in which transactions are recorded in a general ledger system, is referred to as a _____.
a. Thing
b. Journal7
c. Undefined
d. Undefined

70. _____ refers to the total depreciation that has been reported as depreciation expense for the entire life of a long-term tangible asset. It is a contra-asset account.
a. Accumulated depreciation7
b. Thing
c. Undefined
d. Undefined

71. _____ is the name given to the set of legal principles, in countries following the English common law tradition, which supplement strict rules of law where their application would operate harshly, so as to achieve what is sometimes referred to as "natural justice."
a. Equity7
b. Thing
c. Undefined
d. Undefined

72. Movement of funds related to the financing of the company which is reported on the cash flow statement of a company's annual report are _____.
a. Cash flows from financing activities7
b. Thing
c. Undefined
d. Undefined

73. Stock that has specified rights over common stock is a _____.
a. Preferred stock7
b. Thing
c. Undefined
d. Undefined

74. _____ refers to a note payable issued for property, such as a house, usually repaid in equal installments consisting of part principle and part interest, over a specified period.

## Chapter 7. Cash Flow Analysis

    a. Thing                                                b. Mortgage7
    c. Undefined                                      d. Undefined

75. _____ refer to transactions that do not have direct cash flow effects; reported as a supplement to the statement of cash flows in narrative or schedule form.
    a. Noncash investing and financing activities7      b. Thing
    c. Undefined                                      d. Undefined

76. _____ characterizes the process of leading and directing all or part of an organization, often a business, through the deployment and manipulation of resources. Early twentieth-century _____ writer Mary Parker Follett defined _____ as "the art of getting things done through people."
    a. Thing                                                b. Management7
    c. Undefined                                      d. Undefined

77. _____ is a term in Corporate Finance used to indicate a condition when promises to creditors of a company are broken or honored with difficulty. Sometimes _____ can lead to bankruptcy. _____ is usually associated with some costs to the company and these are known as Costs of _____. A common example of a cost of _____ is bankrupty costs.
    a. Thing                                                b. Financial distress7
    c. Undefined                                      d. Undefined

78. In business organization law, the cash or property contributed to a business by its owners is referred to as _____.
    a. Thing                                                b. Contribution7
    c. Undefined                                      d. Undefined

79. Method of accounting for investments in marketable equity securities; is required when the investor owns percent to percent of the investee company. The amount of investments carried under the _____ represents a measure of the book value of the investee rather than the cost or market value of the investment security.
    a. Thing                                                b. Equity method7
    c. Undefined                                      d. Undefined

80. In finance and economics, _____ is the price paid by a borrower for the use of a lender's money. In other words, _____ is the amount of paid to "rent" money for a period of time.
    a. Interest7                                              b. Thing
    c. Undefined                                      d. Undefined

81. _____ is one of a series of accounting transactions dealing with the billing of customers which owe money to a person, company or organization for goods and services that have been provided to the customer. This is typically done in a one person organization by writing an invoice and mailing or delivering it to each customer.
    a. Thing                                                b. Accounts receivable7
    c. Undefined                                      d. Undefined

82. A financial market in which long-term debt and equity instruments are traded is referred to as a _____. The _____ includes the stock market and the bond market.

a. Thing
b. Capital market7
c. Undefined
d. Undefined

83. _____ is a financing technique that allows the corporation to separate credit origination and funding activities. The technique comes under the umbrella of structured finance as it applies to assets that typically are illiquid contracts.
    a. Thing
    b. Securitization7
    c. Undefined
    d. Undefined

84. A _____ is, as defined in economics, a social arrangement that allows buyers and sellers to discover information and carry out a voluntary exchange of goods or services.
    a. Market7
    b. Thing
    c. Undefined
    d. Undefined

85. _____ refers to a person or tool with a primary function of information analysis, generally with a more limited, practical and short term set of goals than a researcher.
    a. Analyst7
    b. Person
    c. Undefined
    d. Undefined

86. _____ is a transaction that is posted to a cardholder's credit card account in which the cardholder receives cash at an ATM, or cash or travelers checks at a branch of a member financial institution or at a qualified and approved agent of a member financial institution.
    a. Cash disbursement7
    b. Thing
    c. Undefined
    d. Undefined

87. _____ refers to a term often used to describe the party charged in an administrative proceeding. The party adverse to the appellant in a case appealed to a higher court.
    a. Respondent7
    b. Thing
    c. Undefined
    d. Undefined

88. A person to whom a debt or legal obligation is owed, and who has the right to enforce payment of that debt or obligation is referred to as _____.
    a. Thing
    b. Creditor7
    c. Undefined
    d. Undefined

89. A signed, written order by which one party instructs another party to pay a specified sum to a third party, at sight or at a specific date is a _____.
    a. Thing
    b. Draft7
    c. Undefined
    d. Undefined

90. Suppliers and financial institutions that lend money to companies is referred to as a _____.
    a. Thing
    b. Lender7
    c. Undefined
    d. Undefined

91. _____ refers to a system by which individuals can reduce their exposure to risk of large losses by spreading the risks among a large number of persons.

## Chapter 7. Cash Flow Analysis

a. Insurance7
b. Thing
c. Undefined
d. Undefined

92. A legal entity chartered by a state or the Federal government that is distinct and separate from the individuals who own it is a _____. This separation gives the _____ unique powers which other legal entities lack.
a. Corporation7
b. Organization
c. Undefined
d. Undefined

93. _____ is the analysis of the accounts and the economic prospects of a firm.
a. Thing
b. Financial analysis7
c. Undefined
d. Undefined

94. A _____ refers to a layout accurate in size, color, scheme, and other necessary details to show how a final ad will look. For presentation only, never for reproduction.
a. Comprehensive7
b. Thing
c. Undefined
d. Undefined

95. _____ refer to a distribution in which the investment banker agrees to work for a commission rather than actually underwriting the issue for resale. It is a procedure that is used by smaller investment bankers with relatively unknown companies. The investment banker is not directly taking the risk for distribution.
a. Thing
b. Best efforts7
c. Undefined
d. Undefined

96. Local television stations that are associated with a major network are called _____. _____ agree to preempt time during specified hours for programming provided by the network and carry the advertising contained in the program.
a. Thing
b. Affiliates7
c. Undefined
d. Undefined

97. A company that is controlled by another company or corporation is a _____.
a. Subsidiary7
b. Thing
c. Undefined
d. Undefined

98. The consumer's appraisal of the product or brand on important attributes is called _____.
a. Evaluation7
b. Thing
c. Undefined
d. Undefined

99. In finance, _____ is the process of estimating the market value of a financial asset or liability. They can be done on assets (for example, investments in marketable securities such as stocks, options, business enterprises, or intangible assets such as patents and trademarks) or on liabilities (e.g., Bonds issued by a company).
a. Valuation7
b. Event
c. Undefined
d. Undefined

100. Deferred is any account where the asset or liability is not realized until a future date, e.g. annuities, charges, taxes, income, etc. The deferred item may be carried, dependent on type of _____, as either an asset or liability.

a. Thing  
b. Deferral7  
c. Undefined  
d. Undefined

101. Method of accounting that records the effects of accounting events in the period in which such events occur regardless of when cash is exchanged is _____.  
a. Thing  
b. Accrual accounting7  
c. Undefined  
d. Undefined

102. _____ is an important accounting concept that describes the value of a business entity not directly attributable to its tangible assets and liabilities.  
a. Goodwill7  
b. Thing  
c. Undefined  
d. Undefined

103. Collecting information and providing feedback to employees about their behavior, communication style, or skills is an _____.  
a. Assessment7  
b. Thing  
c. Undefined  
d. Undefined

104. _____ refers to the long-term movement of an economic variable, such as its average rate of increase or decrease over enough years to encompass several business cycles.  
a. Trend7  
b. Thing  
c. Undefined  
d. Undefined

105. An out-of-court settlement in which creditors agree to accept a fractional settlement on their original claim is referred to as _____.  
a. Composition7  
b. Thing  
c. Undefined  
d. Undefined

106. People's physical and mental talents and efforts that are used to help produce goods and services are called _____.  
a. Thing  
b. Labor7  
c. Undefined  
d. Undefined

107. Characterized by rizing output, falling unemployment, rizing profits, and increasing economic activity following a decline is a _____.  
a. Thing  
b. Recovery7  
c. Undefined  
d. Undefined

108. A short-term investment with original maturities of three months or less that is readily convertible to cash and whose value is unlikely to change is a _____.  
a. Thing  
b. Cash equivalent7  
c. Undefined  
d. Undefined

109. _____ are the most liquid asset found within the asset portion of a company's balance sheet. Cash "equivalents" are typically comprized of assets that are readily convertible into cash such as money market accounts, short-term government bonds and commercial paper.

## Chapter 7. Cash Flow Analysis

a. Thing
c. Undefined
b. Cash and cash equivalents7
d. Undefined

110. _____ is the corporate management term for the act of partially dismantling and reorganizing a company for the purpose of making it more efficient and therefore more profitable.
a. Thing
c. Undefined
b. Restructuring7
d. Undefined

111. _____ refers to assets used to operate the business; frequently called long-term assets. They are property such as land, livestock, and trees that produce income.
a. Thing
c. Undefined
b. Productive assets7
d. Undefined

112. In accounting, the _____ of an asset is its remaining value after depreciation. The estimated value of an asset at the end of its useful life.
a. Salvage value7
c. Undefined
b. Thing
d. Undefined

113. The length of service of a productive facility or piece of equipment is its _____. The period of time during which an asset will have economic value and be usable.
a. Useful life7
c. Undefined
b. Thing
d. Undefined

114. The difference between the cash receipts and cash disbursements that are related to operating activities is referred to as _____.
a. Thing
c. Undefined
b. Cash provided by operations7
d. Undefined

115. A defense that relieves a seller of product liability if the user abnormally misused the product is called _____. Products must be designed to protect against foreseeable _____.
a. Thing
c. Undefined
b. Misuse7
d. Undefined

116. _____ is an American stock investor, businessman and philanthropist. Nicknamed the "Oracle of Omaha" or the "Sage of Omaha", he has amassed an enormous fortune from astute investments, particularly through his company Berkshire Hathaway, in which he holds a greater than 38% stake.
a. Warren Buffett7
c. Undefined
b. Person
d. Undefined

117. _____ refers to a claim on the borrower future income that is sold by the borrower to the lender. A _____ is a type of transferable interest representing financial value.
a. Thing
c. Undefined
b. Security7
d. Undefined

118. _____ refers to the return a businessperson gets on the money he and other owners invest in the firm; for example, a business that earned $100 on a $1,000 investment would have a ROI of 10 percent: 100 divided by 1000.

a. Thing
b. Return on investment7
c. Undefined
d. Undefined

119. _____, also known as property, plant, and equipment (PP&E), is a term used in accountancy for assets and property which cannot easily be converted into cash. This can be compared with current assets such as cash or bank accounts, which are described as liquid assets. In most cases, only tangible assets are referred to as fixed.
a. Thing
b. Fixed asset7
c. Undefined
d. Undefined

120. In Keynesian economics _____ refers to personal _____ expenditure, i.e., the purchase of currently produced goods and services out of income, out of savings (net worth), or from borrowed funds. It refers to that part of disposable income that does not go to saving.
a. Thing
b. Consumption7
c. Undefined
d. Undefined

121. In economic models, the _____ time frame assumes no fixed factors of production. Firms can enter or leave the marketplace, and the cost (and availability) of land, labor, raw materials, and capital goods can be assumed to vary.
a. Long run7
b. Thing
c. Undefined
d. Undefined

122. A worker association that bargains with employers over wages and working conditions is called a _____.
a. Thing
b. Union7
c. Undefined
d. Undefined

123. _____ in a financial context refers to the rate at which a provider of goods cycles through its average inventory. _____ in a human resources context refers to the characteristic of a given company or industry, relative to rate at which an employer gains and loses staff.
a. Thing
b. Turnover7
c. Undefined
d. Undefined

124. A _____ is an industrial action in which employees perform their duties but seek to reduce productivity or efficiency in their performance of these duties. A _____ may be used as either a prelude or an alternative to a strike, as it is seen as less disruptive as well as less risky and costly for workers and their union.
a. Thing
b. Slowdown7
c. Undefined
d. Undefined

125. A _____ is something measured by a number; it is used to analyze what happens to other things when the size of that number changes.
a. Thing
b. Variable7
c. Undefined
d. Undefined

126. _____ or consumption is also known as personal consumption expenditure. It is the largest part of aggregate demand or effective demand at the macroeconomic level.There are two variants of consumption in the aggregate demand model, including induced consumption and autonomous consumption.

a. Thing
b. Consumer demand7
c. Undefined
d. Undefined

127. _____ refers to the amount recognized as an expense in one period resulting from the periodic recognition of the used portion of the cost of a long-term tangible asset over its life.
a. Thing
b. Depreciation expense7
c. Undefined
d. Undefined

128. Asset measure based on the cost of purchasing an asset today identical to the one currently held, or the cost of purchasing an asset that provides services like the one currently held, if an identical one cannot be purchased is a _____.
a. Thing
b. Current cost7
c. Undefined
d. Undefined

129. Similar to a script in that a _____ can be a less than completely rational decision-making method. Involves the use of a pre-existing set of decision steps for any problem that presents itself.
a. Policy7
b. Thing
c. Undefined
d. Undefined

130. A _____ is a generic term for specific types of investments from which payoffs over time are derived from the performance of assets (such as commodities, shares or bonds), interest rates, exchange rates, or indices (such as a stock market index, consumer price index (CPI) or an index of weather conditions).
a. Derivative7
b. Thing
c. Undefined
d. Undefined

131. Cash provided by operating activities adjusted for capital expenditures and dividends paid is referred to as _____.
a. Free cash flow7
b. Thing
c. Undefined
d. Undefined

132. A substantial expenditure that is used by a company to acquire or upgrade physical assets such as equipment, property, industrial buildings, including those which improve the quality and life of an asset is referred to as a _____.
a. Thing
b. Capital expenditure7
c. Undefined
d. Undefined

133. Major investments in long-term assets such as land, buildings, equipment, or research and development are referred to as _____.
a. Thing
b. Capital expenditures7
c. Undefined
d. Undefined

134. Reduction in the selling price of goods extended to the buyer because the goods are defective or of lower quality than the buyer ordered and to encourage a buyer to keep merchandise that would otherwise be returned is the _____.
a. Thing
b. Allowance7
c. Undefined
d. Undefined

135. _____ refers to measures that are important to monitoring and tracking the effectiveness of a company's operations.
   a. Operating results7  
   b. Thing  
   c. Undefined  
   d. Undefined

136. _____ refers to the function in a firm that searches for quality material resources, finds the best suppliers, and negotiates the best price for goods and services.
   a. Purchasing7  
   b. Thing  
   c. Undefined  
   d. Undefined

137. A pro rata distribution of cash to stockholders of corporate stock is called a _____.
   a. Cash dividend7  
   b. Thing  
   c. Undefined  
   d. Undefined

138. A written record of all vendors to whom the business firm owes money is referred to as _____.
   a. Thing  
   b. Accounts payable7  
   c. Undefined  
   d. Undefined

139. A _____ is a "promise" or an "agreement" that is enforced or recognized by the law. In the civil law, a _____ is considered to be part of the general law of obligations.
   a. Thing  
   b. Contract7  
   c. Undefined  
   d. Undefined

140. The use of resources for the deliberate discovery of new information and ways of doing things, together with the application of that information in inventing new products or processes is referred to as _____.
   a. Research and development7  
   b. Thing  
   c. Undefined  
   d. Undefined

141. _____ refers to the amount of accounts receivable that is expected to go uncollected. It is called a contra-asset because it is deducted from the asset, accounts receivable. Also called allowance for doubtful accounts or allowance for bad debts.
   a. Allowance for uncollectible accounts7  
   b. Thing  
   c. Undefined  
   d. Undefined

142. In accounting and finance, _____ is the portion of receivables that can no longer be collected, typically from accounts receivable or loans. _____ in accounting is considered an expense.
   a. Bad debt7  
   b. Thing  
   c. Undefined  
   d. Undefined

143. _____ refers to the price of an asset agreed on between a willing buyer and a willing seller; the price an asset could demand if it is sold on the open market.
   a. Market value7  
   b. Thing  
   c. Undefined  
   d. Undefined

144. A _____ is a type of business loan that leaves the lender the option of taking stock in the company instead of repayment. In theory, the market price of a _____ should never drop below its intrinsic value.

## Chapter 7. Cash Flow Analysis

a. Convertible debenture7  
b. Thing  
c. Undefined  
d. Undefined

145. The nominal or par value of an instrument as expressed on its face is referred to as the _____.  
a. Face value7  
b. Thing  
c. Undefined  
d. Undefined

146. The central value of a pegged exchange rate, around which the actual rate is permitted to fluctuate within set bounds is a _____.  
a. Par value7  
b. Thing  
c. Undefined  
d. Undefined

147. A _____ is a long-term debt instrument used by governments and large companies to obtain funds. It is similar to a bond except the securitization conditions are different.  
a. Debenture7  
b. Thing  
c. Undefined  
d. Undefined

148. The group of individuals elected by the stockholders of a corporation to oversee its operations is a _____.  
a. Thing  
b. Board of directors7  
c. Undefined  
d. Undefined

149. A _____ is an individual or company (including a corporation) that legally owns one or more shares of stock in a joined stock company. The shareholders are the owners of a corporation. Companies listed at the stock market strive to enhance shareholder value.  
a. Stockholder7  
b. Thing  
c. Undefined  
d. Undefined

150. _____ is a liability. It is recorded when an asset (e.g. receivable) is recorded, but the related income (i.e. revenue) will be earned only in the future.  
a. Deferred income7  
b. Thing  
c. Undefined  
d. Undefined

151. _____ refers to an obligation in the form of a written promissory note. It is a balance sheet term referring to a company's outstanding bank loans  
a. Notes payable7  
b. Thing  
c. Undefined  
d. Undefined

152. _____ refers to a corporate action that increases the shares in a public company. The price of the shares are adjusted such that the before and after market capitalization of the company remains the same and dilution does not occur.  
a. Thing  
b. Stock split7  
c. Undefined  
d. Undefined

153. The difference between the face value of a bond and its selling price, when a bond is sold for less than its face value it's referred to as a _____.

a. Thing
b. Discount7
c. Undefined
d. Undefined

154. Assets defined in the broadest legal sense. _____ includes the unrealized receivables of a cash basis taxpayer, but not services rendered.
a. Property7
b. Thing
c. Undefined
d. Undefined

155. _____ refers to the fee charged by an insurance company for an insurance policy. The rate of losses must be relatively predictable: In order to set the _____ (prices) insurers must be able to estimate them accurately.
a. Thing
b. Premium7
c. Undefined
d. Undefined

156. Corporate stock that has been reacquired by the corporation is _____. It is stock which is bought back by the issuing company. It reduces the number of outstanding stocks on the open market ("open market" including insiders holdings).
a. Thing
b. Treasury stock7
c. Undefined
d. Undefined

157. A _____ is a steady income given to a person (usually after retirement). Pensions are typically payments made in the form of a guaranteed annuity to a retired or disabled employee.
a. Pension7
b. Thing
c. Undefined
d. Undefined

158. Cumulative earnings of a company that are not distributed to the owners and are reinvested in the business are called _____.
a. Thing
b. Retained earnings7
c. Undefined
d. Undefined

159. _____ refers to the total costs of goods made or purchased and sold.
a. Thing
b. Cost of sales7
c. Undefined
d. Undefined

160. The total amount of physical capital that has been accumulated, usually in a country is _____. Also refers to the total issued capital of a firm, including ordinary and preferred shares.
a. Capital stock7
b. Thing
c. Undefined
d. Undefined

161. A long-lasting, sometimes permanent team in the organization structure created to deal with tasks that recur regularly is the _____.
a. Committee7
b. Thing
c. Undefined
d. Undefined

162. _____ refers to pro rata distributions of stock or stock rights on common stock. They are usually issued in proportion to shares owned.

## Chapter 7. Cash Flow Analysis

a. Thing
c. Undefined

b. Stock dividend7
d. Undefined

163. All investments in stocks or bonds that are held primarily for the purpose of active trading in the near future are called _____.

a. Trading securities7
c. Undefined

b. Thing
d. Undefined

164. The accountant's concept of income is generally based upon the realization principle. Financial _____ may differ from taxable income. Differences are included in a reconciliation of taxable and _____ on Schedule M-1 of Form 1120.

a. Accounting income7
c. Undefined

b. Thing
d. Undefined

165. _____ in contract law, a basic requirement for an enforceable agreement under traditional contract principles, defined in this text as legal value, bargained for and given in exchange for an act or promise. In corporation law, cash or property contributed to a corporation in exchange for shares, or a promise to contribute such cash or property.

a. Thing
c. Undefined

b. Consideration7
d. Undefined

166. _____ refers to a debt that can reasonably be expected to be paid from existing current assets or through the creation of other current liabilities, within one year or the operating cycle, whichever is longer.

a. Thing
c. Undefined

b. Current liability7
d. Undefined

167. A transfer of property or some right or interest is referred to as _____.

a. Thing
c. Undefined

b. Assignment7
d. Undefined

168. _____ refers to financial results from the disposal of a major segment of the business and are reported net of income tax effects.

a. Discontinued operations7
c. Undefined

b. Thing
d. Undefined

169. The creation of finished goods and services using the factors of _____: land, labor, capital, entrepreneurship, and knowledge.

a. Thing
c. Undefined

b. Production7
d. Undefined

170. Obtaining financing by borrowing money is _____.

a. Debt financing7
c. Undefined

b. Thing
d. Undefined

171. The legal right to the proceeds from and control over the use of an invented product or process, granted for a fixed period of time, usually 20 years. _____ is one form of intellectual property that is subject of the TRIPS agreement.

a. Patent7  
b. Thing  
c. Undefined  
d. Undefined

172. _____ refers to recording as negative in the balance of payments, any transaction that gives rise to a payment out of the country, such as an import, the purchase of an asset, or lending to foreigners. Opposite of credit.
   a. Debit7  
   b. Thing  
   c. Undefined  
   d. Undefined

173. Completed products awaiting sale are called _____. An item considered a finished good in a supplying plant might be considered a component or raw material in a receiving plant.
   a. Thing  
   b. Finished goods7  
   c. Undefined  
   d. Undefined

174. Contra-asset account containing the estimated uncollectible accounts receivable is an _____. Also called allowance for bad debts or allowance for uncollectible accounts.
   a. Allowance for doubtful accounts7  
   b. Thing  
   c. Undefined  
   d. Undefined

175. A company's purchase of the property and obligations of another company is an _____.
   a. Acquisition7  
   b. Thing  
   c. Undefined  
   d. Undefined

176. The expense associated with uncollectible accounts is _____. When it is a significant amount, the _____ is estimated with the allowance method.
   a. Thing  
   b. Bad debt expense7  
   c. Undefined  
   d. Undefined

177. The value today of a stream of payments and/or receipts over time in the future and/or the past, converted to the present using an interest rate. If X t is the amount in period t and r the interest rate, then _____ at time t=0 is V = ?T /t.
   a. Present value7  
   b. Thing  
   c. Undefined  
   d. Undefined

178. _____ refers to the amount at which property would change hands between a willing buyer and a willing seller, neither being under any compulsion to buy or to sell, and both having reasonable knowledge of the relevant facts.
   a. Thing  
   b. Fair market value7  
   c. Undefined  
   d. Undefined

179. _____ refer to an equity security, representing a shareholder's ownership of a corporation. _____ are one of a finite number of equal portions in the capital of a company, entitling the owner to a proportion of distributed, non-reinvested profits known as dividends and to a portion of the value of the company in case of liquidation.
   a. Thing  
   b. Shares7  
   c. Undefined  
   d. Undefined

180. The _____ is a comparison of a firm's current assets to its current liabilities. The _____ is an indication of a firm's market liquidity and ability to meet short-term debt obligations.

a. Thing  
b. Current ratio7  
c. Undefined  
d. Undefined  

181. _____ refer to securities that are readily traded in the secondary securities market.  
a. Marketable securities7  
b. Thing  
c. Undefined  
d. Undefined  

182. _____ refers to a liability that results from the execution of a legal document called a note that describes technical terms, including interest charges, maturity date, collateral, and so on.  
a. Note payable7  
b. Thing  
c. Undefined  
d. Undefined  

183. _____ refers to goods held for resale in the ordinary course of business.  
a. Thing  
b. Merchandise inventory7  
c. Undefined  
d. Undefined  

184. _____, is the world's largest commercial tobacco company by sales. _____ was begun by a London tobacconist of the same name. He was one of the first people to sell hand-rolled cigarettes in the 1860s, selling them under the brand names Oxford and Cambridge Blues, following the adoption of cigarette smoking by British soldiers returning from the Crimean War.  
a. Philip Morris7  
b. Organization  
c. Undefined  
d. Undefined  

185. _____ refers to the price at which one country's currency trades for another, typically on the exchange market.  
a. Exchange rate7  
b. Thing  
c. Undefined  
d. Undefined  

186. A _____ is a specific type of option that uses the stock itself as an underlying instrument to determine the option's pay-off and therefore its value.  
a. Stock option7  
b. Thing  
c. Undefined  
d. Undefined  

187. _____ refers to the final payment date of a loan or other financial instrument, after which point no further interest or principal need be paid.  
a. Maturity7  
b. Thing  
c. Undefined  
d. Undefined  

188. A _____ is a security that entitles the holder to buy or sell a certain additional quantity of an underlying security at an agreed-upon price, at the holder's discretion.  
a. Thing  
b. Warrant7  
c. Undefined  
d. Undefined  

189. A contract that gives the purchaser the _____ to buy or sell the underlying financial instrument at a specified price, called the exercise price or strike price, within a specific period of time.

a. Option7  
b. Thing  
c. Undefined  
d. Undefined

190. _____ refers to an intergovernmental transfer of funds . Since the New Deal, state and local governments have become increasingly dependent upon federal grants for an almost infinite variety of programs.
a. Grant7  
b. Thing  
c. Undefined  
d. Undefined

191. Preferred stock that includes an option for the holder to convert the preferred shares into a fixed number of common shares, usually anytime after a predetermined date is _____.
a. Thing  
b. Convertible preferred stock7  
c. Undefined  
d. Undefined

192. _____ refers to the entity that has a controlling influence over another company. It may have its own operations, or it may have been set up solely for the purpose of owning the Subject Company.
a. Parent company7  
b. Thing  
c. Undefined  
d. Undefined

193. An attempt by employees, management, or a group of investors to purchase an organization primarily through borrowing is a _____.
a. Thing  
b. Leveraged buyout7  
c. Undefined  
d. Undefined

194. Under the Uniform Commercial Code, one who regularly deals in goods of the kind sold in the contract at issue, or holds himself out as having special knowledge or skill relevant to such goods, or who makes the sale through an agent who regularly deals in such goods or claims such knowledge or skill is referred to as _____.
a. Thing  
b. Merchant7  
c. Undefined  
d. Undefined

195. A _____ is an investment transaction by which the entire or a controlling part of the stock of a company is sold. A firm buysout the stake of the company to strengthen its influence on the company's decision making body. A _____ can take the forms of a leveraged _____ or a management _____.
a. Buyout7  
b. Thing  
c. Undefined  
d. Undefined

196. An organization that employs resources to produce a good or service for profit and owns and operates one or more plants is referred to as a _____.
a. Firm7  
b. Thing  
c. Undefined  
d. Undefined

197. The payments made by a borrower on their debt, usually including both interest payments and partial repayment of principal, are called _____.
a. Debt service7  
b. Thing  
c. Undefined  
d. Undefined

198. The _____ is the market for securities, where companies and the government can raise long-term funds.

a. Thing  
c. Undefined  
b. Securities market7  
d. Undefined

199. _____ refer to representation of ownership rights to the corporation.  
a. Thing  
c. Undefined  
b. Equity securities7  
d. Undefined

## Chapter 8. Return on Invested Capital

1. _____ generally refers to financial wealth, especially that used to start or maintain a business. In classical economics, _____ is one of four factors of production, the others being land and labor and entrepreneurship.
   - a. Capital8
   - b. Thing
   - c. Undefined
   - d. Undefined

2. An item of property, such as land, capital, money, a share in ownership, or a claim on others for future payment, such as a bond or a bank deposit is an _____.
   - a. Thing
   - b. Asset8
   - c. Undefined
   - d. Undefined

3. The _____ percentage shows how profitable a company's assets are in generating revenue.
   - a. Thing
   - b. Return on Assets8
   - c. Undefined
   - d. Undefined

4. _____ refer to shareholders who claim the residual profits and assets of a corporation, and usually have the exclusive power and right to elect the directors of the corporation.
   - a. Thing
   - b. Common shareholders8
   - c. Undefined
   - d. Undefined

5. A _____ is an individual or company (including a corporation) that legally owns one or more shares of stock in a joined stock company.
   - a. Shareholder8
   - b. Thing
   - c. Undefined
   - d. Undefined

6. _____ is the name given to the set of legal principles, in countries following the English common law tradition, which supplement strict rules of law where their application would operate harshly, so as to achieve what is sometimes referred to as "natural justice."
   - a. Thing
   - b. Equity8
   - c. Undefined
   - d. Undefined

7. _____ is using given resources in such a way that the potential positive or negative outcome is magnified. In finance, this generally refers to borrowing.
   - a. Thing
   - b. Leverage8
   - c. Undefined
   - d. Undefined

8. In finance, _____ is a profit or an increase in value of an investment such as a stock or bond. _____ is calculated by fair market value or the proceeds from the sale of the investment minus the sum of the purchase price and all costs associated with it.
   - a. Thing
   - b. Gain8
   - c. Undefined
   - d. Undefined

9. In December of 1995, _____ became the first major North American retailer to accept independent monitoring of the working conditions in a contract factory producing its garments. _____ is the largest specialty retailer in the United States.
   - a. Gap8
   - b. Organization
   - c. Undefined
   - d. Undefined

10. A _____ is a ratio of two numbers of reported levels or flows of a company. It may be two financial flows categories divided by each other (profit margin, profit/revenue). It may be a level divided by a financial flow (price/earnings). It may be a flow divided by a level (return on equity or earnings/equity). The numerator or denominator may itself be a ratio (PEG ratio).
   a. Financial ratio8
   b. Thing
   c. Undefined
   d. Undefined

11. _____ refers to a "non tangible product" that is not embodied in a physical good and that typically effects some change in another product, person, or institution. Contrasts with good.
   a. Service8
   b. Thing
   c. Undefined
   d. Undefined

12. In financial terminology, _____ is the capital raized by a corporation, through the issuance and sale of shares.
   a. Stock8
   b. Thing
   c. Undefined
   d. Undefined

13. _____ refers to a debt instrument, issued by a borrower and promising a specified stream of payments to the purchaser, usually regular interest payments plus a final repayment of principal.
   a. Bond8
   b. Thing
   c. Undefined
   d. Undefined

14. A measure of the amount of debt used in the capital structure of the firm is the _____.
   a. Financial leverage8
   b. Thing
   c. Undefined
   d. Undefined

15. Net profit after taxes per dollar of equity capital is referred to as _____.
   a. Return on equity8
   b. Thing
   c. Undefined
   d. Undefined

16. _____ is a measure of profitability. It is calculated using a formula and written as a percentage or a number. _____ = Net income before tax and interest / Revenue.
   a. Profit margin8
   b. Thing
   c. Undefined
   d. Undefined

17. _____ is an accounting term which is commonly used in business. It is equal to the gross revenue for a given time period minus associated expenses.
   a. Net profit8
   b. Thing
   c. Undefined
   d. Undefined

18. A _____ is a present obligation of the enterprise arizing from past events, the settlement of which is expected to result in an outflow from the enterprise of resources embodying economic benefits.
   a. Liability8
   b. Thing
   c. Undefined
   d. Undefined

19. _____ refers to the return to the resource entrepreneurial ability; total revenue minus total cost.

a. Thing
b. Profit8
c. Undefined
d. Undefined

20. A deposit by a buyer in stocks with a seller or a stockbroker, as security to cover fluctuations in the market in reference to stocks that the buyer has purchased but for which he has not paid is a _____. Commodities are also traded on _____.
a. Margin8
b. Thing
c. Undefined
d. Undefined

21. A contract for the possession and use of land or other property, including goods, on one side, and a recompense of rent or other income on the other is the _____.
a. Thing
b. Lease8
c. Undefined
d. Undefined

22. The ability of a company to pay interest as it comes due and to repay the face value of debt at maturity is called _____.
a. Thing
b. Solvency8
c. Undefined
d. Undefined

23. _____ refers to a summary of all the transactions that have occurred over a particular period.
a. Financial statement8
b. Thing
c. Undefined
d. Undefined

24. A standardized method or technique that is performed repetitively, often on different materials resulting in different finished goods is called an _____.
a. Operation8
b. Thing
c. Undefined
d. Undefined

25. _____ in a financial context refers to the rate at which a provider of goods cycles through its average inventory. _____ in a human resources context refers to the characteristic of a given company or industry, relative to rate at which an employer gains and loses staff.
a. Turnover8
b. Thing
c. Undefined
d. Undefined

26. Net sales less cost of goods sold is called _____.
a. Thing
b. Gross profit8
c. Undefined
d. Undefined

27. _____ is equal to the income that a firm has after subtracting costs and expenses from the total revenue. Expenses will typically include tax expense.
a. Net income8
b. Thing
c. Undefined
d. Undefined

28. _____ is a U.S. business term for the amount of money that a company receives from its activities, mostly from sales of products and/or services to customers.

a. Revenue8  
b. Thing  
c. Undefined  
d. Undefined  

29. _____ refers to the return a businessperson gets on the money he and other owners invest in the firm; for example, a business that earned $100 on a $1,000 investment would have a ROI of 10 percent: 100 divided by 1000.
   a. Thing  
   b. Return on investment8  
   c. Undefined  
   d. Undefined  

30. _____ refers to spending for the production and accumulation of capital and additions to inventories. In a financial sense, buying an asset with the expectation of making a return.
   a. Investment8  
   b. Thing  
   c. Undefined  
   d. Undefined  

31. The interest rate that equates a future value or an annuity to a given present value is a _____.
   a. Thing  
   b. Yield8  
   c. Undefined  
   d. Undefined  

32. A person to whom a debt or legal obligation is owed, and who has the right to enforce payment of that debt or obligation is referred to as _____.
   a. Thing  
   b. Creditor8  
   c. Undefined  
   d. Undefined  

33. _____ characterizes the process of leading and directing all or part of an organization, often a business, through the deployment and manipulation of resources. Early twentieth-century _____ writer Mary Parker Follett defined _____ as "the art of getting things done through people."
   a. Management8  
   b. Thing  
   c. Undefined  
   d. Undefined  

34. _____ is an American stock investor, businessman and philanthropist. Nicknamed the "Oracle of Omaha" or the "Sage of Omaha", he has amassed an enormous fortune from astute investments, particularly through his company Berkshire Hathaway, in which he holds a greater than 38% stake.
   a. Person  
   b. Warren Buffett8  
   c. Undefined  
   d. Undefined  

35. _____ is the founder of Dell, Inc., the world's largest computer manufacturer which revolutionized the home computer industry.
   a. Michael Dell8  
   b. Person  
   c. Undefined  
   d. Undefined  

36. _____ is the co-founder, chairman, former chief software architect, and former CEO of Microsoft Corporation. He is one of the best-known entrepreneurs of the personal computer revolution and he is widely respected for his foresight and ambition.
   a. Person  
   b. Bill Gates8  
   c. Undefined  
   d. Undefined

## Chapter 8. Return on Invested Capital

37. While _____ was not the first company to develop and sell a router (a device that forwards computer traffic from one network to another), it did create the first commercially successful multi-protocol router to allow previously incompatible computers to communicate using different network protocols.
    a. Organization
    b. Cisco Systems8
    c. Undefined
    d. Undefined

38. Collecting information and providing feedback to employees about their behavior, communication style, or skills is an _____.
    a. Thing
    b. Assessment8
    c. Undefined
    d. Undefined

39. Other organizations in the same industry or type of business that provide a good or service to the same set of customers is referred to as a _____.
    a. Competitor8
    b. Thing
    c. Undefined
    d. Undefined

40. _____ refers to the return on an asset expected over the next period.
    a. Thing
    b. Expected return8
    c. Undefined
    d. Undefined

41. A management function that involves determining whether or not an organization is progressing toward its goals and objectives, and taking corrective action if it is not is called _____.
    a. Controlling8
    b. Thing
    c. Undefined
    d. Undefined

42. Responsibility center where the manager is accountable for revenues and costs is referred to as a _____.
    a. Thing
    b. Profit center8
    c. Undefined
    d. Undefined

43. _____ refers to a written document that includes the steps the trainee and manager will take to ensure that training transfers to the job.
    a. Thing
    b. Action plan8
    c. Undefined
    d. Undefined

44. Production of goods primarily by the application of labor and capital to raw materials and other intermediate inputs, in contrast to agriculture, mining, forestry, fishing, and services a _____.
    a. Thing
    b. Manufacturing8
    c. Undefined
    d. Undefined

45. An examination of the financial reports to ensure that they represent what they claim and conform with generally accepted accounting principles is referred to as _____.
    a. Thing
    b. Audit8
    c. Undefined
    d. Undefined

46. _____ refer to people in the organization who actually use the product or service purchased by the buying center.

## Chapter 8. Return on Invested Capital

a. Thing
b. Users8
c. Undefined
d. Undefined

47. A _____ is a comparison of the money earned (or lost) on an investment to the amount of money invested.
a. Rate of return8
b. Thing
c. Undefined
d. Undefined

48. _____ refer to securities that are readily traded in the secondary securities market.
a. Marketable securities8
b. Thing
c. Undefined
d. Undefined

49. _____ refers to a claim on the borrower future income that is sold by the borrower to the lender. A _____ is a type of transferable interest representing financial value.
a. Security8
b. Thing
c. Undefined
d. Undefined

50. Assets that have special rights but not physical substance are referred to as _____.
a. Intangible assets8
b. Thing
c. Undefined
d. Undefined

51. An intangible assets is defined as an asset that is not physical in nature. The most common types are trade secrets (e.g., customer lists and know-how), copyrights, patents, trademarks, and goodwill.
a. Intangible asset8
b. Thing
c. Undefined
d. Undefined

52. _____ is an accounting and finance term for the method of attributing the cost of an asset across the useful life of the asset. _____ is a reduction in the value of a currency in floating exchange rate.
a. Thing
b. Depreciation8
c. Undefined
d. Undefined

53. The length of service of a productive facility or piece of equipment is its _____. The period of time during which an asset will have economic value and be usable.
a. Thing
b. Useful life8
c. Undefined
d. Undefined

54. _____ refers to portion of the assets remaining after the creditors' claims have been satisfied; also called equity or residual interest.
a. Net assets8
b. Thing
c. Undefined
d. Undefined

55. _____ refers to the total depreciation that has been reported as depreciation expense for the entire life of a long-term tangible asset. It is a contra-asset account.
a. Thing
b. Accumulated depreciation8
c. Undefined
d. Undefined

56. _____ refers to the plan of organization and all the related methods and measures adopted within a business to safeguard its assets and enhance the accuracy and reliability of its accounting records.
- a. Thing
- b. Internal control8
- c. Undefined
- d. Undefined

57. A company's purchase of the property and obligations of another company is an _____.
- a. Thing
- b. Acquisition8
- c. Undefined
- d. Undefined

58. _____ refers to money raized from within the firm or through the sale of ownership in the firm.
- a. Thing
- b. Equity capital8
- c. Undefined
- d. Undefined

59. Stock that has specified rights over common stock is a _____.
- a. Preferred stock8
- b. Thing
- c. Undefined
- d. Undefined

60. _____ refers to the price of an asset agreed on between a willing buyer and a willing seller; the price an asset could demand if it is sold on the open market.
- a. Market value8
- b. Thing
- c. Undefined
- d. Undefined

61. A _____ is, as defined in economics, a social arrangement that allows buyers and sellers to discover information and carry out a voluntary exchange of goods or services.
- a. Thing
- b. Market8
- c. Undefined
- d. Undefined

62. The common stock or ownership capital of the firm is _____. _____ may be supplied through retained earnings or the sale of new common stock.
- a. Common equity8
- b. Thing
- c. Undefined
- d. Undefined

63. The _____ of an asset or group of assets is sometimes the price at which they were originally acquired, in many cases equal to purchase price.
- a. Book value8
- b. Thing
- c. Undefined
- d. Undefined

64. A group of firms that produce identical or similar products is an _____. It is also used specifically to refer to an area of economic production focused on manufacturing which involves large amounts of capital investment before any profit can be realized, also called "heavy _____".
- a. Industry8
- b. Thing
- c. Undefined
- d. Undefined

65. The cost a business incurs to borrow money. With respect to bonds payable, the _____ is calculated by multiplying the market rate of interest by the carrying value of the bonds on the date of the payment.

a. Thing
b. Interest expense8
c. Undefined
d. Undefined

66. In finance and economics, _____ is the price paid by a borrower for the use of a lender's money. In other words, _____ is the amount of paid to "rent" money for a period of time.
   a. Interest8
   b. Thing
   c. Undefined
   d. Undefined

67. In accounting, an _____ represents an event in which an asset is used up or a liability is incurred. In terms of the accounting equation, expenses reduce owners' equity.
   a. Thing
   b. Expense8
   c. Undefined
   d. Undefined

68. _____ refers to funds raized through various forms of borrowing to finance a company that must be repaid.
   a. Debt capital8
   b. Thing
   c. Undefined
   d. Undefined

69. Amount of corporate profits paid out for each share of stock is referred to as _____.
   a. Thing
   b. Dividend8
   c. Undefined
   d. Undefined

70. A company that is controlled by another company or corporation is a _____.
   a. Subsidiary8
   b. Thing
   c. Undefined
   d. Undefined

71. A statement of the assets, liabilities, and net worth of a firm or individual at some given time often at the end of its "fiscal year," is referred to as a _____.
   a. Thing
   b. Balance sheet8
   c. Undefined
   d. Undefined

72. In banking and accountancy, the outstanding _____ is the amount of money owned, (or due), that remains in a deposit account (or a loan account) at a given date, after all past remittances, payments and withdrawal have been accounted for. It can be positive (then, in the _____ sheet of a firm, it is an asset) or negative (a liability).
   a. Balance8
   b. Thing
   c. Undefined
   d. Undefined

73. _____ - earnings before extraordinary items, less preferred-share dividends, divided by average common shareholders' equity. Shows the rate of return on the investment for the company's common shareholders, the only providers of capital who do not have a fixed return.
   a. Return on common Equity8
   b. Thing
   c. Undefined
   d. Undefined

74. _____ refers to a system by which individuals can reduce their exposure to risk of large losses by spreading the risks among a large number of persons.

## Chapter 8. Return on Invested Capital

a. Insurance8  
b. Thing  
c. Undefined  
d. Undefined  

75. A legal entity chartered by a state or the Federal government that is distinct and separate from the individuals who own it is a _____. This separation gives the _____ unique powers which other legal entities lack.
a. Organization  
b. Corporation8  
c. Undefined  
d. Undefined  

76. The dollar sum of costs that an insured individual must pay before the insurer begins to pay is called _____.
a. Deductible8  
b. Thing  
c. Undefined  
d. Undefined  

77. Tangible property held for sale in the normal course of business or used in producing goods or services for sale is an _____.
a. Thing  
b. Inventory8  
c. Undefined  
d. Undefined  

78. Total shareholders' equity divided by the number of outstanding common shares is referred to as _____.
a. Book value per share8  
b. Thing  
c. Undefined  
d. Undefined  

79. _____ refers to annual profit of the corporation divided by the number of shares outstanding.
a. Earnings per share8  
b. Thing  
c. Undefined  
d. Undefined  

80. Earnings per share unadjusted for dilution are _____.
a. Thing  
b. Basic earnings per share8  
c. Undefined  
d. Undefined  

81. A means of measuring the profitability of the firm's products, customer groups, sales territories, channels of distribution, and order sizes is called _____.
a. Thing  
b. Profitability analysis8  
c. Undefined  
d. Undefined  

82. The consumer's appraisal of the product or brand on important attributes is called _____.
a. Thing  
b. Evaluation8  
c. Undefined  
d. Undefined  

83. The central value of a pegged exchange rate, around which the actual rate is permitted to fluctuate within set bounds is a _____.
a. Thing  
b. Par value8  
c. Undefined  
d. Undefined  

84. Loan origination fees that may be deductible as interest by a buyer of property. A seller of property who pays _____ reduces the selling price by the amount of the _____ paid for the buyer.

## Chapter 8. Return on Invested Capital

a. Points8  
c. Undefined  
b. Thing  
d. Undefined

85. _____ refers to plant resources that are underused when imperfectly competitive firms produce less output than that associated with purely competitive firms, who by definiation, are achieving minimum average total cost.
    a. Excess capacity8
    b. Thing
    c. Undefined
    d. Undefined

86. A group of products that are physically similar or are intended for a similar market are called the _____.
    a. Thing
    b. Product line8
    c. Undefined
    d. Undefined

87. The cost that a firm bears if it does not produce at all and that is independent of its output. The presence of a _____ tends to imply increasing returns to scale. Contrasts with variable cost.
    a. Fixed cost8
    b. Thing
    c. Undefined
    d. Undefined

88. The creation of finished goods and services using the factors of _____: land, labor, capital, entrepreneurship, and knowledge.
    a. Thing
    b. Production8
    c. Undefined
    d. Undefined

89. The body of knowledge and techniques that can be used to combine economic resources to produce goods and services is called _____.
    a. Thing
    b. Technology8
    c. Undefined
    d. Undefined

90. The difference between the face value of a bond and its selling price, when a bond is sold for less than its face value it's referred to as a _____.
    a. Thing
    b. Discount8
    c. Undefined
    d. Undefined

91. _____ refers to a thing that was originally personal property and that has been actually or constructively affixed to the soil itself or to some structure legally a part of the land.
    a. Thing
    b. Fixture8
    c. Undefined
    d. Undefined

92. _____ refers to the pattern followed by macroeconommic variables, such as GDP and unemployment that rise and fall irregularly over time, relative to trend.
    a. Business cycle8
    b. Thing
    c. Undefined
    d. Undefined

93. A short-term investment with original maturities of three months or less that is readily convertible to cash and whose value is unlikely to change is a _____.

a. Thing  
b. Cash equivalent8  
c. Undefined  
d. Undefined  

94. Cash coming into the company as the result of a previous investment is a _____.
   a. Thing
   b. Cash inflow8
   c. Undefined
   d. Undefined

95. _____ refers to the capacity to turn assets into cash, or the amount of assets in a portfolio that have that capacity.
   a. Thing
   b. Liquidity8
   c. Undefined
   d. Undefined

96. _____ are the most liquid asset found within the asset portion of a company's balance sheet. Cash "equivalents" are typically comprized of assets that are readily convertible into cash such as money market accounts, short-term government bonds and commercial paper.
   a. Thing
   b. Cash and cash equivalents8
   c. Undefined
   d. Undefined

97. Situation in which a firm is unable to meet due bills is a _____.
   a. Thing
   b. Liquidity crisis8
   c. Undefined
   d. Undefined

98. The acquisition of an increasing quantity of something. The _____ of factors, especially capital, is a primary mechanism for economic growth.
   a. Thing
   b. Accumulation8
   c. Undefined
   d. Undefined

99. Independent accounting entity with a self-balancing set of accounts segregated for the purposes of carrying on specific activities is referred to as a _____.
   a. Thing
   b. Fund8
   c. Undefined
   d. Undefined

100. _____ refers to a recording as positive in the balance of payments, any transaction that gives rise to a payment into the country, such as an export, the sale of an asset, or borrowing from abroad.
   a. Credit8
   b. Thing
   c. Undefined
   d. Undefined

101. Similar to a script in that a _____ can be a less than completely rational decision-making method. Involves the use of a pre-existing set of decision steps for any problem that presents itself.
   a. Policy8
   b. Thing
   c. Undefined
   d. Undefined

102. A _____ is an industrial action in which employees perform their duties but seek to reduce productivity or efficiency in their performance of these duties. A _____ may be used as either a prelude or an alternative to a strike, as it is seen as less disruptive as well as less risky and costly for workers and their union.

a. Thing  
c. Undefined  
b. Slowdown8  
d. Undefined

103. _____, also known as property, plant, and equipment (PP&E), is a term used in accountancy for assets and property which cannot easily be converted into cash. This can be compared with current assets such as cash or bank accounts, which are described as liquid assets. In most cases, only tangible assets are referred to as fixed.
a. Fixed asset8  
c. Undefined  
b. Thing  
d. Undefined

104. Assets defined in the broadest legal sense. _____ includes the unrealized receivables of a cash basis taxpayer, but not services rendered.
a. Property8  
c. Undefined  
b. Thing  
d. Undefined

105. _____ refers to a good that has not been transformed by production; a primary product.
a. Raw material8  
c. Undefined  
b. Thing  
d. Undefined

106. _____ is the aggregate amount of any material good that can be called into being at a certain price point; it comprises one half of the equation of _____ and demand. In classical economic theory, a curve representing _____ is one of the factors that produce price.
a. Supply8  
c. Undefined  
b. Thing  
d. Undefined

107. The dollar difference between total current assets and total current liabilities is called _____.
a. Thing  
c. Undefined  
b. Working capital8  
d. Undefined

108. _____ refers to financial results from the disposal of a major segment of the business and are reported net of income tax effects.
a. Thing  
c. Undefined  
b. Discontinued operations8  
d. Undefined

109. A self analysis of the strengths and weaknesses of a company is an _____. Includes an analysis of the company's manufacturing, marketing, technological, financial and human resources.
a. Internal analysis8  
c. Undefined  
b. Thing  
d. Undefined

110. A professional that provides expert advice in a particular field or area in which customers occassionaly require this type of knowledge is a _____.
a. Consultant8  
c. Undefined  
b. Concept  
d. Undefined

111. _____ refers to the phase of the promotional planning process that focuses on factors such as the characteristics of an organization's customers, market segments, positioning strategies, competitors, and marketing environment.

a. Thing
c. Undefined
b. External analysis8
d. Undefined

112. _____ refers to the ability to influence the setting of prices or wages, usually arising from some sort of monopoly or monopsony position
a. Thing
c. Undefined
b. Bargaining power8
d. Undefined

113. _____ refer to shareholders who have dividend and liquidation preferences over other classes of shareholders, usually common shareholders. _____ get paid before common shareholders.
a. Preferred shareholders8
c. Undefined
b. Thing
d. Undefined

114. In finance, _____ is the process of estimating the market value of a financial asset or liability. They can be done on assets (for example, investments in marketable securities such as stocks, options, business enterprises, or intangible assets such as patents and trademarks) or on liabilities (e.g., Bonds issued by a company).
a. Valuation8
c. Undefined
b. Event
d. Undefined

115. There are several methods used for _____. They try to give an estimate of their fair value, by using fundamental economic criteria. This theoretical valuation has to be perfected with market criteria, as the final purpose is to determine potential market prices.
a. Stock valuation8
c. Undefined
b. Thing
d. Undefined

116. A system that collects and processes financial information about an organization and reports that information to decision makers is referred to as _____.
a. Thing
c. Undefined
b. Accounting8
d. Undefined

117. _____ refers to the rate of return that investors demand from an investment to compensate them for the amount of risk involved.
a. Required rate of return8
c. Undefined
b. Thing
d. Undefined

118. _____ refers to a bank's capital divided by its assets.
a. Thing
c. Undefined
b. Leverage ratio8
d. Undefined

119. Financing that consists of funds that are invested in exchange for ownership in the company is called _____.
a. Equity financing8
c. Undefined
b. Thing
d. Undefined

120. The _____ is the amount of income tax an individual or firm pays divided by the individual or firm's total taxable income. This ratio is usually expressed as a percentage.

a. Thing
b. Effective tax rate8
c. Undefined
d. Undefined

121. _____ refers to a bank check that has been fraudulently altered to increase its face value.
a. Thing
b. Kite8
c. Undefined
d. Undefined

122. A maximum amount of growth a firm can sustain without increasing financial leverage is called _____.
a. Sustainable growth8
b. Thing
c. Undefined
d. Undefined

123. _____ refers to a debt that can reasonably be expected to be paid from existing current assets or through the creation of other current liabilities, within one year or the operating cycle, whichever is longer.
a. Current liability8
b. Thing
c. Undefined
d. Undefined

124. A pro rata distribution of cash to stockholders of corporate stock is called a _____.
a. Cash dividend8
b. Thing
c. Undefined
d. Undefined

125. That fraction of an industry's output accounted for by an individual firm or group of firms is called _____.
a. Market share8
b. Thing
c. Undefined
d. Undefined

126. _____ is an American electronic stock exchange. It was founded in 1971 by the National Association of Securities Dealers who divested it in a series of sales in 2000 and 2001.
a. NASDAQ8
b. Thing
c. Undefined
d. Undefined

127. _____ refer to an equity security, representing a shareholder's ownership of a corporation. _____ are one of a finite number of equal portions in the capital of a company, entitling the owner to a proportion of distributed, non-reinvested profits known as dividends and to a portion of the value of the company in case of liquidation.
a. Thing
b. Shares8
c. Undefined
d. Undefined

128. A _____ price is a price offered by a buyer when he/she buys a good. In the context of stock trading on a stock exchange, the _____ price is the highest price a buyer of a stock is willing to pay for a share of that given stock.
a. Thing
b. Bid8
c. Undefined
d. Undefined

129. A _____ is the measure of the extent to which two economic or statistical variables move together, normalized so that its values range from -1 to +1. It is defined as the covariance of the two variables divided by the square root of the product of their variances.
a. Correlation8
b. Thing
c. Undefined
d. Undefined

## Chapter 8. Return on Invested Capital

130. Cumulative earnings of a company that are not distributed to the owners and are reinvested in the business are called _____.
   a. Retained earnings8
   b. Thing
   c. Undefined
   d. Undefined

131. _____ is a research-based magazine written for business practitioners, it claims a high ranking business readership and enjoys the reverence of academics, executives, and management consultants. It has been the frequent publishing home for well known scholars and management thinkers.
   a. Harvard Business Review8
   b. Organization
   c. Undefined
   d. Undefined

132. A contract that gives the purchaser the _____ to buy or sell the underlying financial instrument at a specified price, called the exercise price or strike price, within a specific period of time.
   a. Thing
   b. Option8
   c. Undefined
   d. Undefined

133. _____ refers to the basic, normal, voting stock issued by a corporation; called residual equity because it ranks after preferred stock for dividend and liquidation distributions.
   a. Common stock8
   b. Thing
   c. Undefined
   d. Undefined

134. In finance, a _____ is "attached" to a bond, either physically (as with old bonds) or electronically. Each _____ represents a predetermined payment promized to the bond-holder in return for his or her loan of money to the bond-issuer. .
   a. Concept
   b. Coupon8
   c. Undefined
   d. Undefined

135. Total revenues from operation minus cost of goods sold and operating costs are called _____.
   a. Operating income8
   b. Thing
   c. Undefined
   d. Undefined

136. The income from business operations before interest expense and income taxes are subtracted is an _____. Also known as earnings before interest and taxes or EBIT.
   a. Income before interest and taxes8
   b. Thing
   c. Undefined
   d. Undefined

137. _____ refers to the way a corporation finances itself through some combination of equity sales, equity options, bonds, and loans. Optimal _____ refers to the particular combination that minimizes the cost of capital while maximizing the stock price.
   a. Capital structure8
   b. Thing
   c. Undefined
   d. Undefined

138. A _____ in property law is a future interest created in a transferee that is capable of becoming possessory upon the natural termination of a prior estate created by the same instrument.

## Chapter 8. Return on Invested Capital

a. Thing
c. Undefined
b. Remainder8
d. Undefined

139. People who link buyers with sellers by buying and selling securities at stated prices are referred to as a _____.
a. Thing
c. Undefined
b. Dealer8
d. Undefined

140. _____ refers to the percentage cost of funds used for acquiring resources for an organization, typically a weighted average of the firms cost of equity and cost of debt.
a. Cost of capital8
c. Undefined
b. Place
d. Undefined

141. In finance, the _____ is the minimum rate of return a firm must offer shareholders to compensate for waiting for their returns, and for bearing some risk.
a. Cost of equity8
c. Undefined
b. Thing
d. Undefined

142. The minimum acceptable rate of return in a capital budgeting decision is the _____. The _____ should reflect the riskiness of the investment, typically measured by volatility of cash flows, and must take into account the financing mix.
a. Hurdle rate8
c. Undefined
b. Thing
d. Undefined

143. A person in possession of a document of title or an instrument payable or indorsed to him, his order, or to bearer is a _____.
a. Holder8
c. Undefined
b. Thing
d. Undefined

144. _____ refers to the rate, per year, at which future values are diminished to make them comparable to values in the present. Can be either subjective or objective .
a. Thing
c. Undefined
b. Discount rate8
d. Undefined

145. The _____ is the cost of borrowing money (usually denoted by Kd). It is derived by dividing debt's interest payments on the total market value of the debts.
a. Thing
c. Undefined
b. Cost of debt8
d. Undefined

146. In finance, _____ refers to the amounts of cash being received and spent by a business during a defined period of time, sometimes tied to a specific project. Most of the time they are being used to determine gaps in the liquid position of a company.
a. Thing
c. Undefined
b. Cash flow8
d. Undefined

147. _____ refers to a rise in the value of a country's currency on the exchange market, relative either to a particular other currency or to a weighted average of other currencies. The currency is said to appreciate. Opposite of 'depreciation.' _____ can also refer to the increase in value of any asset.
- a. Appreciation8
- b. Thing
- c. Undefined
- d. Undefined

148. An organized marketplace in which common stocks are traded. In the United States, the largest _____ is the New York Stock Exchange, on which are traded the stocks of the largest U.S. companies.
- a. Thing
- b. Stock market8
- c. Undefined
- d. Undefined

149. In finance, the _____ can be the expected rate of return above the risk-free interest rate.
- a. Thing
- b. Risk premium8
- c. Undefined
- d. Undefined

150. An increase in the overall price level of an economy, usually as measured by the CPI or by the implicit price deflator is called _____.
- a. Inflation8
- b. Thing
- c. Undefined
- d. Undefined

151. _____ refers to the fee charged by an insurance company for an insurance policy. The rate of losses must be relatively predictable: In order to set the _____ (prices) insurers must be able to estimate them accurately.
- a. Premium8
- b. Thing
- c. Undefined
- d. Undefined

152. The _____ is a court's determination of a matter of law based on the issue presented in the particular case. In other words: under this law, with these facts, this result.
- a. Holding8
- b. Thing
- c. Undefined
- d. Undefined

153. According to the United Nations Statistics Division _____ is the resale of new and used goods to retailers, to industrial, commercial, institutional or professional users, or to other wholesalers, or involves acting as an agent or broker in buying merchandise for, or selling merchandise, to such persons or companies.
- a. Thing
- b. Wholesale8
- c. Undefined
- d. Undefined

154. A _____ is a long-term debt instrument used by governments and large companies to obtain funds. It is similar to a bond except the securitization conditions are different.
- a. Debenture8
- b. Thing
- c. Undefined
- d. Undefined

155. The portion of a firm or industry's cost that changes with output, in contrast to fixed cost is referred to as _____.
- a. Thing
- b. Variable cost8
- c. Undefined
- d. Undefined

## Chapter 8. Return on Invested Capital

156. A _____ is something measured by a number; it is used to analyze what happens to other things when the size of that number changes.
   a. Thing
   b. Variable8
   c. Undefined
   d. Undefined

157. _____ is the process whereby interested parties resolve disputes, agree upon courses of action, bargain for individual or collective advantage, and/or attempt to craft outcomes which serve their mutual interests.
   a. Negotiation8
   b. Thing
   c. Undefined
   d. Undefined

158. People's physical and mental talents and efforts that are used to help produce goods and services are called _____.
   a. Labor8
   b. Thing
   c. Undefined
   d. Undefined

159. The payment for the service of a unit of labor, per unit time. In trade theory, it is the only payment to labor, usually unskilled labor. In empirical work, _____ data may exclude other compenzation, which must be added to get the total cost of employment.
   a. Wage8
   b. Thing
   c. Undefined
   d. Undefined

160. A _____ is an asset on the balance sheet which is expected to be sold or otherwise used up in the near future, usually within one year.
   a. Thing
   b. Current asset8
   c. Undefined
   d. Undefined

161. A _____ is a 12-month period used for calculating annual ("yearly") financial reports in businesses and other organizations. In many jurisdictions, regulatory laws regarding accounting require such reports once per twelve months, but do not require that the twelve months constitute a calendar year (i.e. January to December).
   a. Fiscal year8
   b. Thing
   c. Undefined
   d. Undefined

162. _____ refers to a financial statement that presents the revenues and expenses and resulting net income or net loss of a company for a specific period of time.
   a. Income statement8
   b. Thing
   c. Undefined
   d. Undefined

163. _____ refers to a person or tool with a primary function of information analysis, generally with a more limited, practical and short term set of goals than a researcher.
   a. Analyst8
   b. Person
   c. Undefined
   d. Undefined

164. _____ refers to assets used to operate the business; frequently called long-term assets. They are property such as land, livestock, and trees that produce income.

a. Productive assets8  
b. Thing  
c. Undefined  
d. Undefined  

165. _____ is an economic concept with commonplace familiarity; it is the price that a good or service is offered at, or will fetch, in the marketplace; it is of interest mainly in the study of microeconomics.
   a. Market price8  
   b. Thing  
   c. Undefined  
   d. Undefined  

166. In finance, a _____ is a collection of investments held by an institution or a private individual. Holding but not always a _____ is part of an investment and risk-limiting strategy called diversification. By owning several assets, certain types of risk (in particular specific risk) can be reduced.
   a. Thing  
   b. Portfolio8  
   c. Undefined  
   d. Undefined  

167. An organization that employs resources to produce a good or service for profit and owns and operates one or more plants is referred to as a _____.
   a. Thing  
   b. Firm8  
   c. Undefined  
   d. Undefined  

168. _____ refers to paid, nonpersonal communication through various media by organizations and individuals who are in some way identified in the _____ message.
   a. Thing  
   b. Advertising8  
   c. Undefined  
   d. Undefined  

169. All activities involved in selling, renting, and providing goods and services to ultimate consumers for personal, family, or household use is referred to as _____.
   a. Thing  
   b. Retailing8  
   c. Undefined  
   d. Undefined  

170. A market in which no buyer or seller has market power is called a _____.
   a. Competitive market8  
   b. Thing  
   c. Undefined  
   d. Undefined  

171. Income from operations before subtracting interest expense and income taxes is an _____.
   a. Thing  
   b. Earnings before interest and taxes8  
   c. Undefined  
   d. Undefined  

172. _____ refers to the long-term movement of an economic variable, such as its average rate of increase or decrease over enough years to encompass several business cycles.
   a. Trend8  
   b. Thing  
   c. Undefined  
   d. Undefined  

173. _____ is one of the largest media and entertainment corporations in the world. Founded on October 16, 1923 by brothers Walt and Roy _____ as a small animation studio, today it is one of the largest Hollywood studios and also owns nine theme parks and several television networks, including the American Broadcasting Company (ABC).

## Chapter 8. Return on Invested Capital

a. Organization
c. Undefined
b. Disney8
d. Undefined

174. _____ in economics, the manner in which total output and income is distributed among individuals or factors.
a. Thing
c. Undefined
b. Distribution8
d. Undefined

175. _____, in communications (sometimes called communications _____), refers to the medium used to convey information from a sender (or transmitter) to a receiver.
a. Channel8
c. Undefined
b. Thing
d. Undefined

176. The combination of product lines offered by a manufacturer is referred to as _____.
a. Product mix8
c. Undefined
b. Thing
d. Undefined

177. _____ is a form of strategic alliance which involves the sale of a right to use certain proprietary knowledge (so called intellectual property) in a defined way.
a. Licensing8
c. Undefined
b. Thing
d. Undefined

178. A _____ is an individual or company (including a corporation) that legally owns one or more shares of stock in a joined stock company. The shareholders are the owners of a corporation. Companies listed at the stock market strive to enhance shareholder value.
a. Thing
c. Undefined
b. Stockholder8
d. Undefined

179. The finalization of a real estate sales transaction that passes title to the property from the seller to the buyer is referred to as a _____. _____ is a sales term which refers to the process of making a sale. It refers to reaching the final step, which may be an exchange of money or acquiring a signature.
a. Closing8
c. Undefined
b. Thing
d. Undefined

## Chapter 9. Profitability Analysis

1. _____ is a U.S. business term for the amount of money that a company receives from its activities, mostly from sales of products and/or services to customers.
   - a. Thing
   - b. Revenue9
   - c. Undefined
   - d. Undefined

2. Net sales less cost of goods sold is called _____.
   - a. Thing
   - b. Gross profit9
   - c. Undefined
   - d. Undefined

3. The consumer's appraisal of the product or brand on important attributes is called _____.
   - a. Evaluation9
   - b. Thing
   - c. Undefined
   - d. Undefined

4. _____ refers to the return to the resource entrepreneurial ability; total revenue minus total cost.
   - a. Profit9
   - b. Thing
   - c. Undefined
   - d. Undefined

5. An _____ expresses the cost of a market basket of goods relative to its cost in some 'base' period, which is simply the year or years used as a basis of comparison.
   - a. Index number9
   - b. Thing
   - c. Undefined
   - d. Undefined

6. In accounting, an _____ represents an event in which an asset is used up or a liability is incurred. In terms of the accounting equation, expenses reduce owners' equity.
   - a. Expense9
   - b. Thing
   - c. Undefined
   - d. Undefined

7. The _____ is the amount of income tax an individual or firm pays divided by the individual or firm's total taxable income. This ratio is usually expressed as a percentage.
   - a. Thing
   - b. Effective tax rate9
   - c. Undefined
   - d. Undefined

8. _____ means the giving out of information, either voluntarily or to be in compliance with legal regulations or workplace rules.
   - a. Disclosure9
   - b. Thing
   - c. Undefined
   - d. Undefined

9. _____ has recently added self checkout registers at most of its stores in North America. These automated kiosks allow the customer to scan the barcode of the item they wish to purchase, then insert money to pay for the items, and receive any change automatically. The customer no longer needs to interact with a store employee during checkout.
   - a. Organization
   - b. Home Depot9
   - c. Undefined
   - d. Undefined

10. _____, in the field of loss prevention, are systems designed to introduce technical barriers to shoplifting.
    - a. Thing
    - b. Inventory control9
    - c. Undefined
    - d. Undefined

## Chapter 9. Profitability Analysis

11. _____ characterizes the process of leading and directing all or part of an organization, often a business, through the deployment and manipulation of resources. Early twentieth-century _____ writer Mary Parker Follett defined _____ as "the art of getting things done through people."
    a. Thing
    b. Management9
    c. Undefined
    d. Undefined

12. Tangible property held for sale in the normal course of business or used in producing goods or services for sale is an _____.
    a. Inventory9
    b. Thing
    c. Undefined
    d. Undefined

13. _____ equals Gross Profit divided by Revenue, expressed as a percentage. The percentage represents the amount of each dollar of Revenue that results in Gross Profit.
    a. Thing
    b. Gross profit margin9
    c. Undefined
    d. Undefined

14. In throughput accounting, the cost accounting aspect of Theory of Constraints (TOC), _____ is the money spent turning inventory into throughput. In TOC, _____ is limited to costs that vary strictly with the quantity produced, like raw materials and purchased components.
    a. Thing
    b. Operating expense9
    c. Undefined
    d. Undefined

15. _____ is a measure of profitability. It is calculated using a formula and written as a percentage or a number. _____ = Net income before tax and interest / Revenue.
    a. Profit margin9
    b. Thing
    c. Undefined
    d. Undefined

16. A deposit by a buyer in stocks with a seller or a stockbroker, as security to cover fluctuations in the market in reference to stocks that the buyer has purchased but for which he has not paid is a _____. Commodities are also traded on _____.
    a. Margin9
    b. Thing
    c. Undefined
    d. Undefined

17. A _____ is, as defined in economics, a social arrangement that allows buyers and sellers to discover information and carry out a voluntary exchange of goods or services.
    a. Market9
    b. Thing
    c. Undefined
    d. Undefined

18. _____ is a measure of a company's earning power from ongoing operations, equal to earnings before the deduction of interest payments and income taxes.
    a. Thing
    b. Operating profit9
    c. Undefined
    d. Undefined

19. Management merely consists of _____ applied to business situations; or in other words: management forms a subset of the broader process of _____.

## Chapter 9. Profitability Analysis

a. Leadership9  
b. Thing  
c. Undefined  
d. Undefined

20. A standardized method or technique that is performed repetitively, often on different materials resulting in different finished goods is called an _____.
a. Operation9  
b. Thing  
c. Undefined  
d. Undefined

21. _____ refers to the function in a firm that searches for quality material resources, finds the best suppliers, and negotiates the best price for goods and services.
a. Purchasing9  
b. Thing  
c. Undefined  
d. Undefined

22. _____ refers to paid, nonpersonal communication through various media by organizations and individuals who are in some way identified in the _____ message.
a. Thing  
b. Advertising9  
c. Undefined  
d. Undefined

23. _____ refers to a person or tool with a primary function of information analysis, generally with a more limited, practical and short term set of goals than a researcher.
a. Person  
b. Analyst9  
c. Undefined  
d. Undefined

24. People's physical and mental talents and efforts that are used to help produce goods and services are called _____.
a. Labor9  
b. Thing  
c. Undefined  
d. Undefined

25. A means of measuring the profitability of the firm's products, customer groups, sales territories, channels of distribution, and order sizes is called _____.
a. Profitability analysis9  
b. Thing  
c. Undefined  
d. Undefined

26. _____ refers to the total costs of goods made or purchased and sold.
a. Cost of sales9  
b. Thing  
c. Undefined  
d. Undefined

27. A system that collects and processes financial information about an organization and reports that information to decision makers is referred to as _____.
a. Accounting9  
b. Thing  
c. Undefined  
d. Undefined

28. Collecting information and providing feedback to employees about their behavior, communication style, or skills is an _____.

## Chapter 9. Profitability Analysis

a. Thing
c. Undefined
b. Assessment9
d. Undefined

29. _____ refers to a summary of all the transactions that have occurred over a particular period.
a. Financial statement9
c. Undefined
b. Thing
d. Undefined

30. _____ refers to a financial statement that presents the revenues and expenses and resulting net income or net loss of a company for a specific period of time.
a. Income statement9
c. Undefined
b. Thing
d. Undefined

31. _____ refers to measures that are important to monitoring and tracking the effectiveness of a company's operations.
a. Operating results9
c. Undefined
b. Thing
d. Undefined

32. _____ refers to the capacity to turn assets into cash, or the amount of assets in a portfolio that have that capacity.
a. Thing
c. Undefined
b. Liquidity9
d. Undefined

33. The ability of a company to pay interest as it comes due and to repay the face value of debt at maturity is called _____.
a. Solvency9
c. Undefined
b. Thing
d. Undefined

34. A person to whom a debt or legal obligation is owed, and who has the right to enforce payment of that debt or obligation is referred to as _____.
a. Creditor9
c. Undefined
b. Thing
d. Undefined

35. _____ is the name given to the set of legal principles, in countries following the English common law tradition, which supplement strict rules of law where their application would operate harshly, so as to achieve what is sometimes referred to as "natural justice."
a. Thing
c. Undefined
b. Equity9
d. Undefined

36. _____ refer to people in the organization who actually use the product or service purchased by the buying center.
a. Thing
c. Undefined
b. Users9
d. Undefined

37. In finance, _____ is a profit or an increase in value of an investment such as a stock or bond. _____ is calculated by fair market value or the proceeds from the sale of the investment minus the sum of the purchase price and all costs associated with it.

a. Gain9  
b. Thing  
c. Undefined  
d. Undefined

38. An _____ is prepared by corporate management that presents financial information including financial statements, footnotes, and the management discussion and analysis.
    a. Thing
    b. Annual report9
    c. Undefined
    d. Undefined

39. The creation of finished goods and services using the factors of _____: land, labor, capital, entrepreneurship, and knowledge.
    a. Production9
    b. Thing
    c. Undefined
    d. Undefined

40. An item of property, such as land, capital, money, a share in ownership, or a claim on others for future payment, such as a bond or a bank deposit is an _____.
    a. Asset9
    b. Thing
    c. Undefined
    d. Undefined

41. _____ is a liability. It is recorded when an asset (e.g. receivable) is recorded, but the related income (i.e. revenue) will be earned only in the future.
    a. Thing
    b. Deferred income9
    c. Undefined
    d. Undefined

42. A _____ is a present obligation of the enterprise arizing from past events, the settlement of which is expected to result in an outflow from the enterprise of resources embodying economic benefits.
    a. Liability9
    b. Thing
    c. Undefined
    d. Undefined

43. Financial standards that corporations must meet before their common stock can be traded on a stock exchange are _____. _____ are not standard, but are set by each exchange. The requirements for the NYSE are the most stringent.
    a. Listing requirements9
    b. Thing
    c. Undefined
    d. Undefined

44. The trade of things of value between buyer and seller so that each is better off after the trade is called the _____.
    a. Thing
    b. Exchange9
    c. Undefined
    d. Undefined

45. _____ refers to a claim on the borrower future income that is sold by the borrower to the lender. A _____ is a type of transferable interest representing financial value.
    a. Thing
    b. Security9
    c. Undefined
    d. Undefined

46. A group of products that are physically similar or are intended for a similar market are called the _____.

## Chapter 9. Profitability Analysis

a. Product line9  
b. Thing  
c. Undefined  
d. Undefined

47. _____ refers to the total number of dollars received by a firm from the sale of a product; equal to the total expenditures for the product produced by the firm; equal to the quantity sold multiplied by the price at which it is sold.
a. Thing  
b. Total revenue9  
c. Undefined  
d. Undefined

48. An out-of-court settlement in which creditors agree to accept a fractional settlement on their original claim is referred to as _____.
a. Composition9  
b. Thing  
c. Undefined  
d. Undefined

49. Cash flow activities that include obtaining cash from issuing debt and repaying the amounts borrowed and obtaining cash from stockholders and paying dividends is referred to as _____.
a. Financing activities9  
b. Thing  
c. Undefined  
d. Undefined

50. A statement of the assets, liabilities, and net worth of a firm or individual at some given time often at the end of its "fiscal year," is referred to as a _____.
a. Thing  
b. Balance sheet9  
c. Undefined  
d. Undefined

51. In finance, _____ refers to the amounts of cash being received and spent by a business during a defined period of time, sometimes tied to a specific project. Most of the time they are being used to determine gaps in the liquid position of a company.
a. Thing  
b. Cash flow9  
c. Undefined  
d. Undefined

52. In banking and accountancy, the outstanding _____ is the amount of money owned, (or due), that remains in a deposit account (or a loan account) at a given date, after all past remittances, payments and withdrawal have been accounted for. It can be positive (then, in the _____ sheet of a firm, it is an asset) or negative (a liability).
a. Thing  
b. Balance9  
c. Undefined  
d. Undefined

53. _____ refers to an agency, commission, or board established by the Federal government or a state government to regulates businesses in the public interest.
a. Thing  
b. Regulatory agency9  
c. Undefined  
d. Undefined

54. A group of firms that produce identical or similar products is an _____. It is also used specifically to refer to an area of economic production focused on manufacturing which involves large amounts of capital investment before any profit can be realized, also called "heavy _____".
a. Industry9  
b. Thing  
c. Undefined  
d. Undefined

## Chapter 9. Profitability Analysis

55. In economics, an _____ is any good or commodity, shipped or otherwise transported out of a country, province, town to another part of the world in a legitimate fashion, typically for use in trade or sale.
   a. Export9
   b. Thing
   c. Undefined
   d. Undefined

56. Total revenues from operation minus cost of goods sold and operating costs are called _____.
   a. Operating income9
   b. Thing
   c. Undefined
   d. Undefined

57. Dealers, who buy products to sell to others, and ultimate customers, who buy products for their own personal use are referred to as _____.
   a. Thing
   b. External customers9
   c. Undefined
   d. Undefined

58. Systematic and rational allocation of the acquisition cost of an intangible asset over its useful life is referred to as _____.
   a. Thing
   b. Amortization9
   c. Undefined
   d. Undefined

59. _____ is an accounting and finance term for the method of attributing the cost of an asset across the useful life of the asset. _____ is a reduction in the value of a currency in floating exchange rate.
   a. Depreciation9
   b. Thing
   c. Undefined
   d. Undefined

60. _____ is the result of computing current and deferred tax payable using the asset-liability method in which the balance sheet is seen as primary and the income statement as secondary.
   a. Thing
   b. Tax expense9
   c. Undefined
   d. Undefined

61. In finance and economics, _____ is the price paid by a borrower for the use of a lender's money. In other words, _____ is the amount of paid to "rent" money for a period of time.
   a. Interest9
   b. Thing
   c. Undefined
   d. Undefined

62. _____ refers to a good that has not been transformed by production; a primary product.
   a. Thing
   b. Raw material9
   c. Undefined
   d. Undefined

63. In agency law, one under whose direction an agent acts and for whose benefit that agent acts is a _____.
   a. Thing
   b. Principal9
   c. Undefined
   d. Undefined

64. _____ refers to a "non tangible product" that is not embodied in a physical good and that typically effects some change in another product, person, or institution. Contrasts with good.

a. Thing  
c. Undefined  
b. Service9  
d. Undefined  

65. The legal right to the proceeds from and control over the use of an invented product or process, granted for a fixed period of time, usually 20 years. _____ is one form of intellectual property that is subject of the TRIPS agreement.
   a. Patent9  
   c. Undefined  
   b. Thing  
   d. Undefined  

66. The use of resources for the deliberate discovery of new information and ways of doing things, together with the application of that information in inventing new products or processes is referred to as _____.
   a. Thing  
   c. Undefined  
   b. Research and development9  
   d. Undefined  

67. Any cost incurred by a utility providing more than one service, but which cannot be assigned solely to one or another function, as they relate to the utility's overall operations is a _____.
   a. Common cost9  
   c. Undefined  
   b. Thing  
   d. Undefined  

68. Production of goods primarily by the application of labor and capital to raw materials and other intermediate inputs, in contrast to agriculture, mining, forestry, fishing, and services a _____.
   a. Thing  
   c. Undefined  
   b. Manufacturing9  
   d. Undefined  

69. An _____ is a company offering debit and credit card acceptance services for merchants. Often the company is partially or wholly owned by a bank, sometimes a bank itself offers acquiring services.
   a. Thing  
   c. Undefined  
   b. Acquirer9  
   d. Undefined  

70. The finalization of a real estate sales transaction that passes title to the property from the seller to the buyer is referred to as a _____. _____ is a sales term which refers to the process of making a sale. It refers to reaching the final step, which may be an exchange of money or acquiring a signature.
   a. Thing  
   c. Undefined  
   b. Closing9  
   d. Undefined  

71. _____ refers to the act of asking an appellate court to overturn a decision after the trial court's final judgment has been entered.
   a. Appeal9  
   c. Undefined  
   b. Thing  
   d. Undefined  

72. _____ refers to the final stage of the creative process where the validity or truthfulness of the insight is determined. The feedback portion of communication in which the receiver sends a message to the source indicating receipt of the message and the degree to which he or she understood the message.
   a. Concept  
   c. Undefined  
   b. Verification9  
   d. Undefined

## Chapter 9. Profitability Analysis

73. _____ refers to the long-term movement of an economic variable, such as its average rate of increase or decrease over enough years to encompass several business cycles.
   a. Trend9
   b. Thing
   c. Undefined
   d. Undefined

74. A substantial expenditure that is used by a company to acquire or upgrade physical assets such as equipment, property, industrial buildings, including those which improve the quality and life of an asset is referred to as a _____.
   a. Capital expenditure9
   b. Thing
   c. Undefined
   d. Undefined

75. Major investments in long-term assets such as land, buildings, equipment, or research and development are referred to as _____.
   a. Capital expenditures9
   b. Thing
   c. Undefined
   d. Undefined

76. _____ generally refers to financial wealth, especially that used to start or maintain a business. In classical economics, _____ is one of four factors of production, the others being land and labor and entrepreneurship.
   a. Capital9
   b. Thing
   c. Undefined
   d. Undefined

77. In financial terminology, _____ is the capital raized by a corporation, through the issuance and sale of shares.
   a. Stock9
   b. Thing
   c. Undefined
   d. Undefined

78. _____ in contract law, a basic requirement for an enforceable agreement under traditional contract principles, defined in this text as legal value, bargained for and given in exchange for an act or promise. In corporation law, cash or property contributed to a corporation in exchange for shares, or a promise to contribute such cash or property.
   a. Consideration9
   b. Thing
   c. Undefined
   d. Undefined

79. Gross sales less sales returns and allowances and sales discounts are referred to as _____.
   a. Thing
   b. Net sales9
   c. Undefined
   d. Undefined

80. This is the term used in the balance of payments statistics, since sometime in the 1990s, for what used to be called the 'capital account are referred to as _____.
   a. Financial account9
   b. Thing
   c. Undefined
   d. Undefined

81. Assistance provided by countries and by international institutions such as the World Bank to developing countries in the form of monetary grants, loans at low interest rates, in kind, or a combination of these is called _____. _____ can also refer to assistance of any type rendered to benefit some group or individual.
   a. Thing
   b. Aid9
   c. Undefined
   d. Undefined

82. Cash flow activities that include the cash effects of transactions that create revenues and expenses and thus enter into the determination of net income is an _____.
   a. Thing
   b. Operating activities9
   c. Undefined
   d. Undefined

83. An increase in the overall price level of an economy, usually as measured by the CPI or by the implicit price deflator is called _____.
   a. Inflation9
   b. Thing
   c. Undefined
   d. Undefined

84. _____ is the aggregate amount of any material good that can be called into being at a certain price point; it comprises one half of the equation of _____ and demand. In classical economic theory, a curve representing _____ is one of the factors that produce price.
   a. Thing
   b. Supply9
   c. Undefined
   d. Undefined

85. An _____ is any factor (financial or non-financial) that provides a motive for a particular course of action, or counts as a reason for preferring one choice to the alternatives.
   a. Thing
   b. Incentive9
   c. Undefined
   d. Undefined

86. _____ is one of a series of accounting transactions dealing with the billing of customers which owe money to a person, company or organization for goods and services that have been provided to the customer. This is typically done in a one person organization by writing an invoice and mailing or delivering it to each customer.
   a. Accounts receivable9
   b. Thing
   c. Undefined
   d. Undefined

87. _____ is most well known for its Unix systems, which have a reputation for system stability and a consistent design philosophy.
   a. Organization
   b. Sun Microsystems9
   c. Undefined
   d. Undefined

88. _____ in a financial context refers to the rate at which a provider of goods cycles through its average inventory. _____ in a human resources context refers to the characteristic of a given company or industry, relative to rate at which an employer gains and loses staff.
   a. Thing
   b. Turnover9
   c. Undefined
   d. Undefined

89. Completed products awaiting sale are called _____. An item considered a finished good in a supplying plant might be considered a component or raw material in a receiving plant.
   a. Finished goods9
   b. Thing
   c. Undefined
   d. Undefined

90. An advertising effectiveness measure of print ads that allows the advertiser to assess the impact of an ad in a single issue of a magazine over time and/or across alternative magazines is called the _____.

a. Recognition method9  
b. Thing  
c. Undefined  
d. Undefined

91. _____ refer to an equity security, representing a shareholder's ownership of a corporation. _____ are one of a finite number of equal portions in the capital of a company, entitling the owner to a proportion of distributed, non-reinvested profits known as dividends and to a portion of the value of the company in case of liquidation.
    a. Shares9
    b. Thing
    c. Undefined
    d. Undefined

92. An organization that employs resources to produce a good or service for profit and owns and operates one or more plants is referred to as a _____.
    a. Thing
    b. Firm9
    c. Undefined
    d. Undefined

93. In many tribunal and administrative law suits, the person who initiates the claim is called the _____.
    a. Applicant9
    b. Person
    c. Undefined
    d. Undefined

94. _____ is an ambiguous phrase that expresses the relationship between gross profit and sales revenue as _____ = Revenue - costs of good sold.
    a. Thing
    b. Gross margin9
    c. Undefined
    d. Undefined

95. The percentage of payments that you receive, such as from installment sales or annuities, which is from your profit or investment earnings is the _____.
    a. Gross profit percentage9
    b. Thing
    c. Undefined
    d. Undefined

96. _____ refers to spending for the production and accumulation of capital and additions to inventories. In a financial sense, buying an asset with the expectation of making a return.
    a. Investment9
    b. Thing
    c. Undefined
    d. Undefined

97. _____ refers to cost computed by dividing some amount of total costs by the related number of units. Also called average cost.
    a. Unit cost9
    b. Thing
    c. Undefined
    d. Undefined

98. _____ refers to the method under which income and expenses are determined for tax purposes. Important accounting methods include the cash basis and the accrual basis.
    a. Accounting method9
    b. Thing
    c. Undefined
    d. Undefined

99. _____ refers to any departure from the ideal of perfect competition that interferes with economic agents maximizing social welfare when they maximize their own.

## Chapter 9. Profitability Analysis

a. Thing
b. Distortion9
c. Undefined
d. Undefined

100. _____ refers to the time period used for comparative analysis; the basis for indexing, e.g., of price change. A _____ may be a month, year or average of years.
a. Thing
b. Base period9
c. Undefined
d. Undefined

101. A _____ refers to a layout accurate in size, color, scheme, and other necessary details to show how a final ad will look. For presentation only, never for reproduction.
a. Thing
b. Comprehensive9
c. Undefined
d. Undefined

102. _____ is one of the most general and applicable methods of analytical thinking, depending only on the division of a problem, decision or situation into a sufficient number of separate cases.
a. Case analysis9
b. Thing
c. Undefined
d. Undefined

103. In accounting, the _____ describes the direct expenses incurred in producing a particular good for sale, including the actual cost of materials that comprise the good, and direct labor expense in putting the good in salable condition.
a. Cost of goods sold9
b. Thing
c. Undefined
d. Undefined

104. Promoting and selling products or services to customers, or prospective customers, is referred to as _____.
a. Marketing9
b. Thing
c. Undefined
d. Undefined

105. _____ refers to the total output of goods and services in a given period of time divided by work hours.
a. Thing
b. Productivity9
c. Undefined
d. Undefined

106. A _____ is something measured by a number; it is used to analyze what happens to other things when the size of that number changes.
a. Thing
b. Variable9
c. Undefined
d. Undefined

107. _____ refers to all the techniques sellers use to motivate people to buy products or services. An attempt by marketers to inform people about products and to persuade them to participate in an exchange.
a. Promotion9
b. Thing
c. Undefined
d. Undefined

108. In accounting and finance, _____ is the portion of receivables that can no longer be collected, typically from accounts receivable or loans. _____ in accounting is considered an expense.

## Chapter 9. Profitability Analysis

a. Bad debt9  
b. Thing  
c. Undefined  
d. Undefined  

109. Reduction in the selling price of goods extended to the buyer because the goods are defective or of lower quality than the buyer ordered and to encourage a buyer to keep merchandise that would otherwise be returned is the _____.
a. Thing  
b. Allowance9  
c. Undefined  
d. Undefined  

110. Contra-asset account containing the estimated uncollectible accounts receivable is an _____. Also called allowance for bad debts or allowance for uncollectible accounts.
a. Thing  
b. Allowance for doubtful accounts9  
c. Undefined  
d. Undefined  

111. _____ refers to the promotional tool that stimulates consumer purchasing and dealer interest by means of short-term activities.
a. Thing  
b. Sales promotion9  
c. Undefined  
d. Undefined  

112. The interest rate that equates a future value or an annuity to a given present value is a _____.
a. Thing  
b. Yield9  
c. Undefined  
d. Undefined  

113. _____ was the United States' second largest long distance phone company (AT&T was the largest). _____ grew largely by acquiring other telecommunications companies, most notably MCI Communications. It also owned the Tier 1 ISP UUNET, a major part of the Internet backbone.
a. Organization  
b. WorldCom9  
c. Undefined  
d. Undefined  

114. The cost that a firm bears if it does not produce at all and that is independent of its output. The presence of a _____ tends to imply increasing returns to scale. Contrasts with variable cost.
a. Thing  
b. Fixed cost9  
c. Undefined  
d. Undefined  

115. The portion of a firm or industry's cost that changes with output, in contrast to fixed cost is referred to as _____.
a. Thing  
b. Variable cost9  
c. Undefined  
d. Undefined  

116. _____ refers to the amount recognized as an expense in one period resulting from the periodic recognition of the used portion of the cost of a long-term tangible asset over its life.
a. Depreciation expense9  
b. Thing  
c. Undefined  
d. Undefined  

117. A _____ is an expense that remains constant as activity changes within the relevant range. Any costs not related directly to the production of your product or service.

## Chapter 9. Profitability Analysis

a. Fixed expense9  
b. Thing  
c. Undefined  
d. Undefined  

118. Loan origination fees that may be deductible as interest by a buyer of property. A seller of property who pays _____ reduces the selling price by the amount of the _____ paid for the buyer.
a. Thing  
b. Points9  
c. Undefined  
d. Undefined  

119. Financing that consists of funds that are invested in exchange for ownership in the company is called _____.
a. Thing  
b. Equity financing9  
c. Undefined  
d. Undefined  

120. The cost a business incurs to borrow money. With respect to bonds payable, the _____ is calculated by multiplying the market rate of interest by the carrying value of the bonds on the date of the payment.
a. Thing  
b. Interest expense9  
c. Undefined  
d. Undefined  

121. The difference between the face value of a bond and its selling price, when a bond is sold for less than its face value it's referred to as a _____.
a. Discount9  
b. Thing  
c. Undefined  
d. Undefined  

122. _____ refers to the fee charged by an insurance company for an insurance policy. The rate of losses must be relatively predictable: In order to set the _____ (prices) insurers must be able to estimate them accurately.
a. Thing  
b. Premium9  
c. Undefined  
d. Undefined  

123. The rate of return on bonds, loans, or deposits. When one speaks of 'the' _____, it is usually in a model where there is only one.
a. Thing  
b. Interest rate9  
c. Undefined  
d. Undefined  

124. The rate that a bank charges its most creditworthy customers is referred to as the _____.
a. Prime rate9  
b. Thing  
c. Undefined  
d. Undefined  

125. _____ in economics, the manner in which total output and income is distributed among individuals or factors.
a. Thing  
b. Distribution9  
c. Undefined  
d. Undefined  

126. _____ refer to representation of ownership rights to the corporation.
a. Thing  
b. Equity securities9  
c. Undefined  
d. Undefined  

127. Effects that fixed costs have on changes in operating income as changes occur in units sold and hence in contribution margin are called _____.

a. Thing
b. Operating leverage9
c. Undefined
d. Undefined

128. _____ refers to the way a corporation finances itself through some combination of equity sales, equity options, bonds, and loans. Optimal _____ refers to the particular combination that minimizes the cost of capital while maximizing the stock price.
a. Thing
b. Capital structure9
c. Undefined
d. Undefined

129. _____ is using given resources in such a way that the potential positive or negative outcome is magnified. In finance, this generally refers to borrowing.
a. Leverage9
b. Thing
c. Undefined
d. Undefined

130. A measure of the amount of debt used in the capital structure of the firm is the _____.
a. Financial leverage9
b. Thing
c. Undefined
d. Undefined

131. An _____ is an accounting event in which the transaction is recognized when the action takes place, instead of when cash is disbursed or received.
a. Accrual9
b. Thing
c. Undefined
d. Undefined

132. _____ refer to gains and losses that are both unusual in nature and infrequent in occurrence; they are reported net of tax on the income statement.
a. Thing
b. Extraordinary items9
c. Undefined
d. Undefined

133. _____ refers to financial results from the disposal of a major segment of the business and are reported net of income tax effects.
a. Discontinued operations9
b. Thing
c. Undefined
d. Undefined

134. _____ is equal to the income that a firm has after subtracting costs and expenses from the total revenue. Expenses will typically include tax expense.
a. Net income9
b. Thing
c. Undefined
d. Undefined

135. A worker association that bargains with employers over wages and working conditions is called a _____.
a. Union9
b. Thing
c. Undefined
d. Undefined

136. _____ refers to the manner in which an economy distributes its resources among the potential uses so as to produce a particular set of final goods.

*Chapter 9. Profitability Analysis* 277

    a. Thing
    b. Resource allocation9
    c. Undefined
    d. Undefined

137. A decline in a stock market or economic cycle is a _____.
    a. Downturn9
    b. Thing
    c. Undefined
    d. Undefined

138. Profit of a firm over and above what provides its owners with a normal return to capital is called _____.
    a. Excess profit9
    b. Thing
    c. Undefined
    d. Undefined

139. _____ refers to the total depreciation that has been reported as depreciation expense for the entire life of a long-term tangible asset. It is a contra-asset account.
    a. Accumulated depreciation9
    b. Thing
    c. Undefined
    d. Undefined

140. Yield rate of bonds, which is usually equal to the market rate of interest on the day the bonds are sold is the _____.
    a. Effective interest rate9
    b. Thing
    c. Undefined
    d. Undefined

141. A legal entity chartered by a state or the Federal government that is distinct and separate from the individuals who own it is a _____. This separation gives the _____ unique powers which other legal entities lack.
    a. Corporation9
    b. Organization
    c. Undefined
    d. Undefined

142. In business organization law, the cash or property contributed to a business by its owners is referred to as _____.
    a. Contribution9
    b. Thing
    c. Undefined
    d. Undefined

143. The combination of product lines offered by a manufacturer is referred to as _____.
    a. Thing
    b. Product mix9
    c. Undefined
    d. Undefined

144. A long-lasting, sometimes permanent team in the organization structure created to deal with tasks that recur regularly is the _____.
    a. Committee9
    b. Thing
    c. Undefined
    d. Undefined

145. Similar to a script in that a _____ can be a less than completely rational decision-making method. Involves the use of a pre-existing set of decision steps for any problem that presents itself.
    a. Policy9
    b. Thing
    c. Undefined
    d. Undefined

146. _____ is an important accounting concept that describes the value of a business entity not directly attributable to its tangible assets and liabilities.
   a. Thing
   b. Goodwill9
   c. Undefined
   d. Undefined

147. The effect of the background under which a message often takes on more and richer meaning is a _____. _____ is especially important in cross-cultural interactions because some cultures are said to be high _____ or low _____.
   a. Context9
   b. Thing
   c. Undefined
   d. Undefined

## Chapter 10. Prospective Analysis

1. Reports inflows and outflows of cash during the accounting period in the categories of operating, investing, and financing is a _____.
   a. Thing
   b. Statement of cash flow10
   c. Undefined
   d. Undefined

2. _____ refers to a financial statement that presents the revenues and expenses and resulting net income or net loss of a company for a specific period of time.
   a. Income statement10
   b. Thing
   c. Undefined
   d. Undefined

3. A statement of the assets, liabilities, and net worth of a firm or individual at some given time often at the end of its "fiscal year," is referred to as a _____.
   a. Thing
   b. Balance sheet10
   c. Undefined
   d. Undefined

4. In finance, _____ refers to the amounts of cash being received and spent by a business during a defined period of time, sometimes tied to a specific project. Most of the time they are being used to determine gaps in the liquid position of a company.
   a. Cash flow10
   b. Thing
   c. Undefined
   d. Undefined

5. In banking and accountancy, the outstanding _____ is the amount of money owned, (or due), that remains in a deposit account (or a loan account) at a given date, after all past remittances, payments and withdrawal have been accounted for. It can be positive (then, in the _____ sheet of a firm, it is an asset) or negative (a liability).
   a. Thing
   b. Balance10
   c. Undefined
   d. Undefined

6. A what-if technique that managers use to examine how a result will change if the original predicted data are not achieved or if an underlying assumption changes is _____.
   a. Sensitivity analysis10
   b. Thing
   c. Undefined
   d. Undefined

7. _____ refer to representation of ownership rights to the corporation.
   a. Equity securities10
   b. Thing
   c. Undefined
   d. Undefined

8. In finance, _____ is the process of estimating the market value of a financial asset or liability. They can be done on assets (for example, investments in marketable securities such as stocks, options, business enterprises, or intangible assets such as patents and trademarks) or on liabilities (e.g., Bonds issued by a company).
   a. Valuation10
   b. Event
   c. Undefined
   d. Undefined

9. _____ refers to a claim on the borrower future income that is sold by the borrower to the lender. A _____ is a type of transferable interest representing financial value.
   a. Thing
   b. Security10
   c. Undefined
   d. Undefined

10. _____ is the name given to the set of legal principles, in countries following the English common law tradition, which supplement strict rules of law where their application would operate harshly, so as to achieve what is sometimes referred to as "natural justice."
- a. Thing
- b. Equity10
- c. Undefined
- d. Undefined

11. In law, a _____ is an agreement such that one party takes ownership of a piece of property from another under the understanding that the ownership will revert to the second party when an agreed event occurs.
- a. Thing
- b. Reversion10
- c. Undefined
- d. Undefined

12. _____ refers to the return to the resource entrepreneurial ability; total revenue minus total cost.
- a. Profit10
- b. Thing
- c. Undefined
- d. Undefined

13. _____ is a style of investment strategy. Followers of this style, known as value investors, generally buy companies whose shares appear underpriced by some forms of fundamental analysis; these may include shares that are trading at, for example, high dividend yields or low price-to-earning or price-to-book ratios, and so on.
- a. Thing
- b. Value investing10
- c. Undefined
- d. Undefined

14. A rising stock market. A _____ exists when stock prices are strong and rising and investors are optimistic about future market performance.
- a. Bull market10
- b. Thing
- c. Undefined
- d. Undefined

15. _____ refers to a falling or lethargic stock market.
- a. Bear market10
- b. Thing
- c. Undefined
- d. Undefined

16. A _____ is, as defined in economics, a social arrangement that allows buyers and sellers to discover information and carry out a voluntary exchange of goods or services.
- a. Market10
- b. Thing
- c. Undefined
- d. Undefined

17. In December of 1995, _____ became the first major North American retailer to accept independent monitoring of the working conditions in a contract factory producing its garments. _____ is the largest specialty retailer in the United States.
- a. Gap10
- b. Organization
- c. Undefined
- d. Undefined

18. Independent accounting entity with a self-balancing set of accounts segregated for the purposes of carrying on specific activities is referred to as a _____.
- a. Thing
- b. Fund10
- c. Undefined
- d. Undefined

19. _____ is the value of anything expressed in money of the day with the effects of inflation removed.
   a. Real value10
   b. Thing
   c. Undefined
   d. Undefined

20. In financial terminology, _____ is the capital raized by a corporation, through the issuance and sale of shares.
   a. Stock10
   b. Thing
   c. Undefined
   d. Undefined

21. The _____ represents the external conditions under which people are engaged in, and benefit from, economic activity. It includes aspects of economic status, paid employment, and finances.
   a. Economic environment10
   b. Thing
   c. Undefined
   d. Undefined

22. A _____ is the instrument by which a business intends to generate revenue and profits. It is a summary of how a company means to serve its employees and customers, and involves both strategy (what an business intends to do) as well as an implementation.
   a. Business model10
   b. Thing
   c. Undefined
   d. Undefined

23. The formal document that presents the ways and means by which a strategic goal will be achieved is a _____. A long-term flexible plan that does not regulate activities but rather outlines the means to achieve certain results, and provides the means to alter the course of action should the desired ends change.
   a. Thing
   b. Strategic plan10
   c. Undefined
   d. Undefined

24. _____ refers to a summary of all the transactions that have occurred over a particular period.
   a. Financial statement10
   b. Thing
   c. Undefined
   d. Undefined

25. _____ is the term used to describe income received based on the production of those others who have become members of one's organization.
   a. Thing
   b. Residual income10
   c. Undefined
   d. Undefined

26. The _____ of an asset or group of assets is sometimes the price at which they were originally acquired, in many cases equal to purchase price.
   a. Book value10
   b. Thing
   c. Undefined
   d. Undefined

27. _____ is an accounting term which is commonly used in business. It is equal to the gross revenue for a given time period minus associated expenses.
   a. Thing
   b. Net profit10
   c. Undefined
   d. Undefined

28. _____ payments can refer to an ongoing stream of payments in respect of the completion of past achievements.

a. Thing  
b. Residual10  
c. Undefined  
d. Undefined  

29. A _____ refers to a layout accurate in size, color, scheme, and other necessary details to show how a final ad will look. For presentation only, never for reproduction.
   a. Thing
   b. Comprehensive10
   c. Undefined
   d. Undefined

30. A legal entity chartered by a state or the Federal government that is distinct and separate from the individuals who own it is a _____. This separation gives the _____ unique powers which other legal entities lack.
   a. Organization
   b. Corporation10
   c. Undefined
   d. Undefined

31. _____ is income minus taxes. More accurately, income minus direct taxes plus transfer payments; that is, the income available to be spent and saved.
   a. Disposable income10
   b. Thing
   c. Undefined
   d. Undefined

32. The sale of goods and services to consumers for their own use is a _____.
   a. Retail sale10
   b. Thing
   c. Undefined
   d. Undefined

33. The income, expenditures, and resources that affect the cost of running a business and household are called an _____.
   a. Economy10
   b. Thing
   c. Undefined
   d. Undefined

34. _____ equals personal income minus personal income tax payments. Also called "take-home pay."
   a. Personal disposable income10
   b. Thing
   c. Undefined
   d. Undefined

35. The combination of product lines offered by a manufacturer is referred to as _____.
   a. Thing
   b. Product mix10
   c. Undefined
   d. Undefined

36. Other organizations in the same industry or type of business that provide a good or service to the same set of customers is referred to as a _____.
   a. Thing
   b. Competitor10
   c. Undefined
   d. Undefined

37. _____ equals Gross Profit divided by Revenue, expressed as a percentage. The percentage represents the amount of each dollar of Revenue that results in Gross Profit.
   a. Gross profit margin10
   b. Thing
   c. Undefined
   d. Undefined

## Chapter 10. Prospective Analysis

38. _____ is a measure of profitability. It is calculated using a formula and written as a percentage or a number. _____ = Net income before tax and interest / Revenue.
    a. Thing
    b. Profit margin10
    c. Undefined
    d. Undefined

39. Net sales less cost of goods sold is called _____.
    a. Thing
    b. Gross profit10
    c. Undefined
    d. Undefined

40. A deposit by a buyer in stocks with a seller or a stockbroker, as security to cover fluctuations in the market in reference to stocks that the buyer has purchased but for which he has not paid is a _____. Commodities are also traded on _____.
    a. Margin10
    b. Thing
    c. Undefined
    d. Undefined

41. In accounting, an _____ represents an event in which an asset is used up or a liability is incurred. In terms of the accounting equation, expenses reduce owners' equity.
    a. Expense10
    b. Thing
    c. Undefined
    d. Undefined

42. _____ refers to the amount recognized as an expense in one period resulting from the periodic recognition of the used portion of the cost of a long-term tangible asset over its life.
    a. Depreciation expense10
    b. Thing
    c. Undefined
    d. Undefined

43. _____ is an accounting and finance term for the method of attributing the cost of an asset across the useful life of the asset. _____ is a reduction in the value of a currency in floating exchange rate.
    a. Depreciation10
    b. Thing
    c. Undefined
    d. Undefined

44. A _____ is an expense that remains constant as activity changes within the relevant range. Any costs not related directly to the production of your product or service.
    a. Fixed expense10
    b. Thing
    c. Undefined
    d. Undefined

45. An item of property, such as land, capital, money, a share in ownership, or a claim on others for future payment, such as a bond or a bank deposit is an _____.
    a. Asset10
    b. Thing
    c. Undefined
    d. Undefined

46. Assets defined in the broadest legal sense. _____ includes the unrealized receivables of a cash basis taxpayer, but not services rendered.
    a. Property10
    b. Thing
    c. Undefined
    d. Undefined

47. The cost a business incurs to borrow money. With respect to bonds payable, the _____ is calculated by multiplying the market rate of interest by the carrying value of the bonds on the date of the payment.
   a. Interest expense10
   b. Thing
   c. Undefined
   d. Undefined

48. In finance and economics, _____ is the price paid by a borrower for the use of a lender's money. In other words, _____ is the amount of paid to "rent" money for a period of time.
   a. Thing
   b. Interest10
   c. Undefined
   d. Undefined

49. The rate of return on bonds, loans, or deposits. When one speaks of 'the' _____, it is usually in a model where there is only one.
   a. Thing
   b. Interest rate10
   c. Undefined
   d. Undefined

50. A substantial expenditure that is used by a company to acquire or upgrade physical assets such as equipment, property, industrial buildings, including those which improve the quality and life of an asset is referred to as a _____.
   a. Capital expenditure10
   b. Thing
   c. Undefined
   d. Undefined

51. Major investments in long-term assets such as land, buildings, equipment, or research and development are referred to as _____.
   a. Thing
   b. Capital expenditures10
   c. Undefined
   d. Undefined

52. An _____ is prepared by corporate management that presents financial information including financial statements, footnotes, and the management discussion and analysis.
   a. Annual report10
   b. Thing
   c. Undefined
   d. Undefined

53. _____ generally refers to financial wealth, especially that used to start or maintain a business. In classical economics, _____ is one of four factors of production, the others being land and labor and entrepreneurship.
   a. Thing
   b. Capital10
   c. Undefined
   d. Undefined

54. _____ refers to the long-term movement of an economic variable, such as its average rate of increase or decrease over enough years to encompass several business cycles.
   a. Thing
   b. Trend10
   c. Undefined
   d. Undefined

55. _____ refers to the final payment date of a loan or other financial instrument, after which point no further interest or principal need be paid.
   a. Maturity10
   b. Thing
   c. Undefined
   d. Undefined

56. _____ refers to the basic, normal, voting stock issued by a corporation; called residual equity because it ranks after preferred stock for dividend and liquidation distributions.
   a. Thing
   b. Common stock10
   c. Undefined
   d. Undefined

57. Cumulative earnings of a company that are not distributed to the owners and are reinvested in the business are called _____.
   a. Thing
   b. Retained earnings10
   c. Undefined
   d. Undefined

58. Amount of corporate profits paid out for each share of stock is referred to as _____.
   a. Dividend10
   b. Thing
   c. Undefined
   d. Undefined

59. _____ is one of a series of accounting transactions dealing with the billing of customers which owe money to a person, company or organization for goods and services that have been provided to the customer. This is typically done in a one person organization by writing an invoice and mailing or delivering it to each customer.
   a. Accounts receivable10
   b. Thing
   c. Undefined
   d. Undefined

60. A measure of the amount of debt used in the capital structure of the firm is the _____.
   a. Thing
   b. Financial leverage10
   c. Undefined
   d. Undefined

61. A written record of all vendors to whom the business firm owes money is referred to as _____.
   a. Thing
   b. Accounts payable10
   c. Undefined
   d. Undefined

62. Expenses that have been incurred by the end of the current accounting period but that will not be paid until a future accounting period are _____.
   a. Thing
   b. Accrued expenses10
   c. Undefined
   d. Undefined

63. _____ is a liability. It is recorded when an asset (e.g. receivable) is recorded, but the related income (i.e. revenue) will be earned only in the future.
   a. Thing
   b. Deferred income10
   c. Undefined
   d. Undefined

64. In accrual basis accounting, _____ is a liability resulting from an expense for which no invoice or other official document is available yet.
   a. Thing
   b. Accrued expense10
   c. Undefined
   d. Undefined

65. A _____ is an individual or company (including a corporation) that legally owns one or more shares of stock in a joined stock company.

a. Thing  
c. Undefined  
b. Shareholder10  
d. Undefined

66. Tangible property held for sale in the normal course of business or used in producing goods or services for sale is an _____.
   a. Inventory10  
   b. Thing  
   c. Undefined  
   d. Undefined

67. A _____ is a present obligation of the enterprise arizing from past events, the settlement of which is expected to result in an outflow from the enterprise of resources embodying economic benefits.
   a. Thing  
   b. Liability10  
   c. Undefined  
   d. Undefined

68. _____ in a financial context refers to the rate at which a provider of goods cycles through its average inventory. _____ in a human resources context refers to the characteristic of a given company or industry, relative to rate at which an employer gains and loses staff.
   a. Thing  
   b. Turnover10  
   c. Undefined  
   d. Undefined

69. _____ is using given resources in such a way that the potential positive or negative outcome is magnified. In finance, this generally refers to borrowing.
   a. Leverage10  
   b. Thing  
   c. Undefined  
   d. Undefined

70. The interest rate that equates a future value or an annuity to a given present value is a _____.
   a. Yield10  
   b. Thing  
   c. Undefined  
   d. Undefined

71. In accounting, the _____ describes the direct expenses incurred in producing a particular good for sale, including the actual cost of materials that comprise the good, and direct labor expense in putting the good in salable condition.
   a. Thing  
   b. Cost of goods sold10  
   c. Undefined  
   d. Undefined

72. _____ refers to the total depreciation that has been reported as depreciation expense for the entire life of a long-term tangible asset. It is a contra-asset account.
   a. Thing  
   b. Accumulated depreciation10  
   c. Undefined  
   d. Undefined

73. _____ is the result of computing current and deferred tax payable using the asset-liability method in which the balance sheet is seen as primary and the income statement as secondary.
   a. Thing  
   b. Tax expense10  
   c. Undefined  
   d. Undefined

74. _____ refers to a balance sheet account. Balance sheet item under shareholders' equity. Increases by the value above an original par value per share that newly issued shares are sold for.

a. Thing  
b. Capital surplus10  
c. Undefined  
d. Undefined  

75. A _____ is a specific type of option that uses the stock itself as an underlying instrument to determine the option's pay-off and therefore its value.  
a. Thing  
b. Stock option10  
c. Undefined  
d. Undefined  

76. _____ is equal to the income that a firm has after subtracting costs and expenses from the total revenue. Expenses will typically include tax expense.  
a. Thing  
b. Net income10  
c. Undefined  
d. Undefined  

77. A contract that gives the purchaser the _____ to buy or sell the underlying financial instrument at a specified price, called the exercise price or strike price, within a specific period of time.  
a. Thing  
b. Option10  
c. Undefined  
d. Undefined  

78. _____ refers to a bank's capital divided by its assets.  
a. Leverage ratio10  
b. Thing  
c. Undefined  
d. Undefined  

79. _____ refers to a measure of the impact of debt on the earnings capability of the firm. The percentage change in earnings per share is divided by the percentage change in earnings before interest and taxes at a given level of operation.  
a. Thing  
b. Degree of financial leverage10  
c. Undefined  
d. Undefined  

80. The _____ is the amount by which expenditure exceed revenue.  
a. Deficit10  
b. Thing  
c. Undefined  
d. Undefined  

81. The _____ percentage shows how profitable a company's assets are in generating revenue.  
a. Return on Assets10  
b. Thing  
c. Undefined  
d. Undefined  

82. In business management, _____ measures the number of times capital invested in goods to be sold turns over in a year.  
a. Inventory turns10  
b. Thing  
c. Undefined  
d. Undefined  

83. _____ refers to a person or tool with a primary function of information analysis, generally with a more limited, practical and short term set of goals than a researcher.  
a. Person  
b. Analyst10  
c. Undefined  
d. Undefined

84. The value today of a stream of payments and/or receipts over time in the future and/or the past, converted to the present using an interest rate. If X t is the amount in period t and r the interest rate, then _____ at time t=0 is V = ?T /t.
   a. Present value10
   b. Thing
   c. Undefined
   d. Undefined

85. _____ refers to the percentage cost of funds used for acquiring resources for an organization, typically a weighted average of the firms cost of equity and cost of debt.
   a. Place
   b. Cost of capital10
   c. Undefined
   d. Undefined

86. A _____ is an individual or company (including a corporation) that legally owns one or more shares of stock in a joined stock company. The shareholders are the owners of a corporation. Companies listed at the stock market strive to enhance shareholder value.
   a. Stockholder10
   b. Thing
   c. Undefined
   d. Undefined

87. _____ refers to the productivity of capital or sales revenue divided by invested capital.
   a. Capital turnover10
   b. Thing
   c. Undefined
   d. Undefined

88. The dollar difference between total current assets and total current liabilities is called _____.
   a. Working capital10
   b. Thing
   c. Undefined
   d. Undefined

89. In finance, the _____ is the minimum rate of return a firm must offer shareholders to compensate for waiting for their returns, and for bearing some risk.
   a. Cost of equity10
   b. Thing
   c. Undefined
   d. Undefined

90. _____ refers to money raized from within the firm or through the sale of ownership in the firm.
   a. Equity capital10
   b. Thing
   c. Undefined
   d. Undefined

91. _____, also known as property, plant, and equipment (PP&E), is a term used in accountancy for assets and property which cannot easily be converted into cash. This can be compared with current assets such as cash or bank accounts, which are described as liquid assets. In most cases, only tangible assets are referred to as fixed.
   a. Fixed asset10
   b. Thing
   c. Undefined
   d. Undefined

92. In finance, the _____ of a security is the present value at a future point in time of all future cash flows. It is most often used in multi-stage discounted cash flow analysis, and allows for the limitation of cash flow projections to a several-year period.
   a. Terminal value10
   b. Thing
   c. Undefined
   d. Undefined

## Chapter 10. Prospective Analysis

93. The difference between the face value of a bond and its selling price, when a bond is sold for less than its face value it's referred to as a _____.
   a. Discount10
   b. Thing
   c. Undefined
   d. Undefined

94. _____ refer to an equity security, representing a shareholder's ownership of a corporation. _____ are one of a finite number of equal portions in the capital of a company, entitling the owner to a proportion of distributed, non-reinvested profits known as dividends and to a portion of the value of the company in case of liquidation.
   a. Shares10
   b. Thing
   c. Undefined
   d. Undefined

95. The discounted price is the original price multiplied by the _____.
   a. Concept
   b. Discount factor10
   c. Undefined
   d. Undefined

96. An increase in the overall price level of an economy, usually as measured by the CPI or by the implicit price deflator is called _____.
   a. Inflation10
   b. Thing
   c. Undefined
   d. Undefined

97. A contract to make regular payments to a person for life or for a fixed period is an _____.
   a. Annuity10
   b. Thing
   c. Undefined
   d. Undefined

98. Total number of shares of stock that are owned by stockholders on any particular date is referred to as _____.
   a. Thing
   b. Outstanding shares10
   c. Undefined
   d. Undefined

99. _____ is an economic term of profit exceeding the normal profit. Normal profit equals the opportunity cost of labor and capital, while supernormal profit is the amount exceeds the normal return from these input factors in production.
   a. Thing
   b. Abnormal profit10
   c. Undefined
   d. Undefined

100. A group of firms that produce identical or similar products is an _____. It is also used specifically to refer to an area of economic production focused on manufacturing which involves large amounts of capital investment before any profit can be realized, also called "heavy _____".
   a. Industry10
   b. Thing
   c. Undefined
   d. Undefined

101. In finance, a _____ is a collection of investments held by an institution or a private individual. Holding but not always a _____ is part of an investment and risk-limiting strategy called diversification. By owning several assets, certain types of risk (in particular specific risk) can be reduced.
   a. Portfolio10
   b. Thing
   c. Undefined
   d. Undefined

## Chapter 10. Prospective Analysis

102. An organization that employs resources to produce a good or service for profit and owns and operates one or more plants is referred to as a _____.
   a. Firm10
   b. Thing
   c. Undefined
   d. Undefined

103. A _____ is something measured by a number; it is used to analyze what happens to other things when the size of that number changes.
   a. Variable10
   b. Thing
   c. Undefined
   d. Undefined

104. A registered representative who works as a market intermediary to buy and sell securities for clients is a _____.
   a. Thing
   b. Stockbroker10
   c. Undefined
   d. Undefined

105. Firms in the process of becoming publicly traded companies will issue shares of stock using an _____, which is merely the process of selling stock for the first time to interested investors.
   a. Thing
   b. Initial public offering10
   c. Undefined
   d. Undefined

106. Cash flow activities that include the cash effects of transactions that create revenues and expenses and thus enter into the determination of net income is an _____.
   a. Thing
   b. Operating activities10
   c. Undefined
   d. Undefined

107. _____ refer to people in the organization who actually use the product or service purchased by the buying center.
   a. Thing
   b. Users10
   c. Undefined
   d. Undefined

108. Forecast that predicts the cash inflows and outflows in future periods is a _____. It is a company's projected cash receipts and disbursements over a set time horizon.
   a. Thing
   b. Cash flow forecast10
   c. Undefined
   d. Undefined

109. A short-term investment with original maturities of three months or less that is readily convertible to cash and whose value is unlikely to change is a _____.
   a. Cash equivalent10
   b. Thing
   c. Undefined
   d. Undefined

110. _____ are the most liquid asset found within the asset portion of a company's balance sheet. Cash "equivalents" are typically comprized of assets that are readily convertible into cash such as money market accounts, short-term government bonds and commercial paper.
   a. Cash and cash equivalents10
   b. Thing
   c. Undefined
   d. Undefined

## Chapter 10. Prospective Analysis

111. _____ characterizes the process of leading and directing all or part of an organization, often a business, through the deployment and manipulation of resources. Early twentieth-century _____ writer Mary Parker Follett defined _____ as "the art of getting things done through people."
- a. Management10
- b. Thing
- c. Undefined
- d. Undefined

112. The amount of goods that money will buy, usually measured by the CPI is referred to as _____.
- a. Thing
- b. Purchasing power10
- c. Undefined
- d. Undefined

113. _____ refers to the function in a firm that searches for quality material resources, finds the best suppliers, and negotiates the best price for goods and services.
- a. Thing
- b. Purchasing10
- c. Undefined
- d. Undefined

114. The _____ is a court's determination of a matter of law based on the issue presented in the particular case. In other words: under this law, with these facts, this result.
- a. Holding10
- b. Thing
- c. Undefined
- d. Undefined

115. _____ refers to any distinct act of dominion wrongfully exerted over another's personal property in denial of or inconsistent with his rights therein. That tort committed by a person who deals with chattels not belonging to him in a manner that is inconsistent with the ownership of the lawful owner.
- a. Conversion10
- b. Thing
- c. Undefined
- d. Undefined

116. Promoting and selling products or services to customers, or prospective customers, is referred to as _____.
- a. Marketing10
- b. Thing
- c. Undefined
- d. Undefined

117. _____ refers to the capacity to turn assets into cash, or the amount of assets in a portfolio that have that capacity.
- a. Liquidity10
- b. Thing
- c. Undefined
- d. Undefined

118. The ability of a company to pay interest as it comes due and to repay the face value of debt at maturity is called _____.
- a. Solvency10
- b. Thing
- c. Undefined
- d. Undefined

119. Characterized by rizing output, falling unemployment, rizing profits, and increasing economic activity following a decline is a _____.
- a. Recovery10
- b. Thing
- c. Undefined
- d. Undefined

120. Completed products awaiting sale are called _____. An item considered a finished good in a supplying plant might be considered a component or raw material in a receiving plant.
   a. Finished goods10
   b. Thing
   c. Undefined
   d. Undefined

121. The creation of finished goods and services using the factors of _____: land, labor, capital, entrepreneurship, and knowledge.
   a. Thing
   b. Production10
   c. Undefined
   d. Undefined

122. Cash flowing out of the business from all sources over a period of time is _____.
   a. Cash outflow10
   b. Thing
   c. Undefined
   d. Undefined

123. _____ is a financial condition experienced by a person or business entity when their assets no longer exceed their liabilities or when the person or entity can no longer meet its debt obligations when they come due.
   a. Thing
   b. Insolvency10
   c. Undefined
   d. Undefined

124. The acquisition of an increasing quantity of something. The _____ of factors, especially capital, is a primary mechanism for economic growth.
   a. Accumulation10
   b. Thing
   c. Undefined
   d. Undefined

125. _____ refers to the total costs of goods made or purchased and sold.
   a. Thing
   b. Cost of sales10
   c. Undefined
   d. Undefined

126. Cash provided by operating activities adjusted for capital expenditures and dividends paid is referred to as _____.
   a. Thing
   b. Free cash flow10
   c. Undefined
   d. Undefined

127. Cash coming into the company as the result of a previous investment is a _____.
   a. Thing
   b. Cash inflow10
   c. Undefined
   d. Undefined

128. _____ refers to the maximum total sales of a product that a firm expects to sell during a specified time period under specified environmental conditions and its own marketing efforts.
   a. Sales forecast10
   b. Thing
   c. Undefined
   d. Undefined

129. _____ refers to cash flow activities that include purchasing and disposing of investments and productive long-lived assets using cash and lending money and collecting on those loans.

## Chapter 10. Prospective Analysis

  a. Investing activities10  
  c. Undefined  
  b. Thing  
  d. Undefined

130. Production of goods primarily by the application of labor and capital to raw materials and other intermediate inputs, in contrast to agriculture, mining, forestry, fishing, and services a _____.
  a. Thing
  b. Manufacturing10
  c. Undefined
  d. Undefined

131. _____ or consumption is also known as personal consumption expenditure. It is the largest part of aggregate demand or effective demand at the macroeconomic level. There are two variants of consumption in the aggregate demand model, including induced consumption and autonomous consumption.
  a. Consumer demand10
  b. Thing
  c. Undefined
  d. Undefined

132. _____ refers to a good that has not been transformed by production; a primary product.
  a. Raw material10
  b. Thing
  c. Undefined
  d. Undefined

133. _____ is a legally declared inability or impairment of ability of an individual or organization to pay their creditors.
  a. Bankruptcy10
  b. Thing
  c. Undefined
  d. Undefined

134. _____ refers to the extent to which an economic variable, such as a price or an exchange rate, moves up and down over time.
  a. Thing
  b. Volatility10
  c. Undefined
  d. Undefined

135. _____ refer to a series of projected financial statements. Of major importance are the pro forma income statement, the pro forma balance sheet, and the cash budget.
  a. Thing
  b. Pro forma financial statements10
  c. Undefined
  d. Undefined

136. A _____ is a ratio of two numbers of reported levels or flows of a company. It may be two financial flows categories divided by each other (profit margin, profit/revenue). It may be a level divided by a financial flow (price/earnings). It may be a flow divided by a level (return on equity or earnings/equity). The numerator or denominator may itself be a ratio (PEG ratio).
  a. Financial ratio10
  b. Thing
  c. Undefined
  d. Undefined

137. The body of knowledge and techniques that can be used to combine economic resources to produce goods and services is called _____.
  a. Technology10
  b. Thing
  c. Undefined
  d. Undefined

138. In many governments, a _____ is the person responsible for running the treasury. Treasurers are also employed by organizations to look after funds.

a. Treasurer10  
b. Thing  
c. Undefined  
d. Undefined  

139. _____ refers to a liability that results from the execution of a legal document called a note that describes technical terms, including interest charges, maturity date, collateral, and so on.
   a. Note payable10  
   b. Thing  
   c. Undefined  
   d. Undefined  

140. The consumer's appraisal of the product or brand on important attributes is called _____.
   a. Evaluation10  
   b. Thing  
   c. Undefined  
   d. Undefined  

141. _____ refers to the regional and economic differences in a country, province, state, or continent
   a. Disparity10  
   b. Thing  
   c. Undefined  
   d. Undefined  

142. _____ refers to the cash inflows and cash outflows from the general operating activities of the business; one of the three sections in the statement of cash flows.
   a. Thing  
   b. Operating cash flows10  
   c. Undefined  
   d. Undefined  

143. _____ refers to spending for the production and accumulation of capital and additions to inventories. In a financial sense, buying an asset with the expectation of making a return.
   a. Investment10  
   b. Thing  
   c. Undefined  
   d. Undefined  

144. Collecting information and providing feedback to employees about their behavior, communication style, or skills is an _____.
   a. Assessment10  
   b. Thing  
   c. Undefined  
   d. Undefined  

145. _____ refers to payments of income to those who supply the economy with capital.
   a. Thing  
   b. Interest income10  
   c. Undefined  
   d. Undefined  

146. A standardized method or technique that is performed repetitively, often on different materials resulting in different finished goods is called an _____.
   a. Operation10  
   b. Thing  
   c. Undefined  
   d. Undefined  

147. _____ refers to the business of acquiring finished goods for resale, either in a wholesale or a retail operation.
   a. Merchandising10  
   b. Thing  
   c. Undefined  
   d. Undefined  

148. Systematic and rational allocation of the acquisition cost of an intangible asset over its useful life is referred to as _____.

a. Thing  
b. Amortization10  
c. Undefined  
d. Undefined

149. _____ is a U.S. business term for the amount of money that a company receives from its activities, mostly from sales of products and/or services to customers.
a. Revenue10  
b. Thing  
c. Undefined  
d. Undefined

150. Corporate stock that has been reacquired by the corporation is _____. It is stock which is bought back by the issuing company. It reduces the number of outstanding stocks on the open market ("open market" including insiders holdings).
a. Thing  
b. Treasury stock10  
c. Undefined  
d. Undefined

151. In throughput accounting, the cost accounting aspect of Theory of Constraints (TOC), _____ is the money spent turning inventory into throughput. In TOC, _____ is limited to costs that vary strictly with the quantity produced, like raw materials and purchased components.
a. Thing  
b. Operating expense10  
c. Undefined  
d. Undefined

152. _____ refers to usually the first stage in the creative process. It includes education and formal training.
a. Thing  
b. Preparation10  
c. Undefined  
d. Undefined

153. _____ refers to a measure of income that usually excludes items that a company thinks are unusual or nonrecurring; forecast income.
a. Pro forma income10  
b. Thing  
c. Undefined  
d. Undefined

154. A projection of anticipated sales, expenses, and income is called _____. If the projections predict a downturn in profitability, you can make operational changes such as increasing prices or decreasing costs before these projections become reality.
a. Pro forma income statement10  
b. Thing  
c. Undefined  
d. Undefined

155. _____ refers to a projection of future asset, liability, and stockholders' equity levels. Notes payable or cash is used as a plug or balancing figure for the statement.
a. Pro forma balance sheet10  
b. Thing  
c. Undefined  
d. Undefined

156. A pro rata distribution of cash to stockholders of corporate stock is called a _____.
a. Thing  
b. Cash dividend10  
c. Undefined  
d. Undefined

157. _____ refers to a debt that can reasonably be expected to be paid from existing current assets or through the creation of other current liabilities, within one year or the operating cycle, whichever is longer.

a. Current liability10  
b. Thing  
c. Undefined  
d. Undefined  

158. _____ is the corporate management term for the act of partially dismantling and reorganizing a company for the purpose of making it more efficient and therefore more profitable.
   a. Restructuring10
   b. Thing
   c. Undefined
   d. Undefined

159. A _____ is an asset on the balance sheet which is expected to be sold or otherwise used up in the near future, usually within one year.
   a. Thing
   b. Current asset10
   c. Undefined
   d. Undefined

160. _____ refers to financial results from the disposal of a major segment of the business and are reported net of income tax effects.
   a. Thing
   b. Discontinued operations10
   c. Undefined
   d. Undefined

161. Stock that has specified rights over common stock is a _____.
   a. Thing
   b. Preferred stock10
   c. Undefined
   d. Undefined

162. _____ is an important accounting concept that describes the value of a business entity not directly attributable to its tangible assets and liabilities.
   a. Thing
   b. Goodwill10
   c. Undefined
   d. Undefined

163. _____ refers to a note payable issued for property, such as a house, usually repaid in equal installments consisting of part principle and part interest, over a specified period.
   a. Thing
   b. Mortgage10
   c. Undefined
   d. Undefined

164. A bank's commitment to provide a firm with loans up to a given amount at an interest rate that is tied to some market interest rate is called _____.
   a. Thing
   b. Loan commitment10
   c. Undefined
   d. Undefined

165. In agency law, one under whose direction an agent acts and for whose benefit that agent acts is a _____.
   a. Principal10
   b. Thing
   c. Undefined
   d. Undefined

166. A person to whom goods are consigned, shipped, or otherwise transmitted, either for sale or for safekeeping is the _____.
   a. Thing
   b. Consignee10
   c. Undefined
   d. Undefined

## Chapter 10. Prospective Analysis

167. _____ refers to a "non tangible product" that is not embodied in a physical good and that typically effects some change in another product, person, or institution. Contrasts with good.
   a. Thing
   b. Service10
   c. Undefined
   d. Undefined

168. _____ is a measure of a company's earning power from ongoing operations, equal to earnings before the deduction of interest payments and income taxes.
   a. Operating profit10
   b. Thing
   c. Undefined
   d. Undefined

169. The total amount of physical capital that has been accumulated, usually in a country is _____. Also refers to the total issued capital of a firm, including ordinary and preferred shares.
   a. Capital stock10
   b. Thing
   c. Undefined
   d. Undefined

170. A person to whom a debt or legal obligation is owed, and who has the right to enforce payment of that debt or obligation is referred to as _____.
   a. Thing
   b. Creditor10
   c. Undefined
   d. Undefined

171. The cost that a firm bears if it does not produce at all and that is independent of its output. The presence of a _____ tends to imply increasing returns to scale. Contrasts with variable cost.
   a. Thing
   b. Fixed cost10
   c. Undefined
   d. Undefined

172. The earnings of employees who work directly on the products being manufactured are _____.
   a. Direct labor10
   b. Thing
   c. Undefined
   d. Undefined

173. People's physical and mental talents and efforts that are used to help produce goods and services are called _____.
   a. Labor10
   b. Thing
   c. Undefined
   d. Undefined

174. Damages made certain by the prior agreement of the parties are called _____.
   a. Thing
   b. Liquidated10
   c. Undefined
   d. Undefined

175. _____ refers to a process whereby the assets of a business are converted to money. The conversion may be coerced by a legal process to pay off the debt of the business, or to satisfy any other business obligation that the business has not voluntarily satisfied.
   a. Liquidation10
   b. Thing
   c. Undefined
   d. Undefined

176. The payment for the service of a unit of labor, per unit time. In trade theory, it is the only payment to labor, usually unskilled labor. In empirical work, _____ data may exclude other compenzation, which must be added to get the total cost of employment.
   a. Wage10
   b. Thing
   c. Undefined
   d. Undefined

177. A worker association that bargains with employers over wages and working conditions is called a _____.
   a. Union10
   b. Thing
   c. Undefined
   d. Undefined

178. _____ is a transaction that is posted to a cardholder's credit card account in which the cardholder receives cash at an ATM, or cash or travelers checks at a branch of a member financial institution or at a qualified and approved agent of a member financial institution.
   a. Cash disbursement10
   b. Thing
   c. Undefined
   d. Undefined

## Chapter 11. Credit Analysis

1. The dollar difference between total current assets and total current liabilities is called _____.
   a. Working capital11
   b. Thing
   c. Undefined
   d. Undefined

2. _____ refers to the capacity to turn assets into cash, or the amount of assets in a portfolio that have that capacity.
   a. Liquidity11
   b. Thing
   c. Undefined
   d. Undefined

3. _____ generally refers to financial wealth, especially that used to start or maintain a business. In classical economics, _____ is one of four factors of production, the others being land and labor and entrepreneurship.
   a. Capital11
   b. Thing
   c. Undefined
   d. Undefined

4. The _____ is a comparison of a firm's current assets to its current liabilities. The _____ is an indication of a firm's market liquidity and ability to meet short-term debt obligations.
   a. Current ratio11
   b. Thing
   c. Undefined
   d. Undefined

5. _____ refers to the time it takes for a company to purchase goods or services from suppliers, sell those goods and services to customers, and collect cash from customers.
   a. Thing
   b. Operating cycle11
   c. Undefined
   d. Undefined

6. _____ in a financial context refers to the rate at which a provider of goods cycles through its average inventory. _____ in a human resources context refers to the characteristic of a given company or industry, relative to rate at which an employer gains and loses staff.
   a. Turnover11
   b. Thing
   c. Undefined
   d. Undefined

7. Similar to a script in that a _____ can be a less than completely rational decision-making method. Involves the use of a pre-existing set of decision steps for any problem that presents itself.
   a. Thing
   b. Policy11
   c. Undefined
   d. Undefined

8. _____ refers to the way a corporation finances itself through some combination of equity sales, equity options, bonds, and loans. Optimal _____ refers to the particular combination that minimizes the cost of capital while maximizing the stock price.
   a. Capital structure11
   b. Thing
   c. Undefined
   d. Undefined

9. The ability of a company to pay interest as it comes due and to repay the face value of debt at maturity is called _____.
   a. Thing
   b. Solvency11
   c. Undefined
   d. Undefined

10. A measure of the amount of debt used in the capital structure of the firm is the _____.

a. Financial leverage11  
b. Thing  
c. Undefined  
d. Undefined

11. _____ is using given resources in such a way that the potential positive or negative outcome is magnified. In finance, this generally refers to borrowing.
   a. Leverage11  
   b. Thing  
   c. Undefined  
   d. Undefined

12. A system that collects and processes financial information about an organization and reports that information to decision makers is referred to as _____.
   a. Thing  
   b. Accounting11  
   c. Undefined  
   d. Undefined

13. The _____ of an asset or group of assets is sometimes the price at which they were originally acquired, in many cases equal to purchase price.
   a. Thing  
   b. Book value11  
   c. Undefined  
   d. Undefined

14. An out-of-court settlement in which creditors agree to accept a fractional settlement on their original claim is referred to as _____.
   a. Composition11  
   b. Thing  
   c. Undefined  
   d. Undefined

15. An item of property, such as land, capital, money, a share in ownership, or a claim on others for future payment, such as a bond or a bank deposit is an _____.
   a. Thing  
   b. Asset11  
   c. Undefined  
   d. Undefined

16. _____ refers to a summary of all the transactions that have occurred over a particular period.
   a. Thing  
   b. Financial statement11  
   c. Undefined  
   d. Undefined

17. A decline in a stock market or economic cycle is a _____.
   a. Thing  
   b. Downturn11  
   c. Undefined  
   d. Undefined

18. In finance, _____ occurs when a debtor has not met its legal obligations according to the debt contract, e.g. it has not made a scheduled payment, or violated a covenant (condition) of the debt contract.
   a. Default11  
   b. Thing  
   c. Undefined  
   d. Undefined

19. _____ refers to a recording as positive in the balance of payments, any transaction that gives rise to a payment into the country, such as an export, the sale of an asset, or borrowing from abroad.
   a. Credit11  
   b. Thing  
   c. Undefined  
   d. Undefined

## Chapter 11. Credit Analysis

20. The income, expenditures, and resources that affect the cost of running a business and household are called an _____.
    a. Thing
    b. Economy11
    c. Undefined
    d. Undefined

21. Independent accounting entity with a self-balancing set of accounts segregated for the purposes of carrying on specific activities is referred to as a _____.
    a. Fund11
    b. Thing
    c. Undefined
    d. Undefined

22. _____ Corportaion's global reputation was undermined by persistent rumours of bribery and political pressure to secure contracts in Central America, South America, Africa, and the Philippines. Especially controversial was its $3 billion contract with the Maharashtra State Electricity Board in India, where it is alleged that _____ officials used political connections within the Clinton and Bush administrations to exert pressure on the board.
    a. Thing
    b. Enron11
    c. Undefined
    d. Undefined

23. _____ is a U.S. business term for the amount of money that a company receives from its activities, mostly from sales of products and/or services to customers.
    a. Thing
    b. Revenue11
    c. Undefined
    d. Undefined

24. The payment to holders of bonds payable, calculated by multiplying the stated rate on the face of the bond by the par, or face, value of the bond. If bonds are issued at a discount or premium, the _____ does not equal the interest expense.
    a. Interest payment11
    b. Thing
    c. Undefined
    d. Undefined

25. In finance and economics, _____ is the price paid by a borrower for the use of a lender's money. In other words, _____ is the amount of paid to "rent" money for a period of time.
    a. Thing
    b. Interest11
    c. Undefined
    d. Undefined

26. A standardized method or technique that is performed repetitively, often on different materials resulting in different finished goods is called an _____.
    a. Thing
    b. Operation11
    c. Undefined
    d. Undefined

27. _____ is the name given to the set of legal principles, in countries following the English common law tradition, which supplement strict rules of law where their application would operate harshly, so as to achieve what is sometimes referred to as "natural justice."
    a. Equity11
    b. Thing
    c. Undefined
    d. Undefined

28. In financial terminology, _____ is the capital raized by a corporation, through the issuance and sale of shares.

a. Thing  
b. Stock11  
c. Undefined  
d. Undefined

29. Other organizations in the same industry or type of business that provide a good or service to the same set of customers is referred to as a _____.
   a. Thing  
   b. Competitor11  
   c. Undefined  
   d. Undefined

30. A _____ is a bond issued by a corporation, as the name suggests. The term is usually applied to longer term debt instruments, generally with a maturity date falling at least 12 months after their issue date (the term "commercial paper" being sometimes used for instruments with a shorter maturity).
   a. Thing  
   b. Corporate bond11  
   c. Undefined  
   d. Undefined

31. _____ refers to a debt instrument, issued by a borrower and promising a specified stream of payments to the purchaser, usually regular interest payments plus a final repayment of principal.
   a. Bond11  
   b. Thing  
   c. Undefined  
   d. Undefined

32. A _____ is an individual or company (including a corporation) that legally owns one or more shares of stock in a joined stock company.
   a. Thing  
   b. Shareholder11  
   c. Undefined  
   d. Undefined

33. A group of firms that produce identical or similar products is an _____. It is also used specifically to refer to an area of economic production focused on manufacturing which involves large amounts of capital investment before any profit can be realized, also called "heavy _____".
   a. Industry11  
   b. Thing  
   c. Undefined  
   d. Undefined

34. In 2001, the _____ purchased Pillsbury, although it was officially described as a "merger." While many of the Pillsbury-branded products are still manufactured by _____, some products had to be sold off to allow the merger since the new company would have held a very strong monopoly position.
   a. Thing  
   b. General Mills11  
   c. Undefined  
   d. Undefined

35. A company's purchase of the property and obligations of another company is an _____.
   a. Acquisition11  
   b. Thing  
   c. Undefined  
   d. Undefined

36. _____ arises from situations in which a party interested in trading an asset cannot do it because nobody in the market wants to trade that asset. _____ becomes particularly important to parties who are about to hold or currently hold an asset, since it affects their ability to trade.
   a. Liquidity risk11  
   b. Thing  
   c. Undefined  
   d. Undefined

## Chapter 11. Credit Analysis

37. Cash coming into the company as the result of a previous investment is a _____.
    a. Thing
    b. Cash inflow11
    c. Undefined
    d. Undefined

38. Cash flow activities that include the cash effects of transactions that create revenues and expenses and thus enter into the determination of net income is an _____.
    a. Operating activities11
    b. Thing
    c. Undefined
    d. Undefined

39. The _____ is a bank regulation, which sets a framework on how banks and depository institutions must handle their capital. The categorization of assets and capital is highly standardized so that it can be risk weighted.
    a. Thing
    b. Capital requirement11
    c. Undefined
    d. Undefined

40. _____ refers to a "non tangible product" that is not embodied in a physical good and that typically effects some change in another product, person, or institution. Contrasts with good.
    a. Service11
    b. Thing
    c. Undefined
    d. Undefined

41. _____ refers to the return to the resource entrepreneurial ability; total revenue minus total cost.
    a. Thing
    b. Profit11
    c. Undefined
    d. Undefined

42. The difference between the face value of a bond and its selling price, when a bond is sold for less than its face value it's referred to as a _____.
    a. Thing
    b. Discount11
    c. Undefined
    d. Undefined

43. _____ characterizes the process of leading and directing all or part of an organization, often a business, through the deployment and manipulation of resources. Early twentieth-century _____ writer Mary Parker Follett defined _____ as "the art of getting things done through people."
    a. Management11
    b. Thing
    c. Undefined
    d. Undefined

44. _____ refers to spending for the production and accumulation of capital and additions to inventories. In a financial sense, buying an asset with the expectation of making a return.
    a. Thing
    b. Investment11
    c. Undefined
    d. Undefined

45. Absence of any limits on the maximum amount that an individual may become legally required to pay is called _____.
    a. Thing
    b. Unlimited liability11
    c. Undefined
    d. Undefined

46. In the common law, a _____ is a type of business entity in which partners share with each other the profits or losses of the business undertaking in which they have all invested.

## Chapter 11. Credit Analysis

a. Thing
c. Undefined
b. Partnership11
d. Undefined

47. A _____ is a present obligation of the enterprise arizing from past events, the settlement of which is expected to result in an outflow from the enterprise of resources embodying economic benefits.
a. Liability11
c. Undefined
b. Thing
d. Undefined

48. In agency law, one under whose direction an agent acts and for whose benefit that agent acts is a _____.
a. Thing
c. Undefined
b. Principal11
d. Undefined

49. A person to whom a debt or legal obligation is owed, and who has the right to enforce payment of that debt or obligation is referred to as _____.
a. Creditor11
c. Undefined
b. Thing
d. Undefined

50. The interest rate that equates a future value or an annuity to a given present value is a _____.
a. Yield11
c. Undefined
b. Thing
d. Undefined

51. A _____ is a "promise" or an "agreement" that is enforced or recognized by the law. In the civil law, a _____ is considered to be part of the general law of obligations.
a. Thing
c. Undefined
b. Contract11
d. Undefined

52. _____ refers to a debt that can reasonably be expected to be paid from existing current assets or through the creation of other current liabilities, within one year or the operating cycle, whichever is longer.
a. Thing
c. Undefined
b. Current liability11
d. Undefined

53. A _____ is an asset on the balance sheet which is expected to be sold or otherwise used up in the near future, usually within one year.
a. Current asset11
c. Undefined
b. Thing
d. Undefined

54. _____ refer to securities that are readily traded in the secondary securities market.
a. Thing
c. Undefined
b. Marketable securities11
d. Undefined

55. _____ is one of a series of accounting transactions dealing with the billing of customers which owe money to a person, company or organization for goods and services that have been provided to the customer. This is typically done in a one person organization by writing an invoice and mailing or delivering it to each customer.
a. Thing
c. Undefined
b. Accounts receivable11
d. Undefined

## Chapter 11. Credit Analysis

56. A statement of the assets, liabilities, and net worth of a firm or individual at some given time often at the end of its "fiscal year," is referred to as a _____.
    a. Thing
    b. Balance sheet11
    c. Undefined
    d. Undefined

57. A _____ is a 12-month period used for calculating annual ("yearly") financial reports in businesses and other organizations. In many jurisdictions, regulatory laws regarding accounting require such reports once per twelve months, but do not require that the twelve months constitute a calendar year (i.e. January to December).
    a. Thing
    b. Fiscal year11
    c. Undefined
    d. Undefined

58. Tangible property held for sale in the normal course of business or used in producing goods or services for sale is an _____.
    a. Inventory11
    b. Thing
    c. Undefined
    d. Undefined

59. _____ refers to a claim on the borrower future income that is sold by the borrower to the lender. A _____ is a type of transferable interest representing financial value.
    a. Security11
    b. Thing
    c. Undefined
    d. Undefined

60. In accounting, an _____ represents an event in which an asset is used up or a liability is incurred. In terms of the accounting equation, expenses reduce owners' equity.
    a. Thing
    b. Expense11
    c. Undefined
    d. Undefined

61. In banking and accountancy, the outstanding _____ is the amount of money owned, (or due), that remains in a deposit account (or a loan account) at a given date, after all past remittances, payments and withdrawal have been accounted for. It can be positive (then, in the _____ sheet of a firm, it is an asset) or negative (a liability).
    a. Thing
    b. Balance11
    c. Undefined
    d. Undefined

62. A written record of all vendors to whom the business firm owes money is referred to as _____.
    a. Accounts payable11
    b. Thing
    c. Undefined
    d. Undefined

63. Expenses that have been incurred by the end of the current accounting period but that will not be paid until a future accounting period are _____.
    a. Thing
    b. Accrued expenses11
    c. Undefined
    d. Undefined

64. In accrual basis accounting, _____ is a liability resulting from an expense for which no invoice or other official document is available yet.
    a. Thing
    b. Accrued expense11
    c. Undefined
    d. Undefined

## Chapter 11. Credit Analysis

65. _____ refers to an obligation in the form of a written promissory note. It is a balance sheet term referring to a company's outstanding bank loans.
- a. Thing
- b. Notes payable11
- c. Undefined
- d. Undefined

66. _____ is the largest specialty retailer of consumer electronics, personal computers and related goods in North America. The company's subsidiaries include Geek Squad, Magnolia Audio Video, and Future Shop in Canada, which together operate over 700 stores in the United States and Canada. _____ is noted for being staffed with non-commissioned sales associates.
- a. Thing
- b. Best Buy11
- c. Undefined
- d. Undefined

67. _____ refers to potential liability that does not currently exist but is probable and reasonably estimable, such as lawsuits and tax disputes, is referred to as a _____.
- a. Contingent liability11
- b. Thing
- c. Undefined
- d. Undefined

68. _____ refers to a contractual arrangement giving the lessee temporary use of the property with continued ownership of the property by the lessor. Accounted for as a rental.
- a. Operating lease11
- b. Thing
- c. Undefined
- d. Undefined

69. A contract for the possession and use of land or other property, including goods, on one side, and a recompense of rent or other income on the other is the _____.
- a. Lease11
- b. Thing
- c. Undefined
- d. Undefined

70. _____ is an accounting term, meaning future tax liability or asset, resulting from temporary differences between book (accounting) value of assets and liabilities, and their tax value.
- a. Thing
- b. Deferred tax11
- c. Undefined
- d. Undefined

71. Bond contract that specifies the stated rate of interest and the face value of the bond as well as other contractual provisions is called the _____. A company's _____ will cover all bonds issued by that company and also list all bond covenants.
- a. Thing
- b. Bond indenture11
- c. Undefined
- d. Undefined

72. A _____ is an agreement made between two parties in legal proceedings. A _____ removes points of contention so that progress can be made during the proceedings.
- a. Thing
- b. Stipulation11
- c. Undefined
- d. Undefined

73. A bond contract that specifies the legal provisions of a bond issue is called an _____.

## Chapter 11. Credit Analysis

a. Indenture11  
b. Thing  
c. Undefined  
d. Undefined

74. _____ refers to a person or tool with a primary function of information analysis, generally with a more limited, practical and short term set of goals than a researcher.
a. Analyst11  
b. Person  
c. Undefined  
d. Undefined

75. _____ is the difference between the intrinsic value of a stock (i.e. value based on stock valuation and what the company is actually worth) and the price that the market sets on a stock (i.e. stock price is a matter of market participants' opinions and is different from the intrinsic value).
a. Thing  
b. Margin of safety11  
c. Undefined  
d. Undefined

76. Breakage and theft of merchandise by customers and employees is referred to as _____.
a. Thing  
b. Shrinkage11  
c. Undefined  
d. Undefined

77. A deposit by a buyer in stocks with a seller or a stockbroker, as security to cover fluctuations in the market in reference to stocks that the buyer has purchased but for which he has not paid is a _____. Commodities are also traded on _____.
a. Margin11  
b. Thing  
c. Undefined  
d. Undefined

78. In finance, _____ refers to the amounts of cash being received and spent by a business during a defined period of time, sometimes tied to a specific project. Most of the time they are being used to determine gaps in the liquid position of a company.
a. Cash flow11  
b. Thing  
c. Undefined  
d. Undefined

79. The withholding of labor services by an organized group of workers is referred to as a _____.
a. Thing  
b. Strike11  
c. Undefined  
d. Undefined

80. A short-term investment with original maturities of three months or less that is readily convertible to cash and whose value is unlikely to change is a _____.
a. Cash equivalent11  
b. Thing  
c. Undefined  
d. Undefined

81. The expected sales price less selling costs is referred to as _____. Gross receivables less allowance for doubtful accounts, representing the expected collectibility of those receivables.
a. Net realizable value11  
b. Thing  
c. Undefined  
d. Undefined

82. _____ is a concept used in finance and economics, defined as a rational and unbiased estimate of the potential market price of a good, service, or asset.

a. Fair value11  
b. Thing  
c. Undefined  
d. Undefined

83. Loan origination fees that may be deductible as interest by a buyer of property. A seller of property who pays _____ reduces the selling price by the amount of the _____ paid for the buyer.
   a. Points11  
   b. Thing  
   c. Undefined  
   d. Undefined

84. The planning, coordinating, and controlling activities related to the flow of inventory into, through, and out of an organization is referred to as _____.
   a. Inventory management11  
   b. Thing  
   c. Undefined  
   d. Undefined

85. _____ is additional inventory planned to buffer against the variability in supply and demand plans, that could otherwise result in inventory shortages.
   a. Safety stock11  
   b. Thing  
   c. Undefined  
   d. Undefined

86. _____ is the aggregate amount of any material good that can be called into being at a certain price point; it comprises one half of the equation of _____ and demand. In classical economic theory, a curve representing _____ is one of the factors that produce price.
   a. Supply11  
   b. Thing  
   c. Undefined  
   d. Undefined

87. Decision model that calculates the optimal quantity of inventory to order under a set of assumptions is called _____.
   a. Economic order quantity11  
   b. Thing  
   c. Undefined  
   d. Undefined

88. _____ refers to any distinct act of dominion wrongfully exerted over another's personal property in denial of or inconsistent with his rights therein. That tort committed by a person who deals with chattels not belonging to him in a manner that is inconsistent with the ownership of the lawful owner.
   a. Thing  
   b. Conversion11  
   c. Undefined  
   d. Undefined

89. Valuation method departing from the cost principle that recognizes a loss when replacement cost or net realizable value drops below cost is called _____.
   a. Lower of cost11  
   b. Thing  
   c. Undefined  
   d. Undefined

90. _____ is a measure of profitability. It is calculated using a formula and written as a percentage or a number. _____ = Net income before tax and interest / Revenue.
   a. Thing  
   b. Profit margin11  
   c. Undefined  
   d. Undefined

## Chapter 11. Credit Analysis

91. A _____ is, as defined in economics, a social arrangement that allows buyers and sellers to discover information and carry out a voluntary exchange of goods or services.
    a. Market11
    b. Thing
    c. Undefined
    d. Undefined

92. _____ is an accounting method used to establish the dollar amount at which assets are recorded on a savings association's books. The amount established is the lower of the cost of the asset or the current market value.
    a. Lower of Cost or Market11
    b. Thing
    c. Undefined
    d. Undefined

93. The process of retiring an old bond issue before maturity and replacing it with a new issue is _____. _____ will occur when interest rates have fallen and new bonds may be sold at lower interest rates.
    a. Thing
    b. Refunding11
    c. Undefined
    d. Undefined

94. _____ are the most liquid asset found within the asset portion of a company's balance sheet. Cash "equivalents" are typically comprized of assets that are readily convertible into cash such as money market accounts, short-term government bonds and commercial paper.
    a. Thing
    b. Cash and cash equivalents11
    c. Undefined
    d. Undefined

95. The _____ is one of two primary components of the balance of payments. It tracks the movement of funds for investments and loans into and out of a country.
    a. Thing
    b. Capital account11
    c. Undefined
    d. Undefined

96. The effect of the background under which a message often takes on more and richer meaning is a _____. _____ is especially important in cross-cultural interactions because some cultures are said to be high _____ or low _____.
    a. Thing
    b. Context11
    c. Undefined
    d. Undefined

97. _____ refers to the long-term movement of an economic variable, such as its average rate of increase or decrease over enough years to encompass several business cycles.
    a. Thing
    b. Trend11
    c. Undefined
    d. Undefined

98. _____ refers to a process whereby the assets of a business are converted to money. The conversion may be coerced by a legal process to pay off the debt of the business, or to satisfy any other business obligation that the business has not voluntarily satisfied.
    a. Liquidation11
    b. Thing
    c. Undefined
    d. Undefined

99. A _____ is a comparison of the money earned (or lost) on an investment to the amount of money invested.

## 310  Chapter 11. Credit Analysis

a. Thing  
c. Undefined  
b. Rate of return11  
d. Undefined

100. Spending by firms on additional holdings of raw materials, parts, and finished goods is called _____.
a. Thing  
c. Undefined  
b. Inventory investment11  
d. Undefined

101. _____ refers to the total costs of goods made or purchased and sold.
a. Thing  
c. Undefined  
b. Cost of sales11  
d. Undefined

102. A legal entity chartered by a state or the Federal government that is distinct and separate from the individuals who own it is a _____. This separation gives the _____ unique powers which other legal entities lack.
a. Organization  
c. Undefined  
b. Corporation11  
d. Undefined

103. The detailed identification and description of the activities conducted in an enterprise is an _____.
a. Thing  
c. Undefined  
b. Activity analysis11  
d. Undefined

104. _____ refers to written promises that require another party to pay the business under specified conditions.
a. Thing  
c. Undefined  
b. Notes receivable11  
d. Undefined

105. Gross sales less sales returns and allowances and sales discounts are referred to as _____.
a. Net sales11  
c. Undefined  
b. Thing  
d. Undefined

106. _____ refers to financial ratio that measures how fast accounts receivable are turned into cash; computed by dividing credit sales by accounts receivable.
a. Thing  
c. Undefined  
b. Accounts receivable turnover ratio11  
d. Undefined

107. A _____ occurs when a customer does not pay cash at the time of the sale but instead agrees to pay later. The sale occurs now, with payment from the customer to follow at a later time.
a. Credit sale11  
c. Undefined  
b. Thing  
d. Undefined

108. A measure of the liquidity of receivables, computed by dividing net credit sales by average gross receivables is called the _____. The _____ is an activity ratio, measuring how efficiently a firm uses its assets.
a. Thing  
c. Undefined  
b. Receivables turnover ratio11  
d. Undefined

109. The _____ is a court's determination of a matter of law based on the issue presented in the particular case. In other words: under this law, with these facts, this result.

## Chapter 11. Credit Analysis

a. Thing
c. Undefined
b. Holding11
d. Undefined

110. In accounting, the _____ describes the direct expenses incurred in producing a particular good for sale, including the actual cost of materials that comprise the good, and direct labor expense in putting the good in salable condition.
a. Thing
c. Undefined
b. Cost of goods sold11
d. Undefined

111. _____ refers to a ratio that measures the number of times on average the inventory sold during the period; computed by dividing cost of goods sold by the average inventory during the period.
a. Thing
c. Undefined
b. Inventory turnover ratio11
d. Undefined

112. Inventory on hand at the end of the accounting period, shown on the balance sheet in the current assets section is called _____.
a. Thing
c. Undefined
b. Ending inventory11
d. Undefined

113. _____ refers to the function in a firm that searches for quality material resources, finds the best suppliers, and negotiates the best price for goods and services.
a. Purchasing11
c. Undefined
b. Thing
d. Undefined

114. The creation of finished goods and services using the factors of _____: land, labor, capital, entrepreneurship, and knowledge.
a. Thing
c. Undefined
b. Production11
d. Undefined

115. In finance, _____ is the process of estimating the market value of a financial asset or liability. They can be done on assets (for example, investments in marketable securities such as stocks, options, business enterprises, or intangible assets such as patents and trademarks) or on liabilities (e.g., Bonds issued by a company).
a. Event
c. Undefined
b. Valuation11
d. Undefined

116. _____ refers to giving workers the education and tools they need to assume their new decision-making powers.
a. Thing
c. Undefined
b. Enabling11
d. Undefined

117. The overall level of prices in a country, as usually measured empirically by a price index, but often captured in theoretical models by a single variable is a _____.
a. Thing
c. Undefined
b. Price level11
d. Undefined

118. A professional that provides expert advice in a particular field or area in which customers occassionaly require this type of knowledge is a _____.

a. Concept
b. Consultant11
c. Undefined
d. Undefined

119. _____ in agency law, refers to an agent's ability to affect his principal's legal relations with third parties. Also used to refer to an actor's legal power or ability to do something. In addition, sometimes used to refer to a statute, case, or other legal source that justifies a particular result.
a. Concept
b. Authority11
c. Undefined
d. Undefined

120. Obligations to make future economic sacrifices, usually cash payments, are referred to as _____. Same as current liabilities.
a. Payables11
b. Thing
c. Undefined
d. Undefined

121. _____ refers to the shortening of the time for the performance of a contract or the payment of a note by the operation of some provision in the contract or note itself.
a. Acceleration11
b. Thing
c. Undefined
d. Undefined

122. The consumer's appraisal of the product or brand on important attributes is called _____.
a. Evaluation11
b. Thing
c. Undefined
d. Undefined

123. The Acid-test or _____ measures the ability of a company to use its "near cash" or quick assets to immediately extinguish its current liabilities. Quick assets include those current assets that presumably can be quickly converted to cash at close to their book values.
a. Thing
b. Quick ratio11
c. Undefined
d. Undefined

124. A _____ is something measured by a number; it is used to analyze what happens to other things when the size of that number changes.
a. Thing
b. Variable11
c. Undefined
d. Undefined

125. _____ in contract law, a basic requirement for an enforceable agreement under traditional contract principles, defined in this text as legal value, bargained for and given in exchange for an act or promise. In corporation law, cash or property contributed to a corporation in exchange for shares, or a promise to contribute such cash or property.
a. Thing
b. Consideration11
c. Undefined
d. Undefined

126. _____ refers to money raized from within the firm or through the sale of ownership in the firm.
a. Equity capital11
b. Thing
c. Undefined
d. Undefined

127. A _____ is where borrowers come together with lenders to determine conditions of exchange such as interest rates and the duration of a loan.

a. Credit market11  
b. Thing  
c. Undefined  
d. Undefined

128. The body of knowledge and techniques that can be used to combine economic resources to produce goods and services is called _____.  
a. Thing  
b. Technology11  
c. Undefined  
d. Undefined

129. Goods on hand at the beginning of the inventory period are referred to as _____.  
a. Thing  
b. Beginning inventory11  
c. Undefined  
d. Undefined

130. _____ is an accounting and finance term for the method of attributing the cost of an asset across the useful life of the asset. _____ is a reduction in the value of a currency in floating exchange rate.  
a. Depreciation11  
b. Thing  
c. Undefined  
d. Undefined

131. Net sales less cost of goods sold is called _____.  
a. Gross profit11  
b. Thing  
c. Undefined  
d. Undefined

132. A _____ is a fixed point of time in the future at which point certain processes will be evaluated or assumed to end. It is necessary in an accounting, finance or risk management regime to assign such a fixed horizon time so that alternatives can be evaluated for performance over the same period of time.  
a. Time horizon11  
b. Thing  
c. Undefined  
d. Undefined

133. Suppliers and financial institutions that lend money to companies is referred to as a _____.  
a. Lender11  
b. Thing  
c. Undefined  
d. Undefined

134. _____ is a term in Corporate Finance used to indicate a condition when promises to creditors of a company are broken or honored with difficulty. Sometimes _____ can lead to bankruptcy. _____ is usually associated with some costs to the company and these are known as Costs of _____. A common example of a cost of _____ is bankrupty costs.  
a. Financial distress11  
b. Thing  
c. Undefined  
d. Undefined

135. _____ is a financial condition experienced by a person or business entity when their assets no longer exceed their liabilities or when the person or entity can no longer meet its debt obligations when they come due.  
a. Thing  
b. Insolvency11  
c. Undefined  
d. Undefined

136. A _____ is a signed written agreement between two or more parties. Also referred to as a contract.

a. Covenant11  
b. Thing  
c. Undefined  
d. Undefined  

137. The _____ is a financial ratio debt divided by shareholders' equity. The two components are often taken from the firm's balance sheet, but they might also be calulated as market values if both the companiy's debt and equity are publicly traded. It is used to calculate a company's "financial leverage" and indicates what proportion of equity and debt the company is using to finance its assets.
   a. Debt to equity ratio11  
   b. Thing  
   c. Undefined  
   d. Undefined  

138. Amount of corporate profits paid out for each share of stock is referred to as _____.
   a. Dividend11  
   b. Thing  
   c. Undefined  
   d. Undefined  

139. Obtaining financing by borrowing money is _____.
   a. Thing  
   b. Debt financing11  
   c. Undefined  
   d. Undefined  

140. Financing that consists of funds that are invested in exchange for ownership in the company is called _____.
   a. Thing  
   b. Equity financing11  
   c. Undefined  
   d. Undefined  

141. The risk related to the inability of the firm to hold its competitive position and maintain stability and growth in earnings is _____.
   a. Thing  
   b. Business risk11  
   c. Undefined  
   d. Undefined  

142. _____ refers to funds raized through various forms of borrowing to finance a company that must be repaid.
   a. Debt capital11  
   b. Thing  
   c. Undefined  
   d. Undefined  

143. _____ refer to shareholders who claim the residual profits and assets of a corporation, and usually have the exclusive power and right to elect the directors of the corporation.
   a. Thing  
   b. Common shareholders11  
   c. Undefined  
   d. Undefined  

144. The _____ percentage shows how profitable a company's assets are in generating revenue.
   a. Thing  
   b. Return on Assets11  
   c. Undefined  
   d. Undefined  

145. The _____ is the cost of borrowing money (usually denoted by Kd). It is derived by dividing debt's interest payments on the total market value of the debts.
   a. Cost of debt11  
   b. Thing  
   c. Undefined  
   d. Undefined  

146. _____ in economics, the manner in which total output and income is distributed among individuals or factors.

## Chapter 11. Credit Analysis

    a. Thing
    b. Distribution11
    c. Undefined
    d. Undefined

147. A person in possession of a document of title or an instrument payable or indorsed to him, his order, or to bearer is a _____.
    a. Holder11
    b. Thing
    c. Undefined
    d. Undefined

148. The rate of return on bonds, loans, or deposits. When one speaks of 'the' _____, it is usually in a model where there is only one.
    a. Thing
    b. Interest rate11
    c. Undefined
    d. Undefined

149. _____ refers to a bank's capital divided by its assets.
    a. Thing
    b. Leverage ratio11
    c. Undefined
    d. Undefined

150. The common stock or ownership capital of the firm is _____. _____ may be supplied through retained earnings or the sale of new common stock.
    a. Thing
    b. Common equity11
    c. Undefined
    d. Undefined

151. The owner/operator. The person who organizes, manages, and assumes the risks of a firm, taking a new idea or a new product and turning it into a successful business is an _____.
    a. Thing
    b. Entrepreneur11
    c. Undefined
    d. Undefined

152. _____ means the giving out of information, either voluntarily or to be in compliance with legal regulations or workplace rules.
    a. Disclosure11
    b. Thing
    c. Undefined
    d. Undefined

153. The difference between the time a transaction occurs and the time the cash related to the transaction is exchanged is referred to as _____.
    a. Timing differences11
    b. Thing
    c. Undefined
    d. Undefined

154. Methods that result in higher depreciation expense in the early years of an asset's life, and lower expense in the later years are referred to as _____.
    a. Accelerated depreciation11
    b. Thing
    c. Undefined
    d. Undefined

155. An obligation of a company to replace defective goods or correct any deficiencies in performance or quality of a product is called a _____.

a. Thing  
b. Warranty11  
c. Undefined  
d. Undefined  

156. A company that is controlled by another company or corporation is a _____.  
a. Thing  
b. Subsidiary11  
c. Undefined  
d. Undefined  

157. A _____ refers to a financial statement of a parent company and its subsidiaries that has been combined into a single set of financial statements as if the companies were one.  
a. Consolidated financial statement11  
b. Thing  
c. Undefined  
d. Undefined  

158. _____ refers to the basic, normal, voting stock issued by a corporation; called residual equity because it ranks after preferred stock for dividend and liquidation distributions.  
a. Thing  
b. Common stock11  
c. Undefined  
d. Undefined  

159. Stock that has specified rights over common stock is a _____.  
a. Preferred stock11  
b. Thing  
c. Undefined  
d. Undefined  

160. An organization that employs resources to produce a good or service for profit and owns and operates one or more plants is referred to as a _____.  
a. Thing  
b. Firm11  
c. Undefined  
d. Undefined  

161. The risk related to the inability of the firm to meet its debt obligations as they come due is called _____.  
a. Thing  
b. Financial risk11  
c. Undefined  
d. Undefined  

162. A _____ refers to a layout accurate in size, color, scheme, and other necessary details to show how a final ad will look. For presentation only, never for reproduction.  
a. Comprehensive11  
b. Thing  
c. Undefined  
d. Undefined  

163. A _____ is an individual or company (including a corporation) that legally owns one or more shares of stock in a joined stock company. The shareholders are the owners of a corporation. Companies listed at the stock market strive to enhance shareholder value.  
a. Stockholder11  
b. Thing  
c. Undefined  
d. Undefined  

164. _____ refers to the calculation of the total liabilities divided by the total liabilities plus capital. This results in the measurment of the debt level of the business (leverage).  
a. Debt ratio11  
b. Thing  
c. Undefined  
d. Undefined

## Chapter 11. Credit Analysis

165. _____ refers to obligations that are not paid within 1 year.
 a. Thing
 b. Noncurrent liabilities11
 c. Undefined
 d. Undefined

166. A _____ is a method by which an organization sets aside money over time to retire its indebtedness. More specifically, it is a fund into which money can be deposited, so that over time its preferred stock, debentures or stocks can be retired.
 a. Sinking fund11
 b. Thing
 c. Undefined
 d. Undefined

167. _____ refers to another name for a business organization. Other similar terms are business firm, sometimes simply business, sometimes simply firm, as well as company, and entity.
 a. Thing
 b. Enterprise11
 c. Undefined
 d. Undefined

168. _____ in economics refers to a strategy of combating adverse selection, one of the potential decision-making complications in cases of asymmetric information.
 a. Thing
 b. Screening11
 c. Undefined
 d. Undefined

169. _____ refers to the final payment date of a loan or other financial instrument, after which point no further interest or principal need be paid.
 a. Maturity11
 b. Thing
 c. Undefined
 d. Undefined

170. _____ refers to the want-satisfying power of a good or service; the satisfaction or pleasure a consumer obtains from the consumption of a good or service.
 a. Thing
 b. Utility11
 c. Undefined
 d. Undefined

171. Assets defined in the broadest legal sense. _____ includes the unrealized receivables of a cash basis taxpayer, but not services rendered.
 a. Thing
 b. Property11
 c. Undefined
 d. Undefined

172. Type of security acquired by loaning assets is called a _____.
 a. Debt security11
 b. Thing
 c. Undefined
 d. Undefined

173. _____ refers to a report detailing a future stock offering containing a set of financial statements; required by the SEC from a company that wishes to make an initial public offering of its stock.
 a. Thing
 b. Prospectus11
 c. Undefined
 d. Undefined

174. _____ refers to restrictions state and federal laws place on business with regard to the conduct of its activities.

a. Thing
b. Regulation11
c. Undefined
d. Undefined

175. The trade of things of value between buyer and seller so that each is better off after the trade is called the _____.
a. Exchange11
b. Thing
c. Undefined
d. Undefined

176. _____ refers to U.S. government agency that determines the financial statements that public companies must provide to stockholders and the measurement rules that they must use in producing those statements.
a. Organization
b. Securities and exchange commission11
c. Undefined
d. Undefined

177. _____ refers to the pattern followed by macroeconommic variables, such as GDP and unemployment that rise and fall irregularly over time, relative to trend.
a. Business cycle11
b. Thing
c. Undefined
d. Undefined

178. The central value of a pegged exchange rate, around which the actual rate is permitted to fluctuate within set bounds is a _____.
a. Par value11
b. Thing
c. Undefined
d. Undefined

179. The cost a business incurs to borrow money. With respect to bonds payable, the _____ is calculated by multiplying the market rate of interest by the carrying value of the bonds on the date of the payment.
a. Thing
b. Interest expense11
c. Undefined
d. Undefined

180. Systematic and rational allocation of the acquisition cost of an intangible asset over its useful life is referred to as _____.
a. Thing
b. Amortization11
c. Undefined
d. Undefined

181. _____ refers to the fee charged by an insurance company for an insurance policy. The rate of losses must be relatively predictable: In order to set the _____ (prices) insurers must be able to estimate them accurately.
a. Thing
b. Premium11
c. Undefined
d. Undefined

182. Reports inflows and outflows of cash during the accounting period in the categories of operating, investing, and financing is a _____.
a. Thing
b. Statement of cash flow11
c. Undefined
d. Undefined

183. _____ refers to pro rata distributions of stock or stock rights on common stock. They are usually issued in proportion to shares owned.

## Chapter 11. Credit Analysis

a. Stock dividend11  
b. Thing  
c. Undefined  
d. Undefined

184. The combination of two or more firms, generally of equal size and market power, to form an entirely new entity is a _____.

a. Thing  
b. Consolidation11  
c. Undefined  
d. Undefined

185. Cash flowing out of the business from all sources over a period of time is _____.

a. Cash outflow11  
b. Thing  
c. Undefined  
d. Undefined

186. _____, also known as property, plant, and equipment (PP&E), is a term used in accountancy for assets and property which cannot easily be converted into cash. This can be compared with current assets such as cash or bank accounts, which are described as liquid assets. In most cases, only tangible assets are referred to as fixed.

a. Fixed asset11  
b. Thing  
c. Undefined  
d. Undefined

187. The discussion by counsel for the respective parties of their contentions on the law and the facts of the case being tried in order to aid the jury in arriving at a correct and just conclusion is called _____.

a. Argument11  
b. Thing  
c. Undefined  
d. Undefined

188. _____ is equal to the income that a firm has after subtracting costs and expenses from the total revenue. Expenses will typically include tax expense.

a. Thing  
b. Net income11  
c. Undefined  
d. Undefined

189. A method for determining the budget for advertising and promotion based on arbitrary decisions of executives is called _____.

a. Arbitrary allocation11  
b. Thing  
c. Undefined  
d. Undefined

190. Large final payment due at the maturity of a debt that otherwise requires systematic smaller payments over the term of the loan prior to maturity is a _____.

a. Balloon payment11  
b. Thing  
c. Undefined  
d. Undefined

191. In economic models, the _____ time frame assumes no fixed factors of production. Firms can enter or leave the marketplace, and the cost (and availability) of land, labor, raw materials, and capital goods can be assumed to vary.

a. Long run11  
b. Thing  
c. Undefined  
d. Undefined

192. Interest expenditures included in the cost of a self-constructed asset is _____.

## Chapter 11. Credit Analysis

a. Thing
c. Undefined
b. Capitalized interest11
d. Undefined

193. Local television stations that are associated with a major network are called _____. _____ agree to preempt time during specified hours for programming provided by the network and carry the advertising contained in the program.
a. Affiliates11
c. Undefined
b. Thing
d. Undefined

194. _____ refer to gains and losses that are both unusual in nature and infrequent in occurrence; they are reported net of tax on the income statement.
a. Extraordinary items11
c. Undefined
b. Thing
d. Undefined

195. _____ refers to financial results from the disposal of a major segment of the business and are reported net of income tax effects.
a. Thing
c. Undefined
b. Discontinued operations11
d. Undefined

196. Method of accounting for investments in marketable equity securities; is required when the investor owns percent to percent of the investee company. The amount of investments carried under the _____ represents a measure of the book value of the investee rather than the cost or market value of the investment security.
a. Equity method11
c. Undefined
b. Thing
d. Undefined

197. In finance, _____ is a profit or an increase in value of an investment such as a stock or bond. _____ is calculated by fair market value or the proceeds from the sale of the investment minus the sum of the purchase price and all costs associated with it.
a. Thing
c. Undefined
b. Gain11
d. Undefined

198. _____ refers to net income before interest and taxes, divided by interest expense; describes a company's ability to make interest payments on its debt.
a. Times interest earned11
c. Undefined
b. Thing
d. Undefined

199. A measure of a company's solvency, calculated by dividing income before interest expense and taxes by interest expense is a _____.
a. Times interest earned ratio11
c. Undefined
b. Concept
d. Undefined

200. _____ is the result of computing current and deferred tax payable using the asset-liability method in which the balance sheet is seen as primary and the income statement as secondary.
a. Tax expense11
c. Undefined
b. Thing
d. Undefined

## Chapter 11. Credit Analysis

201. Characterized by rizing output, falling unemployment, rizing profits, and increasing economic activity following a decline is a _____.
 a. Recovery11
 b. Thing
 c. Undefined
 d. Undefined

202. _____ is an important accounting concept that describes the value of a business entity not directly attributable to its tangible assets and liabilities.
 a. Thing
 b. Goodwill11
 c. Undefined
 d. Undefined

203. _____ refers to the cash inflows and cash outflows from the general operating activities of the business; one of the three sections in the statement of cash flows.
 a. Thing
 b. Operating cash flows11
 c. Undefined
 d. Undefined

204. The dollar sum of costs that an insured individual must pay before the insurer begins to pay is called _____.
 a. Deductible11
 b. Thing
 c. Undefined
 d. Undefined

205. A _____ is the measure of the extent to which two economic or statistical variables move together, normalized so that its values range from -1 to +1. It is defined as the covariance of the two variables divided by the square root of the product of their variances.
 a. Thing
 b. Correlation11
 c. Undefined
 d. Undefined

206. The amount of earnings attributable to higher sales or lower costs rather than artificial profits created by accounting anomalies such as inflation of inventory is the _____.
 a. Quality of earnings11
 b. Thing
 c. Undefined
 d. Undefined

207. In finance, a _____ is a bond that is rated below investment grade. These bonds have a higher risk of defaulting, but typically pay high yields in order to make them attractive to investors.
 a. Junk bond11
 b. Thing
 c. Undefined
 d. Undefined

208. The development of new financial products-new ways of borrowing and lending is referred to as _____.
 a. Financial innovation11
 b. Thing
 c. Undefined
 d. Undefined

209. In finance, when a bond pays in kind, it means that the amount of principal owed to the bondholder is increased in lieu of paying current interest. Often it is referred to as _____.
 a. Thing
 b. Payment in kind11
 c. Undefined
 d. Undefined

210. _____ refers to the first commercially successful introduction of a new product, the use of a new method of production, or the creation of a new form of business organization.

## Chapter 11. Credit Analysis

a. Thing
b. Innovation11
c. Undefined
d. Undefined

211. Referring to a payment made with goods instead of money is an _____. An expression relating to the insurer's right in many Property contracts to replace damaged objects with new or equivalent (_____) material, rather than to pay a cash benefit.
a. In kind11
b. Thing
c. Undefined
d. Undefined

212. _____ is the handing of a task over to another person, usually a subordinate. It is the assignment of authority and responsibility to another person to carry out specific activities.
a. Delegation11
b. Event
c. Undefined
d. Undefined

213. A _____ acts as an agent that provides financial services for its clients. Financial institutions generally fall under financial regulation from a government authority.
a. Thing
b. Financial institution11
c. Undefined
d. Undefined

214. In investment, the _____ assesses the credit worthiness of a corporation. It is analogous to credit ratings for individuals and countries. The credit rating is a financial indicator to potential investors of debt securities such as bonds. These are assigned by credit rating agencies such as Standard & Poor's and have letter designations such as AAA, B, CC.
a. Thing
b. Bond credit rating11
c. Undefined
d. Undefined

215. _____ indicates whether a borrower has in the past made loan payments when due.
a. Creditworthiness11
b. Thing
c. Undefined
d. Undefined

216. The company that borrows money from investors by issuing bonds is referred to as _____. They are legally responsible for the obligations of the issue and for reporting financial conditions, material developments and any other operational activities as required by the regulations of their jurisdictions.
a. Issuer11
b. Thing
c. Undefined
d. Undefined

217. The risk of loss due to a counterparty defaulting on a contract, or more generally the risk of loss due to some "credit event" is called _____.
a. Thing
b. Credit risk11
c. Undefined
d. Undefined

218. The _____, in macroeconomics and international finance, refers to the equilibration of demand for a country's domestic money to its money supply; market for short-term financial instruments.
a. Thing
b. Money market11
c. Undefined
d. Undefined

219. _____ refer to representation of ownership rights to the corporation.

## Chapter 11. Credit Analysis

a. Thing
c. Undefined
b. Equity securities11
d. Undefined

220. A long-lasting, sometimes permanent team in the organization structure created to deal with tasks that recur regularly is the _____.
a. Thing
c. Undefined
b. Committee11
d. Undefined

221. _____ refers to a set of legal techniques for protecting one's belongings against lawsuits and judgments.
a. Thing
c. Undefined
b. Asset protection11
d. Undefined

222. Assets that have physical substance that cannot easily be converted into cash are referd to as a _____.
a. Thing
c. Undefined
b. Tangible asset11
d. Undefined

223. Having a physical existence is referred to as the _____. Personal property other than real estate, such as cars, boats, stocks, or other assets.
a. Thing
c. Undefined
b. Tangible11
d. Undefined

224. An _____ is the totality of the legal rights, interests, entitlements and obligations attaching to property. In the context of wills and probate, it refers to the totality of the property which the deceased owned or in which some interest was held.
a. Estate11
c. Undefined
b. Thing
d. Undefined

225. _____ refers to all the techniques sellers use to motivate people to buy products or services. An attempt by marketers to inform people about products and to persuade them to participate in an exchange.
a. Thing
c. Undefined
b. Promotion11
d. Undefined

226. A short-term immediate decision that, in its totality, leads to the achievement of strategic goals is called a _____.
a. Tactic11
c. Undefined
b. Thing
d. Undefined

227. The use of resources for the deliberate discovery of new information and ways of doing things, together with the application of that information in inventing new products or processes is referred to as _____.
a. Research and development11
c. Undefined
b. Thing
d. Undefined

228. The individual or entity that purchases a bond, thus loaning money to the company that issued the bond is the _____.
a. Thing
c. Undefined
b. Bondholder11
d. Undefined

## Chapter 11. Credit Analysis

229. _____ is a legally declared inability or impairment of ability of an individual or organization to pay their creditors.
   a. Thing
   b. Bankruptcy11
   c. Undefined
   d. Undefined

230. A _____ is a ratio of two numbers of reported levels or flows of a company. It may be two financial flows categories divided by each other (profit margin, profit/revenue). It may be a level divided by a financial flow (price/earnings). It may be a flow divided by a level (return on equity or earnings/equity). The numerator or denominator may itself be a ratio (PEG ratio).
   a. Thing
   b. Financial ratio11
   c. Undefined
   d. Undefined

231. _____ is a statistical technique for analyzing data. It is applicable when there is only one dependent variable but multiple independent variables.
   a. Thing
   b. Discriminant analysis11
   c. Undefined
   d. Undefined

232. Book of original entry, in which transactions are recorded in a general ledger system, is referred to as a _____.
   a. Journal11
   b. Thing
   c. Undefined
   d. Undefined

233. _____ refers to the price of an asset agreed on between a willing buyer and a willing seller; the price an asset could demand if it is sold on the open market.
   a. Market value11
   b. Thing
   c. Undefined
   d. Undefined

234. _____ is one of the constituents of a leasing calculus or operation. It describes the future value of a good in terms of percentage of depreciation of its initial value.
   a. Thing
   b. Residual value11
   c. Undefined
   d. Undefined

235. _____ payments can refer to an ongoing stream of payments in respect of the completion of past achievements.
   a. Residual11
   b. Thing
   c. Undefined
   d. Undefined

236. Notes that clarify information presented in the financial statements, as well as expand upon it where additional detail is needed are _____.
   a. Notes to the financial statements11
   b. Thing
   c. Undefined
   d. Undefined

237. In accounting terminology, _____ describes the original cost of an asset at the time of purchase or payment as opposed to its market value
   a. Historical cost11
   b. Thing
   c. Undefined
   d. Undefined

238. _____ measures and reports financial and nonfinancial information relating to the cost of acquiring or consuming resources in an organization. It provides information for both management accounting and financial accounting.

## Chapter 11. Credit Analysis

a. Cost accounting11
b. Thing
c. Undefined
d. Undefined

239. _____ refers to a good that has not been transformed by production; a primary product.
a. Raw material11
b. Thing
c. Undefined
d. Undefined

240. A subsidiary in which the firm owns 100 percent of the stock is a _____.
a. Wholly owned subsidiary11
b. Thing
c. Undefined
d. Undefined

241. A pro rata distribution of cash to stockholders of corporate stock is called a _____.
a. Thing
b. Cash dividend11
c. Undefined
d. Undefined

242. Commercial paper or instrument in which the maker promises to pay a specific sum of money to another person, to his order, or to bearer is referred to as a _____.
a. Promissory note11
b. Thing
c. Undefined
d. Undefined

243. _____ refers to a system by which individuals can reduce their exposure to risk of large losses by spreading the risks among a large number of persons.
a. Insurance11
b. Thing
c. Undefined
d. Undefined

244. Reduction in the selling price of goods extended to the buyer because the goods are defective or of lower quality than the buyer ordered and to encourage a buyer to keep merchandise that would otherwise be returned is the _____.
a. Thing
b. Allowance11
c. Undefined
d. Undefined

245. Contra-asset account containing the estimated uncollectible accounts receivable is an _____. Also called allowance for bad debts or allowance for uncollectible accounts.
a. Thing
b. Allowance for doubtful accounts11
c. Undefined
d. Undefined

246. The method of presenting the operating activities section of the statement of cash flow statement reports components of cash flows from operating activities as gross receipts and gross payments is called _____.
a. Direct method11
b. Concept
c. Undefined
d. Undefined

247. In accounting and finance, _____ is the portion of receivables that can no longer be collected, typically from accounts receivable or loans. _____ in accounting is considered an expense.
a. Thing
b. Bad debt11
c. Undefined
d. Undefined

248. The value today of a stream of payments and/or receipts over time in the future and/or the past, converted to the present using an interest rate. If X t is the amount in period t and r the interest rate, then _____ at time t=0 is V = ?T /t.
   a. Present value11
   b. Thing
   c. Undefined
   d. Undefined

249. _____ refers to the amount at which property would change hands between a willing buyer and a willing seller, neither being under any compulsion to buy or to sell, and both having reasonable knowledge of the relevant facts.
   a. Thing
   b. Fair market value11
   c. Undefined
   d. Undefined

250. _____ refers to the sale of securities directly to a financial institution by a corporation. This eliminates the middleman and reduces the cost of issue to the corporation.
   a. Private placement11
   b. Concept
   c. Undefined
   d. Undefined

251. _____ refers to a financial organization that specializes in selling primary offerings of securities. Investment bankers can also perform other financial functions, such as advising clients, negotiating mergers and takeovers, and selling secondary offerings.
   a. Thing
   b. Investment banker11
   c. Undefined
   d. Undefined

252. A _____ is a long-term debt instrument used by governments and large companies to obtain funds. It is similar to a bond except the securitization conditions are different.
   a. Thing
   b. Debenture11
   c. Undefined
   d. Undefined

253. Collecting information and providing feedback to employees about their behavior, communication style, or skills is an _____.
   a. Thing
   b. Assessment11
   c. Undefined
   d. Undefined

254. An arbitrary dollar amount assigned to shares by the board of directors, representing the minimum amount of consideration for which the corporation may issue the shares and the portion of consideration that must be allocated to the stated capital account is the _____.
   a. Stated value11
   b. Thing
   c. Undefined
   d. Undefined

255. Difference between the selling price and the face amount of the bond that is sold for more than the face amount is called the _____.
   a. Thing
   b. Bond premium11
   c. Undefined
   d. Undefined

256. Cumulative earnings of a company that are not distributed to the owners and are reinvested in the business are called _____.

## Chapter 11. Credit Analysis

a. Retained earnings11  
b. Thing  
c. Undefined  
d. Undefined

257. _____ refers to a financial statement that presents the revenues and expenses and resulting net income or net loss of a company for a specific period of time.
   a. Income statement11  
   b. Thing  
   c. Undefined  
   d. Undefined

258. Type of secured bond that conditionally transfers title of a designated piece of property to the bondholder until the bond is paid is referred to as _____.
   a. Mortgage bond11  
   b. Thing  
   c. Undefined  
   d. Undefined

259. The total amount of physical capital that has been accumulated, usually in a country is _____. Also refers to the total issued capital of a firm, including ordinary and preferred shares.
   a. Capital stock11  
   b. Thing  
   c. Undefined  
   d. Undefined

260. _____ refer to bonds in an issue that mature periodically over several years, usually at varying interest rates.
   a. Serial bonds11  
   b. Thing  
   c. Undefined  
   d. Undefined

261. _____ refers to a note payable issued for property, such as a house, usually repaid in equal installments consisting of part principle and part interest, over a specified period.
   a. Mortgage11  
   b. Thing  
   c. Undefined  
   d. Undefined

262. In finance the term _____ has two distinct meanings, both relating to securities. The first is a designation for a 'class' of common or preferred stock. _____ of common or preferred stock typically has enhanced voting rights or other benefits compared to the other forms of shares that may have been created. The equity structure, or how many types of shares are offered, is determined by the corporate charter.
   a. A share11  
   b. Thing  
   c. Undefined  
   d. Undefined

263. _____ refer to an equity security, representing a shareholder's ownership of a corporation. _____ are one of a finite number of equal portions in the capital of a company, entitling the owner to a proportion of distributed, non-reinvested profits known as dividends and to a portion of the value of the company in case of liquidation.
   a. Thing  
   b. Shares11  
   c. Undefined  
   d. Undefined

264. The _____ is a feature of preferred stock entitling the stockholder to receive current and unpaid prior-year dividends before common stockholders receive any dividends.
   a. Cumulative dividend11  
   b. Thing  
   c. Undefined  
   d. Undefined

## Chapter 11. Credit Analysis

265. A contract that gives the purchaser the _____ to buy or sell the underlying financial instrument at a specified price, called the exercise price or strike price, within a specific period of time.
   a. Thing
   b. Option11
   c. Undefined
   d. Undefined

266. The income from business operations before interest expense and income taxes are subtracted is an _____. Also known as earnings before interest and taxes or EBIT.
   a. Income before interest and taxes11
   b. Thing
   c. Undefined
   d. Undefined

267. The portion of a firm or industry's cost that changes with output, in contrast to fixed cost is referred to as _____.
   a. Thing
   b. Variable cost11
   c. Undefined
   d. Undefined

268. The cost that a firm bears if it does not produce at all and that is independent of its output. The presence of a _____ tends to imply increasing returns to scale. Contrasts with variable cost.
   a. Thing
   b. Fixed cost11
   c. Undefined
   d. Undefined

269. The sum of fixed cost and variable cost is referred to as _____.
   a. Total cost11
   b. Thing
   c. Undefined
   d. Undefined

270. _____ is a branch of investment analysis that looks into the process of managing money. Investment portfolios can be managed through decisions about security purchases and sales.
   a. Investment management11
   b. Thing
   c. Undefined
   d. Undefined

271. A company that conducts various aspects of securities trading, analysis and advisory services is a _____.
   a. Thing
   b. Brokerage firm11
   c. Undefined
   d. Undefined

272. In finance, a _____ is a collection of investments held by an institution or a private individual. Holding but not always a _____ is part of an investment and risk-limiting strategy called diversification. By owning several assets, certain types of risk (in particular specific risk) can be reduced.
   a. Portfolio11
   b. Thing
   c. Undefined
   d. Undefined

273. _____ refers to the entity that has a controlling influence over another company. It may have its own operations, or it may have been set up solely for the purpose of owning the Subject Company.
   a. Thing
   b. Parent company11
   c. Undefined
   d. Undefined

274. _____ refers to a method of inventory accounting that refers to First In, First Out.

## Chapter 11. Credit Analysis

    a. Thing
    b. Fifo method11
    c. Undefined
    d. Undefined

275. A _____ is a steady income given to a person (usually after retirement). Pensions are typically payments made in the form of a guaranteed annuity to a retired or disabled employee.
    a. Pension11
    b. Thing
    c. Undefined
    d. Undefined

276. _____ is an economic concept with commonplace familiarity; it is the price that a good or service is offered at, or will fetch, in the marketplace; it is of interest mainly in the study of microeconomics.
    a. Market price11
    b. Thing
    c. Undefined
    d. Undefined

277. _____ is the method that a company uses to track fixed assets, for example factory equipment, desks and chairs, computers, even buildings. Although the exact details of the task varies widely from company to company, _____ often includes tracking the physical location of assets, managing demand for scarce resources, and accounting tasks such as amortization.
    a. Asset management11
    b. Thing
    c. Undefined
    d. Undefined

278. A _____ in business refers to one company (the acquirer) purchasing another (the target). Such events resemble mergers, but without the formation of a new company.
    a. Thing
    b. Takeover11
    c. Undefined
    d. Undefined

279. _____ refers to the combination of two firms into a single firm.
    a. Thing
    b. Merger11
    c. Undefined
    d. Undefined

280. A contractual right to sell certain products or services, use certain trademarks, or perform activities in a geographical region is called a _____.
    a. Franchise11
    b. Thing
    c. Undefined
    d. Undefined

281. _____ usually refers to characteristics that permit a firm to compete effectively with other firms due to low cost or superior technology, perhaps internationally.
    a. Competitiveness11
    b. Thing
    c. Undefined
    d. Undefined

282. A substantial expenditure that is used by a company to acquire or upgrade physical assets such as equipment, property, industrial buildings, including those which improve the quality and life of an asset is referred to as a _____.
    a. Capital expenditure11
    b. Thing
    c. Undefined
    d. Undefined

283. Major investments in long-term assets such as land, buildings, equipment, or research and development are referred to as _____.

a. Capital expenditures11  
b. Thing  
c. Undefined  
d. Undefined

284. Total revenues from operation minus cost of goods sold and operating costs are called _____.
a. Thing  
b. Operating income11  
c. Undefined  
d. Undefined

285. _____ refers to the rate of return on a bond; the annual interest payment divided by the bond's price.
a. Thing  
b. Current yield11  
c. Undefined  
d. Undefined

286. One one-hundredth of a percentage point is a _____. Each one percent in interest is equal to 100 basis points.
a. Basis point11  
b. Thing  
c. Undefined  
d. Undefined

287. Income from operations before subtracting interest expense and income taxes is an _____.
a. Thing  
b. Earnings before interest and taxes11  
c. Undefined  
d. Undefined

288. _____ refers to the required rate of return on a bond issue. It is the discount rate used in present-valuing future interest payments and the principal payment at maturity. The term is used interchangeably with market rate of interest.
a. Yield to maturity11  
b. Thing  
c. Undefined  
d. Undefined

289. A decline in performance, in a firm is a _____ in sales or profits, or in a country is a _____ in output or employment.
a. Thing  
b. Slump11  
c. Undefined  
d. Undefined

290. In throughput accounting, the cost accounting aspect of Theory of Constraints (TOC), _____ is the money spent turning inventory into throughput. In TOC, _____ is limited to costs that vary strictly with the quantity produced, like raw materials and purchased components.
a. Operating expense11  
b. Thing  
c. Undefined  
d. Undefined

291. Production of goods primarily by the application of labor and capital to raw materials and other intermediate inputs, in contrast to agriculture, mining, forestry, fishing, and services a _____.
a. Manufacturing11  
b. Thing  
c. Undefined  
d. Undefined

292. _____ refers to the amount recognized as an expense in one period resulting from the periodic recognition of the used portion of the cost of a long-term tangible asset over its life.
a. Depreciation expense11  
b. Thing  
c. Undefined  
d. Undefined

## Chapter 11. Credit Analysis

293. _____ refers to the total depreciation that has been reported as depreciation expense for the entire life of a long-term tangible asset. It is a contra-asset account.
- a. Thing
- b. Accumulated depreciation11
- c. Undefined
- d. Undefined

294. Promoting and selling products or services to customers, or prospective customers, is referred to as _____.
- a. Marketing11
- b. Thing
- c. Undefined
- d. Undefined

295. _____ reports the way that net income and the distribution of dividends affected the financial position of the company during the accounting period.
- a. Thing
- b. Statement of Retained Earnings11
- c. Undefined
- d. Undefined

296. An _____ is all executive, organizational, and clerical costs associated with the general management of an organization rather than with manufacturing, marketing, or selling
- a. Administrative cost11
- b. Thing
- c. Undefined
- d. Undefined

297. _____, is the world's largest commercial tobacco company by sales. _____ was begun by a London tobacconist of the same name. He was one of the first people to sell hand-rolled cigarettes in the 1860s, selling them under the brand names Oxford and Cambridge Blues, following the adoption of cigarette smoking by British soldiers returning from the Crimean War.
- a. Organization
- b. Philip Morris11
- c. Undefined
- d. Undefined

298. Total number of shares of stock that are owned by stockholders on any particular date is referred to as _____.
- a. Outstanding shares11
- b. Thing
- c. Undefined
- d. Undefined

299. A public offer by a bidder to purchase a subject company's shares directly from its shareholders at a specified price for a fixed period of time is called _____.
- a. Thing
- b. Tender offer11
- c. Undeflned
- d. Undefined

300. An unconditional offer of payment, consisting in the actual production in money or legal _____ of a sum not less than the amount due.
- a. Tender11
- b. Thing
- c. Undefined
- d. Undefined

301. _____ is the process whereby interested parties resolve disputes, agree upon courses of action, bargain for individual or collective advantage, and/or attempt to craft outcomes which serve their mutual interests.
- a. Negotiation11
- b. Thing
- c. Undefined
- d. Undefined

## Chapter 11. Credit Analysis

302. A _____ is an employee of an organization with some of the powers and responsibilities of management, occupying a role between true manager and a regular employee. A _____ position is typically the first step towards being promoted into a management role.
   a. Supervisor11
   b. Thing
   c. Undefined
   d. Undefined

303. _____ refers to the legal requirement that anyone seeking to challenge a particular action in court must demonstrate that such action substantially affects his legitimate interests before he will be entitled to bring suit.
   a. Thing
   b. Standing11
   c. Undefined
   d. Undefined

304. A significant decline in economic activity. In the U.S., _____ is approximately defined as two successive quarters of falling GDP, as judged by NBER.
   a. Recession11
   b. Thing
   c. Undefined
   d. Undefined

305. That fraction of an industry's output accounted for by an individual firm or group of firms is called _____.
   a. Market share11
   b. Thing
   c. Undefined
   d. Undefined

306. The relative proportion of an organization's fixed, variable, and mixed costs is referred to as _____.
   a. Cost structure11
   b. Thing
   c. Undefined
   d. Undefined

307. In finance, the _____ approach describes a method to value a project or an entire company. The DCF methods determine the present value of future cash flows by discounting them using the appropriate cost of capital.
   a. Discounted cash flow11
   b. Thing
   c. Undefined
   d. Undefined

## Chapter 12. Equity Analysis and Valuation

1. _____ is a legally declared inability or impairment of ability of an individual or organization to pay their creditors.
   a. Bankruptcy12
   b. Thing
   c. Undefined
   d. Undefined

2. In financial terminology, _____ is the capital raized by a corporation, through the issuance and sale of shares.
   a. Stock12
   b. Thing
   c. Undefined
   d. Undefined

3. A _____ is the set of feasible allocations in an economy that cannot be improved upon by subset of the set of the economy's consumers (a coalition). In construction, when the force in an element is within a certain center section, the _____, the element will only be under compression.
   a. Thing
   b. Core12
   c. Undefined
   d. Undefined

4. _____ is the corporate management term for the act of partially dismantling and reorganizing a company for the purpose of making it more efficient and therefore more profitable.
   a. Thing
   b. Restructuring12
   c. Undefined
   d. Undefined

5. A _____ is a specific type of option that uses the stock itself as an underlying instrument to determine the option's pay-off and therefore its value.
   a. Thing
   b. Stock option12
   c. Undefined
   d. Undefined

6. Amounts of money put aside by corporations, nonprofit organizations, or unions to cover part of the financial needs of members when they retire is a _____.
   a. Thing
   b. Pension fund12
   c. Undefined
   d. Undefined

7. A standardized method or technique that is performed repetitively, often on different materials resulting in different finished goods is called an _____.
   a. Operation12
   b. Thing
   c. Undefined
   d. Undefined

8. A _____ is a steady income given to a person (usually after retirement). Pensions are typically payments made in the form of a guaranteed annuity to a retired or disabled employee.
   a. Pension12
   b. Thing
   c. Undefined
   d. Undefined

9. In accounting, an _____ represents an event in which an asset is used up or a liability is incurred. In terms of the accounting equation, expenses reduce owners' equity.
   a. Thing
   b. Expense12
   c. Undefined
   d. Undefined

10. A contract that gives the purchaser the _____ to buy or sell the underlying financial instrument at a specified price, called the exercise price or strike price, within a specific period of time.

a. Thing  
b. Option12  
c. Undefined  
d. Undefined

11. An item of property, such as land, capital, money, a share in ownership, or a claim on others for future payment, such as a bond or a bank deposit is an _____.
    a. Thing  
    b. Asset12  
    c. Undefined  
    d. Undefined

12. In finance, _____ is a profit or an increase in value of an investment such as a stock or bond. _____ is calculated by fair market value or the proceeds from the sale of the investment minus the sum of the purchase price and all costs associated with it.
    a. Thing  
    b. Gain12  
    c. Undefined  
    d. Undefined

13. Independent accounting entity with a self-balancing set of accounts segregated for the purposes of carrying on specific activities is referred to as a _____.
    a. Fund12  
    b. Thing  
    c. Undefined  
    d. Undefined

14. In 1876, Thomas Alva Edison opened a new laboratory in Menlo Park, New Jersey. Out of the laboratory was to come perhaps the most famous invention of all—a successful development of the incandescent electric lamp. By 1890, Edison had organized his various businesses into the Edison _____ Company.
    a. General Electric12  
    b. Organization  
    c. Undefined  
    d. Undefined

15. _____ refers to an intergovernmental transfer of funds . Since the New Deal, state and local governments have become increasingly dependent upon federal grants for an almost infinite variety of programs.
    a. Grant12  
    b. Thing  
    c. Undefined  
    d. Undefined

16. _____ refers to a summary of all the transactions that have occurred over a particular period.
    a. Financial statement12  
    b. Thing  
    c. Undefined  
    d. Undefined

17. In finance, _____ is the process of estimating the market value of a financial asset or liability. They can be done on assets (for example, investments in marketable securities such as stocks, options, business enterprises, or intangible assets such as patents and trademarks) or on liabilities (e.g., Bonds issued by a company).
    a. Event  
    b. Valuation12  
    c. Undefined  
    d. Undefined

18. _____ is the name given to the set of legal principles, in countries following the English common law tradition, which supplement strict rules of law where their application would operate harshly, so as to achieve what is sometimes referred to as "natural justice."
    a. Thing  
    b. Equity12  
    c. Undefined  
    d. Undefined

## Chapter 12. Equity Analysis and Valuation

19. _____ refers to the long-term movement of an economic variable, such as its average rate of increase or decrease over enough years to encompass several business cycles.
    a. Thing
    b. Trend12
    c. Undefined
    d. Undefined

20. _____ characterizes the process of leading and directing all or part of an organization, often a business, through the deployment and manipulation of resources. Early twentieth-century _____ writer Mary Parker Follett defined _____ as "the art of getting things done through people."
    a. Management12
    b. Thing
    c. Undefined
    d. Undefined

21. That which involves playing down differences and finding areas of agreement are referred to as accommodation or _____.
    a. Thing
    b. Smoothing12
    c. Undefined
    d. Undefined

22. _____ refers to measures that are important to monitoring and tracking the effectiveness of a company's operations.
    a. Operating results12
    b. Thing
    c. Undefined
    d. Undefined

23. _____ refers to any departure from the ideal of perfect competition that interferes with economic agents maximizing social welfare when they maximize their own.
    a. Distortion12
    b. Thing
    c. Undefined
    d. Undefined

24. _____ refers to a financial statement that presents the revenues and expenses and resulting net income or net loss of a company for a specific period of time.
    a. Income statement12
    b. Thing
    c. Undefined
    d. Undefined

25. A system that collects and processes financial information about an organization and reports that information to decision makers is referred to as _____.
    a. Thing
    b. Accounting12
    c. Undefined
    d. Undefined

26. Ability to compare the accounting information of different companies because they use the same accounting principles is known as _____.
    a. Thing
    b. Comparability12
    c. Undefined
    d. Undefined

27. Assistance provided by countries and by international institutions such as the World Bank to developing countries in the form of monetary grants, loans at low interest rates, in kind, or a combination of these is called _____. _____ can also refer to assistance of any type rendered to benefit some group or individual.

a. Aid12
b. Thing
c. Undefined
d. Undefined

28. _____ is equal to the income that a firm has after subtracting costs and expenses from the total revenue. Expenses will typically include tax expense.
   a. Net income12
   b. Thing
   c. Undefined
   d. Undefined

29. _____ means the giving out of information, either voluntarily or to be in compliance with legal regulations or workplace rules.
   a. Thing
   b. Disclosure12
   c. Undefined
   d. Undefined

30. _____ refers to a recording as positive in the balance of payments, any transaction that gives rise to a payment into the country, such as an export, the sale of an asset, or borrowing from abroad.
   a. Credit12
   b. Thing
   c. Undefined
   d. Undefined

31. Systematic and rational allocation of the acquisition cost of an intangible asset over its useful life is referred to as _____.
   a. Amortization12
   b. Thing
   c. Undefined
   d. Undefined

32. _____ is an accounting and finance term for the method of attributing the cost of an asset across the useful life of the asset. _____ is a reduction in the value of a currency in floating exchange rate.
   a. Thing
   b. Depreciation12
   c. Undefined
   d. Undefined

33. In finance and economics, _____ is the reduction of some kind of asset, for either financial or social goals. A divestment is the opposite of an investment.
   a. Thing
   b. Divestiture12
   c. Undefined
   d. Undefined

34. _____ refers to paid, nonpersonal communication through various media by organizations and individuals who are in some way identified in the _____ message.
   a. Thing
   b. Advertising12
   c. Undefined
   d. Undefined

35. A company that is controlled by another company or corporation is a _____.
   a. Subsidiary12
   b. Thing
   c. Undefined
   d. Undefined

36. Promoting and selling products or services to customers, or prospective customers, is referred to as _____.
   a. Thing
   b. Marketing12
   c. Undefined
   d. Undefined

## Chapter 12. Equity Analysis and Valuation

37. An _____ is any factor (financial or non-financial) that provides a motive for a particular course of action, or counts as a reason for preferring one choice to the alternatives.
    a. Thing
    b. Incentive12
    c. Undefined
    d. Undefined

38. _____ refers to a process whereby the assets of a business are converted to money. The conversion may be coerced by a legal process to pay off the debt of the business, or to satisfy any other business obligation that the business has not voluntarily satisfied.
    a. Thing
    b. Liquidation12
    c. Undefined
    d. Undefined

39. _____ refers to the extent to which an economic variable, such as a price or an exchange rate, moves up and down over time.
    a. Thing
    b. Volatility12
    c. Undefined
    d. Undefined

40. _____ is a U.S. business term for the amount of money that a company receives from its activities, mostly from sales of products and/or services to customers.
    a. Revenue12
    b. Thing
    c. Undefined
    d. Undefined

41. _____ refers to the method under which income and expenses are determined for tax purposes. Important accounting methods include the cash basis and the accrual basis.
    a. Accounting method12
    b. Thing
    c. Undefined
    d. Undefined

42. _____ is an important accounting concept that describes the value of a business entity not directly attributable to its tangible assets and liabilities.
    a. Goodwill12
    b. Thing
    c. Undefined
    d. Undefined

43. The social science dealing with the use of scarce resources to obtain the maximum satisfaction of society's virtually unlimited economic wants is an _____.
    a. Thing
    b. Economics12
    c. Undefined
    d. Undefined

44. _____ is a term in Corporate Finance used to indicate a condition when promises to creditors of a company are broken or honored with difficulty. Sometimes _____ can lead to bankruptcy. _____ is usually associated with some costs to the company and these are known as Costs of _____. A common example of a cost of _____ is bankrupty costs.
    a. Financial distress12
    b. Thing
    c. Undefined
    d. Undefined

45. Management merely consists of _____ applied to business situations; or in other words: management forms a sub-set of the broader process of _____.

a. Leadership12  
b. Thing  
c. Undefined  
d. Undefined

46. The finalization of a real estate sales transaction that passes title to the property from the seller to the buyer is referred to as a _____. _____ is a sales term which refers to the process of making a sale. It refers to reaching the final step, which may be an exchange of money or acquiring a signature.
   a. Thing  
   b. Closing12  
   c. Undefined  
   d. Undefined

47. _____ refer to gains and losses that are both unusual in nature and infrequent in occurrence; they are reported net of tax on the income statement.
   a. Thing  
   b. Extraordinary items12  
   c. Undefined  
   d. Undefined

48. Collecting information and providing feedback to employees about their behavior, communication style, or skills is an _____.
   a. Assessment12  
   b. Thing  
   c. Undefined  
   d. Undefined

49. The consumer's appraisal of the product or brand on important attributes is called _____.
   a. Thing  
   b. Evaluation12  
   c. Undefined  
   d. Undefined

50. _____ refer to securities that are readily traded in the secondary securities market.
   a. Marketable securities12  
   b. Thing  
   c. Undefined  
   d. Undefined

51. _____ refers to a claim on the borrower future income that is sold by the borrower to the lender. A _____ is a type of transferable interest representing financial value.
   a. Thing  
   b. Security12  
   c. Undefined  
   d. Undefined

52. _____ refers to the speed of the up and down movements of a fluctuating economic variable; that is, the number of times per unit of time that the variable completes a cycle of up and down movement.
   a. Frequency12  
   b. Thing  
   c. Undefined  
   d. Undefined

53. _____ is an airline of the United States. Based in Houston, Texas, it is the 6th largest airline in the U.S. and the 8th largest in the world. Continental's tagline, since 1998, has been Work Hard, Fly Right.
   a. Continental Airlines12  
   b. Organization  
   c. Undefined  
   d. Undefined

54. During its life, _____ was one of the largest shipbuilding companies in the world and was one of the most powerful symbols of American manufacturing leadership. It was the second largest steel producer in the United States, but following its 2001 bankruptcy, the company was dissolved and the remaining assets sold to International Steel Group in 2003.

a. Thing
b. Bethlehem Steel12
c. Undefined
d. Undefined

55. _____ generally refers to financial wealth, especially that used to start or maintain a business. In classical economics, _____ is one of four factors of production, the others being land and labor and entrepreneurship.
   a. Thing
   b. Capital12
   c. Undefined
   d. Undefined

56. _____ refers to the return a businessperson gets on the money he and other owners invest in the firm; for example, a business that earned $100 on a $1,000 investment would have a ROI of 10 percent: 100 divided by 1000.
   a. Thing
   b. Return on investment12
   c. Undefined
   d. Undefined

57. _____ refers to spending for the production and accumulation of capital and additions to inventories. In a financial sense, buying an asset with the expectation of making a return.
   a. Investment12
   b. Thing
   c. Undefined
   d. Undefined

58. _____ is the auditor's assessment that there are material misstatements in the financial statements before considering the effectiveness of internal controls. If the auditor concludes that there is a high likelihood of misstamtement, ignoring internal controls, the auditor would conclude that the _____ is high.
   a. Inherent Risk12
   b. Thing
   c. Undefined
   d. Undefined

59. The income, expenditures, and resources that affect the cost of running a business and household are called an _____.
   a. Economy12
   b. Thing
   c. Undefined
   d. Undefined

60. _____ refers to a "non tangible product" that is not embodied in a physical good and that typically effects some change in another product, person, or institution. Contrasts with good.
   a. Service12
   b. Thing
   c. Undefined
   d. Undefined

61. _____ refer to people in the organization who actually use the product or service purchased by the buying center.
   a. Thing
   b. Users12
   c. Undefined
   d. Undefined

62. In finance, the _____ approach describes a method to value a project or an entire company. The DCF methods determine the present value of future cash flows by discounting them using the appropriate cost of capital.
   a. Thing
   b. Discounted cash flow12
   c. Undefined
   d. Undefined

63. In finance, _____ refers to the amounts of cash being received and spent by a business during a defined period of time, sometimes tied to a specific project. Most of the time they are being used to determine gaps in the liquid position of a company.

## Chapter 12. Equity Analysis and Valuation

a. Cash flow12  
b. Thing  
c. Undefined  
d. Undefined

64. _____ is the term used to describe income received based on the production of those others who have become members of one's organization.
   a. Residual income12  
   b. Thing  
   c. Undefined  
   d. Undefined

65. _____ refers to the percentage cost of funds used for acquiring resources for an organization, typically a weighted average of the firms cost of equity and cost of debt.
   a. Cost of capital12  
   b. Place  
   c. Undefined  
   d. Undefined

66. The _____ of an asset or group of assets is sometimes the price at which they were originally acquired, in many cases equal to purchase price.
   a. Book value12  
   b. Thing  
   c. Undefined  
   d. Undefined

67. _____ payments can refer to an ongoing stream of payments in respect of the completion of past achievements.
   a. Thing  
   b. Residual12  
   c. Undefined  
   d. Undefined

68. A _____ refers to a layout accurate in size, color, scheme, and other necessary details to show how a final ad will look. For presentation only, never for reproduction.
   a. Thing  
   b. Comprehensive12  
   c. Undefined  
   d. Undefined

69. _____ in contract law, a basic requirement for an enforceable agreement under traditional contract principles, defined in this text as legal value, bargained for and given in exchange for an act or promise. In corporation law, cash or property contributed to a corporation in exchange for shares, or a promise to contribute such cash or property.
   a. Thing  
   b. Consideration12  
   c. Undefined  
   d. Undefined

70. In finance and economics, _____ is the price paid by a borrower for the use of a lender's money. In other words, _____ is the amount of paid to "rent" money for a period of time.
   a. Interest12  
   b. Thing  
   c. Undefined  
   d. Undefined

71. A _____ is an individual or company (including a corporation) that legally owns one or more shares of stock in a joined stock company. The shareholders are the owners of a corporation. Companies listed at the stock market strive to enhance shareholder value.
   a. Stockholder12  
   b. Thing  
   c. Undefined  
   d. Undefined

72. _____ refers to a person or tool with a primary function of information analysis, generally with a more limited, practical and short term set of goals than a researcher.

## Chapter 12. Equity Analysis and Valuation

a. Person  
b. Analyst12  
c. Undefined  
d. Undefined

73. _____ refers to money raized from within the firm or through the sale of ownership in the firm.
    a. Equity capital12
    b. Thing
    c. Undefined
    d. Undefined

74. The _____ is the cost of borrowing money (usually denoted by Kd). It is derived by dividing debt's interest payments on the total market value of the debts.
    a. Thing
    b. Cost of debt12
    c. Undefined
    d. Undefined

75. The difference between the face value of a bond and its selling price, when a bond is sold for less than its face value it's referred to as a _____.
    a. Discount12
    b. Thing
    c. Undefined
    d. Undefined

76. A person in possession of a document of title or an instrument payable or indorsed to him, his order, or to bearer is a _____.
    a. Thing
    b. Holder12
    c. Undefined
    d. Undefined

77. A nation's currency is said to _____ when exchange rates change so that a unit of its currency can buy fewer units of foreign currency.
    a. Depreciate12
    b. Thing
    c. Undefined
    d. Undefined

78. In finance, the _____ is the minimum rate of return a firm must offer shareholders to compensate for waiting for their returns, and for bearing some risk.
    a. Cost of equity12
    b. Thing
    c. Undefined
    d. Undefined

79. Amount of corporate profits paid out for each share of stock is referred to as _____.
    a. Dividend12
    b. Thing
    c. Undefined
    d. Undefined

80. The interest rate that equates a future value or an annuity to a given present value is a _____.
    a. Thing
    b. Yield12
    c. Undefined
    d. Undefined

81. _____ refers to the price of an asset agreed on between a willing buyer and a willing seller; the price an asset could demand if it is sold on the open market.
    a. Thing
    b. Market value12
    c. Undefined
    d. Undefined

## Chapter 12. Equity Analysis and Valuation

82. A _____ is, as defined in economics, a social arrangement that allows buyers and sellers to discover information and carry out a voluntary exchange of goods or services.
   a. Market12
   b. Thing
   c. Undefined
   d. Undefined

83. _____ refers to financial results from the disposal of a major segment of the business and are reported net of income tax effects.
   a. Discontinued operations12
   b. Thing
   c. Undefined
   d. Undefined

84. An increase in the overall price level of an economy, usually as measured by the CPI or by the implicit price deflator is called _____.
   a. Inflation12
   b. Thing
   c. Undefined
   d. Undefined

85. An organization that employs resources to produce a good or service for profit and owns and operates one or more plants is referred to as a _____.
   a. Thing
   b. Firm12
   c. Undefined
   d. Undefined

86. _____ refers to the return to the resource entrepreneurial ability; total revenue minus total cost.
   a. Profit12
   b. Thing
   c. Undefined
   d. Undefined

87. Cash flowing out of the business from all sources over a period of time is _____.
   a. Thing
   b. Cash outflow12
   c. Undefined
   d. Undefined

88. _____ refers to an input that exists as a stock, providing services that contribute to production. The stock is not used up in production, although it may deteriorate with use, providing a smaller flow of services later.
   a. Primary factor12
   b. Thing
   c. Undefined
   d. Undefined

89. _____ is the analysis of the accounts and the economic prospects of a firm.
   a. Thing
   b. Financial analysis12
   c. Undefined
   d. Undefined

90. Cash flow activities that include the cash effects of transactions that create revenues and expenses and thus enter into the determination of net income is an _____.
   a. Operating activities12
   b. Thing
   c. Undefined
   d. Undefined

91. _____ refers to the pattern followed by macroeconommic variables, such as GDP and unemployment that rise and fall irregularly over time, relative to trend.

## Chapter 12. Equity Analysis and Valuation

a. Thing
b. Business cycle12
c. Undefined
d. Undefined

92. A _____ is a fixed point of time in the future at which point certain processes will be evaluated or assumed to end. It is necessary in an accounting, finance or risk management regime to assign such a fixed horizon time so that alternatives can be evaluated for performance over the same period of time.
a. Time horizon12
b. Thing
c. Undefined
d. Undefined

93. A group of firms that produce identical or similar products is an _____. It is also used specifically to refer to an area of economic production focused on manufacturing which involves large amounts of capital investment before any profit can be realized, also called "heavy _____".
a. Industry12
b. Thing
c. Undefined
d. Undefined

94. _____ is a business magazine published by McGraw-Hill. It was first published in 1929 under the direction of Malcolm Muir, who was serving as president of the McGraw-Hill Publishing company at the time. It is considered to be the standard both in industry and among students.
a. Business Week12
b. Organization
c. Undefined
d. Undefined

95. The company that borrows money from investors by issuing bonds is referred to as _____. They are legally responsible for the obligations of the issue and for reporting financial conditions, material developments and any other operational activities as required by the regulations of their jurisdictions.
a. Thing
b. Issuer12
c. Undefined
d. Undefined

96. _____ refers to annual profit of the corporation divided by the number of shares outstanding.
a. Earnings per share12
b. Thing
c. Undefined
d. Undefined

97. The _____ is the amount of income tax an individual or firm pays divided by the individual or firm's total taxable income. This ratio is usually expressed as a percentage.
a. Thing
b. Effective tax rate12
c. Undefined
d. Undefined

98. A group of products that are physically similar or are intended for a similar market are called the _____.
a. Thing
b. Product line12
c. Undefined
d. Undefined

99. Assets defined in the broadest legal sense. _____ includes the unrealized receivables of a cash basis taxpayer, but not services rendered.
a. Property12
b. Thing
c. Undefined
d. Undefined

# Chapter 12. Equity Analysis and Valuation

100. A media scheduling strategy where a continuous pattern of advertising is used over the time span of the advertising campaign is _____.
- a. Continuity12
- b. Thing
- c. Undefined
- d. Undefined

101. _____ is the method that a company uses to track fixed assets, for example factory equipment, desks and chairs, computers, even buildings. Although the exact details of the task varies widely from company to company, _____ often includes tracking the physical location of assets, managing demand for scarce resources, and accounting tasks such as amortization.
- a. Asset management12
- b. Thing
- c. Undefined
- d. Undefined

102. _____ refers to the way a corporation finances itself through some combination of equity sales, equity options, bonds, and loans. Optimal _____ refers to the particular combination that minimizes the cost of capital while maximizing the stock price.
- a. Thing
- b. Capital structure12
- c. Undefined
- d. Undefined

103. _____ refers to the capacity to turn assets into cash, or the amount of assets in a portfolio that have that capacity.
- a. Thing
- b. Liquidity12
- c. Undefined
- d. Undefined

104. _____ is the sale of assets when an entity is being liquidated.
- a. Thing
- b. Realization12
- c. Undefined
- d. Undefined

105. A _____ functions as a form of shark repellent used to thwart hostile takeovers. Under implementation of this provision, a target company will acquire a troublesome firm in order to raise the acquisition price and make acquisition by other parties economically unattractive.
- a. Thing
- b. Safe harbor12
- c. Undefined
- d. Undefined

106. An _____ is an accounting event in which the transaction is recognized when the action takes place, instead of when cash is disbursed or received.
- a. Accrual12
- b. Thing
- c. Undefined
- d. Undefined

107. The creation of finished goods and services using the factors of _____: land, labor, capital, entrepreneurship, and knowledge.
- a. Production12
- b. Thing
- c. Undefined
- d. Undefined

108. A cost that results from a discretionary management decision to spend a particular amount of money is called _____.

## Chapter 12. Equity Analysis and Valuation

a. Thing
c. Undefined
b. Discretionary cost12
d. Undefined

109. The cost that a firm bears if it does not produce at all and that is independent of its output. The presence of a _____ tends to imply increasing returns to scale. Contrasts with variable cost.
a. Fixed cost12
c. Undefined
b. Thing
d. Undefined

110. A statement of the assets, liabilities, and net worth of a firm or individual at some given time often at the end of its "fiscal year," is referred to as a _____.
a. Thing
c. Undefined
b. Balance sheet12
d. Undefined

111. An _____ is prepared by corporate management that presents financial information including financial statements, footnotes, and the management discussion and analysis.
a. Thing
c. Undefined
b. Annual report12
d. Undefined

112. In agency law, one under whose direction an agent acts and for whose benefit that agent acts is a _____.
a. Principal12
c. Undefined
b. Thing
d. Undefined

113. In banking and accountancy, the outstanding _____ is the amount of money owned, (or due), that remains in a deposit account (or a loan account) at a given date, after all past remittances, payments and withdrawal have been accounted for. It can be positive (then, in the _____ sheet of a firm, it is an asset) or negative (a liability).
a. Thing
c. Undefined
b. Balance12
d. Undefined

114. Employees who are not covered by the Fair Labor Standards Act are _____. _____ employees are not eligible for overtime pay.
a. Thing
c. Undefined
b. Exempt12
d. Undefined

115. Two or more balance sheets from the same company for consecutive accounting periods, shown together to reflect the company's financial situation over time are refrred to as _____.
a. Comparative balance sheets12
c. Undefined
b. Thing
d. Undefined

116. _____ refers to restrictions state and federal laws place on business with regard to the conduct of its activities.
a. Regulation12
c. Undefined
b. Thing
d. Undefined

117. The trade of things of value between buyer and seller so that each is better off after the trade is called the _____.
a. Exchange12
c. Undefined
b. Thing
d. Undefined

## Chapter 12. Equity Analysis and Valuation

118. _____ refers to a written statement-also called an accountant's certificate, accountant's opinion, or audit report- prepared by an independent accountant or auditor after an audit.
   a. Financial report12
   b. Thing
   c. Undefined
   d. Undefined

119. The amount of earnings attributable to higher sales or lower costs rather than artificial profits created by accounting anomalies such as inflation of inventory is the _____.
   a. Thing
   b. Quality of earnings12
   c. Undefined
   d. Undefined

120. A company owned in a foreign country by another company is referred to as _____.
   a. Foreign subsidiary12
   b. Thing
   c. Undefined
   d. Undefined

121. In finance, _____ means currencies, such as U.S. Dollars and Euros. These are traded on _____ markets.
   a. Foreign exchange12
   b. Thing
   c. Undefined
   d. Undefined

122. _____ refers to the price at which one country's currency trades for another, typically on the exchange market.
   a. Thing
   b. Exchange rate12
   c. Undefined
   d. Undefined

123. Tangible property held for sale in the normal course of business or used in producing goods or services for sale is an _____.
   a. Inventory12
   b. Thing
   c. Undefined
   d. Undefined

124. Other organizations in the same industry or type of business that provide a good or service to the same set of customers is referred to as a _____.
   a. Competitor12
   b. Thing
   c. Undefined
   d. Undefined

125. The withholding of labor services by an organized group of workers is referred to as a _____.
   a. Thing
   b. Strike12
   c. Undefined
   d. Undefined

126. The use of resources for the deliberate discovery of new information and ways of doing things, together with the application of that information in inventing new products or processes is referred to as _____.
   a. Research and development12
   b. Thing
   c. Undefined
   d. Undefined

127. In accounting and finance, _____ is the portion of receivables that can no longer be collected, typically from accounts receivable or loans. _____ in accounting is considered an expense.
   a. Bad debt12
   b. Thing
   c. Undefined
   d. Undefined

## Chapter 12. Equity Analysis and Valuation

128. _____ is the act of removing from control the owner of an item of property. The term is used to both refer to acts by a government or by any group of people.
   a. Expropriation12
   b. Thing
   c. Undefined
   d. Undefined

129. _____ in law, is the relinquishment of an interest, claim, privilege or possession. This broad meaning has a number of applications in different branches of law.
   a. Thing
   b. Abandonment12
   c. Undefined
   d. Undefined

130. A contract for the possession and use of land or other property, including goods, on one side, and a recompense of rent or other income on the other is the _____.
   a. Thing
   b. Lease12
   c. Undefined
   d. Undefined

131. A _____ is a "promise" or an "agreement" that is enforced or recognized by the law. In the civil law, a _____ is considered to be part of the general law of obligations.
   a. Thing
   b. Contract12
   c. Undefined
   d. Undefined

132. The extent to which a physical unit of production has been finished with respect to direct material or conversion activity is called _____.
   a. Thing
   b. Percentage of completion12
   c. Undefined
   d. Undefined

133. _____ is one of a series of accounting transactions dealing with the billing of customers which owe money to a person, company or organization for goods and services that have been provided to the customer. This is typically done in a one person organization by writing an invoice and mailing or delivering it to each customer.
   a. Thing
   b. Accounts receivable12
   c. Undefined
   d. Undefined

134. _____ refers to capital stock that has been issued and is being held by stockholders.
   a. Thing
   b. Outstanding stock12
   c. Undefined
   d. Undefined

135. Cumulative earnings of a company that are not distributed to the owners and are reinvested in the business are called _____.
   a. Retained earnings12
   b. Thing
   c. Undefined
   d. Undefined

136. Stock that has specified rights over common stock is a _____.
   a. Thing
   b. Preferred stock12
   c. Undefined
   d. Undefined

137. _____ refers to an obligation in the form of a written promissory note. It is a balance sheet term referring to a company's outstanding bank loans.

a. Notes payable12  
b. Thing  
c. Undefined  
d. Undefined

138. _____ is usually a long term liability account containing the face amount, par amount, or maturity amount of the bonds issued by a company that are outstanding as of the balance sheet date.
   a. Thing
   b. Bonds payable12
   c. Undefined
   d. Undefined

139. _____ refers to the basic, normal, voting stock issued by a corporation; called residual equity because it ranks after preferred stock for dividend and liquidation distributions.
   a. Thing
   b. Common stock12
   c. Undefined
   d. Undefined

140. A _____ is a present obligation of the enterprise arizing from past events, the settlement of which is expected to result in an outflow from the enterprise of resources embodying economic benefits.
   a. Liability12
   b. Thing
   c. Undefined
   d. Undefined

141. At equality refers to _____. Two currencies are said to be '_____' if they are trading one-for-one.
   a. At par12
   b. Thing
   c. Undefined
   d. Undefined

142. _____ refers to a debt instrument, issued by a borrower and promising a specified stream of payments to the purchaser, usually regular interest payments plus a final repayment of principal.
   a. Thing
   b. Bond12
   c. Undefined
   d. Undefined

143. _____ refers to the total depreciation that has been reported as depreciation expense for the entire life of a long-term tangible asset. It is a contra-asset account.
   a. Accumulated depreciation12
   b. Thing
   c. Undefined
   d. Undefined

144. A company's purchase of the property and obligations of another company is an _____.
   a. Thing
   b. Acquisition12
   c. Undefined
   d. Undefined

145. _____ refers to a method of inventory accounting that refers to First In, First Out.
   a. Thing
   b. Fifo method12
   c. Undefined
   d. Undefined

146. Total revenues from operation minus cost of goods sold and operating costs are called _____.
   a. Operating income12
   b. Thing
   c. Undefined
   d. Undefined

## Chapter 12. Equity Analysis and Valuation

147. In accounting, the _____ describes the direct expenses incurred in producing a particular good for sale, including the actual cost of materials that comprise the good, and direct labor expense in putting the good in salable condition.
    a. Thing
    b. Cost of goods sold12
    c. Undefined
    d. Undefined

148. Gross sales less sales returns and allowances and sales discounts are referred to as _____.
    a. Net sales12
    b. Thing
    c. Undefined
    d. Undefined

149. The _____ is a bank regulation, which sets a framework on how banks and depository institutions must handle their capital. The categorization of assets and capital is highly standardized so that it can be risk weighted.
    a. Capital requirement12
    b. Thing
    c. Undefined
    d. Undefined

150. The dollar difference between total current assets and total current liabilities is called _____.
    a. Working capital12
    b. Thing
    c. Undefined
    d. Undefined

151. The _____ is a comparison of a firm's current assets to its current liabilities. The _____ is an indication of a firm's market liquidity and ability to meet short-term debt obligations.
    a. Thing
    b. Current ratio12
    c. Undefined
    d. Undefined

152. _____ is an ambiguous phrase that expresses the relationship between gross profit and sales revenue as _____ = Revenue - costs of good sold.
    a. Gross margin12
    b. Thing
    c. Undefined
    d. Undefined

153. A deposit by a buyer in stocks with a seller or a stockbroker, as security to cover fluctuations in the market in reference to stocks that the buyer has purchased but for which he has not paid is a _____. Commodities are also traded on _____.
    a. Thing
    b. Margin12
    c. Undefined
    d. Undefined

154. Reduction in the selling price of goods extended to the buyer because the goods are defective or of lower quality than the buyer ordered and to encourage a buyer to keep merchandise that would otherwise be returned is the _____.
    a. Thing
    b. Allowance12
    c. Undefined
    d. Undefined

155. Reduction of sales revenues for return of or allowances for unsatisfactory goods are _____.
    a. Sales returns and allowances12
    b. Thing
    c. Undefined
    d. Undefined

156. Inventory on hand at the end of the accounting period, shown on the balance sheet in the current assets section is called _____.

a. Thing
c. Undefined
b. Ending inventory12
d. Undefined

157. Goods on hand at the beginning of the inventory period are referred to as _____.
a. Thing
c. Undefined
b. Beginning inventory12
d. Undefined

158. _____ refers to a debt that can reasonably be expected to be paid from existing current assets or through the creation of other current liabilities, within one year or the operating cycle, whichever is longer.
a. Current liability12
c. Undefined
b. Thing
d. Undefined

159. A written record of all vendors to whom the business firm owes money is referred to as _____.
a. Accounts payable12
c. Undefined
b. Thing
d. Undefined

160. Depreciation methods that recognize more depreciation expense in the early years of an asset's life and less in later years are referred to asan _____.
a. Accelerated method12
c. Undefined
b. Thing
d. Undefined

161. Taxes not paid until future years because of the difference in accounting methods selected for financial statements and methods required for tax purposes are _____.
a. Deferred tax liability12
c. Undefined
b. Thing
d. Undefined

162. _____ is an accounting term, meaning future tax liability or asset, resulting from temporary differences between book (accounting) value of assets and liabilities, and their tax value.
a. Thing
c. Undefined
b. Deferred tax12
d. Undefined

163. _____ is using given resources in such a way that the potential positive or negative outcome is magnified. In finance, this generally refers to borrowing.
a. Thing
c. Undefined
b. Leverage12
d. Undefined

164. A _____ is an individual or company (including a corporation) that legally owns one or more shares of stock in a joined stock company.
a. Thing
c. Undefined
b. Shareholder12
d. Undefined

165. The _____ percentage shows how profitable a company's assets are in generating revenue.
a. Return on Assets12
c. Undefined
b. Thing
d. Undefined

## Chapter 12. Equity Analysis and Valuation

166. The body of knowledge and techniques that can be used to combine economic resources to produce goods and services is called _____.
    a. Thing
    b. Technology12
    c. Undefined
    d. Undefined

167. Economic _____ refers to reducing barriers among countries to transactions and to movements of goods, capital, and labor, including harmonization of laws, regulations, and standards. Integrated markets theoretically function as a unified market.
    a. Integration12
    b. Thing
    c. Undefined
    d. Undefined

168. The combination of two or more firms, generally of equal size and market power, to form an entirely new entity is a _____.
    a. Consolidation12
    b. Thing
    c. Undefined
    d. Undefined

## Chapter 1

| | | | | | | | | | |
|---|---|---|---|---|---|---|---|---|---|
| 1. b | 2. b | 3. a | 4. a | 5. b | 6. b | 7. b | 8. b | 9. a | 10. a |
| 11. a | 12. b | 13. b | 14. b | 15. a | 16. a | 17. a | 18. a | 19. a | 20. b |
| 21. b | 22. a | 23. b | 24. b | 25. a | 26. b | 27. b | 28. b | 29. a | 30. a |
| 31. b | 32. a | 33. a | 34. b | 35. b | 36. a | 37. b | 38. a | 39. b | 40. b |
| 41. b | 42. b | 43. b | 44. a | 45. a | 46. a | 47. a | 48. a | 49. b | 50. b |
| 51. b | 52. b | 53. a | 54. a | 55. a | 56. b | 57. a | 58. b | 59. a | 60. a |
| 61. a | 62. a | 63. a | 64. a | 65. a | 66. a | 67. b | 68. b | 69. a | 70. a |
| 71. a | 72. a | 73. b | 74. b | 75. a | 76. b | 77. a | 78. a | 79. b | 80. b |
| 81. b | 82. a | 83. a | 84. b | 85. b | 86. b | 87. a | 88. b | 89. a | 90. a |
| 91. b | 92. b | 93. a | 94. a | 95. a | 96. a | 97. a | 98. a | 99. a | 100. a |
| 101. a | 102. a | 103. b | 104. b | 105. a | 106. b | 107. a | 108. a | 109. b | 110. b |
| 111. b | 112. b | 113. a | 114. b | 115. b | 116. a | 117. b | 118. a | 119. a | 120. a |
| 121. a | 122. b | 123. a | 124. b | 125. b | 126. b | 127. b | 128. a | 129. b | 130. b |
| 131. a | 132. b | 133. a | 134. a | 135. b | 136. b | 137. b | 138. b | 139. b | 140. a |
| 141. a | 142. a | 143. b | 144. a | 145. b | 146. b | 147. a | 148. b | 149. a | 150. b |
| 151. b | 152. a | 153. b | 154. a | 155. b | 156. b | 157. a | 158. b | 159. b | 160. b |
| 161. b | 162. a | 163. a | 164. b | 165. a | 166. a | 167. b | 168. a | 169. b | 170. b |
| 171. a | 172. a | 173. a | 174. b | 175. b | 176. a | 177. b | 178. b | 179. b | 180. b |
| 181. b | 182. a | 183. a | 184. a | 185. b | 186. a | 187. a | 188. b | 189. a | 190. b |
| 191. b | 192. a | 193. a | 194. a | 195. a | 196. a | 197. a | 198. b | 199. b | 200. b |
| 201. b | 202. a | 203. a | 204. b | 205. b | 206. a | 207. b | 208. b | 209. b | 210. a |
| 211. a | 212. b | 213. a | 214. a | 215. b | 216. a | 217. a | 218. b | 219. b | 220. b |
| 221. a | 222. a | 223. b | 224. a | 225. b | 226. b | 227. a | 228. a | 229. a | 230. a |
| 231. a | 232. a | 233. a | 234. b | 235. b | 236. a | 237. a | 238. a | 239. b | 240. a |
| 241. a | 242. b | 243. b | 244. a | 245. b | 246. b | 247. a | 248. a | 249. a | 250. a |
| 251. b | 252. b | 253. a | 254. a | 255. a | 256. a | 257. b | 258. a | 259. b | 260. a |
| 261. b | 262. a | 263. b | 264. b | 265. a | 266. b | 267. b | 268. a | 269. b | 270. b |
| 271. a | 272. b | 273. a | 274. b | 275. a | 276. a | 277. b | 278. b | 279. a | 280. a |
| 281. b | 282. a | 283. b | 284. a | 285. a | 286. b | 287. a | 288. b | 289. b | 290. b |
| 291. b | 292. a | 293. b | 294. a | 295. b | 296. a | 297. b | 298. b | 299. a | 300. a |
| 301. a | 302. b | 303. b | 304. a | 305. a | 306. a | 307. a | 308. a | 309. a | 310. a |
| 311. a | 312. b | 313. b | 314. a | 315. b | 316. b | 317. a | 318. a | 319. a | 320. a |
| 321. b | 322. b | 323. b | 324. b | 325. b | 326. b | 327. a | 328. a | 329. a | 330. a |
| 331. b | 332. a | 333. a | 334. a | 335. a | 336. a | 337. a | 338. a | 339. a | 340. a |
| 341. b | 342. a | 343. a | 344. b | 345. a | 346. a | 347. a | 348. a | 349. b | 350. b |
| 351. a | 352. b | 353. a | 354. b | 355. a | 356. b | 357. b | 358. a | 359. b | 360. a |

# ANSWER KEY

## Chapter 2

| | | | | | | | | | |
|---|---|---|---|---|---|---|---|---|---|
| 1. b | 2. b | 3. b | 4. a | 5. a | 6. a | 7. b | 8. a | 9. a | 10. b |
| 11. a | 12. a | 13. b | 14. b | 15. b | 16. a | 17. a | 18. b | 19. a | 20. b |
| 21. a | 22. a | 23. b | 24. a | 25. a | 26. a | 27. b | 28. a | 29. a | 30. a |
| 31. b | 32. a | 33. b | 34. a | 35. b | 36. a | 37. b | 38. b | 39. a | 40. b |
| 41. a | 42. b | 43. b | 44. a | 45. b | 46. a | 47. a | 48. b | 49. b | 50. b |
| 51. a | 52. a | 53. b | 54. b | 55. a | 56. a | 57. b | 58. a | 59. a | 60. b |
| 61. a | 62. a | 63. b | 64. b | 65. a | 66. a | 67. b | 68. a | 69. a | 70. a |
| 71. b | 72. b | 73. a | 74. a | 75. b | 76. b | 77. b | 78. b | 79. b | 80. a |
| 81. b | 82. a | 83. b | 84. a | 85. b | 86. a | 87. b | 88. b | 89. b | 90. b |
| 91. b | 92. b | 93. b | 94. a | 95. b | 96. b | 97. a | 98. b | 99. b | 100. b |
| 101. b | 102. a | 103. b | 104. a | 105. a | 106. a | 107. a | 108. b | 109. b | 110. b |
| 111. b | 112. a | 113. b | 114. b | 115. b | 116. a | 117. b | 118. a | 119. b | 120. a |
| 121. a | 122. b | 123. a | 124. a | 125. a | 126. a | 127. a | 128. a | 129. a | 130. b |
| 131. b | 132. a | 133. b | 134. a | 135. b | 136. b | 137. b | 138. b | 139. a | 140. b |
| 141. a | 142. a | 143. a | 144. a | 145. a | 146. b | 147. a | 148. a | 149. a | 150. a |
| 151. a | 152. b | 153. a | 154. b | 155. b | 156. a | 157. b | 158. b | 159. a | 160. a |
| 161. a | 162. b | 163. a | 164. b | 165. a | 166. b | 167. b | 168. a | 169. b | 170. a |
| 171. b | 172. b | 173. a | 174. a | 175. a | 176. a | 177. b | 178. b | 179. b | 180. b |
| 181. a | 182. b | 183. a | 184. a | 185. b | 186. b | 187. b | 188. b | 189. a | 190. b |
| 191. b | 192. b | 193. b | 194. b | 195. b | 196. a | 197. b | 198. b | 199. a | 200. a |
| 201. a | 202. b | 203. b | 204. a | 205. b | 206. b | 207. a | 208. a | 209. b | 210. a |
| 211. b | 212. a | 213. a | 214. a | 215. b | 216. a | 217. a | 218. a | 219. a | 220. a |
| 221. a | 222. b | 223. b | 224. b | 225. b | 226. b | 227. a | 228. b | 229. b | 230. b |
| 231. b | 232. a | 233. a | 234. a | 235. b | 236. b | 237. a | 238. a | 239. b | 240. a |
| 241. b | 242. a | 243. a | 244. b | 245. b | 246. b | 247. a | 248. a | 249. a | 250. a |
| 251. a | 252. b | 253. a | 254. b | 255. a | 256. a | 257. b | 258. b | 259. b | 260. a |
| 261. b | 262. a | 263. b | 264. b | 265. a | | | | | |

## Chapter 3

| | | | | | | | | | |
|---|---|---|---|---|---|---|---|---|---|
| 1. b | 2. b | 3. b | 4. a | 5. b | 6. a | 7. b | 8. b | 9. a | 10. b |
| 11. a | 12. a | 13. b | 14. a | 15. a | 16. a | 17. b | 18. a | 19. a | 20. b |
| 21. b | 22. b | 23. a | 24. a | 25. b | 26. b | 27. b | 28. a | 29. a | 30. b |
| 31. a | 32. b | 33. b | 34. a | 35. b | 36. a | 37. a | 38. b | 39. b | 40. b |
| 41. b | 42. a | 43. b | 44. b | 45. b | 46. a | 47. b | 48. a | 49. a | 50. b |
| 51. a | 52. a | 53. a | 54. b | 55. a | 56. a | 57. b | 58. b | 59. a | 60. b |
| 61. b | 62. b | 63. b | 64. a | 65. b | 66. b | 67. b | 68. b | 69. a | 70. b |
| 71. a | 72. b | 73. a | 74. a | 75. a | 76. b | 77. b | 78. a | 79. a | 80. b |
| 81. b | 82. b | 83. b | 84. a | 85. b | 86. a | 87. b | 88. a | 89. a | 90. b |
| 91. b | 92. b | 93. b | 94. a | 95. a | 96. a | 97. b | 98. a | 99. a | 100. a |
| 101. a | 102. b | 103. a | 104. a | 105. a | 106. b | 107. b | 108. a | 109. a | 110. a |
| 111. b | 112. a | 113. b | 114. a | 115. a | 116. b | 117. a | 118. a | 119. a | 120. a |
| 121. a | 122. a | 123. a | 124. b | 125. b | 126. a | 127. b | 128. a | 129. a | 130. a |
| 131. a | 132. a | 133. a | 134. a | 135. a | 136. b | 137. a | 138. a | 139. a | 140. b |
| 141. a | 142. b | 143. a | 144. a | 145. a | 146. b | 147. a | 148. a | 149. a | 150. b |
| 151. b | 152. b | 153. a | 154. a | 155. a | 156. b | 157. a | 158. a | 159. a | 160. a |
| 161. a | 162. b | 163. a | 164. a | 165. b | 166. a | 167. b | 168. a | 169. b | 170. b |
| 171. b | 172. a | 173. a | 174. b | 175. a | 176. a | 177. a | 178. a | 179. a | 180. b |
| 181. b | 182. a | 183. b | 184. a | 185. a | 186. a | 187. a | 188. b | 189. a | 190. a |
| 191. a | 192. a | 193. b | 194. b | 195. a | 196. a | 197. a | 198. b | 199. a | 200. b |
| 201. a | 202. a | 203. a | 204. b | 205. b | 206. b | 207. b | 208. b | 209. a | 210. b |
| 211. b | 212. b | 213. b | 214. a | 215. b | 216. b | 217. a | 218. b | 219. b | 220. a |
| 221. a | 222. b | 223. a | 224. b | 225. b | 226. b | 227. a | 228. b | 229. b | 230. a |
| 231. b | 232. b | 233. b | 234. a | 235. b | 236. a | 237. a | 238. a | 239. b | 240. b |
| 241. b | 242. b | 243. b | 244. b | 245. b | 246. a | 247. b | 248. b | 249. a | 250. b |
| 251. a | 252. a | 253. b | 254. a | 255. b | 256. a | 257. a | 258. b | 259. b | 260. a |
| 261. a | 262. a | 263. b | 264. b | 265. b | 266. a | 267. a | 268. a | 269. a | 270. a |
| 271. a | 272. b | 273. b | 274. a | 275. b | 276. b | 277. a | 278. b | 279. b | 280. a |
| 281. b | 282. b | 283. b | 284. a | 285. a | 286. b | 287. b | 288. a | 289. a | 290. b |
| 291. a | 292. b | 293. b | 294. b | 295. b | 296. a | 297. b | 298. a | 299. a | 300. a |
| 301. b | 302. a | 303. b | 304. a | 305. a | 306. a | 307. b | 308. a | 309. b | 310. a |
| 311. b | 312. a | 313. b | 314. a | 315. a | 316. a | 317. a | 318. b | 319. a | 320. b |
| 321. b | 322. a | 323. a | 324. b | 325. a | 326. b | 327. b | 328. b | 329. a | 330. a |
| 331. a | 332. b | 333. b | 334. a | 335. a | 336. b | 337. a | 338. a | 339. b | 340. a |
| 341. b | 342. b | 343. b | 344. b | 345. a | 346. a | 347. a | 348. a | 349. b | 350. b |
| 351. a | 352. b | 353. b | 354. a | 355. b | 356. b | 357. b | 358. a | 359. a | 360. b |
| 361. b | 362. a | 363. a | 364. b | 365. b | 366. b | 367. b | 368. a | 369. b | 370. a |
| 371. a | 372. a | 373. b | 374. b | 375. a | 376. a | 377. b | 378. a | | |

# ANSWER KEY

**Chapter 4**

| | | | | | | | | | |
|---|---|---|---|---|---|---|---|---|---|
| 1. b | 2. b | 3. a | 4. b | 5. a | 6. b | 7. a | 8. a | 9. a | 10. a |
| 11. b | 12. b | 13. a | 14. a | 15. b | 16. b | 17. a | 18. a | 19. b | 20. a |
| 21. a | 22. b | 23. a | 24. b | 25. a | 26. a | 27. b | 28. a | 29. b | 30. b |
| 31. a | 32. b | 33. b | 34. b | 35. b | 36. a | 37. b | 38. b | 39. a | 40. b |
| 41. a | 42. a | 43. b | 44. b | 45. a | 46. a | 47. b | 48. a | 49. a | 50. b |
| 51. a | 52. a | 53. b | 54. a | 55. b | 56. b | 57. b | 58. a | 59. a | 60. a |
| 61. a | 62. a | 63. a | 64. a | 65. a | 66. a | 67. b | 68. a | 69. a | 70. a |
| 71. a | 72. a | 73. b | 74. a | 75. a | 76. a | 77. a | 78. b | 79. b | 80. a |
| 81. b | 82. b | 83. a | 84. b | 85. b | 86. a | 87. a | 88. a | 89. b | 90. a |
| 91. a | 92. b | 93. a | 94. a | 95. a | 96. a | 97. b | 98. b | 99. b | 100. a |
| 101. b | 102. b | 103. b | 104. b | 105. a | 106. a | 107. b | 108. b | 109. a | 110. b |
| 111. b | 112. b | 113. a | 114. b | 115. b | 116. a | 117. a | 118. a | 119. b | 120. b |
| 121. a | 122. b | 123. b | 124. a | 125. b | 126. a | 127. b | 128. a | 129. a | 130. b |
| 131. b | 132. a | 133. b | 134. a | 135. a | 136. b | 137. b | 138. b | 139. a | 140. b |
| 141. a | 142. b | 143. b | 144. a | 145. b | 146. a | 147. b | 148. b | 149. b | 150. b |
| 151. b | 152. a | 153. b | 154. a | 155. a | 156. b | 157. a | 158. a | 159. a | 160. b |
| 161. a | 162. b | 163. a | 164. b | 165. b | 166. a | 167. a | 168. a | 169. a | 170. b |
| 171. b | 172. a | 173. b | 174. a | 175. b | 176. a | 177. b | 178. b | 179. b | 180. b |
| 181. a | 182. b | 183. b | 184. b | 185. b | 186. b | 187. a | 188. a | 189. a | 190. b |
| 191. a | 192. a | 193. b | 194. a | 195. a | 196. b | 197. b | 198. b | 199. a | 200. b |
| 201. a | 202. a | 203. a | 204. b | 205. b | 206. b | 207. b | 208. b | 209. b | 210. a |
| 211. a | 212. a | 213. b | 214. b | 215. b | 216. a | 217. b | 218. a | 219. b | 220. a |
| 221. b | 222. b | 223. a | 224. a | 225. a | 226. b | 227. b | 228. b | 229. a | 230. a |
| 231. b | 232. b | 233. a | 234. b | 235. a | 236. b | 237. b | 238. a | 239. a | 240. a |
| 241. a | 242. a | 243. b | 244. b | 245. a | 246. b | 247. b | 248. b | 249. a | 250. a |
| 251. b | 252. a | 253. b | 254. b | 255. a | 256. a | 257. a | 258. b | 259. a | 260. a |
| 261. b | 262. b | 263. b | 264. a | 265. a | 266. b | 267. b | 268. a | 269. a | 270. b |
| 271. b | 272. b | 273. a | 274. a | 275. a | 276. b | 277. a | 278. a | 279. b | 280. a |
| 281. a | 282. a | 283. a | 284. b | 285. a | 286. b | 287. a | 288. a | 289. b | 290. b |
| 291. a | 292. b | 293. b | 294. b | 295. b | 296. a | 297. b | 298. a | 299. b | 300. a |
| 301. b | 302. b | 303. a | 304. a | 305. b | 306. b | 307. b | 308. a | 309. b | 310. b |
| 311. b | 312. a | 313. a | 314. b | 315. b | 316. b | 317. b | 318. a | 319. a | 320. b |
| 321. a | 322. b | 323. b | 324. b | 325. a | 326. b | 327. a | 328. b | 329. b | 330. a |
| 331. a | 332. b | 333. b | 334. a | 335. b | 336. a | 337. a | 338. b | 339. b | 340. b |
| 341. b | 342. b | 343. b | 344. b | 345. a | 346. a | 347. a | | | |

## Chapter 5

| | | | | | | | | | |
|---|---|---|---|---|---|---|---|---|---|
| 1. b | 2. b | 3. a | 4. a | 5. a | 6. b | 7. b | 8. a | 9. b | 10. b |
| 11. a | 12. a | 13. b | 14. a | 15. b | 16. a | 17. b | 18. b | 19. b | 20. b |
| 21. a | 22. b | 23. a | 24. a | 25. a | 26. b | 27. b | 28. a | 29. b | 30. a |
| 31. b | 32. b | 33. a | 34. b | 35. b | 36. a | 37. a | 38. b | 39. a | 40. a |
| 41. b | 42. b | 43. b | 44. b | 45. a | 46. b | 47. b | 48. b | 49. a | 50. a |
| 51. a | 52. b | 53. b | 54. a | 55. a | 56. a | 57. a | 58. b | 59. a | 60. a |
| 61. a | 62. a | 63. b | 64. a | 65. a | 66. a | 67. a | 68. b | 69. b | 70. b |
| 71. b | 72. a | 73. a | 74. b | 75. b | 76. b | 77. b | 78. a | 79. b | 80. a |
| 81. a | 82. b | 83. a | 84. a | 85. b | 86. a | 87. b | 88. a | 89. a | 90. a |
| 91. a | 92. a | 93. b | 94. a | 95. b | 96. b | 97. b | 98. a | 99. b | 100. a |
| 101. b | 102. a | 103. a | 104. a | 105. b | 106. a | 107. b | 108. a | 109. b | 110. b |
| 111. a | 112. b | 113. b | 114. a | 115. a | 116. a | 117. b | 118. b | 119. a | 120. a |
| 121. a | 122. b | 123. b | 124. a | 125. a | 126. a | 127. a | 128. b | 129. b | 130. b |
| 131. b | 132. b | 133. b | 134. b | 135. b | 136. b | 137. a | 138. a | 139. a | 140. a |
| 141. a | 142. b | 143. a | 144. b | 145. a | 146. b | 147. b | 148. b | 149. b | 150. a |
| 151. b | 152. a | 153. b | 154. a | 155. b | 156. b | 157. a | 158. a | 159. a | 160. b |
| 161. a | 162. b | 163. b | 164. a | 165. b | 166. b | 167. b | 168. b | 169. b | 170. a |
| 171. b | 172. b | 173. b | 174. b | 175. a | 176. b | 177. a | 178. a | 179. a | 180. b |
| 181. b | 182. b | 183. b | 184. b | 185. b | 186. a | 187. a | 188. b | 189. a | 190. a |
| 191. a | 192. b | 193. a | 194. b | 195. b | 196. a | 197. a | 198. b | 199. a | 200. a |
| 201. b | 202. b | 203. a | 204. a | 205. b | 206. b | 207. b | 208. b | 209. a | 210. a |
| 211. a | 212. a | 213. b | 214. b | 215. b | 216. b | 217. b | 218. b | 219. b | 220. a |
| 221. b | 222. a | 223. a | 224. b | 225. a | 226. a | 227. b | 228. b | 229. b | 230. b |
| 231. a | 232. b | 233. a | 234. a | 235. a | 236. a | 237. b | 238. a | 239. a | 240. a |
| 241. a | 242. a | 243. a | 244. b | 245. a | 246. b | 247. b | 248. a | 249. a | 250. b |
| 251. b | 252. b | 253. b | 254. b | 255. a | 256. a | 257. b | 258. a | 259. a | 260. a |
| 261. a | 262. a | 263. a | 264. a | 265. a | | | | | |

# ANSWER KEY

## Chapter 6

| | | | | | | | | | |
|---|---|---|---|---|---|---|---|---|---|
| 1. b | 2. a | 3. a | 4. b | 5. a | 6. a | 7. b | 8. b | 9. a | 10. b |
| 11. b | 12. b | 13. a | 14. a | 15. a | 16. a | 17. b | 18. a | 19. b | 20. a |
| 21. b | 22. a | 23. b | 24. b | 25. b | 26. b | 27. b | 28. b | 29. b | 30. b |
| 31. b | 32. a | 33. b | 34. a | 35. b | 36. b | 37. b | 38. b | 39. b | 40. b |
| 41. b | 42. b | 43. a | 44. b | 45. b | 46. a | 47. a | 48. a | 49. b | 50. b |
| 51. b | 52. b | 53. b | 54. b | 55. a | 56. b | 57. b | 58. b | 59. a | 60. a |
| 61. b | 62. a | 63. b | 64. a | 65. a | 66. a | 67. a | 68. b | 69. b | 70. a |
| 71. b | 72. a | 73. a | 74. b | 75. a | 76. a | 77. a | 78. a | 79. b | 80. b |
| 81. b | 82. a | 83. a | 84. b | 85. a | 86. b | 87. a | 88. b | 89. a | 90. b |
| 91. b | 92. b | 93. a | 94. a | 95. b | 96. b | 97. b | 98. a | 99. b | 100. b |
| 101. a | 102. b | 103. a | 104. b | 105. b | 106. a | 107. b | 108. a | 109. a | 110. a |
| 111. a | 112. b | 113. b | 114. a | 115. b | 116. b | 117. a | 118. b | 119. a | 120. b |
| 121. a | 122. b | 123. a | 124. a | 125. a | 126. b | 127. a | 128. b | 129. a | 130. b |
| 131. b | 132. b | 133. a | 134. b | 135. b | 136. a | 137. a | 138. a | 139. a | 140. a |
| 141. a | 142. a | 143. a | 144. b | 145. a | 146. a | 147. b | 148. a | 149. a | 150. b |
| 151. a | 152. b | 153. b | 154. a | 155. b | 156. a | 157. a | 158. b | 159. b | 160. b |
| 161. b | 162. a | 163. b | 164. a | 165. b | 166. a | 167. a | 168. b | 169. a | 170. a |
| 171. b | 172. a | 173. a | 174. b | 175. a | 176. b | 177. b | 178. b | 179. b | 180. b |
| 181. a | 182. a | 183. a | 184. a | 185. b | 186. a | 187. a | 188. b | 189. a | 190. a |
| 191. b | 192. a | 193. a | 194. b | 195. b | 196. a | 197. a | 198. a | 199. b | 200. b |
| 201. b | 202. b | 203. b | 204. b | 205. a | 206. a | 207. b | 208. a | 209. b | 210. a |
| 211. a | 212. a | 213. a | 214. b | 215. b | 216. b | 217. b | 218. b | 219. a | 220. a |
| 221. b | 222. b | 223. b | 224. a | 225. b | 226. b | 227. b | 228. a | 229. b | 230. b |
| 231. a | 232. a | 233. a | 234. b | 235. b | 236. b | 237. b | 238. b | 239. a | 240. b |
| 241. a | 242. b | 243. a | 244. b | 245. a | 246. b | 247. a | 248. b | 249. a | 250. b |
| 251. a | 252. b | 253. a | 254. b | 255. b | 256. a | 257. b | 258. a | 259. a | 260. a |
| 261. a | 262. b | 263. b | 264. b | 265. b | 266. a | 267. b | 268. a | 269. b | 270. b |
| 271. a | 272. b | 273. b | 274. a | 275. a | 276. a | 277. b | 278. a | 279. b | 280. b |
| 281. a | 282. a | 283. a | 284. b | 285. a | 286. b | 287. b | 288. b | 289. b | 290. b |
| 291. b | 292. b | 293. a | 294. a | 295. b | 296. b | 297. b | 298. b | 299. a | 300. b |
| 301. a | 302. b | 303. b | 304. a | 305. b | 306. a | 307. b | 308. b | 309. a | 310. b |
| 311. a | 312. b | 313. a | 314. a | 315. a | 316. b | 317. a | 318. b | 319. b | 320. a |
| 321. a | 322. a | 323. b | 324. b | 325. b | 326. b | 327. a | 328. b | 329. b | 330. b |
| 331. b | 332. a | | | | | | | | |

## Chapter 7

| | | | | | | | | | |
|---|---|---|---|---|---|---|---|---|---|
| 1. b | 2. a | 3. b | 4. b | 5. a | 6. a | 7. b | 8. a | 9. a | 10. a |
| 11. b | 12. a | 13. b | 14. a | 15. b | 16. b | 17. b | 18. a | 19. b | 20. a |
| 21. a | 22. b | 23. a | 24. b | 25. b | 26. b | 27. a | 28. a | 29. b | 30. a |
| 31. b | 32. b | 33. a | 34. b | 35. a | 36. b | 37. a | 38. b | 39. b | 40. b |
| 41. a | 42. a | 43. b | 44. a | 45. b | 46. b | 47. a | 48. b | 49. b | 50. b |
| 51. b | 52. a | 53. a | 54. b | 55. a | 56. b | 57. a | 58. b | 59. a | 60. a |
| 61. b | 62. a | 63. a | 64. a | 65. a | 66. b | 67. b | 68. a | 69. b | 70. a |
| 71. a | 72. a | 73. a | 74. b | 75. a | 76. b | 77. b | 78. b | 79. b | 80. a |
| 81. b | 82. b | 83. b | 84. a | 85. a | 86. a | 87. a | 88. b | 89. b | 90. b |
| 91. a | 92. a | 93. b | 94. a | 95. b | 96. b | 97. a | 98. a | 99. a | 100. b |
| 101. b | 102. a | 103. a | 104. a | 105. a | 106. b | 107. b | 108. b | 109. b | 110. b |
| 111. b | 112. a | 113. a | 114. b | 115. b | 116. a | 117. b | 118. b | 119. b | 120. b |
| 121. a | 122. b | 123. b | 124. b | 125. b | 126. b | 127. b | 128. b | 129. a | 130. a |
| 131. a | 132. b | 133. b | 134. b | 135. a | 136. a | 137. a | 138. b | 139. b | 140. a |
| 141. a | 142. a | 143. a | 144. a | 145. a | 146. a | 147. a | 148. b | 149. a | 150. a |
| 151. a | 152. b | 153. b | 154. a | 155. b | 156. b | 157. a | 158. b | 159. b | 160. a |
| 161. a | 162. b | 163. a | 164. a | 165. b | 166. b | 167. b | 168. a | 169. b | 170. a |
| 171. a | 172. a | 173. b | 174. a | 175. a | 176. b | 177. a | 178. b | 179. b | 180. b |
| 181. a | 182. a | 183. b | 184. a | 185. a | 186. a | 187. a | 188. b | 189. a | 190. a |
| 191. b | 192. a | 193. b | 194. b | 195. a | 196. a | 197. a | 198. b | 199. b | |

## Chapter 8

| | | | | | | | | | |
|---|---|---|---|---|---|---|---|---|---|
| 1. a | 2. b | 3. b | 4. b | 5. a | 6. b | 7. b | 8. b | 9. a | 10. a |
| 11. a | 12. a | 13. b | 14. a | 15. a | 16. a | 17. a | 18. a | 19. b | 20. a |
| 21. b | 22. b | 23. a | 24. a | 25. a | 26. b | 27. a | 28. a | 29. b | 30. a |
| 31. b | 32. b | 33. a | 34. b | 35. a | 36. b | 37. b | 38. b | 39. a | 40. b |
| 41. a | 42. b | 43. b | 44. b | 45. b | 46. b | 47. a | 48. a | 49. a | 50. a |
| 51. a | 52. b | 53. b | 54. a | 55. b | 56. b | 57. b | 58. b | 59. a | 60. a |
| 61. b | 62. a | 63. a | 64. a | 65. b | 66. a | 67. b | 68. a | 69. b | 70. a |
| 71. b | 72. a | 73. a | 74. a | 75. b | 76. a | 77. b | 78. a | 79. a | 80. b |
| 81. b | 82. b | 83. b | 84. a | 85. a | 86. b | 87. a | 88. b | 89. b | 90. b |
| 91. b | 92. a | 93. b | 94. b | 95. b | 96. b | 97. b | 98. b | 99. b | 100. a |
| 101. a | 102. b | 103. a | 104. a | 105. a | 106. a | 107. b | 108. b | 109. a | 110. a |
| 111. b | 112. b | 113. a | 114. a | 115. a | 116. b | 117. a | 118. b | 119. a | 120. b |
| 121. b | 122. a | 123. a | 124. a | 125. a | 126. a | 127. b | 128. b | 129. a | 130. a |
| 131. a | 132. b | 133. a | 134. b | 135. a | 136. a | 137. a | 138. b | 139. b | 140. a |
| 141. a | 142. a | 143. a | 144. b | 145. b | 146. b | 147. a | 148. b | 149. b | 150. a |
| 151. a | 152. a | 153. b | 154. a | 155. b | 156. b | 157. a | 158. a | 159. a | 160. b |
| 161. a | 162. a | 163. a | 164. a | 165. a | 166. b | 167. b | 168. b | 169. b | 170. a |
| 171. b | 172. a | 173. b | 174. b | 175. a | 176. a | 177. a | 178. b | 179. a | |

# ANSWER KEY

**Chapter 9**

| | | | | | | | | | |
|---|---|---|---|---|---|---|---|---|---|
| 1. b | 2. b | 3. a | 4. a | 5. a | 6. a | 7. b | 8. a | 9. b | 10. b |
| 11. b | 12. a | 13. b | 14. b | 15. a | 16. a | 17. a | 18. b | 19. a | 20. a |
| 21. a | 22. b | 23. b | 24. a | 25. a | 26. a | 27. a | 28. b | 29. a | 30. a |
| 31. a | 32. b | 33. a | 34. a | 35. b | 36. b | 37. a | 38. b | 39. a | 40. a |
| 41. b | 42. a | 43. a | 44. b | 45. b | 46. a | 47. b | 48. a | 49. a | 50. b |
| 51. b | 52. b | 53. b | 54. a | 55. a | 56. a | 57. b | 58. b | 59. a | 60. b |
| 61. a | 62. b | 63. b | 64. b | 65. a | 66. b | 67. a | 68. b | 69. b | 70. b |
| 71. a | 72. b | 73. a | 74. a | 75. a | 76. a | 77. a | 78. a | 79. b | 80. a |
| 81. b | 82. b | 83. a | 84. b | 85. b | 86. a | 87. b | 88. b | 89. a | 90. a |
| 91. a | 92. b | 93. a | 94. b | 95. a | 96. a | 97. a | 98. a | 99. b | 100. b |
| 101. b | 102. a | 103. a | 104. a | 105. b | 106. b | 107. a | 108. a | 109. b | 110. b |
| 111. b | 112. b | 113. b | 114. b | 115. b | 116. a | 117. a | 118. b | 119. b | 120. b |
| 121. a | 122. b | 123. b | 124. a | 125. b | 126. b | 127. b | 128. b | 129. a | 130. a |
| 131. a | 132. b | 133. a | 134. a | 135. a | 136. b | 137. a | 138. a | 139. a | 140. a |
| 141. a | 142. a | 143. b | 144. a | 145. a | 146. b | 147. a | | | |

**Chapter 10**

| | | | | | | | | | |
|---|---|---|---|---|---|---|---|---|---|
| 1. b | 2. a | 3. b | 4. a | 5. b | 6. a | 7. a | 8. a | 9. b | 10. b |
| 11. b | 12. a | 13. b | 14. a | 15. a | 16. a | 17. a | 18. b | 19. a | 20. a |
| 21. a | 22. a | 23. b | 24. a | 25. b | 26. a | 27. b | 28. b | 29. b | 30. b |
| 31. a | 32. a | 33. a | 34. a | 35. b | 36. b | 37. a | 38. b | 39. b | 40. a |
| 41. a | 42. a | 43. a | 44. a | 45. a | 46. a | 47. a | 48. b | 49. b | 50. a |
| 51. b | 52. a | 53. b | 54. b | 55. a | 56. b | 57. b | 58. a | 59. a | 60. b |
| 61. b | 62. b | 63. b | 64. b | 65. b | 66. a | 67. b | 68. b | 69. b | 70. a |
| 71. b | 72. b | 73. b | 74. b | 75. b | 76. b | 77. b | 78. a | 79. b | 80. a |
| 81. a | 82. a | 83. b | 84. a | 85. b | 86. a | 87. a | 88. a | 89. a | 90. a |
| 91. a | 92. a | 93. a | 94. a | 95. b | 96. a | 97. a | 98. b | 99. b | 100. a |
| 101. a | 102. a | 103. a | 104. b | 105. b | 106. b | 107. b | 108. b | 109. a | 110. a |
| 111. a | 112. b | 113. b | 114. a | 115. a | 116. a | 117. a | 118. a | 119. a | 120. a |
| 121. b | 122. a | 123. b | 124. a | 125. b | 126. b | 127. b | 128. a | 129. a | 130. b |
| 131. a | 132. a | 133. a | 134. b | 135. b | 136. a | 137. a | 138. a | 139. a | 140. a |
| 141. a | 142. b | 143. a | 144. a | 145. b | 146. a | 147. a | 148. b | 149. a | 150. b |
| 151. b | 152. b | 153. a | 154. a | 155. a | 156. b | 157. a | 158. a | 159. b | 160. b |
| 161. b | 162. b | 163. b | 164. b | 165. a | 166. b | 167. b | 168. a | 169. a | 170. b |
| 171. b | 172. a | 173. a | 174. b | 175. a | 176. a | 177. a | 178. a | | |

## Chapter 11

| | | | | | | | | | |
|---|---|---|---|---|---|---|---|---|---|
| 1. a | 2. a | 3. a | 4. a | 5. b | 6. a | 7. b | 8. a | 9. b | 10. a |
| 11. a | 12. b | 13. b | 14. a | 15. b | 16. b | 17. b | 18. a | 19. a | 20. b |
| 21. a | 22. b | 23. b | 24. a | 25. b | 26. b | 27. a | 28. b | 29. b | 30. b |
| 31. a | 32. b | 33. a | 34. b | 35. a | 36. a | 37. b | 38. a | 39. b | 40. a |
| 41. b | 42. b | 43. a | 44. b | 45. b | 46. b | 47. a | 48. b | 49. a | 50. a |
| 51. b | 52. b | 53. a | 54. b | 55. b | 56. b | 57. b | 58. a | 59. a | 60. b |
| 61. b | 62. a | 63. b | 64. b | 65. b | 66. b | 67. a | 68. a | 69. a | 70. b |
| 71. b | 72. b | 73. a | 74. a | 75. b | 76. b | 77. a | 78. a | 79. b | 80. a |
| 81. a | 82. a | 83. a | 84. a | 85. a | 86. a | 87. a | 88. b | 89. a | 90. b |
| 91. a | 92. a | 93. b | 94. b | 95. b | 96. b | 97. b | 98. a | 99. b | 100. b |
| 101. b | 102. b | 103. b | 104. b | 105. a | 106. b | 107. a | 108. b | 109. b | 110. b |
| 111. b | 112. b | 113. a | 114. b | 115. b | 116. b | 117. b | 118. b | 119. b | 120. a |
| 121. a | 122. a | 123. b | 124. b | 125. b | 126. a | 127. a | 128. b | 129. b | 130. a |
| 131. a | 132. a | 133. a | 134. a | 135. b | 136. a | 137. a | 138. a | 139. b | 140. b |
| 141. b | 142. a | 143. b | 144. b | 145. a | 146. b | 147. a | 148. b | 149. b | 150. b |
| 151. b | 152. a | 153. a | 154. a | 155. b | 156. b | 157. a | 158. a | 159. a | 160. b |
| 161. b | 162. a | 163. a | 164. a | 165. b | 166. a | 167. b | 168. a | 169. a | 170. b |
| 171. b | 172. a | 173. b | 174. b | 175. a | 176. b | 177. a | 178. a | 179. b | 180. b |
| 181. b | 182. b | 183. a | 184. b | 185. a | 186. a | 187. a | 188. b | 189. a | 190. a |
| 191. a | 192. b | 193. a | 194. a | 195. b | 196. a | 197. b | 198. a | 199. a | 200. a |
| 201. a | 202. b | 203. b | 204. a | 205. b | 206. a | 207. a | 208. a | 209. b | 210. b |
| 211. a | 212. a | 213. b | 214. b | 215. a | 216. a | 217. b | 218. b | 219. b | 220. b |
| 221. b | 222. b | 223. b | 224. a | 225. b | 226. a | 227. a | 228. b | 229. b | 230. b |
| 231. b | 232. a | 233. a | 234. b | 235. a | 236. a | 237. a | 238. a | 239. a | 240. a |
| 241. b | 242. a | 243. a | 244. b | 245. b | 246. a | 247. b | 248. a | 249. b | 250. a |
| 251. b | 252. b | 253. a | 254. a | 255. b | 256. a | 257. a | 258. a | 259. a | 260. a |
| 261. a | 262. a | 263. b | 264. a | 265. b | 266. a | 267. b | 268. b | 269. a | 270. a |
| 271. b | 272. a | 273. b | 274. b | 275. a | 276. a | 277. a | 278. b | 279. b | 280. a |
| 281. a | 282. a | 283. a | 284. b | 285. b | 286. a | 287. b | 288. a | 289. b | 290. a |
| 291. a | 292. a | 293. b | 294. a | 295. b | 296. a | 297. b | 298. a | 299. b | 300. a |
| 301. a | 302. a | 303. b | 304. a | 305. a | 306. a | 307. a | | | |

# ANSWER KEY

**Chapter 12**

| | | | | | | | | | |
|---|---|---|---|---|---|---|---|---|---|
| 1. a | 2. a | 3. b | 4. b | 5. b | 6. b | 7. a | 8. a | 9. b | 10. b |
| 11. b | 12. b | 13. a | 14. a | 15. a | 16. a | 17. b | 18. b | 19. b | 20. a |
| 21. b | 22. a | 23. a | 24. a | 25. b | 26. b | 27. a | 28. a | 29. b | 30. a |
| 31. a | 32. b | 33. b | 34. b | 35. a | 36. b | 37. b | 38. b | 39. b | 40. a |
| 41. a | 42. a | 43. b | 44. a | 45. a | 46. b | 47. b | 48. a | 49. b | 50. a |
| 51. b | 52. a | 53. a | 54. b | 55. b | 56. b | 57. a | 58. a | 59. a | 60. a |
| 61. b | 62. b | 63. a | 64. a | 65. a | 66. a | 67. b | 68. b | 69. b | 70. a |
| 71. a | 72. b | 73. a | 74. b | 75. a | 76. b | 77. a | 78. a | 79. a | 80. b |
| 81. b | 82. a | 83. a | 84. a | 85. b | 86. a | 87. b | 88. a | 89. b | 90. a |
| 91. b | 92. a | 93. a | 94. a | 95. b | 96. a | 97. b | 98. b | 99. a | 100. a |
| 101. a | 102. b | 103. b | 104. b | 105. b | 106. a | 107. a | 108. b | 109. a | 110. b |
| 111. b | 112. a | 113. b | 114. b | 115. a | 116. a | 117. a | 118. a | 119. b | 120. a |
| 121. a | 122. b | 123. a | 124. a | 125. b | 126. a | 127. a | 128. a | 129. b | 130. b |
| 131. b | 132. b | 133. b | 134. b | 135. a | 136. b | 137. a | 138. b | 139. b | 140. a |
| 141. a | 142. b | 143. a | 144. b | 145. b | 146. a | 147. b | 148. a | 149. a | 150. a |
| 151. b | 152. a | 153. b | 154. b | 155. a | 156. b | 157. b | 158. a | 159. a | 160. a |
| 161. a | 162. b | 163. b | 164. b | 165. a | 166. b | 167. a | 168. a | | |

www.ingramcontent.com/pod-product-compliance
Lightning Source LLC
Chambersburg PA
CBHW060244240426
43673CB00047B/1874